Player Won-Lost
Records in Baseball

Player Won-Lost Records in Baseball

Measuring Performance in Context

TOM THRESS

McFarland & Company, Inc., Publishers
Jefferson, North Carolina

LIBRARY OF CONGRESS CATALOGUING-IN-PUBLICATION DATA

Names: Thress, Tom.
Title: Player won-lost records in baseball : measuring performance in context / Tom Thress.
Description: Jefferson, North Carolina : McFarland & Comapny, Inc., Publishers, 2017. | Includes bibliographical references and index.
Identifiers: LCCN 2017033631 | ISBN 9781476670249 (softcover : acid free paper) ∞
Subjects: LCSH: Baseball—Records—United States. | Baseball—United States—Statistics. | Baseball players—United States—Statistics. | Baseball—History.
Classification: LCC GV877 .T57 2017 | DDC 796.357021—dc23
LC record available at https://lccn.loc.gov/2017033631

BRITISH LIBRARY CATALOGUING DATA ARE AVAILABLE

ISBN (print) 978-1-4766-7024-9
ISBN (ebook) 978-1-4766-2923-0

© 2017 Tom Thress. All rights reserved

No part of this book may be reproduced or transmitted in any form or by any means, electronic or mechanical, including photocopying or recording, or by any information storage and retrieval system, without permission in writing from the publisher.

Front cover image © 2017 Shutterstock

Printed in the United States of America

*McFarland & Company, Inc., Publishers
Box 611, Jefferson, North Carolina 28640
www.mcfarlandpub.com*

Table of Contents

Preface   1

Introduction   3

1. Player Won-Lost Records—The Basics   13
2. Impact of Context on Player Won-Lost Records   30
3. Using Player Won-Lost Records to Compare Players   53
4. Components of Player Won-Lost Records   75
5. Offensive Player Won-Lost Records   145
6. Pitching Player Won-Lost Records   158
7. Fielding Player Won-Lost Records   178
8. Baseball Player Won-Lost Records vs. WAR   215
9. Win Probabilities   245
10: Ballpark Adjustments to Player Won-Lost Records   255

Glossary   281
Bibliography   287
Index   289

Preface

The job of a major league baseball player is to help his team win games, for the ultimate purpose of making the playoffs and winning the World Series. Since the early history of major league baseball, pitchers have been credited with wins and losses as official measures of the effectiveness of their pitching. Of course, pitcher wins are a fairly crude measure of how well a pitcher did his job, as wins are the product of the performance of the entire team—batters, baserunners, and fielders, in addition to pitchers.

While the implementation of pitcher wins as a measure of pitcher effectiveness is less than ideal, nevertheless the concept is perfectly sound. The ultimate measure of a player's contribution—be he a pitcher, a hitter, a baserunner, or a fielder—is in how much he contributes to his team's wins.

Using play-by-play data, I have constructed a set of player won-lost records that attempt to quantify the precise extent to which individual players contribute directly to wins and losses in major league baseball on the baseball field.

Player won-lost (pW-L) records are calculated using play-by-play data obtained from Retrosheet. The information used here was obtained free of charge from and is copyrighted by Retrosheet. Interested parties may contact Retrosheet at www.retrosheet.org.

Retrosheet releases data twice per year. The data used in preparing this book were released by Retrosheet on June 29, 2016. As of that time, Retrosheet had released complete play-by-play data for every major-league season since 1945. Retrosheet has also released play-by-play data for a majority of games for 20 seasons prior to this: 1921 (NL only), 1922, 1925, 1927, and 1930–45. For seasons prior to 1945 for which I have play-by-play data, I calculated pW-L records for the games for which Retrosheet has released data. For purposes of calculating season and career records, I extrapolate these partial-season totals out to full-season estimates based on the actual number of games played by players. For example, Rogers Hornsby, who won the National League Triple Crown in 1922, played in 154 games for the St. Louis Cardinals that year. So far, pW-L records have been calculated for 97 of these games. Hence, Rogers Hornsby's pW-L records for 1922 are multiplied by 1.59 (154/97).

Player records that include extrapolations for missing games are italicized throughout the book.

Introduction

This book describes the construction of player won-lost records and looks at the results of such work.

Chapter 1 provides a general overview of player wins (pWins), present career leaders in total player wins as well as player wins over average and replacement level, and describe how I construct pWins.

Chapter 2 breaks down the contextual factors that affect pW-L records.

Chapter 3 analyzes how to use pW-L records to compare players across position. The derivation of pWins over Positional Average (pWOPA) and pWins over Replacement Level (pWORL) are presented here. Chapter 3 ends with an evaluation of the 2005 American League MVP race between Alex Rodriguez and David Ortiz as an example of how pW-L records can be used to compare players.

Chapter 4 walks through the nine components of pW-L records. Chapters 5, 6, and 7 then look at pW-L records by offense, pitching, and fielding, respectively. All of these chapters include a number of leaderboards of the best players at various aspects of play. I compare pW-L records to several alternate fielding measures (UZR, DRA, and DRS) at the conclusion of Chapter 7.

Chapter 8 presents a case that pW-L records are the ultimate baseball statistic. This is done by showing how pW-L records are superior to wins above replacement (WAR) as measured by Baseball-Reference.com and Fangraphs.com.

Finally, Chapter 9 explains win probabilities in some detail, and Chapter 10 looks at how pW-L records control for ballpark effects.

While the bulk of this book looks at pW-L records for players at the season and career level, pW-L records are actually constructed at a game-by-game—and, really, play-by-play—level. So, let's start by looking at a game.

2007: Game 163

The 2007 regular season was so good that they added an extra game, which was so good that it lasted thirteen innings.

PRELUDE

After the games of September 15, 2007, the Colorado Rockies were in 4th place in the NL West with a record of 76–72, 4.5 games behind the San Diego Padres for the NL Wild Card.

The Padres closed the season by winning 9 of their final 12 games that didn't involve the Rockies. Unfortunately for them, they went 0–3 against the Rockies. They were in excellent company in that, though, as the Rockies closed the regular season by winning 13 of their final 14 games, erasing all of the Padres' wild card lead and forcing a Game 163 between the two teams at Coors Field on Monday, October 1, 2007.

Technical Interlude: Tracking pW-L Records Play by Play

The calculation of pW-L records are explained in great detail in this book—primarily in Chapter 1. The core of the pW-L calculations is win probability (which is discussed in detail in Chapter 9).

For every play of a game, I calculate the change in win probability for the teams playing and assign it to the appropriate players. Also calculated is what the average change in win probability for the play would have been across all possible contexts: e.g., in the latter case, all line drive singles to left field are worth the same number of batting wins and all ground outs to the third baseman are worth the same number of batting losses.

The in-context numbers that come out of this step are similar to, but not exactly the same as, the concept of win probability advancements (WPA). One important difference between most implementations of WPA and my work is that most WPA metrics assign all credit and blame to batters and pitchers while I apportion wins and losses to baserunners and fielders as well.

The more important difference between WPA and pWins, however, is that I make a final adjustment at the end of the game based on which team won and which team lost. This is necessary to (a) tie player wins and losses back to team wins and losses, and (b) treat all games as equally valuable (obviously, you can make an argument that Game 163 is more "valuable" than, say, game 25; but that rests on the timing of Game 163 vis-à-vis Game 25, not because Game 163 happened to go 13 innings—especially since, in fact, the 2007 Padres' 25th game went 17 innings).

All of this is discussed in more detail through the course of this book.

Now, on to the big game!

Game 163, as It Unfolded in Real-Time

The starting pitchers for Game 163 were Jake Peavy for the Padres and Josh Fogg for the Rockies. Jake Peavy was looking for his 20th pitching win of the 2007 season, against only 6 losses, and would win the 2007 NL Cy Young award (unanimously) later that fall. Josh Fogg had been a consistently below-average pitcher outside of his first big-league season in 2001, which consisted of 13.1 innings pitched.

Innings 1–2

Given that pitching matchup, the first two innings went pretty much the exact opposite of what you'd expect. Josh Fogg pitched two shutout innings, allowing a solitary single in each of the first two innings while mixing in three strikeouts.

Meanwhile, in the bottom of the first inning, the Rockies opened with a double, single, and walk, to load the bases. Todd Helton put the Rockies on the scoreboard with a sacrifice fly to deep centerfield and Garrett Atkins singled in a second run. A foul pop-up and a flyout ended the inning without any more damage. But catcher Yorvit Torrealba led off the bottom of the second inning with a home run to stake the Rockies to a 3–0 lead.

INNING 3

In the top of the third inning, Josh Fogg began to pitch like Josh Fogg. It began with a single by the Padres' pitcher, Peavy—never a good way to start an inning. That was followed by a walk and a single to load the bases with nobody out. Fogg got Kevin Kouzmanoff to fly out to left field and the bases remained loaded with one out. Adrian Gonzalez proceeded to unload the bases with a grand slam to right field, giving the Padres their first lead of the day, 4–3.

Unfortunately for Fogg and the Rockies, the bases didn't actually stay unloaded very long as a single, double, and intentional walk promptly re-loaded them, still with only one out. Brady Clark grounded out to third base for the second out of the inning, but it was a mixed blessing, as the fifth run of the inning scored on the play.

Jake Peavy came out to pitch the bottom of the third inning with a new lease on life. The Padres' offense had bailed him out and he now had a 5–3 lead to work with. Unfortunately for Peavy and the Padres, the second batter of the inning, Todd Helton, cut the Padres' lead in half with a home run to right-center field. Peavy managed to escape the inning with no further damage, however, and the Padres led 5–4 with the game one-third over.

INNINGS 4–5

Josh Fogg and Jake Peavy both pitched their first 1–2–3 inning of the game in the fourth inning.

Adrian Gonzalez led off the top of the fifth inning with a double, prompting the Rockies to replace Fogg with Taylor Buchholz. Buchholz retired the next three Padres' batters to hold the Padres' lead at a single run, 5–4.

The Padres' lead lasted for only two more batters. A Troy Tulowitzki double, followed by a Matt Holliday single tied the score at five. Peavy got a groundout and two strikeouts (with an intentional walk sandwiched in between) to keep the score tied at 5 through 5.

INNING 6

The Padres threatened to break the tie in the top of the sixth with a leadoff single by Brady Clark. Jake Peavy popped up a bunt attempt for the first out. Jeremy Affeldt came on to pitch for the Rockies, replacing Taylor Buchholz, and proceeded to throw a wild pitch, putting the go-ahead run in scoring position. He got Brian Giles to pop out to shortstop for the second out of the inning. Ryan Speier, the fourth Rockies' pitcher of the game, then came in and struck out Ryan Spilborghs to end the inning.

The bottom of the sixth started okay for Peavy and the Padres with Yorvit Torrealba grounding out. But pinch-hitter Seth Smith tripled to deep right-center and Kaz Matsui gave the Rockies their first lead since the third inning with a sacrifice fly. Troy Tulowitzki tripled to left-center, but Peavy struck Matt Holliday out to end the inning with Tulowitzki stranded on third base.

Inning 7

LaTroy Hawkins, the fifth Rockies pitcher of the night, worked around a one-out infield single to shut the Padres down and hold the Rockies lead at 6–5.

The Rockies threatened to add to their lead in the bottom of the seventh thanks to a one-out double by Garrett Atkins. That was followed by an intentional walk of Brad Hawpe, who was the last batter faced by Jake Peavy. For the day, Peavy gave up 6 runs—all earned, including two home runs, in 6.1 innings and left with the Padres trailing 6–5 with six more outs left to catch up.

Heath Bell struck out Spilborghs and Torrealba to end the inning.

Innings 8–9

The Rockies brought in their sixth pitcher of the game, Brian Fuentes, to try to hold on to their one-run lead heading into the eighth inning. After a leadoff single by Geoff Blum, Fuentes came back to get Brady Clark (foul popup) and Michael Barrett (strikeout) for two outs (although Blum advanced to scoring position on a wild pitch). With the Padres four outs away from their season ending, Brian Giles hit a 1–1 pitch from Fuentes to deep left field for a double, scoring Geoff Blum with the tying run. Suddenly, the situation for the Padres had turned from being one out away from heading into the ninth inning trailing to having the go-ahead run in scoring position. Fuentes got Scott Hairston to ground out to the shortstop and the threat was over; but not before the Padres had tied the score, 6–6, heading to the bottom of the eighth inning.

The Rockies wasted a leadoff walk in the bottom of the 8th inning. The Padres went down 1–2–3 in the top of the ninth inning for only the second time all game. The Rockies managed a two-out walk in the bottom of the ninth but no more as Heath Bell completed a pitching stint in which he retired 8 of the 10 batters he faced (two walks) with 5 strikeouts.

Inning 10

On to extra innings. The Rockies brought on their eighth pitcher of the game (Manny Corpas pitched the 1–2–3 ninth inning), Matt Herges. He got the first two Padres of the inning before walking pinch-hitter Terrmel Sledge and giving up a single to Michael Barrett. But Herges got Brian Giles to ground into a force play to end the inning.

The bottom of the tenth inning was the second inning of the game that saw the Rockies go down 1–2–3. And so the game moved on to the 11th inning.

Inning 11

The 11th inning started dubiously for the Rockies with Scott Hairston reaching on a throwing error by Jamey Carroll. Kouzmanoff bunted Hairston to second base. An intentional walk to Adrian Gonzalez brought Khalil Greene to the plate with the go-ahead runner in scoring position and only one out. Greene promptly hit a weak ground ball to Carroll, who made up for his error by starting a 5–3 double play to end the inning.

In the bottom of the 11th, after two quick outs, the Rockies put runners on 1st and

2nd, bringing Brad Hawpe to the plate. The Padres brought in Joe Thatcher to face him (the Padres' fourth pitcher of the game). Thatcher struck Hawpe out swinging and the game moved on to the 12th inning.

Inning 12

The 12th inning was probably the most uneventful inning of the game since the teams traded 1-2-3 innings in the fourth. Morgan Ensberg led off the top of the 12th with a walk but the two teams combined for six straight outs after that to end the 12th inning, with the score still tied at 6-6.

Inning 13

The Rockies started the 13th inning with their 9th pitcher of the game (this game was being played with expanded September rosters), Jorge Julio. As in the 12th inning, the Padres led off the top of the 13th with a walk. This time, however, the runner was not stranded, as Scott Hairston followed with a two-run home run to finally break the tie. Chase Headley singled and that was it for Julio. The Rockies' 10th pitcher, Ramon Ortiz retired the Padres in order, but the damage was done. The Padres were three outs away from the playoffs, heading to the bottom of the thirteenth inning with an 8-6 lead.

In to pitch the bottom of the 13th inning for the Padres was the man who held the major-league record for career saves at the time, including 42 in 2007, Trevor Hoffman. One thing that the Rockies did have going for them was that they were sending up the top of their batting order.

Kaz Matsui greeted Hoffman with a double to right-center field. Troy Tulowitzki followed with a double to left-center and the Rockies were within a run, 8-7. On the next pitch, Matt Holliday sent a fly ball to deep right field, over the head of Brian Giles for a triple, scoring Troy Tulowitzki with the tying run and putting the winning run 90 feet away with nobody out for the Rockies.

Todd Helton was intentionally walked (the 5th intentional walk of the game between the two teams), bringing Jamey Carroll to the plate. Carroll could easily have been the goat of this game earlier with his throwing error leading off the top of the 11th inning. He had already evened the scales that inning by starting the inning-ending double play. Now was his chance to move firmly into positive territory. And he did so—barely. His fly ball to right field was caught by Brian Giles, Matt Holliday tagged up from third base, and the home plate umpire (Tim McClelland) ruled that Holliday touched home plate safely. And the Colorado Rockies won the 2007 NL Wild Card with a 9-8 win over the San Diego Padres in perhaps the most exciting elimination game ever played.

Aftermath: Doling Out the Wins and Losses

The table below summarizes how Player wins and losses were assigned for this game. The first three columns show pWins, pLosses, and net pWins (pWins minus pLosses). As explained above and elsewhere, pWins tie to team wins. The middle column shows WPA as calculated by Baseball-Reference.com. The final three columns show expected wins (eWins), expected losses (eLosses), and net eWins, which are context-neutral.

Game 163: pW-L Records
(sorted by net pWins)

Colorado	pWins	pLosses	Net pWins	WPA	eWins	eLosses	Net eWins
Matt Holliday	0.37	0.12	0.24	0.41	0.32	0.21	0.11
Troy Tulowitzki	0.25	0.07	0.18	0.28	0.32	0.18	0.14
Matt Herges	0.25	0.07	0.18	0.45	0.19	0.17	0.02
Kazuo Matsui	0.16	0.06	0.10	0.13	0.21	0.18	0.03
Jamey Carroll	0.13	0.05	0.08	0.06	0.13	0.09	0.04
Brian Fuentes	0.11	0.04	0.07	-0.12	0.07	0.07	-0.00
Garrett Atkins	0.08	0.01	0.06	0.08	0.16	0.05	0.11
Todd Helton	0.10	0.05	0.05	0.05	0.20	0.12	0.08
LaTroy Hawkins	0.06	0.00	0.05	0.10	0.06	0.01	0.04
Taylor Buchholz	0.06	0.01	0.05	0.12	0.08	0.04	0.04
Manuel Corpas	0.05	0.00	0.05	0.15	0.04	0.00	0.04
Seth Smith	0.05	0.00	0.04	0.11	0.08	0.01	0.07
Ryan Speier	0.02	0.00	0.02	0.05	0.02	0.00	0.02
Ramon Ortiz	0.01	0.00	0.01	0.03	0.06	0.00	0.06
Jeremy Affeldt	0.02	0.00	0.01	0.03	0.02	0.01	0.01
Cory Sullivan	0.04	0.03	0.01	-0.03	0.05	0.06	-0.01
Yorvit Torrealba	0.05	0.06	-0.01	-0.14	0.16	0.13	0.03
Jeff Baker	0.00	0.01	-0.01	-0.06	0.00	0.02	-0.02
Joe Koshansky	0.00	0.01	-0.01	-0.07	0.00	0.02	-0.02
Brad Hawpe	0.06	0.08	-0.02	-0.15	0.12	0.20	-0.09
Josh Fogg	0.14	0.16	-0.03	0.38	0.26	0.40	-0.14
Ryan Spilborghs	0.00	0.04	-0.04	-0.16	0.00	0.10	-0.10
Jorge Julio	0.00	0.12	-0.11	-0.43	0.00	0.20	-0.20
Team Totals	**2**	**1**	**1**	**0.5**	**2.53**	**2.27**	**0.27**

San Diego	pWins	pLosses	Net pWins	WPA	eWins	eLosses	Net eWins
Adrian Gonzalez	0.14	0.06	0.09	0.32	0.29	0.10	0.20
Joe Thatcher	0.05	0.00	0.05	0.27	0.08	0.00	0.08
Heath Bell	0.11	0.08	0.03	0.34	0.18	0.09	0.09
Doug Brocail	0.06	0.04	0.01	0.18	0.09	0.07	0.02
Morgan Ensberg	0.02	0.01	0.01	0.07	0.03	0.03	0.01
Terrmel Sledge	0.01	0.00	0.01	0.03	0.03	0.00	0.03
Chase Headley	0.00	0.00	0.00	0.01	0.04	0.01	0.03
Scott Hairston	0.15	0.15	-0.00	0.33	0.26	0.22	0.04
Mike Cameron	0.00	0.01	-0.01	0.00	0.00	0.01	-0.01
Brian Myrow	0.00	0.02	-0.02	-0.10	0.00	0.02	-0.02
Josh Bard	0.04	0.06	-0.03	0.02	0.15	0.10	0.05
Oscar Robles	0.00	0.03	-0.03	-0.06	0.00	0.02	-0.02
Geoff Blum	0.05	0.10	-0.05	-0.03	0.13	0.14	-0.01
Jason Lane	0.00	0.06	-0.05	0.00	0.01	0.04	-0.03
Kevin Kouzmanoff	0.04	0.11	-0.08	-0.21	0.13	0.19	-0.06
Michael Barrett	0.02	0.10	-0.09	-0.13	0.05	0.05	0.00
Brady Clark	0.04	0.16	-0.11	-0.02	0.12	0.22	-0.10
Trevor Hoffman	0.03	0.17	-0.14	-0.90	0.03	0.10	-0.07
Brian S. Giles	0.11	0.30	-0.19	0.16	0.15	0.24	-0.09
Khalil Greene	0.01	0.21	-0.20	-0.38	0.07	0.25	-0.18
Jake Peavy	0.11	0.32	-0.21	-0.41	0.41	0.64	-0.23
Team Totals	**1**	**2**	**-1**	**-0.5**	**2.27**	**2.53**	**-0.27**

The star of the game for the Rockies was Matt Holliday who tied the game with his RBI single in the bottom of the 5th inning and then tied the game again with an RBI triple in the bottom of the 13th inning before scoring the winning run himself on a sacrifice fly. Other key contributors for the Rockies included Troy Tulowitzki who scored both game-tying runs that Holliday drove in as well as scoring a third run and driving in one, and Matt Herges, who pitched 3 scoreless innings.

Had the Rockies not rallied in the bottom of the 13th inning, the goat of the game for the Rockies would have been Jorge Julio who allowed a walk, home run, and single (in that order) to the three batters he faced in the top of the 13th inning.

On the Padres side of things, the hero of the game, had they won, in terms of net wins, would have been Adrian Gonzalez, whose 3rd-inning grand slam turned a 3–0 Rockies lead into a 4–3 Padres' one. The most pWins accumulated by any Padre was Scott Hairston, thanks mostly to his 13th-inning two-run home run.

Not surprisingly, when a team scores 8 runs (6 in regulation) and nevertheless loses, the blame is likely to fall on the defensive side of things. Interestingly, the top Padres' pitcher (and player) in net pLosses (the negative of net pWins) is not the relief pitcher who blew the save in the 13th inning, but the starting pitcher who couldn't hold a 5–3 lead and gave up 6 runs in 6.1 innings of work. Brian Giles' appearance near the bottom of the list for the Padres is also largely for defensive reasons, as the fielder who shares responsibility for the Matt Holliday triple and Jamey Carroll sacrifice fly in the bottom of the 13th.

Let's take a closer look below at a few of the players whose pW-L records for this game seemed the most interesting to me.

How Context Affects Player Value: Matt Holliday and Garrett Atkins

Looking at context-neutral net eWins, Matt Holliday and Garrett Atkins end up dead even at +0.11 net eWins. Matt Holliday was 2-for-6 in this game with three strikeouts. Ignoring context, Atkins had a somewhat better (but shorter) day at the plate, going 2-for-3 with a walk (Holliday also had 1 walk) and 1 strikeout. Holliday had one more total base than Atkins (he tripled, Atkins doubled; they both also singled), but also made three more outs (two via strikeout). Holliday's performance in left field also scores as a (context-neutral) net positive for the game (+0.05 wins), while Atkins rates pretty much dead-average defensively (+0.002 wins).

Mix it all together and they're very, very similar context-neutral performances, different perhaps in the mix of how they got there—Holliday had more batting losses but made up for them with more fielding wins—but very similar in overall value.

Except that Garrett Atkins' double was with one out and the bases empty in the seventh inning, with the Rockies already leading 6–5, and was subsequently wasted when Spilborghs and Torrealba struck out to end the inning (although Atkins wouldn't have gotten any baserunning credit had a run scored since Jamey Carroll pinch-ran for him), while Matt Holliday's triple tied the score in the bottom of the thirteenth inning and he followed that up by scoring the winning run two batters later (incidentally, that batter would have been Atkins if he hadn't been pinch-run for 6 innings earlier).

Is the difference in net pWins between Matt Holliday and Garrett Atkins a fair representation of their relative value in this game? I think that it is. I would also, however, point out that the difference in their net pWins (0.18 wins) is far less than the difference in their WPA (0.33 wins) which, in my opinion, over-values Matt Holliday's late-inning heroics at the expense of the early-inning events (by Atkins and others) that made it possible.

How pWins Differ from WPA: Brian Fuentes and Trevor Hoffman

According to Baseball-Reference.com's account of this game, Brian Fuentes' performance was worth –0.12 WPA. This makes some sense as Fuentes was the only Rockies pitcher of the night to be charged with a blown save. I actually credit Brian Fuentes with a net positive performance in context and essentially a dead-average context-neutral performance. That seems odd.

Brian Fuentes pitched the entire top of the 8th inning. That inning went as follows: single (line drive), foul pop-out, strikeout (swinging), wild pitch, double (fly ball), ground-out.

It's not hard to see the average context-neutral rating: Fuentes basically gets full credit for the pop-out and the strikeout, he takes most of the blame for the wild pitch, and then shares credit/blame for three balls-in-play—a groundball, fly ball, and line drive. There are a lot of ways to put those events together in ways that result in a scoreless inning; heck, there are a good number of ways to put those results together in a way that results in no baserunners at all (which, of course, makes even the wild pitch go away).

It's also not hard to see what WPA was thinking. The Rockies needed to get six outs without allowing a run to win the game. Fuentes got two but didn't get the third in time, a run scored, the Padres tied the game.

But what the heck is the net pWins seeing? It's seeing that pitchers don't have a whole lot of control over what happens to a ball once it leaves the batter's bat. In the 2007 National League, a fly ball to left field that stayed in the ballpark turned into an out 90% of the time. The fly ball that Fuentes allowed to Brian Giles was one of the 10%. That's to Fuentes's dis-credit. But, as far as pW-L records are concerned, it's also to the left fielder's dis-credit, Matt Holliday. I discuss the technical details of how event probabilities translate into pW-L records in Chapter 4.

The story is similar for Trevor Hoffman. WPA sees Hoffman's line as double-double-triple-walk-sac fly, game over, Padres lose. For pWins, the story is more subtle and, ultimately, less damning to Trevor Hoffman, partly at the expense of Padres rightfielder Brian Giles, whose net pWins here (-0.19) ranks him as far more responsible for the Padres loss than his WPA (+0.16). The latter is all about Giles's offense, most notably the aforementioned double off of Brian Fuentes. To some extent, Hoffman's job is to put the ball in the field of play and let his defense do its job and, to some (admittedly limited) extent, Hoffman did that: he kept the ball in the ballpark; heck, he even got Jamey Carroll out.

That said, I'm not pretending that Trevor Hoffman was anything but bad that night. He amassed a pWin percentage of 0.140. By that measure, Giles was better (albeit not actually "good"): 0.262. As with Holliday and Atkins above, I think this gives a fair breakdown of the value of their respective performances that night.

He Could Have Been a Hero: Adrian Gonzalez

The top Padres player in net pWins was Adrian Gonzalez, largely on the strength of his third-inning grand slam that gave the Padres a 4–3 lead. For the game, he batted 3-for-6 with a single, double, and (intentional) walk to go with his grand slam, and, arguably, none of his outs came at particularly key moments (although, in any 13-inning loss, trading any out for a home run changes the outcome of the game)—two outs and a man on first in the first inning, in the middle of a 1–2–3 inning in the 9th (again, any at-bat in the 9th inning of a tie game has the potential to be a key moment), as the 1st out in the 13th after the Padres had already taken the lead. It was a solid performance that, ultimately, to some extent, went for naught when Matt Holliday slid in safely.

Comparing their batting lines, it's easy to say that Adrian Gonzalez had a better game that day than Matt Holliday. And their context-neutral pW-L records reflect that: Gonzalez had nearly twice as many net eWins as Holliday. In context, though, Holliday did more to help his team win and his team did, in fact, win. Is that a fair reflection of their respective abilities? No, probably not. But pWins don't measure ability, they measure value.

You Take the Good, You Take the Bad: Scott Hairston

Finally, it is, perhaps, a bit of a surprise to see the man who hit a two-run tiebreaking home run in the top of the 13th inning fairly well down the net PWin list among Padres (and basically dead even). What gives?

Surely, Hairston's home run was the most value play of the game for the Padres. Yes, it was. And, in fact, if you look at the table above, you can see that Scott Hairston did, in fact, lead the San Diego Padres in pWins in this game. He was also among the top six Padres in pLosses for the game, however.

For the game, Scott Hairston went 2-for-7. His other hit was a third-inning single in front of Adrian Gonzalez's grand slam; he also reached on a throwing error to lead off the 11th inning before being forced out at third at the front end of an inning-ending double play. He struck out to end the 6th inning with the score tied and a runner on second base. He grounded out weakly to short to end the 8th inning with the score tied and a runner on second base.

Was Scott Hairston's 13th-inning home run valuable? Sure. Was making the final out of an inning in a tie game with the go-ahead run in scoring position damaging? Absolutely, and Hairston did it twice. The net effect: pretty close to zero.

Conclusion

So there you have it: one game—and a helluva game at that—as seen and measured by pW-L records.

I hope you enjoy reading about pW-L records as much as I enjoyed creating and writing about them. Player won-lost records can be studied more closely at my website, http://baseball.tomthress.com.

1. Player Won-Lost Records—The Basics

The job of a major league baseball player is to help his team win games, for the ultimate purpose of making the playoffs and winning the World Series. Since the early history of major league baseball, pitchers have been credited with Wins and Losses as official measures of the effectiveness of their pitching. Of course, pitcher wins are a fairly crude measure of how well a pitcher did his job, as wins are the product of the performance of the entire team—batters, baserunners, and fielders, in addition to pitchers.

While the implementation of pitcher wins as a measure of pitcher effectiveness is less than ideal, nevertheless the concept is perfectly sound. The ultimate measure of a player's contribution—be he a pitcher, a hitter, a baserunner, or a fielder—is in how much he contributes to his team's wins.

Using play-by-play data, I have constructed a set of pW-L records that attempt to quantify the precise extent to which individual players contribute directly to wins and losses in major league baseball on the baseball field.

Player Wins

Player wins are calculated such that the players on a team earn 3 Player decisions per game. I calculate two sets of player wins: pWins are tied to team wins—the players on a winning team earn 2 pWins and 1 pLoss, the players on a losing team earn 1 pWin and 2 pLosses—while eWins attempt to control for the context in which they were earned, as well as controlling for the abilities of a player's teammates. The contextual factors affecting pW-L records are discussed in detail in Chapter 2.

Player wins end up being on a similar scale to traditional pitcher wins: 20 wins is a good season total, 300 wins is an excellent career total.

There are a total of 72 major-league players who have accumulated 300 or more pWins over the seasons for which I have calculated pW-L records (extrapolating to incorporate missing games). They are shown below. The last two columns present pWins over positional average (pWOPA) and replacement level (pWORL). The calculations of these statistics are described briefly later in this Chapter and in more detail in Chapter 3.

300 pGame Winners of the Retrosheet Era*

Player	*pWins*	*pLosses*	*pWin Pct.*	*pWOPA*	*pWORL*
Hank Aaron	**496.0**	373.2	0.571	43.3	79.8
Barry Bonds	**462.0**	316.8	0.593	59.3	89.7
Willie Mays	**461.0**	333.3	0.580	50.9	83.6
Pete Rose	**436.7**	391.4	0.527	11.9	45.2

Player	pWins	pLosses	pWin Pct.	pWOPA	pWORL
Rickey Henderson	**428.0**	352.9	0.548	29.5	60.2
Carl Yastrzemski	**425.4**	360.7	0.541	18.3	51.7
Stan Musial	***419.9***	*311.2*	*0.574*	*39.7*	*70.3*
Frank Robinson	**398.0**	307.5	0.564	29.7	60.0
Dave Winfield	**395.2**	344.7	0.534	15.0	45.1
Al Kaline	**380.5**	302.4	0.557	25.5	54.2
Cal Ripken	**380.3**	350.1	0.521	27.1	55.2
Mel Ott	***378.5***	*269.3*	*0.584*	*43.3*	*71.9*
Ted Williams	***372.4***	*251.2*	*0.597*	*46.7*	*73.1*
Alex Rodriguez	**369.6**	291.5	0.559	43.4	69.7
Reggie Jackson	**369.2**	298.8	0.553	26.0	55.1
Derek Jeter	**367.2**	318.2	0.536	34.3	60.7
Joe Morgan	**364.6**	281.8	0.564	46.9	73.1
Warren Spahn	***360.6***	*299.9*	*0.546*	*44.0*	*72.7*
Robin Yount	**360.0**	337.9	0.516	18.8	45.9
Nolan Ryan	**359.9**	333.1	0.519	23.5	54.9
Mickey Mantle	**354.5**	232.4	0.604	50.5	74.8
Roberto Clemente	**354.2**	300.8	0.541	13.0	40.0
Craig Biggio	**353.9**	319.4	0.526	18.0	44.1
Andre Dawson	**350.3**	315.9	0.526	7.6	33.9
Eddie Murray	**347.0**	285.2	0.549	19.2	45.7
Brooks Robinson	**346.7**	308.2	0.529	14.0	40.8
Steve Carlton	**344.7**	309.5	0.527	32.5	60.1
Gary Sheffield	**344.1**	291.0	0.542	17.9	43.8
Lou Brock	**342.0**	331.9	0.508	-8.9	18.7
Ken Griffey, Jr.	**339.1**	300.6	0.530	16.3	41.7
Chipper Jones	**337.7**	259.6	0.565	33.3	56.5
Phil Niekro	**337.0**	326.2	0.508	18.2	47.3
Mike Schmidt	**336.3**	256.9	0.567	33.2	56.2
Greg Maddux	**330.9**	273.1	0.548	45.2	74.1
Ozzie Smith	**329.8**	305.3	0.519	20.4	44.7
Billy Williams	**329.2**	281.5	0.539	10.6	36.6
Dwight Evans	**328.9**	275.8	0.544	20.2	44.5
George Brett	**328.1**	273.6	0.545	23.5	48.5
Gaylord Perry	**326.4**	297.0	0.524	24.2	52.4
Rusty Staub	**325.6**	309.2	0.513	-2.2	25.8
Don Sutton	**324.8**	300.0	0.520	24.3	51.5
Vada Pinson	**322.3**	299.2	0.519	1.6	27.2
Tony Gwynn	**321.0**	289.5	0.526	4.6	28.2
Eddie Mathews	**319.4**	238.7	0.572	34.5	57.4
Omar Vizquel	**319.1**	329.7	0.492	3.4	28.4
Roger Clemens	**318.9**	228.4	0.583	51.3	79.9
Sammy Sosa	**318.8**	285.5	0.528	6.3	30.5
Manny Ramirez	**318.4**	252.6	0.558	26.1	49.6
Luis Aparicio	**317.6**	312.1	0.504	12.7	38.6
Luis Gonzalez	**317.0**	294.3	0.519	1.7	25.6
Adrian Beltre	**316.6**	284.0	0.527	14.6	37.5
Paul Molitor	**316.3**	271.1	0.539	20.0	47.5
Tom Seaver	**313.4**	260.5	0.546	38.5	63.0
Luke Appling	***313.4***	*292.8*	*0.517*	*14.1*	*40.5*
Tim Raines	**312.9**	274.8	0.532	11.0	34.1
Dave Parker	**312.8**	276.8	0.531	7.9	32.4
Roberto Alomar	**309.6**	275.9	0.529	21.0	43.8
Steve Finley	**309.5**	290.8	0.516	4.7	28.2
Bobby Abreu	**309.0**	268.1	0.535	11.9	34.6
Rafael Palmeiro	**307.6**	266.6	0.536	9.3	33.6
Albert Pujols	**305.8**	216.2	0.586	33.5	54.1
Tony Perez	**305.3**	253.6	0.546	14.9	38.1
Graig Nettles	**304.7**	269.0	0.531	14.9	37.8
Willie Davis	**304.6**	277.7	0.523	4.9	28.8

Player	pWins	pLosses	pWin Pct.	pWOPA	pWORL
Ernie Banks	304.5	271.1	0.529	12.8	36.5
Enos Slaughter	*303.3*	*257.2*	*0.541*	*14.0*	*38.1*
Carlos Beltran	303.3	268.6	0.530	13.6	35.8
Darrell Evans	302.9	258.2	0.540	15.2	38.1
Torii Hunter	302.7	291.0	0.510	4.2	26.9
Robin Roberts	301.7	274.7	0.523	24.7	50.1
Early Wynn	*301.7*	*279.5*	*0.519*	*22.3*	*48.2*
Harmon Killebrew	301.5	235.4	0.562	21.4	44.2
Robin Roberts	301.6	274.8	0.523	24.6	50.0
Harmon Killebrew	301.4	235.4	0.562	21.4	44.1

*Play-by-play data are missing for many games prior to 1945. Records for missing games are extrapolated based on games for which I have data. Data which include extrapolated data are shown in italics.

Accumulating 300 pWins is certainly an accomplishment. But it's fairly clear looking at the above list that the list of the top players in pWins is not necessarily a list of the best players, period. Just to pick out two examples: Omar Vizquel actually has a career winning percentage under 0.500 and Rusty Staub was (slightly) below average over the course of his career.

Don't get me wrong: Omar Vizquel and Rusty Staub both had fine, noteworthy major-league careers. But did they have better careers than, say, 5-time Cy Young winner Randy Johnson, who "only" amassed 281.7 pWins in his illustrious career?

Wins Over Positional Average

In constructing Player wins and losses, all events are measured against expected, or average, results across the event. Because of this, fielding pW-L records are constructed such that aggregate winning percentages are 0.500 for all fielding positions. Hence, one can say that a shortstop with a defensive winning percentage of 0.475 was a below-average defensive shortstop and a first baseman with a defensive winning percentage of 0.510 was an above-average defensive first baseman, but there is no basis for determining which of these two players was a better fielder—the below-average fielder at the more difficult position or the above-average fielder at the easier position.

From an offensive perspective, batting pW-L records are constructed by comparing across all batters, not simply batters who share the same fielding position. In the National League, this means that offensive comparisons include pitcher hitting, so that, on average, non-pitcher hitters will be slightly above average in the National League, while, of course, because of the DH rule, the average non-pitcher hitter will define the average in the American League.

In order to compare players across positions, it is therefore necessary to normalize players' records relative to an average player at the position(s) a player played. Doing this, we can see, in the above table, that while Rusty Staub amassed a better career winning percentage (0.513) than Omar Vizquel (0.492), Vizquel was above-average for the position(s) he played (mostly shortstop), with 3.4 pWins above "positional average" (pWOPA), while Staub was below-average for the position(s) he played (mostly right field), with −2.2 pWins "above" positional average (pWOPA). I describe the calculation of positional averages in more detail in Chapter 3.

The top 50 players in career pWOPA (for whom I have calculated pW-L records) are shown in the table below.

Top 50 Players in Wins over Positional Average*

	Player	pWins	pLosses	pWin Pct.	pWOPA	pWORL
1	Barry Bonds	462.0	316.8	0.593	**59.3**	89.7
2	Roger Clemens	318.9	228.4	0.583	**51.3**	79.9
3	Willie Mays	461.0	333.3	0.580	**50.9**	83.6
4	Mickey Mantle	354.5	232.4	0.604	**50.5**	74.8
5	Joe Morgan	364.6	281.8	0.564	**46.9**	73.1
6	*Ted Williams*	*372.4*	*251.2*	*0.597*	**46.7**	*73.1*
7	Greg Maddux	330.9	273.1	0.548	**45.2**	74.1
8	*Warren Spahn*	*360.6*	*299.9*	*0.546*	**44.0**	*72.7*
9	Alex Rodriguez	369.6	291.5	0.559	**43.4**	69.7
10	Hank Aaron	496.0	373.2	0.571	**43.3**	79.8
11	*Mel Ott*	*378.5*	*269.3*	*0.584*	**43.3**	*71.9*
12	*Stan Musial*	*419.9*	*311.2*	*0.574*	**39.7**	*70.3*
13	*Joe DiMaggio*	*286.5*	*195.2*	*0.595*	**39.3**	*59.9*
14	Tom Seaver	313.4	260.5	0.546	**38.5**	63.0
15	Randy Johnson	281.7	222.2	0.559	**38.2**	64.1
16	*Lefty Grove*	*219.0*	*153.4*	*0.588*	**37.4**	*55.1*
17	*Lou Gehrig*	*241.8*	*144.5*	*0.626*	**37.0**	*53.6*
18	Eddie Mathews	319.4	238.7	0.572	**34.5**	57.4
19	Bob Gibson	268.7	222.4	0.547	**34.5**	56.0
20	Derek Jeter	367.2	318.2	0.536	**34.3**	60.7
21	Pee Wee Reese	288.1	228.7	0.557	**33.8**	55.6
22	Albert Pujols	305.8	216.2	0.586	**33.5**	54.1
23	Pedro Martinez	194.0	138.6	0.583	**33.4**	51.0
24	Jim Palmer	246.4	190.2	0.564	**33.3**	53.3
25	Chipper Jones	337.7	259.6	0.565	**33.3**	56.5
26	Mike Schmidt	336.3	256.9	0.567	**33.2**	56.2
27	Yogi Berra	245.4	181.9	0.574	**32.9**	50.7
28	Whitey Ford	217.6	168.5	0.564	**32.6**	49.8
29	Steve Carlton	344.7	309.5	0.527	**32.5**	60.1
30	Juan Marichal	235.7	190.9	0.553	**32.3**	50.9
31	*Jimmie Foxx*	*258.7*	*175.2*	*0.596*	**30.3**	*49.5*
32	Frank Robinson	398.0	307.5	0.564	**29.7**	60.0
33	Mariano Rivera	126.7	61.1	0.675	**29.5**	42.2
34	Rickey Henderson	428.0	352.9	0.548	**29.5**	60.2
35	Mike Mussina	224.2	173.5	0.564	**29.3**	51.1
36	Tom Glavine	281.1	250.7	0.529	**29.3**	54.9
37	John Smoltz	240.0	201.3	0.544	**29.0**	51.1
38	Lou Whitaker	298.5	253.2	0.541	**28.7**	50.0
39	*Babe Ruth*	*182.9*	*114.9*	*0.614*	**28.0**	*40.7*
40	Cal Ripken	380.3	350.1	0.521	**27.1**	55.2
41	Duke Snider	270.3	200.9	0.574	**26.7**	46.3
42	Barry Larkin	289.9	246.9	0.540	**26.6**	47.5
43	Fergie Jenkins	290.9	255.7	0.532	**26.4**	50.6
44	Manny Ramirez	318.4	252.6	0.558	**26.1**	49.6
45	Jackie Robinson	192.0	136.5	0.585	**26.0**	39.6
46	Reggie Jackson	369.2	298.8	0.553	**26.0**	55.1
47	Kevin Brown	205.5	166.4	0.553	**25.9**	45.0
48	Al Kaline	380.5	302.4	0.557	**25.5**	54.2
49	*Bob Feller*	*261.5*	*225.5*	*0.537*	**25.4**	*48.2*
50	Johnny Bench	246.5	196.0	0.557	**25.4**	43.4

*Play-by-play data are missing for many games prior to 1945. Records for missing games are extrapolated based on games for which I have data. Data which include extrapolated data are shown in italics.

Focusing on players' wins above average helps to highlight players who had relatively short but brilliant careers, players like Pedro Martinez, whose 194.0 career pWins rank a fairly low 419th across all seasons for which I have calculated pW-L records, while his 33.4 pWOPA rank a much more impressive 23rd, or Mariano Rivera, whose 126.7

pWins rank even lower than Pedro's (1,091st) but who ranks 33rd in career pWOPA with 29.5.

Wins Over Replacement Level

Replacement Level is the level of performance which a team should be able to get from a player who they can find easily on short notice—such as a minor-league call-up or a veteran waiver-wire pickup. The theory here is that major league baseball players only have value to a team above and beyond what the team could get from basically pulling players off the street. That is, there's no real marginal value to having a third baseman make routine plays that anybody who's capable of playing third base at the high school or college level could make, since if a major-league team were to lose its starting third baseman, they would fill the position with somebody and that somebody would, in fact, make at least those routine plays at third base. This is similar to the economic concept of Opportunity Cost.

For my work, I define Replacement Level as equal to a winning percentage one weighted standard deviation below Positional Average, with separate standard deviations calculated for pitchers and non-pitchers. Unique standard deviations are calculated in this way for each year. These standard deviations are then applied to the unique Positional Averages of each individual player. Overall, this works out to an average Replacement Level of about 0.455 (0.464 for non-pitchers, and 0.439 for pitchers). A team of 0.455 players would have an expected winning percentage of 0.366 (59–103 over a 162-game season). I describe the calculation of replacement levels and wins over replacement level (WORL) in more detail in Chapter 3.

The top 50 players in career pWORL (for whom I have calculated pW-L records) are shown in the table below.

Top 50 Players in Wins Over Replacement Level

	Player	pWins	pLosses	pWin Pct.	pWOPA	pWORL
1	Barry Bonds	462.0	316.8	0.593	59.3	**89.7**
2	Willie Mays	461.0	333.3	0.580	50.9	**83.6**
3	Roger Clemens	318.9	228.4	0.583	51.3	**79.9**
4	Hank Aaron	496.0	373.2	0.571	43.3	**79.8**
5	Mickey Mantle	354.5	232.4	0.604	50.5	**74.8**
6	Greg Maddux	330.9	273.1	0.548	45.2	**74.1**
7	*Ted Williams*	*372.4*	*251.2*	*0.597*	*46.7*	***73.1***
8	Joe Morgan	364.6	281.8	0.564	46.9	**73.1**
9	*Warren Spahn*	*360.6*	*299.9*	*0.546*	*44.0*	***72.7***
10	Mel Ott	378.5	269.3	0.584	43.3	**71.9**
11	Stan Musial	419.9	311.2	0.574	39.7	**70.3**
12	Alex Rodriguez	369.6	291.5	0.559	43.4	**69.7**
13	Randy Johnson	281.7	222.2	0.559	38.2	**64.1**
14	Tom Seaver	313.4	260.5	0.546	38.5	**63.0**
15	Derek Jeter	367.2	318.2	0.536	34.3	**60.7**
16	Rickey Henderson	428.0	352.9	0.548	29.5	**60.2**
17	Steve Carlton	344.7	309.5	0.527	32.5	**60.1**
18	Frank Robinson	398.0	307.5	0.564	29.7	**60.0**
19	*Joe DiMaggio*	*286.5*	*195.2*	*0.595*	*39.3*	***59.9***
20	Eddie Mathews	319.4	238.7	0.572	34.5	**57.4**
21	Chipper Jones	337.7	259.6	0.565	33.3	**56.5**
22	Mike Schmidt	336.3	256.9	0.567	33.2	**56.2**

	Player	pWins	pLosses	pWin Pct.	pWOPA	pWORL
23	Bob Gibson	268.7	222.4	0.547	34.5	56.0
24	Pee Wee Reese	288.1	228.7	0.557	33.8	55.6
25	Cal Ripken	380.3	350.1	0.521	27.1	55.2
26	Reggie Jackson	369.2	298.8	0.553	26.0	55.1
27	*Lefty Grove*	*219.0*	*153.4*	*0.588*	*37.4*	**55.1**
28	Nolan Ryan	359.9	333.1	0.519	23.5	54.9
29	Tom Glavine	281.1	250.7	0.529	29.3	54.9
30	Al Kaline	380.5	302.4	0.557	25.5	54.2
31	Albert Pujols	305.8	216.2	0.586	33.5	54.1
32	*Lou Gehrig*	*241.8*	*144.5*	*0.626*	*37.0*	**53.6**
33	Jim Palmer	246.4	190.2	0.564	33.3	53.3
34	Gaylord Perry	326.4	297.0	0.524	24.2	52.4
35	Carl Yastrzemski	425.4	360.7	0.541	18.3	51.7
36	Don Sutton	324.8	300.0	0.520	24.3	51.5
37	John Smoltz	240.0	201.3	0.544	29.0	51.1
38	Mike Mussina	224.2	173.5	0.564	29.3	51.1
39	Pedro Martinez	194.0	138.6	0.583	33.4	51.0
40	Juan Marichal	235.7	190.9	0.553	32.3	50.9
41	Yogi Berra	245.4	181.9	0.574	32.9	50.7
42	Fergie Jenkins	290.9	255.7	0.532	26.4	50.6
43	Robin Roberts	301.7	274.7	0.523	24.7	50.1
44	Lou Whitaker	298.5	253.2	0.541	28.7	50.0
45	Whitey Ford	217.6	168.5	0.564	32.6	49.8
46	Manny Ramirez	318.4	252.6	0.558	26.1	49.6
47	*Jimmie Foxx*	*258.7*	*175.2*	*0.596*	*30.3*	**49.5**
48	Tommy John	286.7	253.7	0.531	25.1	49.3
49	George Brett	328.1	273.6	0.545	23.5	48.5
50	Bert Blyleven	295.7	264.0	0.528	22.3	48.3

Measuring against replacement level instead of average helps to weed out pure compilers such as Rusty Staub while showing a mix of short excellent careers (e.g., Pedro Martinez) together with long, more modestly above-average careers, such as Don Sutton.

The choice between wins, WOPA, and WORL will likely depend on exactly what one is looking for. The calculation of WOPA and WORL are described in more detail in Chapter 3. Wins, WOPA, and WORL are compared to the popular baseball statistic, WAR, in Chapter 8.

The next section of this Chapter explains how I calculate pW-L records.

Calculating pW-L Records: pWins and pLosses

The starting point for constructing pWins and pLosses is Win Probabilities. The concept of Win Probability was first developed by Eldon and Harlan Mills in 1969 and published in their book, *Player Win Averages*. Win Probabilities, and my calculation of them, are described in more detail in Chapter 9.

The basic concept underlying win probability systems is elegantly simple. At any point in time, the situation in a baseball game can be uniquely described by considering the inning, the number and location of any baserunners, the number of outs, and the difference in score between the two teams. Given these four things, one can calculate a probability of each team winning the game. Hence, at the start of a batter's plate appearance, one can calculate the probability of the batting team winning the game.

After the completion of the batter's plate appearance, one can once again calculate the probability of the batting team winning the game. The difference between these two probabilities, typically called the Win Probability Advancement or something similar, is the value added by the offensive team during that particular plate appearance (where such value could, of course, be negative).

If we assume that the two teams are evenly matched, then the initial probability of winning is 50% for each team. At the end of the game, the probability of one team winning will be 100%, while the probability of the other team winning will be 0%. The sum of the Win Probability advancements for a particular team will add up to exactly 50% for a winning team (100% minus 50%) and exactly –50% for a losing team (0% minus 50%). Hence, Win Probability Advancement is a perfect accounting structure for allocating credit for team wins and losses to individual players.

Changes in Win Probabilities are credited to the individual players responsible for these changes. These contributions are called Player Decisions here. Positive changes in Win Probabilities are credited as Positive Player Decisions, while negative changes in Win Probabilities are credited as Negative Player Decisions.

Player Decisions are assigned to both offensive and defensive players on each individual play. Anything which increases the probability of the offensive team winning is credited as positive decisions to the offensive player(s) involved and as negative decisions to the defensive player(s) involved. Anything which increases the probability of the defensive team winning is credited as positive decisions to the defensive player(s) involved and as negative decisions to the offensive player(s) involved. Within any individual game, the number of positive Player Decisions by offensive players on one team will be exactly equal to the number of negative Player Decisions by defensive players on the other team and vice versa. Similarly, the number of positive Player Decisions collected by members of the winning team will exactly equal the number of negative Player Decisions accumulated by the losing team (and, again, vice versa).

Player Decisions assigned in this way provide a perfect accounting structure for assigning 100% of the credit for all changes in Win Probability to players on both teams involved in a game. The sum of the positive Player Decisions minus the sum of the negative Player Decisions for one team in one game will always be the same for any team win (0.5) or loss (-0.5). Most Win Probability systems which I have seen focus on a single number, which is (more or less) the difference between positive Player Decisions and negative Player Decisions, and define this number as something like Win Probability Advancements.

Personally, I find such a construction unsatisfactory. To my mind, net Win Probabilities added don't reveal the full context in which a player's performance took place. From my perspective, 9 wins and 2 losses is a different performance than 15 wins and 8 losses, and that difference needs to be maintained. Moreover, expressing Win Probability Added (WPA) as a single number does not enable one to isolate the specific contextual factors underlying that performance, thereby assessing the extent to which a player's performance was influenced by the performances of his teammates and the specific timing of his performance.

Hence, I convert these Player Decisions into Context-Dependent Player Wins and Losses, which I call pWins and pLosses. I simultaneously construct Context-Neutral Player Wins and Losses, called eWins and eLosses, as well, which can be compared to pWins and pLosses, to identify the contextual factors affecting players' performances and how those contextual factors affect the translation of player wins and losses into team wins and losses.

For both context-dependent and context-neutral player decisions, two adjustments (#1 and #2 below) are made to these results to move from initial player decisions to my final pW-L records.

#1. Normalizing Component Won-Lost Records to 0.500

A key implicit assumption underlying Player Won-Loss Records is that major league baseball players will have a combined winning percentage of 0.500. While this is trivially true at the aggregate level, almost regardless of what you do, it should also be true at finer levels of detail as well.

So, for example, if Player Won-Loss records are calculated correctly, the total number of wins accumulated by baserunners on third base for advancing on wild pitches and passed balls should be exactly equal to the total number of losses accumulated by baserunners on third base for failing to advance on wild pitches or passed balls. Likewise, the total number of wins accumulated by second basemen for turning double plays on ground balls in double-play situations should be exactly equal to the total number of losses accumulated by second basemen for failing to turn double plays on ground balls in double-play situations.

To ensure this symmetry, therefore, I normalize player decisions to ensure that the total number of positive player decisions is exactly equal to the number of negative player decisions for every component of player decisions as well as by sub-component, at the finest level of detail which makes logical sense in each case. The components of pW-L records are discussed in detail in Chapter 4.

#2. Normalizing Player Decisions by Game

The total number of player decisions accumulated in an average major league baseball game is around 3.3 per team. This number varies tremendously game-to-game, however, with some teams earning 2 wins in some team victories while some other teams may earn 6 wins in team losses. At the end of the day (or season), however, all wins are equal. Hence, in my work, I have chosen to assign each team one player win and one player loss for each team game. In addition, the winning team earns a second full win, while the losing team earns a second full loss. Ties are allocated as 1.5 Wins and 1.5 Losses for both teams. Context-neutral player decisions (eWins and eLosses) are also normalized to average three Player decisions per game. For eWins and eLosses, this normalization is done at the season level, however, rather than the game level, so that different numbers of context-neutral player decisions will be earned in different games.

Why 3 Player Decisions Per Game?

The choice of three Player Decisions per game here is largely arbitrary. I chose three because the resulting pW-L records end up being on a similar scale to traditional pitcher won-lost records, with which most baseball fans are quite familiar. For example, expressed in this way, Jayson Werth led the major leagues in 2010 with 23.6 (Context-Dependent) Player Wins, while Ichiro Suzuki led the majors with 21.8 losses.

In comparison, C.C. Sabathia and Roy Halladay led all major league pitchers in 2010 with 21 wins (Sabathia amassed 16.2 Player Wins, while Halladay had 17.0) while Joe Saunders (14.4 Player losses) led the major leagues with 17 losses. Across all seasons for which I have calculated pW-L records, the most pWins accumulated by a player in a single season was 30.7 by Babe Ruth in 1927 (against 15.3 pLosses). The most single-season pLosses were accumulated by Vladimir Guerrero in 2001 with 23.2 pLosses (and 25.5 pWins).

This normalization process has no effect on the relative ordering of players—if pWins and pLosses were normalized to be equal to 6 per game, Jayson Werth would have continued to lead the major leagues in wins in 2010; he simply would have had twice as many of them. Nor does it affect player winning percentages, as pWins and pLosses are scaled proportionally.

One consequence of my choice of three Player Decisions per team game is that, as a result of this normalization process, total Player Wins for a league as a whole will be equal to total Win Shares as constructed by Bill James. Hence, one might think of pW-L records as calculated here as measuring "true" win shares.

Because the players on a team receive only two team-dependent wins for each team win, however, the total number of team-dependent wins will be less than the total number of Win Shares for teams with winning records. On the other hand, because the players on a team receive one team-dependent win for each team loss, the total number of team-dependent wins will be greater than the total number of Win Shares for teams with losing records.

Why Do Players Get Wins in Games Their Team Loses?

If one is interested in assigning credit to players for team wins or blame to players for team losses, one might think that it would make sense to only credit a player with pWins in games which his team won and only credit pLosses in games which his team lost. I have chosen instead to give players some wins even in team losses and some losses even in team wins. I do this for a couple of reasons.

Most simply put, baseball players do tons of positive things in team losses and baseball players do tons of negative things in team wins. Throwing away all of those things based solely on the final score of the game leads, in my opinion, to too much valuable data simply being lost. It makes the results too dependent on context.

As I noted above, in the average major league baseball game for which I have calculated pW-L records, the average team amasses 3.3 player decisions. The win probability for the winning team goes from 50% at the start of the game to 100% at the end, so that the winning team will amass exactly 0.5 more positive player decisions than negative player decisions by construction. This means that the players on an average winning team will amass a combined record of something like 1.9–1.4 in a typical game. That works out to a 0.576 winning percentage, or about 93 wins in a 162-game schedule (93–69). Put another way, more than 40% of all Player Decisions (1–0.576) would be zeroed out in a system that credited no Player wins in team losses (or Player losses in team wins). That's simply too much for me to be comfortable making such an adjustment.

There are two reasons why such a large percentage of plays do not contribute to victory. First, it is indicative, I think, of the fairly high level of competitive balance within major league baseball. Put simply, even very bad major league baseball teams are not that much worse than very good major league baseball teams.

But the other reason why such a large percentage of plays do not contribute to victory, and why I assign player wins even in team losses and vice-versa, is because of the rules of baseball. Because there is no clock in baseball, the only way for a game to end is for the winning team to do some things that reduce its chances of winning: it has to make 3 outs per inning for at least 8 innings (not counting rain-shortened games). Likewise, a losing team is guaranteed to do some things that increase its chance of winning: it must get the other team out 3 times per inning.

My system still rewards players who do positive things that contribute to wins more favorably than players who do positive things that lead to losses. As I noted above, an average team will amass a player winning percentage of approximately 0.576 in team wins (and 0.424 in team losses). By assigning 2 wins and only 1 loss in team wins, however, players will amass a 0.667 player winning percentage in team wins (and 0.333 in team losses). So, player wins that lead to team wins will still be more valuable than player wins that happen in team losses. The latter are simply not worthless.

Relationship of Player Decisions to Team Decisions

Under my system, to move from players' team-dependent won-lost records (pWins and pLosses) to a team won-lost record, one subtracts out what I call "background wins" and "background losses." One-third of a player's decisions are background wins and one-third of a player's decisions are background losses. Mathematically, then, if the sum of the team-dependent won-lost records of the players on a team is W wins and L losses, then the team's won-lost record will be as follows:

$$\text{Team Wins} = W - (W + L) / 3; \quad \text{Team Losses} = L - (W + L) / 3$$

What this means is that a team of, say, .450 players will not play .450 ball, but will instead play something closer to .350 ball. Consider, for example, the 2011 Houston Astros. The 2011 Astros finished with a record of 56–106 (a .346 winning percentage). I view them as having been essentially a replacement-level team. The players on the 2011 Astros earned a total of −3.6 pWORL. The combined winning percentage of the Astros' players, however, was not the .346 winning percentage the Astros amassed, but, instead, was 0.449.

The relationship between player and team wins, expressed as wins in a 162-game season are shown in the table below.

Team Wins	Team Win Pct.	Player Wins	Player Win Pct.
50	0.309	212	0.436
60	0.370	222	0.457
70	0.432	232	0.477
75	0.463	237	0.488
80	0.494	242	0.498
81	0.500	243	0.500
82	0.506	244	0.502
85	0.525	247	0.508
90	0.556	252	0.519
95	0.586	257	0.529
100	0.617	262	0.539
110	0.679	272	0.560

There are two implications to this relationship between player wins and team wins. First, the range of winning percentages for players is narrower than the range of team winning percentages. This is important in evaluating the concept of replacement level.

As noted above, in my work, team-level replacement level is a winning percentage between 0.340 and 0.350. But, *player*-level replacement level is closer to 0.450.

The second implication is that player wins and losses do not have a purely additive effect on team wins and losses; instead, the effect is somewhat more multiplicative. In an average game, the players on the winning team will amass a (context-neutral) winning percentage of approximately 0.576–not all that much above 0.500. Having players who are a little bit better than average will translate into a team that is a lot better than average. In fact, as the above table shows, a team of 0.576 players would win well over 100 games in a 162-game season. The reverse is true of below-average players. A team of slightly below-average players will lose far more often than they win: as noted earlier, the players on the 2011 Houston Astros amassed a pWin percentage of 0.449. In fact, that number has already been adjusted to reflect the Astros' team record of 56–106, and hence understates the raw context-neutral performance of the Astros' players. In terms of raw context-neutral numbers, with no adjustments, the combined performance of the players on the 2011 Houston Astros was a player winning percentage of 0.482. In other words, in this case, a team of 0.482 players became a 0.346 team.

Players' final won-lost records will be pushed away from 0.500 depending on exactly how their performance translates into team wins and losses. So, the final Player records of the Astros' players fell from 0.483 to 0.449 because the players' losses contributed more to losses than the players' wins were able to contribute to team victories. By tying to team wins and losses, pWins and pLosses for a player will be dependent on the context in which they take place. Part of that context is the quality of a player's teammates. The contextual factors affecting pW-L records are discussed in more detail in Chapter 2.

But even beyond the actual context of pWins and pLosses, this tendency of player records to push away from 0.500 also affects eWins and eLosses for a player as well. We can expect players with context-neutral won-lost records over 0.500 to have their record translate into (slightly) more wins than might be implied by their raw record, and players with context-neutral won-lost records below 0.500 to have their record translate into (slightly) more losses than their raw record. This expected team win adjustment to context-neutral pW-L records (eWins and eLosses) is discussed briefly later in this Chapter and in more detail in Chapter 2.

Context-Neutral pW-L Records: eWins and eLosses

In addition to pWins and pLosses, which tie to team wins, I also construct a set of player wins and losses which attempt to control for context. I call these **eWins** and **eLosses**, where the "e" stands for "expected." These are, in effect, how many wins (and losses) a player would have been expected to contribute to a team if he played in a perfectly neutral context with perfectly average teammates.

These eWins and eLosses are built up from three pieces: context-neutral win probabilities, expected context, and an expected team win adjustment.

Context-Neutral Win Probabilities

Traditionally, win-probability systems are purely context-dependent. In fact, however, I do not think that this is necessarily the appropriate starting point for measuring player value. Rather, I am interested in beginning with an assessment of players' performances in the absence of the contexts in which the players actually performed. That is, what would be the expected won-lost record for a player, given his actual performance, assuming that performance had come in a neutral context? To answer this question, I construct a set of context-neutral Player Decisions. Once these are constructed, I can then add back in the contextual information in a way that clearly identifies how players' values were affected by the context in which they performed. The contextual factors affecting pW-L records and their impact on pWins and eWins are discussed in Chapter 2.

Player Decisions are divided into three categories (#1, #2 and #3 below) for the purpose of calculating context-neutral win probabilities: independent events, base-state dependent events, and purely contextual events.

#1. INDEPENDENT EVENTS

Most events can happen regardless of the base-out situation. One can strike out at any time, regardless of how many baserunners or outs there are. Similarly, a triple could happen at any time regardless of the number of baserunners. All batter results, except for double plays (which are base-state dependent), intentional walks, and bunts, fall into the category of independent events. Intentional walks and bunts are treated as purely contextual events, which are described below.

For independent events, the expected win probability of such an event is calculated for each event within the league-year using the Win Probability Matrix for the ballpark in which the event took place.

For example, the win probability of a home run at Wrigley Field in 2005 is calculated by taking every plate appearance that took place in a National League ballpark in 2005 and calculating, for that plate appearance, what the added win probability would have been had the game been played in Wrigley Field and the batter hit a home run. The context-neutral win probability of a home run at Wrigley Field in 2005 is then equal to the average of all of these probabilities. In this case, the average win probability added by a home run at Wrigley Field in 2005 was 0.141 wins.

In the case of events which may or may not lead to baserunner advancement—e.g., outs, singles, doubles—expected results are calculated based on average baserunner advancement, just as is done with contextual Player Decisions.

#2. BASE-STATE DEPENDENT EVENTS

Some events can only happen given certain baserunners or a certain number of outs. For example, one can only ground into a double play with at least one baserunner on and less than two outs. Any player decisions accumulated by a baserunner on third base can, of course, only be accumulated in a base-out state that includes a runner on third base.

For baserunner game points (except for stolen bases, which are treated as purely contextual events and discussed below) and double plays, the context-neutral win probability of the event is calculated the same as for independent events, except that the average win probability is only calculated across events with relevant base-out states.

So, for example, the context-neutral player decisions associated with a double play are calculated as the average win probability, given the ballpark in which the game takes place, added from hitting into a double play across double-play situations (runner on first base and less than two out). For a ground ball to the shortstop at Wrigley Field in 2005, the average win probability added by a double play is 0.011 losses (from the batter's perspective) (on top of the 0.046 losses accrued from the initial ground-out).

For baserunner advancements and baserunner outs, context-neutral win probabilities are only averaged given the specific batting event and hit type. That is, the context-neutral player decisions for a runner on third base advancing on a fly out are calculated only considering plays in which a runner on third base advances on a fly out. Similarly, the context-neutral player decisions for a runner on first base who only advances to second base on a single are calculated only considering plays in which a runner on first base does not advance to third on a single.

#3. Purely Contextual Events

While it is possible to remove much, if not all, of the context from most plays, there are certain plays which are, essentially, purely elective plays, and are therefore inextricably tied to the context in which they take place. In my opinion, it would be wrong to attempt to divorce these plays from their context.

Three types of plays fall into this category: intentional walks, stolen base attempts (including stolen bases, caught stealings, pickoffs, and balks), and bunts (regardless of either situation or outcome). In each of these three cases, the context-neutral player decisions are simply set equal to context-dependent player decisions.

Constructing eWins and eLosses from Context-Neutral Win Probabilities

Context-neutral Player Wins and Losses are normalized to be equal to aggregate Context-dependent Player Wins and Losses for each component and sub-component. Hence, the total number of Context-Neutral Player Wins accumulated for a particular type of event or sub-event—say, home runs—will equal the total number of Context-Dependent Player Wins accumulated over the same set of events. This normalization is done at the season/league level. At the game or team level, however, the total number of context-neutral player decisions need not be equal to the number of context-dependent decisions, either at the component level (the Components of pW-L records are described in detail in Chapter 4) or in the aggregate.

Having completed this normalization process, one might think that the construction of eWins and eLosses is complete. In fact, however, eWins and eLosses are intended to reflect *expected* wins and losses. As such, two more adjustments are made to produce final eWins and eLosses.

Specifically, context-neutral player decisions are converted into eWins and eLosses by making two expected contextual adjustments: Context and Win Adjustments.

Expected Context

In relating player wins and losses to team wins and losses, the context in which a player's performance takes place matters. This is reflected in two context measures related to Context-Dependent player decisions: inter-game context and intra-game context. These terms are defined and discussed in Chapter 2.

In calculating context-neutral player decisions, one might think that the most obvious thing to do would be to simply set inter-game and intra-game context both equal to 1 for all players. In fact, however, this will lead to there being a clear and obvious relationship between players' positions and their tendency to have more or fewer context-dependent player decisions (pWins, pLosses) than context-neutral decisions (eWins, eLosses). Because of this, I think that it is more appropriate to calculate an Expected Context for each player, based on the position(s) which the player played. This is done as follows.

OFFENSE: BATTING AND BASERUNNING

Expected contexts are calculated for four different positions: pinch hitter, pinch runner, pitcher, and other. For each of these positions, expected context is set equal to the average context for the position for the league and season in question.

PITCHING

Starting pitchers have an average inter-game context of 1.002 and an average intra-game context of 1.076, a combined average context of 1.078. For relief pitchers, the numbers are 0.995, 0.821, and 0.816, respectively. Expected contexts for starting pitchers are set equal to the average context for starting pitchers for the relevant league and season. The same is true for relief pitchers: expected context is set equal for all relief pitchers—closers, setup men, mop-up men—regardless of their actual context.

FIELDING

Across all seasons for which I have calculated pW-L records, there is no obvious relationship between context and fielding position. Hence, expected context is set equal to 1 for all fielding player decisions.

FINAL RESULTS

Expected context for a player is calculated by taking the weighted average of the expected contexts for the player's offensive, pitching, and fielding decisions.

Expected Win Adjustments

One of the key implications of my work is that the difference between winning and losing is very small in major league baseball. In an average major league baseball game across all seasons for which I have calculated pW-L records, for example, the winning team accumulated around 1.9 positive player decisions—the building block of pWins—and 1.4 negative player decisions—the building block of pLosses. In other words, the average winning team compiled a team winning percentage of 1.000 (by definition), but the *players* on that team compiled a combined winning percentage of something like 0.576, which works out to about a 93–69 record in a 162-game schedule.

Looking at the issue from the opposite direction, teams whose players compiled a combined player winning percentage around 0.510 (0.505–0.515) had an average team winning percentage of about 0.565 (92–70), while teams whose players compiled a combined player winning percentage around 0.490 (0.485–0.495) had an average team winning percentage around 0.443 (72–90).

Being a little above average helps a lot in producing team victories.

For pWins and pLosses, this is reflected in the Intra-Game Win Adjustment which ties pW-L records to team won-lost records. Intra-game win adjustments are defined and discussed in Chapter 2. In looking at intra-game win adjustments, it is obvious that intra-game win adjustments correlate at least somewhat reasonably well with player winning percentages: good players tend to have positive intra-game win adjustments, while weaker players tend to have negative intra-game win adjustments. This correlation is not perfect, as one's intra-game win adjustments are also affected by one's teammates.

To recognize this correlation, eWins and eLosses are adjusted for intra-game win adjustments. But to maintain the context-neutrality of the results, these records are adjusted based upon *expected* intra-game win adjustments.

Expected intra-game win adjustments for a player are calculated based on the expected impact of the player on the record of a 0.500 team. The exact process by which these are calculated is described in some detail in Chapter 2. Expected win adjustments will be positive for players with context-neutral winning percentages over .500 and negative for players with context-neutral winning percentages below .500. Hence, this has the effect of increasing the spread in context-neutral player winning percentages among players.

The top 50 players in career regular-season pWins over positional average and replacement level were presented earlier in this chapter. The corresponding figures for eWins are presented next. As in the earlier tables, eWins and eLosses are extrapolated for players for whom I am missing some games in seasons prior to 1945. Records which include extrapolated games are italicized in these tables.

Top 50 Players in eWins Over Positional Average

	Player	eWins	eLosses	eWin Pct.	eWOPA	eWORL
1	Barry Bonds	452.5	309.5	0.594	**58.5**	88.2
2	*Ted Williams*	*374.0*	*249.2*	*0.600*	**48.5**	*74.9*
3	Roger Clemens	311.9	228.2	0.577	**47.9**	76.0
4	Greg Maddux	323.6	263.6	0.551	**46.0**	74.1
5	*Mel Ott*	*369.0*	*258.9*	*0.588*	**44.1**	*71.8*
6	Mickey Mantle	341.4	235.1	0.592	**42.8**	66.6
7	Alex Rodriguez	365.2	289.8	0.558	**42.2**	68.3
8	Willie Mays	438.1	329.6	0.571	**41.7**	73.4
9	Joe Morgan	356.3	285.1	0.556	**41.2**	67.1
10	Hank Aaron	478.9	364.8	0.568	**39.4**	74.9
11	*Warren Spahn*	*346.0*	*295.9*	*0.539*	**38.2**	*66.3*
12	*Stan Musial*	*414.1*	*310.0*	*0.572*	**37.5**	*67.9*
13	Mike Schmidt	332.0	247.8	0.573	**35.7**	58.2
14	Randy Johnson	268.0	219.3	0.550	**32.5**	57.6
15	Frank Robinson	387.1	295.5	0.567	**30.7**	59.9
16	Tom Seaver	303.2	266.0	0.533	**30.5**	54.9
17	Pedro Martinez	182.2	132.9	0.578	**30.2**	46.9
18	Kevin Brown	206.9	159.6	0.565	**29.8**	48.7
19	Eddie Mathews	309.6	239.5	0.564	**29.4**	51.9
20	Mike Mussina	221.7	171.1	0.565	**29.3**	50.7
21	*Lou Gehrig*	*227.7*	*147.3*	*0.607*	**28.9**	*45.0*

	Player	eWins	eLosses	eWin Pct.	eWOPA	eWORL
22	Rickey Henderson	421.1	347.8	0.548	**28.7**	59.0
23	Gaylord Perry	327.6	291.1	0.530	**27.6**	55.6
24	*Jimmie Foxx*	*247.3*	*170.4*	*0.592*	**27.5**	*46.0*
25	Bob Gibson	257.9	225.3	0.534	**27.5**	48.6
26	*Joe DiMaggio*	*265.8*	*198.9*	*0.572*	**27.3**	*47.2*
27	Albert Pujols	294.5	218.5	0.574	**26.9**	47.2
28	Cal Ripken	372.8	344.2	0.520	**26.1**	53.7
29	*Babe Ruth*	*175.2*	*112.5*	*0.609*	**25.5**	*37.8*
30	John Smoltz	220.2	188.6	0.539	**25.3**	45.5
31	Duke Snider	276.8	210.2	0.568	**25.1**	45.4
32	Chipper Jones	320.8	259.6	0.553	**25.1**	47.6
33	Jim Thome	269.5	205.4	0.567	**24.7**	46.6
34	Tom Glavine	281.2	260.8	0.519	**24.6**	50.8
35	*Arky Vaughan*	*250.1*	*206.5*	*0.548*	**24.4**	*44.5*
36	*Charlie Gehringer*	*255.1*	*210.3*	*0.548*	**24.4**	*44.9*
37	Al Kaline	378.3	303.2	0.555	**24.1**	52.8
38	Curt Schilling	205.1	173.2	0.542	**23.9**	43.3
39	Nolan Ryan	335.1	306.1	0.523	**23.8**	52.9
40	Frank Thomas	249.0	186.1	0.572	**23.6**	46.1
41	Ken Griffey, Jr.	345.5	293.1	0.541	**23.3**	48.5
42	Manny Ramirez	304.1	244.6	0.554	**23.3**	45.8
43	Tim Hudson	196.3	165.7	0.542	**23.2**	41.5
44	*Red Ruffing*	*244.8*	*215.6*	*0.532*	**22.6**	*43.5*
45	Carl Yastrzemski	441.2	367.1	0.546	**22.5**	56.8
46	Jim Palmer	239.6	205.0	0.539	**22.5**	42.9
47	Steve Carlton	330.9	315.3	0.512	**22.5**	49.7
48	Johnny Bench	234.9	190.5	0.552	**22.5**	39.7
49	Don Sutton	321.8	300.4	0.517	**22.4**	49.6
50	Bobby Grich	242.9	209.7	0.537	**22.4**	40.1

Top 50 Players in eWins Over Replacement Level

	Player	eWins	eLosses	eWin Pct.	eWOPA	eWORL
1	Barry Bonds	452.5	309.5	0.594	58.5	**88.2**
2	Roger Clemens	311.9	228.2	0.577	47.9	**76.0**
3	*Ted Williams*	*374.0*	*249.2*	*0.600*	*48.5*	**74.9**
4	Hank Aaron	478.9	364.8	0.568	39.4	**74.9**
5	Greg Maddux	323.6	263.2	0.551	46.0	**74.1**
6	Willie Mays	438.1	329.6	0.571	41.7	**73.4**
7	*Mel Ott*	*369.0*	*258.9*	*0.588*	*44.1*	**71.8**
8	Alex Rodriguez	365.2	289.8	0.558	42.2	**68.3**
9	*Stan Musial*	*414.1*	*310.0*	*0.572*	*37.5*	**67.9**
10	Joe Morgan	356.3	285.1	0.556	41.2	**67.1**
11	Mickey Mantle	341.4	235.1	0.592	42.8	**66.6**
12	*Warren Spahn*	*346.0*	*295.9*	*0.539*	*38.2*	**66.3**
13	Frank Robinson	387.1	295.5	0.567	30.7	**59.9**
14	Rickey Henderson	421.1	347.8	0.548	28.7	**59.0**
15	Mike Schmidt	332.0	247.8	0.573	35.7	**58.2**
16	Randy Johnson	268.0	219.3	0.550	32.5	**57.6**
17	Carl Yastrzemski	441.2	367.1	0.546	22.5	**56.8**
18	Gaylord Perry	327.6	291.1	0.530	27.6	**55.6**
19	Tom Seaver	303.2	266.0	0.533	30.5	**54.9**
20	Cal Ripken	372.8	344.2	0.520	26.1	**53.7**
21	Nolan Ryan	335.1	306.1	0.523	23.8	**52.9**
22	Al Kaline	378.3	303.2	0.555	24.1	**52.8**
23	Eddie Mathews	309.6	239.5	0.564	29.4	**51.9**
24	Tom Glavine	281.2	260.8	0.519	24.6	**50.8**
25	Mike Mussina	221.7	171.1	0.565	29.3	**50.7**
26	Steve Carlton	330.9	315.3	0.512	22.5	**49.7**
27	Reggie Jackson	352.0	290.7	0.548	21.7	**49.7**

	Player	eWins	eLosses	eWin Pct.	eWOPA	eWORL
28	Don Sutton	321.8	300.4	0.517	22.4	**49.6**
29	Kevin Brown	206.9	159.6	0.565	29.8	**48.7**
30	Bert Blyleven	301.2	270.2	0.527	22.1	**48.6**
31	Bob Gibson	257.9	225.3	0.534	27.5	**48.6**
32	Ken Griffey, Jr.	345.5	293.1	0.541	23.3	**48.5**
33	Robin Roberts	303.0	281.5	0.518	22.1	**47.9**
34	Derek Jeter	355.0	331.9	0.517	21.4	**47.7**
35	Chipper Jones	320.8	259.6	0.553	25.1	**47.6**
36	*Joe DiMaggio*	*265.8*	*198.9*	*0.572*	*27.3*	***47.2***
37	Albert Pujols	294.5	218.5	0.574	26.9	**47.2**
38	Pedro Martinez	182.2	132.9	0.578	30.2	**46.9**
39	Jim Thome	269.5	205.4	0.567	24.7	**46.6**
40	Frank Thomas	249.0	186.1	0.572	23.6	**46.1**
41	*Jimmie Foxx*	*247.3*	*170.4*	*0.592*	*27.5*	***46.0***
42	Manny Ramirez	304.1	244.6	0.554	23.3	**45.8**
43	Robin Yount	354.3	332.1	0.516	18.8	**45.5**
44	John Smoltz	220.2	188.6	0.539	25.3	**45.5**
45	George Brett	325.4	277.1	0.540	20.4	**45.4**
46	Duke Snider	276.8	210.2	0.568	25.1	**45.4**
47	Tommy John	286.4	263.0	0.521	20.5	**45.1**
48	*Lou Gehrig*	*227.7*	*147.3*	*0.607*	*28.9*	***45.0***
49	*Charlie Gehringer*	*255.1*	*210.3*	*0.548*	*24.4*	***44.9***
50	Dwight Evans	330.6	277.5	0.544	20.1	**44.5**

2. Impact of Context on Player Won-Lost Records

The basic process by which I calculate player won-lost records was described in Chapter 1. In my work, I construct two sets of pW-L records: pWins and pLosses, which tie player wins directly to team wins, and eWins and eLosses, which attempt to measure expected Player wins (and losses), given a neutral context and average teammates.

Differences between pWins and eWins arise due to differences in contextual factors. The relationship between pWins and eWins can therefore be explored to identify the contextual factors affecting player performance and, hence, team performance.

Both pWins / pLosses and eWins / eLosses can be constructed from basic context-neutral wins and losses based on the following formulas:

Formulas Relating pWins/pLosses to eWins/eLosses

$$eGames = Games_B * e_{CM}$$
$$eWinPct = (Wins_B / Games_B) + eWinAdj$$
$$eWins = eWinPct * eGames; \quad eLosses = eGames - eWins$$

$$pGames = Games_B * CM_{Inter} * CM_{Intra}$$
$$pWinPct = ((Wins_B + Tm_{Adj}) / Games_B) + WinAdj_{Inter} + WinAdj_{Intra}$$
$$pWins = pWinPct * pGames; \quad pLosses = pGames - pWins$$

The terms above are defined as follows:

Games = Player Wins plus Player Losses

CM stands for Context Multiplier, which measures the relative importance of the player's performance compared to an average player

Tm$_{Adj}$ is an adjustment for the player's teammates, and is defined below

WinAdj is an adjustment to winning percentage to reflect the timing of the player's performance

B stands for Basic context-neutral player games

e stands for Expected, measuring Context-Neutral won-lost records, adjusted for expected contextual factors

p stands for pW-L records, which incorporate actual contextual factors such that player won-lost records are tied directly to team wins and losses

Inter stands for Inter-Game and measures the importance of the player's performance given the immediate context within the game

Intra stands for Intra-Game and measures the importance of the player's performance relative to other games

These factors are here discussed in some more detail.

#1. Context Multipliers

Context multipliers quantify how the total number of context-dependent player games (pGames) relates to an expected number of player games if the player had played in an average context. As part of the normalization processes undertaken to construct player wins and losses, for a given league, league-wide context is set equal to one by construction. For individual players (and individual teams), however, this will likely not be the case. A context greater than one means that a player tended to play in more win-important situations than average, while a context less than one means that a player tended to play in less win-important situations than average.

For example, in 2006, Francisco Rodriguez of the Anaheim Angels had a pWin-pLoss record of 8.8 pWins against 3.2 pLosses, for a total of 12.0 Context-Dependent Player Decisions.

Stripped of its context, however, Rodriguez's basic won-lost record was only 4.5 wins against 3.1 losses, for a total of only 7.6 Basic Player Decisions.

Hence, Francisco Rodriguez's context multiplier for 2006 was 1.582 (12.0 ÷ 7.6), meaning that, on average, Rodriguez's performance was 58.2% more valuable than would have been expected.

There are two types of context: inter-game and intra-game.

Inter-Game Context

Inter-game context measures the importance of the situations in which a player performed within the context of a single game. This is similar to the concept of Leverage, which (to the best of my knowledge) was developed and introduced by Tom Tango (e.g., http://www.hardballtimes.com/crucial-situations/).

One difference between Inter-Game Context and Leverage, as calculated by Tom Tango, is that Leverage is calculated before the play and is, hence, independent of the result of the play. Inter-game context, however, is calculated retrospectively, so that it is dependent on the results of the plays that go into the calculation. This may introduce a slight positive correlation between inter-game context and Player winning percentage.

A simple calculation of the weighted correlation between inter-game context and basic player winning percentage suggests a correlation of 0.21. Much of this correlation, however, is due to the fact that better pitchers are used in higher-context situations. Looking only at non-pitchers, for example, the correlation between winning percentage and inter-game context is only 0.15. And even here, this correlation may be due in part to the occasional use of better hitters as pinch hitters in higher-context situations.

For pitchers, inter-game context is slightly higher, on average, for relief pitchers (average inter-game context of 1.023 since 2000) than for starting pitchers (0.988).

Inter-game context varies considerably, of course, across relief pitchers, depending on their role. For example, in 2010, among players who appeared in at least 10 games, the top 43 players in inter-game context were relief pitchers, as were the 6 lowest inter-game contexts among players with at least 10 games played.

For batters, baserunners, and fielders, inter-game context is largely simply the luck of the draw. There are some exceptions. Pinch hitters and pinch runners, for example, tend to be used in higher-context situations (average inter-game context of 1.45 for pinch hitters and 1.40 for pinch runners across all seasons for which I have calculated pW-L records). There are also some slight variations in average inter-game context across lineup positions, but, in general, inter-game contexts are not particularly persistent across players outside of relief pitchers.

Intra-Game Context

Intra-game context normalizes the number of player decisions across games. Games with close scores, a lot of lead changes and/or multiple ties will earn more total Player decisions than less competitive games. For batters, baserunners, and fielders, intra-game context multipliers will be very highly correlated across teammates depending on how many close games a team plays over the course of a particular season. For example, in 2005, 8 of the top 10 non-pitchers in games reduced by Intra-Game (or "Team") Context played for either the Minnesota Twins or the Washington Nationals. Not coincidentally, in 2005, the Twins led the major leagues with 23 extra-inning games and played in 57 one-run games, while the Nationals led the major leagues with 61 one-run games.

Because intra-game contexts are more likely to be below one the closer a game is, while inter-game contexts are more likely to be above one the closer a game is, these two measures have a tendency to be fairly strongly negatively correlated. This is especially true for pitchers. While relief pitchers have higher inter-game context, on average (1.023 vs. 0.988 for starters since 2000), starting pitchers have higher intra-game context on average (1.093 vs. 0.826 for relievers) as starting pitchers pitch longer in low inter-game context games. Also, as explained later in this chapter, intra-game context is much higher in the early innings of games—when starting pitchers are likely to be pitching—than in the late innings of games. This strong negative relationship between inter-game and intra-game context among pitchers is accounted for by including a measure of expected context in the construction of eWins and eLosses. The derivation of Expected Context is discussed later in this Chapter.

Inter-Game vs. Intra-Game Context

For all player-seasons for which I have calculated pW-L records, inter-game and intra-game context have a weighted correlation of –0.48.

Inter-game context measures the importance of a situation within the context of the individual game being played, relative to an average situation. So, for example, a plate appearance with the bases loaded and two outs in the bottom of the ninth inning of a game with the home team trailing by one run will have a higher inter-game context than, say, a plate appearance with two outs and the bases empty in the top of the fifth inning of a game in which the visiting team is already leading by eight runs.

Some games—e.g., extra-inning games, one-run games—will have more situations that are high-context than other games—e.g., blowouts. In addition, higher scoring games will tend to have more player decisions in general than lower scoring games simply by virtue of having more plate appearances. In calculating pWins and pLosses, total player decisions are normalized per game, so that all games are treated equally.

Consider two games with an average number of total player decisions (i.e., 3 per team after normalization). Now, suppose one game (call it game A) has one extra high-context plate appearance, say an inter-game context of 2. Game A will now have more inter-context Player games than Game B. To normalize the two games to have the same number of Context-Dependent player games—as all games have by construction—then, the average intra-game context for Game B will have to be higher than for Game A to offset the higher inter-game context of Game A.

What does this mean? I believe that it means that inter-game context measures—i.e., traditional win-probability measures, including, for example, Leverage overstate the importance of high-context situations within a game. This has its most profound implications on two specific sets of players: starting pitchers, who are under-rated by typical inter-game context measures, and closers, who are over-rated by inter-game context measures.

In the case of starting pitchers, over all of the years for which I have calculated pW-L records, they had an average inter-game context of 1.002, essentially average. But, starting pitchers had an average intra-game context of 1.076, 7.6% above average. Taken together, starting pitchers pitched in an average context of 1.078, 7.8% above average, which means that, on average, starting pitchers are nearly 8% more valuable than a context-neutral evaluation would suggest. This result is accounted for in my work by adjusting players' context-neutral won-lost records based on Expected Context based on the players' positions. The calculation of Expected Context is described next.

By failing to take intra-game context into account, Leverage, which only considers inter-game context, has a tendency to over-state the value of high-leverage relief pitchers. For example, in 2006, Francisco Rodriguez's inter-game context was 1.905. His intra-game context, however, was 0.830 as 51 of his 69 appearances were in save situations, which tend to occur in games which generate an above-average number of Player decisions. Combining inter- and intra-game context, then, reduces Francisco Rodriguez's true context for 2006 to 1.582.

Expected Context

In relating player wins and losses to team wins and losses, the context in which a player's performance takes place matters. This is reflected in two context measures related to Context-Dependent player decisions that were described earlier in this chapter: Inter-Game Context and Intra-Game Context.

In calculating Context-Neutral player decisions, one might think that the most obvious thing to do would be to simply set inter-game and intra-game context both equal to one for all players. In fact, however, this will lead to there being a clear and obvious relationship between players' positions and their tendency to have more or fewer context-dependent player decisions (pWins, pLosses) than context-neutral decisions (eWins, eLosses). Because of this, I think that it is more appropriate to calculate an Expected Context for each player, based on the position(s) which the player played. This is done as follows.

Offense: Batting and Baserunning

Across all seasons for which I have calculated pW-L records, inter-game and intra-game contexts for offensive player decisions, by player position, were as follows:

Offensive Position	Inter-Game	Intra-Game	Combined
Pinch Hitter	1.4536	0.8561	1.2444
Pitcher	0.8967	1.0273	0.9212
Catcher	0.9797	1.0004	0.9801
First Base	1.0065	1.0068	1.0134
Second Base	0.9745	1.0062	0.9805
Third Base	0.9935	1.0045	0.9980
Shortstop	0.9707	1.0033	0.9739
Left Field	0.9959	1.0090	1.0049
Center Field	0.9841	1.0095	0.9934
Right Field	0.9987	1.0074	1.0061
Designated Hitter	1.0015	1.0183	1.0198
Pinch Runner	1.3972	0.7884	1.1016

There are three positions for which the combined context is noticeably different from 1.0: pinch hitters (1.24), pinch runners (1.10), and pitchers (0.92). Expected contexts for offensive player decisions are calculated, therefore, for four different positions: pinch hitter, pinch runner, pitcher, and other. For each of these positions, expected context is set equal to the average context for the position for the league and season in question.

One could, perhaps, point to differences in the contexts of shortstops (0.97), catchers (0.98), and second basemen (0.98) as compared to DHs (1.02), first basemen (1.01), and corner outfielders (1.01). In fact, however, those differences reflect differences in player talent. Shortstops, catchers, and second basemen tend to be weaker hitters which means that they are more likely to be pinch-hit for and they also bat in lineup positions that are slightly less likely to face high-context situations. In these cases, however, it is not the fielding position that drives these differences in context, but player quality. I do not incorporate these differences into my calculation of expected context.

Pitching

Starting pitchers have an average inter-game context of 1.002 and an average intra-game context of 1.076, a combined average context of 1.078. For relief pitchers, the numbers are 0.995, 0.821, and 0.816, respectively. Expected contexts for starting pitchers are set equal to the average context for starting pitchers for the relevant league and season. Ditto for relief pitchers—expected context is set equal for all relief pitchers—closers, setup men, mop-up men—regardless of their actual context.

Fielding

Across all seasons for which I have calculated pW-L records, for fielding decisions, average context varies across fielding positions between 0.983 and 1.011—in other words, there is no relationship between context and fielding position. Hence, expected context is set equal to 1.0 for all fielding player decisions.

Final Results

Expected context for a player is calculated by taking the weighted average of the expected contexts for the player's offensive, pitching, and fielding decisions as outlined above. The numbers presented above represent averages across all seasons for which I have estimated pW-L records. The actual numbers used in calculating Expected Context are calculated uniquely by season, so that, for example, the Expected Context associated with starting pitching will vary (slightly) by season to reflect differences in the actual context faced by starting pitchers over time.

#2. Win Adjustments

There are two fundamental ways in which contextual factors can affect player value. The first is that the relative importance of the situations in which a player performs can increase or decrease a player's relative value. This is measured via "context," which was just described. The other way in which contextual factors can affect value is if player performance differs across contexts. That is, in addition to a player having more player decisions because of context, some players may perform better in higher-context situations than in lower-context situations (or vice-versa). This will not merely affect the total number of Player decisions, then, but can also affect a player's winning percentage.

I call adjustments to player winning percentage based on differences across different contexts "win adjustments." As with "context," there are two types of "win adjustments": Inter-Game and Intra-Game. And as with "context," I also calculate a set of expected win adjustments which I incorporate into my calculation of expected Player wins and losses (eWins and eLosses). These are described next.

Inter-Game Win Adjustments

As with Inter-Game Context, Inter-Game Win Adjustments refer to differences in performance within a game.

In 2006, hitters put up a batting line (batting average / on-base percentage / slugging percentage) of .197/.276/.333 against Francisco Rodriguez. With the bases empty, batters hit .201/.281/.377 against Rodriguez with 5 home runs in 171 plate appearances. While this is an impressive performance by Rodriguez, he did even better with men on base. With runners on base, Rodriguez allowed a batting line of .191/.270/.273 and allowed only one home run in 125 plate appearances. With two outs and runners in scoring position, his performance improved still further: .128/.227/.154 in 44 plate appearances.

Not only was Rodriguez's performance better with runners on base but it was also noticeably better the closer the game. When the Angels were within four runs of their opponent, batters hit .179/.264/.286 against Rodriguez with 3 home runs in 264 plate appearances. When the difference in the score was more than four runs, however, opponents hit .333/.375/.700 against Rodriguez with 3 home runs in 32 plate appearances.

By just about any measure, Francisco Rodriguez's performance in 2006 was "clutch." That is, Rodriguez clearly performed better in more win-important situations within games than in less win-important situations. Whether Rodriguez's performance here is indicative of a real "clutch" skill or not is considered a bit later in this Chapter. Regardless of whether this is a "skill" or not, however, the timing of Rodriguez's performance unquestionably contributed to more wins for the Angels in 2006 than a more balanced performance would have. In fact, the inter-game "clutchness" of Frankie Rodriguez's performance improved his pW-L percentage by 7.2% (0.072) or by an additional 0.9 wins (incorporating the context in which Rodriguez performed).

Intra-Game Win Adjustments

Francisco Rodriguez appeared in 69 games for the Angels in 2006. The Angels went 59–10 in those games. This was largely a function of Rodriguez's role as the team's closer, which meant that he was primarily used in the late innings of games which the Angels were already winning.

In the 59 Angels wins in which Rodriguez pitched, he was 2–0, 47 saves, 2 blown saves, 60⅔ innings pitched, and a 1.34 earned run average. In the 10 Angels losses in which Rodriguez pitched, he was 0–3 with 2 blown saves, 12⅓ innings pitched, and a 3.65 ERA.

Regardless of the reason why Rodriguez appeared so often in Angels wins, the facts that (a) he performed so well in so many Angels' victories and (b) he performed better in Angels' wins than in Angels' losses both made Rodriguez's performance more valuable to the Angels than if his best performances had occurred more often in Angels' losses. I calculate that Rodriguez's intra-game wins over expectation improved his team-dependent pW-L percentage by 6.6% or an additional 0.8 wins (again, taking account of Rodriguez's actual context).

Very crudely, a positive intra-game win adjustment will reflect the extent to which a player's Player wins are concentrated in team wins, and a negative intra-game win adjustment will reflect the extent to which a player's Player losses are concentrated in team losses.

Before adjusting pW-L records to tie to team won-lost records, on average, players will accumulate a combined winning percentage of approximately 0.576 in games which their team wins and 0.424 in games that their team loses. After adjusting pW-L records to tie to team won-lost records, players accumulate a combined winning percentage of 0.667 in games which their team wins by construction. Within team wins, then, Player wins will be increased by approximately 16% (0.667 / 0.576) while Player losses will be reduced by 21% (0.333 / 0.424). For team losses, the results are exactly reversed—Player wins will be reduced by 21% and Player losses will be increased by approximately 16%.

If a player accumulates a winning percentage of 0.576 in team wins (the .576 varies by season) and 0.424 in team losses and if that same player plays in an equal number of team wins and team losses, then these adjustments will all balance out such that the player's adjusted winning percentage will be equal to his raw winning percentage, leading to an intra-game win adjustment of 0.0%. If, however, a player compiles a winning percentage greater than 0.576 in team wins and/or if the player plays in more team wins than team losses, his intra-game win adjustment may be positive. On the other hand, if a player compiles a winning percentage greater than 0.424 in team losses and/or if the player plays in more team losses than team wins, his intra-game win adjustment may be negative.

Players' intra-game win adjustments will therefore be correlated to team winning percentage. To the extent that team winning percentages are correlated to player winning percentages—which they must be in the aggregate, since team winning percentages will just equal the sum of player winning percentages—then, a player's intra-game win adjustment is (weakly) correlated with his own winning percentage. To account for this correlation, eWins and eLosses are constructed including an Expected Intra-Game Win Adjustment, which is described next.

Expected Team Win Adjustment

One of the key implications of my work is that the difference between winning and losing is very small in major league baseball. In an average major league baseball game across all seasons for which I have calculated pW-L records, for example, the winning team accumulated around 1.9 positive Player Decisions—the building block of Player Wins—and 1.4 negative Player Decisions—the building block of Player Losses. In other words, the average winning team compiled a team winning percentage of 1.000 (by definition), but the Players on that team compiled a combined winning percentage of something like 0.576, which works out to about a 93–69 record in a 162-game schedule.

Looking at the issue from the opposite direction, teams whose players compiled a combined Player winning percentage around 0.510 (0.505–0.515) had an average team winning percentage of about 0.565 (92–70), while teams whose players compiled a combined player winning percentage around 0.490 (0.485–0.495) had an average team winning percentage around 0.441 (72–90).

Being a little above average helps a lot in producing team victories.

In pWins and pLosses, this is reflected in the Intra-Game Win Adjustment which ties pW-L records to team won-lost records. In looking at intra-game win adjustments, it is obvious that intra-game win adjustments correlate at least somewhat reasonably well with player winning percentages—good players tend to have positive intra-game win adjustments, while weaker players tend to have negative intra-game win adjustments. This correlation is not perfect, as one's intra-game win adjustments are also affected by one's teammates.

To recognize this correlation, eWins and eLosses are also adjusted for intra-game win adjustments. To maintain the context-neutrality of the results, however, these records are adjusted based upon Expected intra-game win adjustments.

Expected intra-game win adjustments for a player are calculated based on the expected impact of the player on the record of a 0.500 team. The first step is to calculate what the cumulative pW-L record of a 0.500 team would be if this player replaced an average player. The expected intra-game win adjustment for a team with that record is then estimated.

An example is probably the easiest way to explain this. I will use Dontrelle Willis's 2005 season. Dontrelle Willis appeared in 40 games for the Marlins in 2005. The players on a team will accumulate 3 player decisions per game, meaning that the Florida Marlins would have accumulated 120 Player decisions in the 40 games in which Willis appeared. A 0.500 team would be expected, then, to have 60 Player Wins and 60 Player Losses in these 40 games. Willis accumulated 26.2 (context-neutral) player decisions—14.9 wins and 11.3 losses (a 0.569 winning percentage). Willis's Positional Average was 0.467, meaning that an average player would have been expected to have 12.2 Player wins given Willis's decisions (26.2*0.467 = 12.2). So, Dontrelle Willis would have been expected to add 2.7 wins to an average team (14.9–12.2). So, an otherwise average team with Dontrelle Willis would have been expected to have a cumulative pW-L record of 62.7–57.3, a 0.522 winning percentage.

The next step, then, is to figure out how many wins a team with a cumulative player winning percentage of 0.522 would win, or, more precisely, what the intra-game win adjustment would be for such a team. To figure this out, I look at all major-league teams and estimate an equation to predict intra-game win adjustment as a function of the team's cumulative player winning percentage. I do this separately for each year, so, in the case of Dontrelle Willis, the results here are based on the 30 major-league teams in 2005.

If the team's cumulative player winning percentage is equal to 0.500, we would expect the team to have a team winning percentage of 0.500 and an intra-game win adjustment of zero. The team's intra-game win adjustment (W_A) is hence modeled as a function of the team's cumulative player winning percentage minus 0.500 (call this W).

That is,

$$W_A = a \cdot W$$

At the team level, cumulative player winning percentage incorporates teammate adjustments and inter-game win adjustments. This is done in order to allow for a clean analysis of how player wins convert to team wins. For individual players, to calculate "context-neutral" expected win adjustments, teammate adjustments and inter-game win adjustments are not included, as these factors are not "context-neutral."

For 2005, "a" is estimated to have a value of 1.150 with a standard error of 0.070 (t-statistic of 16.44). This equation has an adjusted-R^2 of 0.903, meaning that about 90.3% of the variance in intra-game win adjustment can be explained by differences in cumulative player win percentage at the team level.

The expected intra-game win adjustment for a player is then calculated by plugging the estimated cumulative team win percentage for the player calculated above (0.522 in the case of Dontrelle Willis in 2005) into the above equation. So, for Dontrelle Willis, his expected intra-game win adjustment is the following:

$$W_A = 1.150 * (0.522 - .500) = 0.025$$

Adjusting Dontrelle Willis's context-neutral won-lost record by this gives him an expected context-neutral winning percentage of 0.594.

Dontrelle Willis's actual intra-game win adjustment for 2005 was 0.028, very close to the expected value of 0.025.

Overall, the average value of "a" in the above equation is approximately 1.1 across all of the years for which I have estimated pW-L records. So, for example, a group of players with a combined context-neutral winning percentage of, say, 0.510, would have an expected team win adjustment of 0.011, leading to a team-wide winning percentage of 0.521. Over a 162-game season, then, this would work out to a combined record of about 253–233 (at 3 Player decisions per team game).

Subtracting background wins, this works out to approximately 91 team wins.

Teammate Adjustments

Player wins and losses are shared between teammates for certain events. For example, pitchers and catchers share responsibility for stolen bases and wild pitches, while pitchers and fielders share responsibility for balls in play. For pWins and pLosses, which tie out to team wins and losses, all that can be done in terms of dividing responsibility for, say, allowing a stolen base, is to divide the pLosses accrued on the play between the pitcher and catcher. Because of this, the cumulative winning percentage of a team's pitchers on shared plays will be exactly equal to the winning percentage of a team's fielders on shared plays. As such, it can be difficult, if not impossible, to judge how much of a particular player's (or team's) performance in shared components is due to his talent and how much is due to his teammates' talents.

The process by which Player decisions are shared is described in more detail in Chapter 4. One of the steps in that process is controlling for the talent of other players involved in the play. The basics of this process are described next via example.

In 2004, the Montreal Expos allowed only 58 stolen bases on the season, while catching 41 opposing baserunners attempting to steal. Based on this, the Montreal Expos compiled a team-wide Component 1.1 (base stealing by runners on first base) winning percentage of 0.645. This winning percentage was the same (by construction) for Expos' pitchers as well as Expos' catchers. But there is no reason to think that the actual performance of Expos' pitchers and catchers were identical in terms of preventing stolen bases in 2004.

On the other hand, the 2002 New York Mets allowed 151 stolen bases against only 53 caught stealing, leading to a team-wide Component 1.1 winning percentage of 0.431, due, in part, to the notorious problems of their catcher, Mike Piazza, who allowed 125 stolen bases (which led the National League) against 27 caught stealing in 121 games caught, for a Component 1.1 winning percentage of 0.320.

The first step before one can accurately assess "true-talent" Component 1 winning percentages is to adjust player winning percentages for the context in which these percentages were amassed. Specifically, pitchers' Component 1 winning percentages are adjusted to control for the Component 1 winning percentages of their catchers, and catchers' Component 1 winning percentages are adjusted to control for the Component 1 winning percentages of their pitchers. Similar adjustments are done for all Components for which Player Decisions are to be shared (the nine Components of pW-L records are described in detail in Chapter 4).

This is done iteratively. First, pitchers' Component 1 winning percentages are adjusted to control for the Component 1 winning percentages of their catchers. This is done using the Matchup Formula (which is also described in Chapter 4). After pitchers' winning percentages are adjusted based on catcher winning percentages, catcher winning percentages are then adjusted based on these newly-adjusted pitcher winning percentages. Ideally, one would continue the iterative process until all Component 1 winning percentages do not change between iterations. For computational simplicity, I simply repeat this process three more times for both pitchers and catchers.

The adjusted Component 1.1 winning percentage for Montreal Expos pitchers was 0.539 in 2004 (versus 0.645 unadjusted), while Montreal Expos catchers put up a combined adjusted Component 1.1 winning percentage of 0.641 (versus 0.645 unadjusted). Here, because Expos pitchers and catchers were both above-average in this component in 2004, their combined winning percentage ends up being greater than either of their individual winning percentages. The whole is greater than the sum of the parts.

For the 2002 New York Mets, their pitchers' adjusted winning percentage was 0.519 (versus 0.431 unadjusted) while Mets' catchers had an adjusted winning percentage of 0.415 (0.304 for Mike Piazza and 0.689 for other Mets' catchers). Mets pitchers weren't bad at preventing stolen bases in 2002; they simply had the misfortune of pitching to one of the worst catchers in modern baseball history at stopping an opponent's running game.

Teammate adjustments are simply equal to the number of context-neutral wins earned by a player minus the number of such wins, after going through the iterative adjustment process described above. For the 2004 Montreal Expos, the combined Component 1.1 teammate adjustments were +0.03 for pitchers and +0.005 for catchers. Pitchers and catchers were both positively influenced by each other, since Montreal's pitchers and catchers were both above-average (as a group) at controlling the opposition's running game.

For the 2002 Mets, on the other hand, the combined teammate adjustments for pitchers were −0.39. Mets' pitchers suffered from pitching mostly to a poor-throwing catcher, Mike Piazza. Piazza, on the other hand, benefitted from catching pitchers who, as a group, were (slightly) above-average at controlling base stealing, so his (Component 1.1) teammate adjustment in 2002 was +0.02.

Teammate adjustments tend to be fairly small in magnitude. Across all of the seasons for which I have calculated pW-L records, for example, the spread of defensive teammate adjustments (adjusting pitchers for fielders and vice-versa), expressed in wins over the course of a full season ranged from −0.39 for Manny Ramirez in 2004 to +0.68 for Reggie Jackson in 1976. The spread in offensive teammate adjustments (adjusting batters for baserunners and vice-versa) ranged (in wins over the course of a full season) from −0.57 for Ricky Gutierrez in 1993 to +0.32 for Minnie Minoso in 1954. The largest adjustments over a career (offensive and defensive adjustments combined) were Lou Brock (−1.5 net wins) and Ozzie Smith (+2.3 net wins). The relationship between player ability and teammate adjustments is explored a bit more next.

Correlation Between Teammate Adjustments and Player Records

As I just noted, the player with the largest positive teammate adjustment for his career was Ozzie Smith. Ozzie Smith is widely regarded as the greatest defensive shortstop in major-league history—and, by extension, arguably the greatest defensive player ever, regardless of position.

Is it merely coincidence that the most extreme player in teammate adjustments was also arguably the most extreme player in fielding ability? Or is there a correlation between a player's fielding record and what I call his teammate adjustment? And if the answer to the latter question is yes, might this mean that I am actually adjusting away actual ability from a player and (mistakenly) attributing it to his teammates?

This section takes a look at these questions.

The table below shows the top 10 players for whom I have calculated pW-L records in net Fielding wins (Fielding wins minus Fielding losses) and net Fielding losses (Fielding losses minus Fielding wins).

Player	Wins	Losses	Win Pct.	Net Wins	Teammate Adj.
Carl Furillo	75.7	63.1	0.545	12.6	0.5
Ozzie Smith	111.0	98.5	0.530	12.5	2.0
Brooks Robinson	84.8	72.6	0.539	12.2	1.1
Ichiro Suzuki	90.9	78.9	0.535	12.0	−1.0
Al Kaline	99.6	88.3	0.530	11.2	0.9
Barry Bonds	115.6	105.0	0.524	10.7	0.5
Jesse Barfield	63.2	52.8	0.545	10.5	0.4
Mark Belanger	67.8	57.7	0.541	10.2	1.3
Roberto Clemente	110.1	100.3	0.523	9.9	0.4
Pee Wee Reese	80.1	70.6	0.532	9.5	0.2

Player	Wins	Losses	Win Pct.	Net Wins	Teammate Adj.
Jeff Burroughs	47.0	57.2	0.451	−10.3	−0.4
Frank Howard	54.1	63.1	0.462	−9.0	−0.4
Ralph Kiner	57.2	65.8	0.465	−8.6	−0.8
Gary Sheffield	78.5	87.0	0.474	−8.6	−0.5
Derek Jeter	87.9	95.9	0.478	−8.0	−0.1
Greg Luzinski	42.6	50.4	0.458	−7.8	−0.9
Dante Bichette	60.1	67.7	0.470	−7.6	−0.9
Don Baylor	30.8	38.3	0.445	−7.5	−0.3
Gary Matthews, Sr.	73.7	81.0	0.476	−7.3	−0.4
Gus Bell	63.1	70.2	0.473	-7.1	-0.2

There does appear to be some correlation between net wins and teammate adjustments. The only player whose net wins and teammate adjustments are not the same sign in the above tables is Ichiro Suzuki, who shows up as a great fielder who played behind pitching staffs which were below-average at preventing hits on balls in play.

On the other hand, there are two sets of teammates on the top 10 list, at least one of whom played behind famously great pitching staffs: the Baltimore Orioles of the 1960s and 1970s. There is, I suppose, a little bit of a chicken-or-an-egg question of whether these pitching staffs made these fielders look better, these fielders made these pitching staffs look better, or (as my work suggests) both. Nevertheless, the ideas that (a) Mark Belanger was one of the best defensive shortstops in history, and (b) Mark Belanger played in front of above-average pitching staffs in his career both seem eminently reasonable to me.

As for the bottom 10, it would appear that most of them played the majority of their career behind a pitching staff that was at least somewhat below-average at preventing hits on balls in play. It is, perhaps, a bit harder to link these players to "famously" poor pitching staffs, largely, I think, because bad pitching staffs tend to be less "famous" in general. Jeff Burroughs and Gary Matthews were teammates, however, on the Atlanta Braves for four years from 1977 to 1980. The first three of those Braves teams were pretty bad (although perhaps not "famously" so), losing 101, 93, and 94 games (the 1980 Braves were 81–80). All three of these teams ranked dead last in the National League in runs allowed per game (although Atlanta-Fulton County Stadium was a very strong hitters' park in those years). Having 2 of perhaps the 10 worst fielders of the past 60 years in the outfield together certainly didn't help those Braves' defenses, but outside of Hall-of-Famer Phil Niekro, those pitching staffs were nothing to write home about either, featuring the likes of Eddie Solomon, Preston Hanna, and Mickey Mahler.

Still, there definitely appears to be a correlation between players' fielding records and the quality of the pitchers on their teams implied by my teammate adjustments.

Expanding beyond the 20 players shown above, I calculated a weighted correlation between a player's net fielding wins and his defensive teammate adjustment. I did this at both the season and career levels for all non-pitchers for whom I have calculated pW-L records. At the seasonal level, I found a correlation between net fielding wins and teammate adjustments of 0.214 (21.4%). The correlation (weighted by the total number of fielding decisions earned by the player) for career values was 0.493 (49.3%).

Going back to the questions I raised in the second paragraph of this section, it does appear that there is a correlation between a player's fielding record and his teammate adjustment. The follow-up question then, is whether this is a problem: am I adjusting away actual ability from players and (mistakenly) attributing it to their teammates? It is certainly possible that I am, in fact, adjusting away actual ability and crediting (blaming) it on a player's teammates. Frankly, I'm not sure how one would "prove" such a thing, one way or the other. I also think, however, that much, if not all, of this observed correlation is, in fact, real.

That is, I think it may simply be the case that good fielders and good pitchers are more likely to be teammates (Jim Palmer and Brooks Robinson and Mark Belanger; Andruw Jones and Greg Maddux, Tom Glavine, and John Smoltz) and bad fielders and bad pitchers are more likely to be teammates (e.g., the 1962 New York Mets).

The table below shows correlations between winning percentages by factor–batting, baserunning, pitching, and fielding–by team for all teams for whom I have estimated pW-L records.

Team Winning Percentages: Correlation Between Factors

	Baserunning	*Pitching*	*Fielding*
Batting	25.8%	9.9%	14.8%
Baserunning		13.8%	16.4%
Pitching			16.6%

This table indicates that team quality is positively correlated across factors: i.e., teams with good batting are more likely to also have good baserunning, good pitching, and good fielding. The strongest correlation is between batting and baserunning, which makes sense since, as will be discussed somewhat in Chapter 5, these are fairly correlated for individual players. The weakest correlations are between batting and pitching, which makes a certain amount of sense to me: these factors are provided by almost entirely different players; there are plenty of examples through history of teams that were all-offense, no-defense, or the reverse.

The correlation between fielding and pitching—which, remember, reflects different players—is the second-highest correlation in the above table and is essentially the same as the correlation between fielding and baserunning—which measure the same set of players. In other words, the evidence that there is a tendency for good pitchers to have teammates who are good fielders and bad pitchers to have teammates who are bad fielders is similar to the evidence that good fielders tend to be good baserunners (and vice versa).

Based on these results, I believe that this explains the apparent correlation I observed above between player performance and teammate adjustments and that these teammate adjustments adequately reflect the "true talent" of a player's teammates.

pWins vs. eWins

I calculate two measures of pW-L records: pWins/pLosses and eWins/eLosses.

pWins and pLosses are tied to team wins: the players on a team earn a total of 2 pWins and 1 pLoss in every team win, and 1 pWin and 2 pLosses in every team loss. As this Chapter has discussed, these records are highly contextual. That is, hitting a grand slam with two outs in the bottom of the ninth inning with your team trailing by three runs will earn more pWins than hitting a solo home run leading off the top of the 8th inning with your team trailing 13–1. Positive events that contribute to wins are more valuable than positive events that end up going for naught in team losses. As such, I believe that pWins and pLosses do a better job of truly capturing player value—which is an inevitable function of the context in which it occurs—than any other baseball statistic available. Nevertheless, calculating Player wins and losses in this way leads to player value being due, at least in part, to factors outside of a player's control—the quality of his teammates, the timing of his performance.

Because of this, I also calculate a set of pW-L records which attempt to control for the quality of a player's teammates and the context in which he performed. I call these expected pW-L records, or eWins and eLosses.

Most sabermetric measures—e.g., WAR—are designed to be context-neutral, and are therefore most comparable to my eWins and eLosses. Bill James's Win Shares do tie to team wins, but the linkage of team wins to player Win Shares is done via an across-the-board adjustment based on end-of-season data, rather than linking to team wins on a game-by-game basis, like my pWins and pLosses. Context does come into play for some subsets of players for some statistics. For example, both Baseball-Reference.com and Fangraphs incorporate leverage into their WAR statistics for relief pitchers. In my opinion, these *ad hoc* contextual adjustments are inadequate to fully reflect actual player value and create inconsistencies in the evaluation of differing players. I compare pW-L records to WAR later in this book, in Chapter 8.

There are many reasons why a player's pWins might differ from his eWins.

- Trevor Hoffman, for example, earned 45.9 more pWins than eWins in his career (84%) mostly because the actual context in which he performed was 68% greater than his expected context.
- Derek Jeter earned 12.2 more pWins than eWins in his career largely because he had the good fortune to play with above-average teammates, so that Jeter's positive contributions were more likely to contribute to victories than would have been expected. This is reflected in what I call Jeter's intra-game win adjustment, which raised his pWin percentage by 0.019 (to 0.536) over Jeter's expected winning percentage (accounting for 13.0 additional wins).
- David Ortiz earned 2.3 more pWins than eWins in 2005 mostly because of the timing of his hits (i.e., Big Papi was a great clutch hitter that year). The timing of Ortiz's hits, which I call his inter-game win adjustment, increased his winning percentage by 0.034 that year, adding 1.1 wins to Ortiz's record.

Certainly, some people may feel that some of these differences are more "real" than others. In theory, one could adjust player records based on individual contextual factors.

The choice between pWins and eWins will likely depend on one's purposes in putting together a list. One could think of pWins as measuring what actually happened, while eWins perhaps measure what *should have* happened. Personally, I think both of these measures provide us with useful and interesting information.

Context by Inning

The table below shows inter-game and intra-game context by inning across all games for which I have calculated pW-L records.

Context by Inning

Inning	Inter-Game	Context Intra-Game	Combined
Top 1	0.9644	1.1942	1.1517
Bottom 1	0.9825	1.2243	1.2029

Inning	Inter-Game	Context Intra-Game	Combined
Top 2	0.9498	1.1532	1.0952
Bottom 2	0.9453	1.1626	1.0990
Top 3	0.9526	1.1220	1.0689
Bottom 3	0.9438	1.1205	1.0575
Top 4	0.9639	1.0774	1.0385
Bottom 4	0.9479	1.0654	1.0098
Top 5	0.9529	1.0370	0.9882
Bottom 5	0.9282	1.0145	0.9417
Top 6	0.9659	0.9883	0.9546
Bottom 6	0.9439	0.9601	0.9063
Top 7	0.9636	0.9446	0.9103
Bottom 7	0.9311	0.9103	0.8476
Top 8	0.9621	0.9017	0.8675
Bottom 8	0.9235	0.8577	0.7921
Top 9	0.9348	0.8559	0.8001
Bottom 9	1.6304	0.8034	1.3098
Top Extras	2.0820	0.5478	1.1406
Bottom Extras	2.3794	0.5452	1.2973

This table takes some thought to understand. But working through it is well worth it, I think, as, in some ways, the results here are perhaps the most interesting and revealing results in all of my work.

Inter-Game Context

The first column of the above table shows inter-game context, which, as I explain elsewhere, is comparable to the concept of Leverage. Not surprisingly, inter-game context is highest in extra innings. In fact, the only other inning with an average inter-game context above one is the bottom of the ninth inning. Interestingly, this means that in games in which the home team wins before their final at-bat, there are no innings in which the average inter-game context is above-average. Of course, this doesn't mean that there are no individual at-bats which are above-average in context. For that matter, in any specific game, there are probably specific half-innings that are above average in context. But, in a typical game that doesn't go into the bottom of the ninth inning, there's simply no way to know which inning is likely to be the decisive inning of the game.

Looking only at the first 8½ innings, two other facts are worth noting. First, after the first inning, inter-game contexts for the home team are an average of 2.2% lower than for the visiting team. This is in stark contrast to extra-inning games, where home-team inter-game context is 14% higher than for the visiting team. Overall, across all innings, the average inter-game context for the visiting team is 0.984; average inter-game context for the home team is 3.3% higher at 1.017.

Second, and I think more interesting, average inter-game context declines as the game progresses (until the bottom of the ninth inning and extra innings). The highest-context half-inning before the bottom of the ninth inning is the bottom of the first inning, with an average inter-game context of 0.983. The lowest-context half-inning, on average, is the bottom of the eighth inning at 0.924. Overall, through the first 8½ innings of the game, the average inter-game context declines by an average of 0.6% per inning.

At first blush, this seems counter-intuitive. When people think of "clutch" situations, they often think of "close and late" situations—situations late in close games. Yet, on average, late situations are relatively un-"clutch" situations. In fact, these two ideas do not conflict. Late innings of close games are, indeed, high-context situations. For example, relief pitchers pitching in hold or save situations pitch in an average inter-game context of 2.027. Relief pitchers pitching in tie games pitch in an average inter-game context of 1.939. The reason why inter-game contexts decline as the game goes on, in spite of this, is because such situations are not the norm. For relief pitchers as a whole, 64.1% of all context-neutral player decisions were earned in non-save/hold, non-tie situations. And these situations, not surprisingly, had an average inter-game context of 0.437.

In the early innings of a typical baseball game, there are no situations that have exceptionally high inter-game context. But, there are also very few situations that have exceptionally low inter-game context. As the game progresses, the chances of higher-context situations rises, but the chance of the game getting completely out of hand, leading to a complete lack of high-context situations, also increases. And, in fact, the latter, a game with nothing but low-context situations in the late innings, is more common in major league baseball, than the former, a close game with high average inter-game contexts in the late innings.

The table below shows the percentage of games in which the winning team took a lead that it held for the remainder of the game, by inning, from 2000 to 2009:

Percentage of Game-Winners with Lead They Never Relinquish Through X Innings Winning Team Takes Lead It Never Relinquishes

Inning	In This Inning	Through This Inning
1	24.07%	24.07%
2	12.81%	36.88%
3	9.67%	46.55%
4	8.82%	55.37%
5	7.60%	62.97%
6	7.59%	70.56%
7	6.93%	77.49%
8	7.48%	84.97%
9	6.77%	91.74%
10+	8.26%	100.00%

That is, in 24.1% of all games, one of the two teams took a lead in the first inning which it proceeded to then hold for the remainder of the game. Note two things about this table. First, by far the most common inning for a team to take a lead which it never relinquished was actually the first inning. In fact, the second-most common inning for a team to take a lead which it never relinquished (again, by a fairly large margin over the third-most common inning) is the second inning. Second, over half of all games were decided by the end of the fourth inning—less than halfway through the game. In such games, there may be relatively few high-context situations in the later innings.

Intra-Game Context

Going back to the table of context by half-inning, the most striking result there and, frankly, the result which I had the hardest time wrapping my head around in all of this work, is that average intra-game context is extremely dependent on the inning. On average, through the first nine innings, intra-game context declines by approximately 4.1% per inning. Intra-game contexts by inning are shown in the table below.

Inning	Intra-Game Context
1	1.2099
2	1.1579
3	1.1212
4	1.0714
5	1.0258
6	0.9742
7	0.9276
8	0.8799
9	0.8301
Extras	0.5464

At first blush, this makes no sense. Except for the bottom of the ninth and extra innings (where the intra-game numbers make perfect sense to me), every game (except for rain-shortened games) includes every half-inning. Any official game will include a top of the first as well as a bottom of the fourth inning. How, then, can it make sense for the average intra-game context of the top of the first inning to be 12% higher than the average intra-game context of the bottom of the fourth?

To understand this, you have to really understand what intra-game context is. Intra-game context adjusts player decisions to reflect the fact that, at the end of the day, the game is the unit of value being measured here and all games have the same value. What does a high intra-game context mean? It means that a relatively low number of player decisions were accumulated within this particular game. Similarly, a low intra-game context means that a relatively high number of player decisions were accumulated within a particular game.

Examples of the latter are extra-inning games. There are more plate appearances than usual in extra-inning games and, because the game is tied late, there are likely to be an above-average number of situations within the game with very high inter-game context levels. Not surprisingly, then, extra-inning games generate nearly twice as many player decisions as nine-inning games. This is reflected in an average intra-game context of 0.546 for extra innings.

Extra-inning games or one-run games are good and fairly obvious examples of low intra-context games. What, then, are the characteristics of high intra-context games?

Basically, just the opposite of low intra-context games: games that are not particularly close, games with no lead changes, perhaps most notably, games in which one team jumps out to an early lead and never relinquishes it. Go back, then, to the table that I showed earlier: the percentage of games in which the winning team had taken the lead which it would never relinquish by inning. As I noted above, the most common inning for a team to take a lead which it would never relinquish was the first inning; the second-most common such inning was the second inning; in over half of all major-league games, the winning team has taken a lead which it will never relinquish by the end of the fourth inning.

Plate appearances that result in runs scoring are, on average, higher inter-context plate appearances than plate appearances that do not result in runs scoring. Plate appearances that result in lead changes are extremely high inter-context plate appearances, on average. But this is all much less true in the early innings of a game than in the late innings of a game. While, as noted above, the average inter-game context in the first inning is actually higher than in any subsequent innings before the bottom of the ninth, peak inter-game context in the first inning is the lowest of any inning. In 2009, for example, inter-game context by inning showed the same basic pattern across all seasons for which I have calculated pW-L records as a whole:

Inter-Game Context by Inning: 2009 American League

Inning	Average	Std Deviation
1	0.981	0.505
2	0.954	0.549
3	0.963	0.577
4	0.971	0.625
5	0.953	0.704
6	0.962	0.814
7	0.957	0.968
8	0.924	1.144
9	1.139	1.525

The last column here shows the standard deviation of inter-game context in the 2009 American League. Standard deviation is a statistical calculation which measures the spread of the inter-game context by inning.

In other words, inter-game contexts in the first inning mostly range from 0.981 +/− 0.505 — i.e., they mostly fall between 0.476 and 1.485. For the second inning, the range is 0.405–1.503. By the sixth inning, the range has increased to 0.148–1.776. And, by the seventh inning and later, the standard deviation is so large that it is actually greater than the mean. For the eighth and ninth innings, the mean plus one standard deviation for these innings is over 2 in both cases.

So, in games in which the winning team jumps out to an early lead, that early lead will likely occur in a relatively low inter-game context, as compared to a similar lead change that might occur later in a game. Then, in the late innings of such a game, the average inter-game context of the game could be very low. The result is that (a) the highest-context portion of the game will be the early innings when the lead was taken for good, and (b) the overall number of player decisions will be exceedingly low. Because of (b), such games will have very high intra-game contexts, on average. For games in which the lead is taken late, on the other hand, the highest-context portion of the game will be in the late innings and the overall number of player decisions is likely to be relatively high, leading to low intra-game contexts. But note that, because the range of inter-game contexts is lower in the early innings than in the late innings, the difference in these two situations in early innings will be far less than in late innings.

A simple example might be helpful. We'll simplify to two types of innings: early and late. Consider the following player decisions for two games: one which was decided early and one which was decided late.

	Early-Inning Decisions		Late-Inning Decisions	
	Context-Neutral	*Contextual*	*Context-Neutral*	*Contextual*
Game decided early	1.5	1.8	1.5	0.5
Game decided late	1.5	1.2	1.5	3.0

In this example, the first game has an early-inning inter-game context of 1.2 (1.8 ÷ 1.5), a late-inning inter-game context of 0.3 (0.5 ÷ 1.5), and an intra-game context of **1.3** (3 ÷ [1.8 + 0.5]).

The second game has an early-game context of 0.8 (1.2 ÷ 1.5), a late-inning inter-game context of 2.0 (3.0 ÷ 1.5), and an intra-game context of **0.7** (3 / [1.2 + 3.0]).

Putting it all together, then, total early-inning decisions for the two games would equal

$$1.8*1.3 + 1.2*0.7 = 3.2$$

for an average early-inning intra-game context of **1.07** (3.2 / 3.0).

Total late-inning decisions for the two games would equal
$$0.5*1.3 + 3.0*0.7 = 2.8$$
for an average late-inning intra-game context of **0.80** (2.8 / 3.0).

This pattern in intra-game context across innings has important implications in valuing starting versus relief pitchers.

Total Context

Putting inter-game and intra-game context together, total context varies by inning as follows:

Total Context by Half-Inning

Inning	Total Context
Top 1	1.1517
Bottom 1	1.2029
Top 2	1.0952
Bottom 2	1.0990
Top 3	1.0689
Bottom 3	1.0575
Top 4	1.0385
Bottom 4	1.0098
Top 5	0.9882
Bottom 5	0.9417
Top 6	0.9546
Bottom 6	0.9063
Top 7	0.9103
Bottom 7	0.8476
Top 8	0.8675
Bottom 8	0.7921
Top 9	0.8001
Bottom 9	1.3098
Top Extras	1.1406
Bottom Extras	1.2973

In order, the highest-context half-innings, on average, are the bottom of the ninth inning, the bottom of extra innings, the bottom of the first inning, the top of the first inning, and the top of extra innings. The lowest-context half-innings, on average, are the bottom of the eighth inning and the top of the ninth. This is not to say, of course, that all first-inning events are higher-context than later-inning events. On the contrary, as noted above, the standard deviation of context is much higher in later innings: there are many more much lower-context situations, but there are also more higher-context situations.

Persistence of Clutch Performance

In 2005, David Ortiz finished second in the voting for AL MVP, thanks to a strong clutch performance. In pW-L records, "clutch" performance can be equated to the inter-game win adjustment, which measures the extent to which a player's context-dependent winning percentage differs from his context-neutral winning percentage. In 2005, David Ortiz's inter-game win adjustment was +3.4%. This translates into an extra 1.1 net wins earned by David Ortiz due to his "clutchiness." This accounted for approximately one-fifth of Ortiz's pWins over Replacement Level (5.5), which was enough to push him up from 3rd place in the American League to 2nd place (behind Alex Rodriguez) in this statistic. Based on his 2005 season, together with back-to-back extra-inning game-winning hits in games 4 and 5 of the 2004 ALCS, David Ortiz is regarded by some as the greatest clutch hitter of his generation.

There has been a great deal of research and debate within the sabermetric community on the question of whether clutch hitting is, in fact, a skill. The most common way of testing whether things are "skill" or "luck" in sabermetrics is to look at the extent to which players' clutch performances persist. I constructed persistence equations for inter-game win adjustments for each of the four basic types of pW-L decisions: batting, baserunning, pitching, and fielding for all of the seasons over which I have estimated pW-L records.

Persistence Equations: A Brief Overview

In theory, the extent to which a factor persists should be a very good indicator of the extent to which that factor represents an actual skill. In practice, however, comparing one year to another can be problematic. A straight comparison of one year to another is only valid if the player's underlying "true talent" skill level is the same both years. Otherwise, differences in "true talent" between the years will be incorrectly viewed as evidence of unexplained, or random, variance between the two years. In such a case, the extent to which something involves a real skill will likely be underestimated. But, of course, we know that players' talent levels change from year to year. Young players improve as they get older, while old players lose their skills. Players may be injured one year but healthy the next. Or players' actual value may be affected by a change in home ballpark, from, for example, a ballpark to which a player is particularly well-suited to one which adversely affects that player's specific strengths.

Player won-lost records are not constructed from aggregated year-end data, however, but are, instead, constructed from play-by-play data. Rather than comparing results across years, therefore, it is possible for me to compare results across plays. As a general rule, players' "true talent" should be much more stable from play to play than from year to year.

For the purpose of developing what I call "Persistence Equations," I divide the plays that took place in a particular season into two pools: odd and even. That is, the first plate appearance of the season is identified as play number 1, the next plate appearance is play number 2, etc. Even-numbered plays (2, 4 ...) go into one pool; odd-numbered plays go into the other one.

To evaluate the persistence of skills, I can then fit a simple equation which attempts to explain the relevant factor (e.g., inter-game win adjustment, etc.) on even plays as a function of the same factor for odd plays. That is,

$$(\text{Factor A})_{\text{Even}} = a + b \cdot (\text{Factor A})_{\text{Odd}}$$

Interpretation of Persistence Equation

The coefficient b in the Persistence Equation measures the persistence of Factor A between the two samples (even plays v. odd plays). The value of Factor A in the odd and the even period here are both samples of Factor A's true value. Sample statistics have a tendency to trend toward their long-run value as the sample size increases. Statisticians call this "regression to the mean."

The constant term, a, can be thought of as a measure of the extent to which Factor A regresses toward the mean. That is, one could re-write the Persistence Equation as follows:

$$(\text{Factor A})_{Even} = b \cdot (\text{Factor A})_{Odd} + (1-b) \cdot (\text{Factor A})_{Baseline}$$

where $(\text{Factor A})_{Baseline}$ represents a baseline toward which Factor A regresses over time.

There are two relevant results in interpreting the extent to which Factor A persists. The one most commonly used by sabermetricians is the correlation coefficient, or r (or r^2). The value, R^2, measures the percentage of variation in the left-hand side variable—$(\text{Factor A})_{Even}$—that can be explained by the right-hand side variable(s)—i.e. $(\text{Factor A})_{Odd}$. This provides some indication of the magnitude of the persistence of Factor A.

To assess the significance of the persistence, however, one must look at the significance of the persistence coefficient, b. The estimated value of b will have a standard error associated with it. If one divides b by this standard error, the resulting variable is called a t-statistic. The larger the t-statistic (in absolute value), the less likely that the true persistence coefficient is zero. As a (somewhat crude) rule of thumb, if the t-statistic is greater than 2, then we can be 95% certain that the true value of b is greater than zero (given that certain statistical assumptions about our equation are true).

Persistence of Inter-Game Win Adjustments

Persistence equations of this type were estimated for inter-game win adjustments for the four basic factors: batting, baserunning, pitching, and fielding.

The dependent variable in each case was the inter-game win adjustment within a season on even-numbered plays. The explanatory variable, then, was the inter-game win adjustment within the season on odd-numbered plays. In addition to inter-game win adjustment, I also included context-neutral win percentage (for even-numbered plays) as a second explanatory variable. I did this to consider the possibility that, perhaps, there might be some correlation between a player's winning percentage and his inter-game win adjustment—that is, it could be the case that better hitters are better (or worse) "clutch hitters" in general—perhaps simply due to measurement errors in my calculations. These persistence equations were estimated using Weighted Least Squares (WLS), where the observations were weighted by the harmonic mean of context-neutral player decisions squared. Finally, winning percentages were subtracted from 0.500 so that all three variables (Inter-Game WinAdj$_{Even}$, WinPct$_{Even}$, and Inter-Game WinAdj$_{Odd}$) are centered on zero, and the constant term was set equal to zero by construction. The weighting scheme and value of the constant term were both tested empirically. The results shown here seemed the most robust to me.

The results are summarized below.

The number n is the number of players over whom the equation was estimated, that is, who accumulated any Player wins and/or losses on both odd- and even-numbered plays within a particular season. The value R^2 measures the percentage of variation in the dependent variable (Inter-Game WinAdj$_{Even}$) explained by the equation (i.e., explained by WinPct$_{Even}$ and Inter-Game WinAdj$_{Odd}$). The numbers in parentheses below the equation are t-statistics. T-statistics measure the significance of the regression coefficients, that is, the confidence we have that these coefficients are greater than zero. The greater the t-statistic, the more confident we are that the true value of a particular coefficient is greater than zero. Roughly, if the t-statistic is greater than 2, then we can be at least 95% certain that the true value of b is greater than zero (given that certain statistical assumptions underlying our model hold).

Persistence of Inter-Game Win Adjustments

Batters: n	=	60,134	,	R^2	=	0.0006
WinAdj$_{Even}$	=	(-0.0109) (-5.708)	•	(WinPct$_{Even}$	−	0.500)
	+	(0.0375) (9.131)	•	WinAdj$_{Odd}$		
Baserunners: n	=	59,525	,	R^2	=	0.0160
WinAdj$_{Even}$	=	(-0.1014) (-42.40)	•	(WinPct$_{Even}$	−	0.500)
	+	(0.0267) (9.041)	•	WinAdj$_{Odd}$		
Pitchers: n	=	35,842	,	R^2	=	0.0068
WinAdj$_{Even}$	=	(-0.0221) (-7.125)	•	(WinPct$_{Even}$	−	0.500)
	+	(0.0755) (13.67)	•	WinAdj$_{Odd}$		
Fielders: n	=	76,587	,	R^2	=	0.0109
WinAdj$_{Even}$	=	(-0.0787) (-29.18)	•	(WinPct$_{Even}$	−	0.500)
	+	(0.0013) (0.301)	•	WinAdj$_{Odd}$		

Is "Clutch" a Significant Skill?

So, is "clutch" performance a persistent skill? For Batting, Baserunning, and Pitching, the answer is a fairly unambiguous "Yes," there is some small but significant persistence in clutch batting, baserunning, and pitching.

While the "persistence coefficient" on Inter-Game Win Adjustments is highly significant (t-statistic > 9) for batting, baserunning, and pitching, this "skill" explains less than two percent of the overall variation in inter-game win adjustments in all three cases.

Interestingly, clutch batting, which has generated by far the most discussion in the debate over whether "clutch" is real, is actually smaller and less significant than clutch pitching.

Exactly how significant is "clutch batting" as a persistent skill? The persistence coefficient in the batting equation above, 0.0375, suggests that if somebody has an inter-game win adjustment of, say, 0.050 on odd-numbered plays (which would improve them from a 0.500 hitter to a 0.550 hitter, say), we would expect the same player to have an inter-game win adjustment on even-numbered plays of 0.002 (0.05 * 0.0375), enough to improve from a 0.500 batter to a 0.502 batter.

The one factor for which the persistence coefficient is not significant is Fielding, suggesting that "clutch fielding" is not a persistent skill.

What About David Ortiz, "the greatest clutch hitter in the history of the Boston Red Sox"?

As noted above, in 2005, David Ortiz had an inter-game win adjustment of +3.4% (1.1 net wins).

How clutch was David Ortiz outside of 2005? It turns out that in David Ortiz's regular-season career (through 2015) outside of the 2005 season, he accumulated an inter-game win adjustment of –0.6%, good for –2.2 net wins.

3. Using Player Won-Lost Records to Compare Players

The basics of how pW-L records are constructed and interpreted were discussed in some detail in Chapter 1. This Chapter looks at how pW-L records can be used to compare players. The calculation of wins over positional average (WOPA) and wins over replacement level (WORL) are described in some detail.

Wins Over Positional Average (WOPA)

pW-L Records are an excellent overall measure of player value. When context and the effects of teammates are controlled for, pW-L records can also, in my opinion, serve as an excellent starting point for measuring player talent. As a means of comparing players who play different positions, however, raw pW-L records are not really an ideal comparative tool.

In constructing pW-L records, all events are measured against expected, or average, results across the event. Because of this, fielding pW-L records are constructed such that aggregate winning percentages are 0.500 for all fielding positions. Hence, one can say that a shortstop with a defensive winning percentage of 0.475 was a below-average defensive shortstop and a first baseman with a defensive winning percentage of 0.510 was an above-average defensive first baseman, but there is no basis for determining which of these two players was a better fielder—the below-average fielder at the more difficult position or the above-average fielder at the easier position.

From an offensive perspective, batting pW-L records are constructed by comparing across all batters, not simply batters who share the same fielding position. In the National League, this means that offensive comparisons include pitcher hitting, so that, on average, non-pitcher hitters will be slightly above average in the National League, while, of course, because of the DH rule, the average non-pitcher hitter will define the average in the American League.

These are, in fact, two sides of the same coin. There is a nearly perfect negative correlation between the average offensive production at a defensive position and the importance and/or difficulty associated with playing that position. That is, players at the toughest defensive positions tend to be weaker hitters than players at easier defensive positions.

Bill James used this observation to define what he called the Defensive Spectrum:

$$1B - LF - RF - 3B - CF - 2B - SS - C$$

Positions get more difficult/valuable defensively moving left to right (e.g., shortstop is a more defensive position than second base) while offensive production increases moving right to left (e.g., first basemen out-hit left fielders).

When comparing, for example, a left fielder to a shortstop, one has to somehow balance the fact that left fielders are expected to hit better than shortstops against the fact that shortstops are, on average, better defensive players than left fielders.

There are three ways to do this:

1. One can adjust offensive pW-L records based on the defensive position of the player,
2. One can adjust defensive pW-L records based on the defensive position of the player, or
3. One can adjust the baseline against which players are measured.

I believe that the best choice is (3), measuring players against different baselines based on the position(s) which they played.

Positional Averages

The table below shows (context-neutral) pW-L records based on the defensive position of the player for every season for which I have estimated pW-L records. Offensive pW-L records are shown first, followed by overall records. Results here distinguish between DH leagues (the American League since 1973) and non–DH Leagues.

Context-Neutral pW-L Records by Defensive Position
(Offensive Player Decisions)

Position	DH Leagues			Non-DH Leagues		
	Wins	Losses	Win Pct.	Wins	Losses	Win Pct.
Pinch Hitter	1,347.0	1,482.9	0.476	5,233.7	5,802.2	0.474
Pitcher	2.5	5.5	0.315	6,294.3	11,853.2	0.347
Catcher	6,839.0	7,414.2	0.480	15,822.2	16,413.4	0.491
First Base	8,400.7	7,709.5	0.521	19,318.4	17,052.6	0.531
Second Base	7,587.8	8,056.4	0.485	17,337.0	17,825.2	0.493
Third Base	7,752.1	7,785.4	0.499	18,056.2	17,304.7	0.511
Shortstop	7,126.1	7,817.0	0.477	16,233.2	17,437.1	0.482
Left Field	8,285.2	7,966.2	0.510	19,436.9	17,353.5	0.528
Center Field	8,285.3	8,189.2	0.503	19,090.0	17,783.6	0.518
Right Field	8,272.2	7,816.6	0.514	19,340.9	17,332.2	0.527
Designated Hitter	7,922.7	7,577.5	0.511	4.2	3.6	0.538
Pinch Runner	164.2	164.6	0.499	281.6	287.1	0.495
Non-P Fielders	62,548.5	62,754.4	0.499	144,634.8	138,502.3	0.511

Context-Neutral pW-L Records by Defensive Position
(Total Player Decisions)

Position	DH Leagues			Non-DH Leagues		
	Wins	Losses	Win Pct.	Wins	Losses	Win Pct.
Pinch Hitter	1,347.0	1,482.9	0.476	5,233.7	5,802.2	0.474
Pitcher	47,440.0	47,500.3	0.500	108,229.3	113,887.5	0.487
Catcher	7,999.3	8,575.8	0.483	18,519.8	19,114.2	0.492
First Base	9,995.4	9,306.7	0.518	22,716.2	20,453.9	0.526
Second Base	10,921.9	11,371.6	0.490	24,598.9	25,055.7	0.495
Third Base	10,767.4	10,805.1	0.499	24,654.3	23,915.6	0.508

| | DH Leagues | | | Non-DH Leagues | | |
Position	Wins	Losses	Win Pct.	Wins	Losses	Win Pct.
Shortstop	10,848.6	11,520.0	0.485	24,536.9	25,709.2	0.488
Left Field	12,343.2	12,015.1	0.507	28,304.1	26,202.2	0.519
Center Field	11,955.5	11,853.5	0.502	27,492.5	26,170.7	0.512
Right Field	12,264.5	11,796.8	0.510	28,325.7	26,294.8	0.519
Designated Hitter	7,922.7	7,577.5	0.511	4.2	3.6	0.538
Pinch Runner	164.2	164.6	0.499	281.6	287.1	0.495
Non-P Fielders	87,096.0	87,244.6	0.500	199,148.3	192,916.5	0.508

A few comments:

1. Non-pitchers have an offensive winning percentage about 1.2% higher in the National League than in the American League,
2. Designated hitters are above-average hitters, but are comparable hitters to corner outfielders and are slightly worse hitters, on average, than first basemen,
3. Pinch hitters are among the worst hitters of any position (comparable to catchers and shortstops).

Positional Averages for Non-Pitchers

Comparisons of this nature are based on an implicit expectation that an average player at every position is equally valuable. Over a long enough time period, such as the 80+ years over which I have calculated pW-L records, offensive winning percentages tend to follow the defensive spectrum fairly closely, suggesting that such an assumption is probably at least generally reasonable. For specific leagues in specific seasons, however, there may be exceptions. In the 1999 American League, for example, 3 of the 14 teams' shortstops were Derek Jeter (who batted .349/.438/.552 in 739 plate appearances), Nomar Garciaparra (.357/.418/.603 in 595 PAs), and Alex Rodriguez (.285/.357/.586 in 572 PAs). That same season, the AL Silver Slugger for third basemen went to Dean Palmer, who batted .263/.339/.518 for Detroit. For that particular league-season, AL shortstops were comparable to AL third basemen in offensive win percentage, 0.486–0.487. It is perfectly reasonable to think that AL shortstops as a group were "above-average" in the 1999 American League. Similarly, centerfielders—led by Willie Mays, Mickey Mantle, Duke Snider, Larry Doby, et al., out-hit corner outfielders in several years of the 1950s.

One way to ameliorate this problem is to combine the two leagues—American and National—so that individual performances are less important (e.g., 3 shortstops represent only 10% of all starting shortstops in the major leagues as a whole). Before doing this, however, one has to adjust National League non-pitchers' offensive winning percentages to account for the lack of a DH in these leagues. This produces the following offensive winning percentages:

Context-Neutral pW-L Records by Defensive Position

	Major League Wide: DH-Adjusted		
Position	Wins	Losses	Win Pct.
Catcher	22,337.1	24,151.7	0.480
First Base	27,323.4	25,157.8	0.521
Second Base	24,569.7	26,236.6	0.484
Third Base	25,438.3	25,460.1	0.500
Shortstop	23,026.9	25,586.5	0.474

	Major League Wide: DH-Adjusted		
Position	Wins	Losses	Win Pct.
Left Field	27,323.6	25,718.1	0.515
Center Field	26,984.3	26,363.9	0.506
Right Field	27,216.7	25,545.2	0.516

Ranking them from highest winning percentage to lowest produces the following "defensive spectrum":

1B—RF—LF—CF—3B—2B—C—SS

This is extremely close to Bill James's defensive spectrum. Third basemen and center fielders are reversed, although the basic conclusion one can draw here is that third basemen and center fielders are both basically average hitters. Shortstops and catchers are also slightly reversed, although, again, the broad conclusion is simply that both positions are populated by relatively poor hitters through major-league history.

Another way to think about these results is to figure out what defensive winning percentage would be needed for each position to have a cumulative 0.500 winning percentage. This is done below.

Implied Defensive Won-Lost Records

	Major League Wide: DH-Adjusted		
Position	Wins	Losses	Win Pct.
Catcher	4,767.5	2,952.8	0.618
First Base	3,912.7	6,078.3	0.392
Second Base	11,404.3	9,737.4	0.539
Third Base	9,632.9	9,611.1	0.501
Shortstop	13,280.4	10,720.8	0.553
Left Field	12,108.7	13,714.2	0.469
Center Field	11,751.9	12,372.3	0.487
Right Field	12,124.3	13,795.8	0.468

Is there a way to compare players' defensive value across fielding positions without resorting to comparisons of offensive performance?

One possible way to do so is to compare the performance of a single player at multiple positions. For example, across all seasons for which I have calculated pW-L records, players who played both left field and center field within the same season had an average winning percentage of 0.489 in center field and 0.509 in left field. From this, one could reasonably conclude that center field is a more difficult position to play and one could also use this difference as a basis for adjusting these winning percentages to reflect a common base.

Comparisons of this type were done for all of the infield and outfield positions. Pitchers and catchers are not considered here. In the case of pitchers, this is because pitchers virtually never play a different position. This is also true, although to a lesser extent, of catchers. More problematic, however, in the case of catchers, is the fact that the skill set needed to be a good major-league catcher isn't really the same skill set needed to be a good fielder at any other position. The same is true to a lesser extent, of course, when comparing infielders to outfielders, and, really, is true to at least some extent in every case here.

Average Winning Percentage at Position X

	1B	2B	3B	SS	LF	CF	RF
1B		0.531	0.520	0.547	0.504	0.504	0.504
2B	0.492		0.494	0.499	0.489	0.489	0.487

	1B	*2B*	*3B*	*SS*	*LF*	*CF*	*RF*
3B	0.479	0.496		0.500	0.479	0.478	0.477
SS	0.485	0.490	0.489		0.486	0.482	0.485
LF	0.487	0.501	0.496	0.507		0.511	0.501
CF	0.485	0.491	0.491	0.502	0.488		0.489
RF	0.480	0.493	0.490	0.494	0.492	0.506	

This table is read as follows. For a player who played both first base and second base, the average winning percentage at first base is shown in the top row, 0.531—this is the average winning percentage of second basemen when they are playing first base. The average winning percentage of first basemen when they are playing second base is shown in the first column, 0.492. In all cases here, average winning percentages are calculated as weighted averages where the weights used are the harmonic mean between the player decisions at the two fielding positions being compared.

The average "normalized" winning percentage for a player at position Y when playing other positions can then be calculated as the weighted average of the numbers down the relevant column. The weights used to calculate these averages were the number of games upon which the comparison was based, which, as noted above, was the harmonic mean of the number of Player decisions accumulated at the two positions being compared.

Doing so produces the following average winning percentages by fielding position:

1B	0.484
2B	0.495
3B	0.495
SS	0.501
LF	0.491
CF	0.506
RF	0.495

This says that, on average, a first baseman amasses an average winning percentage of 0.484 at other positions. These numbers are only comparable, however, if we assume that the players being considered here are 0.500 fielders. Averaging across the rows, we can calculate the average winning percentage at first base of players who also played other positions: in this case, 0.511. Doing this for every position produces the following baseline winning percentages by position to which the above percentages should be compared:

1B	0.511
2B	0.495
3B	0.490
SS	0.489
LF	0.503
CF	0.489
RF	0.496

The first set of winning percentages was adjusted via the Matchup Formula based on this latter set to ensure a combined winning percentage of 0.500 across all positions. The Matchup Formula is described in Chapter 4.

These results are as follows:

1B	0.472
2B	0.500
3B	0.505
SS	0.512
LF	0.488
CF	0.518
RF	0.499

In words, if a set of first basemen with an average winning percentage of 0.511 amass an average winning percentage of 0.484 at other positions, then we would expect a set of first basemen with an average winning percentage of 0.500 to amass an average winning percentage of 0.472 at other positions.

Based on these winning percentages, the defensive spectrum looks something like this:

1B < LF < RF < 2B < 3B < SS < CF

Several aspects of these results are noteworthy. First, the range of winning percentages is very narrow. The other interesting comparison, I think, is that third base appears to be a tougher position to play than second base. Bill James discussed this in his *Win Shares* book, where he discussed the historical shift of the defensive spectrum with second base becoming more important than third base over time. As James puts it:

> Third basemen need quicker reactions, since they are nearer the batter, and they need a stronger arm, since they are further from first base. Without the double play, third base is obviously the more demanding position [*Win Shares*, p. 183].

The results here confirm this. Second base is, in one sense, the more valuable position, with approximately 10 percent more player decisions accumulated at second base than at third base, a difference which comes mostly from Component 7 (double plays) (see Chapter 4). Yet, comparing how well fielders do when they play both second base and third base in the same season, third base is the (slightly) more difficult position.

The final table here compares these results with relative fielding winning percentages implied by average offensive performances by position, which I derived above.

Adjusted Fielding Winning Percentage by Fielding Position Implied By

Position	Offensive Performance	Relative Fielding
1B	0.392	0.472
2B	0.539	0.500
3B	0.501	0.505
SS	0.553	0.512
LF	0.469	0.488
CF	0.487	0.518
RF	0.468	0.499

The most striking difference between relative fielding winning percentages implied by offensive performances and those based on comparing players who played more than one position is the former results in a much wider spread of implied fielding talent across positions. There are also several differences in the relative difficulty implied by position. Perhaps most strikingly, offensive performances by position imply that middle infielders are much better fielders than center fielders.

So, Which Methodology Produces Better Results?

For my work, I have chosen to calculate my positional averages based on relative offensive performances by position. I do this for several reasons which, I believe, make this a better choice for my purposes.

First, the mathematics here, attempting to normalize winning percentages across fielding positions, is fairly murky. In contrast, simply setting the positional average equal to the average winning percentage compiled at that position seems to me to be much cleaner and more elegant mathematically.

Second, I believe that limiting the analysis only to players who have played more than one position in the same season, as is done here, may lead to issues of selection bias. That is, we are not looking at the full population of all major-league players here—since most major-league players never played a game at shortstop, for example—or a random sample of major-league players. Instead, we are looking at a selected sample of major-league players, who were selected, in part, on the basis of exactly what we're attempting to study: with very few exceptions, the only major-league players who are selected to play shortstop are those whose manager thought they were capable of playing a major-league caliber shortstop (and the few exceptions likely only played an inning or two in an emergency situation, so they will be weighted very lightly in the above calculations).

I think that this is probably the primary reason why the winning percentages found here are generally closer to 0.500 than those implied by differences across offensive performances. The players considered here are self-selected for their ability to play multiple positions similarly well. Truly bad players at "offense-first" positions—think Frank Thomas at 1B, Manny Ramirez in LF—are so bad that nobody would ever consider trying to play Frank Thomas at 3B or Manny Ramirez in CF. But, at the other end of the spectrum, great defensive players at "defense-first" positions are so great defensively that, for example, Ozzie Smith never played an inning of major league baseball at any defensive position besides SS; Willie Mays never played a corner outfield position until he was 34 years old.

Finally, I believe that setting positional averages based on actual empirical winning percentages is more consistent with what I am attempting to measure with my pW-L records. pW-L records are a measure of player value. At the bottom-line theoretical level, every team must field a player at all nine positions. If one team has a second baseman that is one win above average and another team has a left fielder who is one win above average, then these two teams will win the same number of games (all other things being equal). Hence, in some sense, not only is it a reasonable assumption to view an average second baseman as equal in value to an average left fielder, it is, in fact, a necessary assumption.

Pitchers

As a general rule, pitchers tend to perform better—lower ERA, more strikeouts, better context-neutral winning percentage—as relief pitchers than as starters. This can be measured in two ways.

First, one can compare the average winning percentage for starting pitchers and relief pitchers. Since 2000, starting pitchers compiled an average winning percentage of 0.496, while relief pitchers amassed a 0.506 winning percentage. From this, one could conclude that the positional average for starting pitchers is about 0.010 lower than for relief pitchers.

Such a conclusion would assume, however, that an average starting pitcher is equal in value to an average relief pitcher (on a per-inning basis). This may not be a reasonable assumption. In general, starting pitchers tend to be better pitchers than relief pitchers, particularly than non-closers.

Alternately, one can look at individual pitchers who both started and relieved in the same season. Over the seasons for which I constructed pW-L records, a total of 14,849 player-seasons included both starting pitching and relief pitching. Weighting each of these players' performances by the harmonic mean of their starting and relief pitching Player Decisions, these pitchers compiled a weighted average winning percentage of 0.476 as starting pitchers and 0.496 as relief pitchers. Using the Matchup Formula to re-center these winning percentages around 0.500, the average winning percentage for these pitchers as starters was 0.490 and for these pitchers as relievers was 0.520. Looked at in this way, the positional average for starting pitchers appears to be about 0.030 lower than for relief pitchers.

For my work, I use this latter difference. That is, the positional average for starting pitchers is set about 0.030 lower than the positional average for relief pitchers. Because this gap is wider than the observed gap in the cumulative winning percentage for all starting pitchers vis-à-vis all relief pitchers, the result of this is that starting pitchers are, on average, slightly above-average pitchers, while relief pitchers are, on average, slightly below-average pitchers. I believe that this fairly represents the reality of how pitchers are used in major league baseball.

Positional Averages for Individual Players

Unique positional averages by position are calculated by season. A positional average winning percentage is then constructed for each individual player based on the positions at which the player accumulated his wins and losses. This is done as follows.

#1. OFFENSIVE PLAYER DECISIONS

For offensive player games (wins plus losses), the positional average is the average (DH-adjusted) offensive winning percentage for that position for that season. For games played under NL rules, then, a "pitcher hitting penalty" is added to the positional average. This is equal to the difference in the average winning percentage of non-pitcher position players (i.e., excluding pinch hitters, pinch runners, and designated hitters) in NL games versus the average winning percentage of these players in AL games. As the table presented near the beginning of this Chapter shows, the "pitcher hitting penalty" has been just over 1% on average. The specific penalty used in this calculation is calculated uniquely each year.

For players who accumulated offensive player decisions while playing multiple defensive positions (where, for lack of a better term, I include "pinch hitter," "pinch runner," and "designated hitter" as unique "defensive positions") or who played some games under AL rules and some games under NL rules (so that the "pitcher hitting penalty" is only applied to some of his player decisions), the overall offensive positional average is simply equal to the weighted average of the unique positional averages across positions and across leagues, weighted by the number of player decisions accumulated by position and league.

#2. PITCHING PLAYER DECISIONS

For pitchers, unique positional averages are calculated for starting pitchers and relief pitchers. These averages are calculated by year (with both leagues combined, with no

DH-adjustments since an average pitcher is a 0.500 pitcher in both leagues by definition) by looking at pitchers who started and relieved in the same season (for the same team) and comparing average winning percentages of these pitchers as starters and as relievers. These average winning percentages are adjusted to an average 0.500 winning percentage using the Matchup Formula. As noted above, on average, the Positional Average for starting pitchers is around 0.490, while for relievers the Positional Average for relief pitchers is around 0.520. These averages vary, however, by year.

#3. Fielding Player Decisions

By construction, cumulative fielding winning percentages will be 0.500 for every defensive position in every league every year. Hence, the Positional Average for fielding player decisions is 0.500 for all players.

Overall Positional Average

The overall Positional Average for a player is then simply a weighted average of his offensive, pitching, and fielding averages where the weights used are the relative offensive, pitching, and fielding decisions compiled by the player.

These Positional Averages form the basis for comparing players across positions, either by comparing players to "average" or to "replacement level."

Wins Over Replacement Level (WORL)

Even having calculated Positional Averages to make comparisons possible across positions, a problem still exists in attempting to compare Won-Lost records of different players. This problem is best illustrated by example. For simplicity, assume that all of the players discussed here had a Positional Average of 0.500.

Which player is more valuable: a player who earns a pW-L record of 5–2 (0.714 winning percentage) or a player who puts up a Won-Lost record of 9–5 (0.667)? The first player (call him A) has a better winning percentage, but the second player (call him B) has more wins. In this case, the answer is fairly simple: Player B is almost certainly more valuable. His value is basically the same as Player A (5–2) plus the value of another player who went 4–3.

Let's try another one. Which player is more valuable, a player who puts up a Won-Lost record of 9–5 (player B) or a player who puts up a won-lost record of 9–8 (player C)? Again, this one seems fairly simple. Clearly, the player who won 9 games with fewer losses is more valuable. Breaking value down, Player C is basically the same as Player B (9–5) plus the value of a player who went 0–3. Notice the logical inference from those last two sentences. If Player B has *more* value than Player C, then the value of a player who goes 0–3 isn't zero (otherwise Player C would have the same value as Player B); it's negative.

Finally, let's make the problem a little harder. Who's more valuable, Player A (5–2) or Player C (9–8)? Now the problem gets trickier. Player C has the same value as Player A plus a second player with a Won-Lost record of 4–6 (0.400). Well, how valuable is a 0.400 winning percentage from a player?

Replacement Level

The question really is, "how valuable compared to what?" And the answer to that question is, "Compared to what the team's other alternatives would have been," which leads nicely to the theory of Replacement Level.

Replacement Level is the level of performance which a team should be able to get from a player who they can find easily on short notice—such as a minor-league call-up or a veteran waiver-wire pickup. The theory here is that major league baseball players only have value to a team above and beyond what the team could get from basically pulling players off the street. That is, there's no real marginal value to having a third baseman make routine plays that anybody who's capable of playing third base at the high school or college level could make, since if a major-league team were to lose its starting third baseman, they would fill the position with somebody and that somebody would, in fact, make at least those routine plays at third base. This is similar to the economic concept of Opportunity Cost.

For my work, I define Replacement Level as equal to a winning percentage one weighted standard deviation below Positional Average. Separate standard deviations are calculated for players at fielding positions, players at offense-only positions (DH, PH, PR), starting pitchers, and relief pitchers. Unique standard deviations are calculated in this way for each year. These standard deviations are then applied to the unique Positional Averages of each individual player. Overall, this works out to an average Replacement Level of about 0.455 (0.464 for non-pitchers, and 0.439 for pitchers). A team of 0.455 players would have an expected winning percentage of 0.366 (59–103 over a 162-game season). The derivation of my choice of Replacement Level is described next.

Derivation of Replacement Level: Hitting Versus Fielding

Some analysts distinguish between replacement-level hitting—the level of hitting that could be found from freely-available talent—and replacement-level fielding—the level of fielding that could be found amongst freely-available talent. The problem with this is that, except for designated hitters, a team can't actually replace a player's hitting and a player's fielding independent of one another. In fact, in many cases, it's quite reasonable to think of situations where a player's replacement is actually better than the player he is replacing at either hitting or fielding, but is nevertheless a worse overall player. Instead, a team must make a tradeoff and settle for the replacement player who provides the best combination of hitting and fielding. Hence, in my opinion, it only makes sense to talk about replacement level at an overall level, taking into account all aspects of a player's game: batting, baserunning, fielding, and, if appropriate, pitching.

Replacement Level by Position

Some analysts also argue that replacement level differs by position—that is, one should calculate the replacement level for first basemen differently from the replacement level for second basemen. This seems to me to be a more reasonable position and is certainly worth investigating. On the other hand, the pool of replacement third basemen is likely to overlap considerably with the pool of replacement shortstops, for example, and any possible replacement starting pitcher is likely to also be a replacement relief pitcher. Certainly, however, at a minimum, the pool of replacement non-pitchers will be distinct from the pool of replacement pitchers.

I will begin by investigating all players to get a sense of where a general Replacement Level might be. From there, I will investigate Replacement Level by position.

Replacement Player Winning Percentages

So, how does one go about determining Replacement Level? The first step, it seems to me, would be to define precisely what is meant by Replacement Level. The most obvious definition of Replacement Level to me, or, perhaps more precisely, the definition of Replacement Level which leads most obviously to a means of measuring it, would be the average winning percentage of marginal major league baseball players.

Over all seasons for which I have calculated pW-L records, there have been a total of 2,006 team seasons and 79,425 player-seasons for which the player accumulated a non-zero number of player decisions, where a player-season is defined as a unique player-season-team combination (so, for example, Aramis Ramirez's 2003 performance with the Pittsburgh Pirates and Ramirez's 2003 performance with the Chicago Cubs are treated as two distinct player-seasons).

I sorted these 79,425 player-seasons by total basic player games (wins plus losses). The total number of games ranged from a high of 47.8 for Mickey Lolich for the 1971 Detroit Tigers to a low of 0.00008 for Walt McKeel for the 1996 Boston Red Sox. Actually, 18 players have appeared in a game but amassed exactly zero Player decisions during a player-season during the time period for which I have calculated pW-L records. This was done most recently by Kevin Kiermaier in 2013, who played one inning in CF for the Tampa Bay Rays. Kiermaier's performance that day, such as it was, becomes wholly irrelevant to the results presented here.

As noted above, there have been 2,006 team-seasons across all seasons for which I have calculated pW-L records. That works out to a total of 50,150 major-league roster spots available over this time period (2,006 teams times 25 roster spots per team). So, one could view the top 50,150 player-seasons over this time period as being "roster-level" player-seasons and the remaining 29,275 player-seasons (15 per team) as being "replacement-level" player-seasons.

As I just explained earlier in this chapter, a .500 winning percentage by a first baseman isn't strictly comparable to a .500 winning percentage by a shortstop. To account for that, I adjusted player winning percentages here; adjusted winning percentage is equal to the player's winning percentage plus (0.500—the player's positional average).

Sorting by total Player games (wins plus losses), the aggregate adjusted winning percentage for "roster-level" players was 0.504, and the aggregate winning percentage for "replacement-level" player seasons was 0.451, with "roster-level" players accounting for 94.7% of all Player decisions when measured in this way. This would imply a Replacement Level approximately 5.2% below Positional Average.

Is This Really the Best Way to Measure Replacement Level?

Conceptually, I think that it is. The question, however, is where to draw the line between "roster-level" and "replacement-level." Drawing the line at 25 players per team makes some obvious sense, of course, as (before September 1st) there are 25 roster spots per team. Of course, no team uses only 25 players in a single season. On average, for the seasons for which I have calculated pW-L records, the average major-league team played 39.6 players per season (which is quite a bit higher than I would have guessed). Given that, how much difference is there between, say, the 23rd player on a typical team and the 28th player on a typical team?

The table below sets out to answer that question. The winning percentages shown here are the aggregate adjusted winning percentage for all players who ranked at a given roster level as well as the aggregate adjusted winning percentage for all players who ranked below the given roster level. For example, the top 18,054 players in terms of Player Games would constitute roster spots 1–9 (2,006 teams times 9 roster spots = 18,054). These players posted an aggregate adjusted winning percentage of 0.513, while players who occupied roster spots 10–40 posted an aggregate adjusted winning percentage of 0.484. The cumulative percentage of team games is also shown for those who occupied roster spots 1 through the particular roster spot(s) shown.

Roster Spot	at Roster Spot	Winning Percentage Below Roster Spot	Cumulative % of Total Games
1–9	0.513	0.484	57.6%
10	0.499	0.482	61.9%
11	0.496	0.481	65.9%
12	0.493	0.479	69.5%
13	0.492	0.478	72.8%
14	0.490	0.476	75.7%
15	0.487	0.475	78.4%
16	0.486	0.474	80.9%
17	0.484	0.472	83.1%
18	0.486	0.470	85.0%
19	0.481	0.469	86.8%
20	0.483	0.467	88.5%
21	0.482	0.465	90.0%
22	0.484	0.462	91.3%
23	0.482	0.458	92.6%
24	0.477	0.455	93.7%
25	0.475	0.451	94.7%
26	0.468	0.448	95.6%
27	0.462	0.445	96.4%
28	0.463	0.441	97.0%
29	0.458	0.437	97.6%
30	0.454	0.432	98.1%
31	0.446	0.428	98.6%
32	0.443	0.423	98.9%
33	0.439	0.417	99.2%
34	0.430	0.411	99.4%
35	0.424	0.404	99.6%
36	0.415	0.397	99.8%
37	0.405	0.389	99.9%
38	0.396	0.376	100.0%
39	0.383	0.333	100.0%
40	0.333	–	100.0%

So what exactly do all of these numbers really mean and how do they help us calculate Replacement Level? Well, the first thing to notice, which shouldn't be too surprising is that, in general, average winning percentages decline as one works one's way deeper into the roster. In fact, looking at the column showing the aggregate winning percentage for players below a given roster level, this value declines uniformly through the entire table. In terms of winning percentage by roster spot, the trend is slightly less perfect, but is still fairly clear nevertheless.

Looking at the above table, is there any obvious break-point where the data seem to indicate that below a certain roster spot players are "replacement-level"? To me, the answer is "Sort of."

Below the first 10 or 11 roster spots, roster spots 12–23 hover just below 0.500, in a relatively narrow range between 0.481 and 0.493. Changes in winning percentage by roster spot are somewhat erratic in this area of the roster, suggesting that differences in player decisions at this level are the result of differences in decisions earned across positions more so than differences in the quality of the players occupying the various spots (e.g., outfielders tend to earn more decisions than infielders even though there's no reason to think that outfielders are better players than infielders on average).

Roster spots 24 and 25 are fairly close to each other and are just a tick below the roster spots just above them. There is a bit more of a clear break, however, in moving from roster spot 25 to roster spot 26.

This might suggest setting "replacement level" as the level just below roster spot 25– which conveniently matches up with the 25-man roster. If players at roster spots below 25 are viewed as "replacement-level," this would put replacement level at approximately 0.451.

This ends up being very close to the result setting replacement level one standard deviation below Positional Average, 0.455, which I have used for my work.

Replacement Levels by Position

I noted earlier that some people like to calculate unique Replacement Levels by position. This is an idea worth at least examining.

To do so, I looked at what a one-standard-deviation standard would imply regarding unique replacement levels by player position. Standard deviations for winning percentage by position are shown below calculated in two ways. The numbers on the left were calculated based on basic context-neutral, teammate-adjusted records. The numbers on the right also incorporate Expected Team Win Adjustments.

Position	Raw Wins	Adjusted Wins
C	4.5%	4.7%
1B	4.5%	4.7%
2B	3.7%	3.9%
3B	4.1%	4.3%
SS	3.6%	3.8%
LF	4.3%	4.5%
CF	3.9%	4.1%
RF	4.1%	4.3%
DH	7.1%	7.3%
PH	15.5%	15.5%
PR	26.6%	26.6%
Pitcher (Offense)	10.7%	10.9%
Starting Pitcher	4.3%	5.2%
Relief Pitcher	6.6%	7.0%
Non-Pitcher Offense	4.8%	5.1%

A few comments about this table. First, the positions of DH, PH, PR, and pitcher offense give somewhat odd results that don't necessarily make a lot of sense and are likely plagued to some extent by small-sample problems, even over the 80+ year time period considered here.

The other problem with PH, PR, and pitcher offense, I think, is that the correlation between winning percentage and total games is almost certainly weaker for these positions, especially pitcher offense, than for other positions. That is, better catchers will catch more games, which will serve to reduce the weighted standard deviation of catcher winning percentage. Pitchers, on the other hand, are chosen almost exclusively for their pitching ability, not their hitting ability. As a result, there is likely to be very little correlation between the number of batting decisions earned by a pitcher and his hitting ability. The same is probably due, albeit to a lesser extent, for pinch hitting and pinch running. In many cases, a team's best pinch-hitting option on a particular day will be the best-hitting regular who has the day off, but, for any given regular, the number of times when that will be him will be very small; if he had too many days off, he'd no longer be a regular.

Excluding these positions, the results are actually quite stable across positions. For non-pitchers at fielding positions, the standard deviation for basic wins averages out to 3.8%, with a fairly narrow range across positions (3.6%–4.5%). For pitchers, the standard deviation for basic wins averages out to 4.5%.

The final row shows the standard deviation for non-pitcher offense—i.e., batting and baserunning only. The standard deviation for offense is somewhat greater than the standard deviation for non-pitchers at fielding positions. This is because poor hitters can improve their overall value with good fielding (and good hitters can reduce their overall value with poor fielding).

The gap between the standard deviations for position players and pitchers is even greater when expected intra-game win adjustments are taken into consideration. As I explained in Chapter 2, expected team win adjustments adjust for the fact that player differences from .500 will tend to have an exaggerated impact on leading to team wins; the reverse is true of below-average players as well. Being a little bit better than average has a multiplicative impact on a team's winning percentage. Because of this effect, when one adjusts basic player winning percentages for this expected team win adjustment, this will have the effect of increasing the spread of player winning percentages: player winning percentages above 0.500 will move farther above 0.500, while player winning percentages below 0.500 will move farther below 0.500. As a result, the standard deviation of player winning percentages is greater when expected team win adjustments are accounted for.

This effect of players on team wins is stronger for pitchers than it is for non-pitchers, because pitchers concentrate their performance into fewer team games. Adding, for example 0.3 player wins in one game will have more of an impact on a team than adding 0.1 player wins in each of three separate games. Because of this, when one incorporates expected team win adjustments for pitchers, especially starting pitchers, this has a much more significant impact on their standard deviation—which rises from 4.3% to 5.2%—than is the case for non-pitchers.

Overall, non-pitcher fielders see their average standard deviation increase from 3.8% to 4.0%. Pitchers, on the other hand, see their average standard deviation increase of 4.5% to 5.2%. This increased separation in the standard deviations of winning percentages for pitchers and non-pitchers further strengthens my decision to calculate separate standard deviations for these two groups. Note that making this adjustment also increases the difference in standard deviation between starting pitchers and relief pitchers. This difference is also recognized in my calculation of replacement level, as described below.

Even with these adjustments, the differences in standard deviation across fielding positions, however, are still very narrow—ranging from 3.8% to 4.7%. Because of this, I have chosen to calculate a single standard deviation for calculating Replacement Levels for all non-pitcher fielding positions.

Final Results

Putting all of this together, these results lead to my final decision to set Replacement Level at one standard deviation below Positional Average with standard deviations calculated separately for non-pitchers and pitchers. A single standard deviation is used for non-pitcher position players across all fielding positions. In the case of DH's, PH's, and PR's, however, all of their value is offensive. Hence, the overall standard deviation for non-pitcher offense is used to calculate replacement level at these positions.

Separate standard deviations are calculated for starting pitchers and relief pitchers based on the differences observed above. The standard deviation for pitcher offense is set equal to zero for purposes of calculating replacement level, on the grounds that, because hitting ability is not (generally) selected for in pitchers, there is no reason to believe that a replacement-level pitcher would be any worse at hitting than an average pitcher.

Putting all of this together, across all seasons for which I have calculated pW-L records, this works out to an average Replacement Level for non-pitchers of 0.464, and for pitchers of 0.439. Across all players, this works out to an average replacement level of 0.455. Going back to the table by roster level, this puts Replacement Level at about the level of players below the 24th-best player on an average major-league roster, with Replacement-Level players accounting for just over 6% of all Player decisions.

Combining these, a team of replacement-level players would have an expected winning percentage of around 0.366 (59–103 over a 162-game season).

For an individual player, Wins over Replacement Level (pWORL, eWORL) are equal to Player Wins minus (Player Decisions times Replacement Level). I compare my wins over replacement level (WORL) to Baseball-Reference.com's Wins above Replacement Level (WAR) in Chapter 8.

Having set up the basics of pW-L records so far in the first three chapters, an example may help to give a flavor of how pW-L records can be used to compare and contrast major league baseball players.

David Ortiz v. Alex Rodriguez: Who Was the 2005 American League MVP?

The 2005 American League Most Valuable Player race was a two-man race between Alex Rodriguez of the New York Yankees and David Ortiz of the Boston Red Sox. Rodriguez received 16 first-place votes to 11 for Ortiz (Vlad Guerrero received one first-place vote) and beat Ortiz overall 331–307. A comparison of the pW-L records of Ortiz and Rodriguez is very instructive, I think, at highlighting the real strengths of this system.

#1. Basic Offensive Statistics

Alex Rodriguez and David Ortiz put up similar offensive statistics in 2005. Their traditional statistics are shown below.

Basic Offensive Statistics, 2005

	G	PA	AB	H	2B	3B	HR
Alex Rodriguez	162	715	605	194	29	1	48
David Ortiz	159	713	601	180	40	1	47

	R	RBI	BB	SO	BA	OBP	SLG
Alex Rodriguez	124	130	91	139	0.321	0.421	0.610
David Ortiz	119	148	102	124	0.300	0.397	0.604

Rodriguez had 2 more plate appearances and 14 more hits, the latter of which was nearly offset by Ortiz drawing 11 additional walks. Ortiz hit 11 more doubles, but Rodriguez hit one more home run. While Ortiz drove in 18 more runs, Rodriguez managed to score 5 more runs. All in all, these are extremely similar season lines.

Turning to more advanced offensive metrics simply reinforces the same thing.

Advanced Offensive Statistics, 2005

	OPS	RC	RC/27	OPS+
Alex Rodriguez	1.031	163	10.2	173
David Ortiz	1.001	149	9.0	158

Not surprisingly (in fact, encouragingly), the similarity between these two players carries over to their context-neutral batting Player Wins and Losses:

pW-L Record: Batting, Context-Neutral

	eWins	eLosses	eWinPct	eWins Over .500
Alex Rodriguez	17.2	10.8	0.614	3.2
David Ortiz	17.0	11.5	0.596	2.7

Once again, Rodriguez comes out slightly, but clearly, ahead, with 0.2 more wins and 0.7 fewer losses.

#2. Everything Else

There's more to playing baseball than simply batting, of course.

Baserunning

David Ortiz is a rather notoriously slow baserunner with 17 career stolen bases. Alex Rodriguez stole more bases than that in 2005 alone (21). Even beyond stolen bases, Rodriguez is, in general, a much better baserunner than David Ortiz. The context-neutral baserunning Player Decisions accumulated by each of them are shown below.

pW-L Record: Baserunning, Context-Neutral

	eWins	eLosses	eWinPct	eWins Over .500
Alex Rodriguez	1.2	1.3	0.484	−0.0
David Ortiz	0.5	0.9	0.372	−0.2

While Rodriguez was a better baserunner than Ortiz, they were actually both below-average baserunners in 2005. Nevertheless, Rodriguez gains about 0.2 net wins (Wins minus Losses) on Ortiz thanks to his baserunning.

Fielding

David Ortiz is a poor-fielding first baseman who played a total of 78 innings in the field in 2005. Alex Rodriguez is a former Gold-Glove winning shortstop who played 1,390 innings in the field in 2005.

Let's see how they compare.

pW-L Record: Fielding, Context-Neutral

	eWins	eLosses	eWinPct	eWins Over .500
Alex Rodriguez	4.9	5.3	0.478	−0.2
David Ortiz	0.2	0.2	0.396	-0.0

While A-Rod looks to have been a below-average third baseman, he was nevertheless a better fielder, relative to his position, than Ortiz (by 0.082), and, perhaps more importantly, because Ortiz was primarily a designated hitter in 2005, A-Rod accumulated 24 times as many context-neutral Fielding Wins as Big Papi. Because Rodriguez was a sub-.500 fielder, those extra decisions actually lead to Rodriguez accumulating fewer Fielding wins over .500, though.

Adding up what we have so far, here is how Alex Rodriguez and David Ortiz compare in terms of basic, context-neutral Player Wins and Losses.

pW-L Record: Context-Neutral

	eWins	eLosses	eWinPct	eWins Over .500
Alex Rodriguez	23.3	17.5	0.571	2.9
David Ortiz	17.7	12.7	0.583	2.5

So far, this really isn't much of a race. David Ortiz has the better winning percentage, 0.583 to 0.571, but because Rodriguez played the field all season, he leads Ortiz in Wins over .500, 2.9 to 2.5 and in total wins, 23.3 to 17.7.

#3. Contextual Adjustments

So why did David Ortiz do as well as he did in the MVP voting?

The answer is hinted at in the one basic offensive statistic in which Ortiz beat Rodriguez fairly convincingly: RBI. David Ortiz led the American League with 148 runs batted in, while Rodriguez, despite one more home run as well as a higher batting average and slugging percentage, managed to finish only 4th in the American League with 130 RBIs.

So how did Ortiz lead the league in RBIs? Well, supposedly, he had a phenomenal season batting in the clutch. The MVP argument in support of David Ortiz basically revolved around the notion that he was the best clutch hitter in all of baseball.

There is an argument that invariably arises every year at MVP voting time, that the "Most Valuable Player" is not the *best* player, but the player who contributed most to his team's success. In other words, the argument goes, to be the MVP, it doesn't just matter *what* you do, it also matters *when* you do it.

Of course, Player Wins and Losses are perfectly designed to exactly measure the extent to which a player's performance contributed to real wins and real losses by his team.

Player Wins and Losses are adjusted in two ways to reflect the impact of the timing of player performance: Inter-Game and Intra-Game.

Inter-Game Adjustments: Performance in the Clutch

Inter-game contextual factors adjust for the relative importance of a player's performance within the context of a given game. In other words, hitting a home run in the bottom of the ninth inning of a tie game is worth more than hitting a home run leading off the top of the 5th inning of a game in which the player's team is already leading 12–1.

There are two inter-game adjustments to pW-L records: Context and Win Adjustments.

Inter-Game Context

Inter-game context is basically what some other people refer to as Leverage. This measures the relative importance of situations within the context of a single game. In 2005, Alex Rodriguez performed in an average inter-game context of 0.991, about 0.9% below average. This served to lower A-Rod's total player decisions by 0.4 games.

In contrast, David Ortiz performed in an average inter-game context of 1.039, about 3.9% above average, which increased Big Papi's total player decisions by 1.2 games.

Inter-Game Win Adjustment

Of course, the issue is not simply how many high-leverage situations a player performs in, but how well he does in those situations. The MVP argument for David Ortiz was not simply that he had a lot of high-leverage at-bats (which, as we just saw, he did), but that he rose to the occasion in those situations, performing even better in those high-leverage situations than his already-excellent self.

In this regard, David Ortiz excelled. Overall, in 2005, Ortiz batted .300/.397/.604. With runners in scoring position, he improved that to .352/.462/.580. With two outs and runners in scoring position, he batted .368/.507/.719. In "late and close" situations, Ortiz batted .346/.447/.846. No matter how you slice the data, Big Papi delivered big time in the clutch in 2005. Because of this, his effective winning percentage was better than his context-neutral winning percentage of 0.583. In fact, his inter-game win adjustment increased his winning percentage by 0.034 to an inter-game adjusted winning percentage of 0.617.

Alex Rodriguez, on the other hand, while not as "un-clutch" as maybe some people thought at the time, performed almost exactly the same regardless of the inter-game context, so that his inter-game win adjustment was –0.001.

Taking inter-game context and inter-game win adjustments into account, the comparison between Alex Rodriguez and David Ortiz looks like this.

pW-L Records, Inter-Game Adjusted: 2005*

	Wins	Losses	WinPct	Wins Over .500
Alex Rodriguez	23.1	17.3	0.572	2.9
David Ortiz	19.6	12.0	0.620	3.8

*Player wins are also adjusted to control for the performance of one's teammates in shared components.

Now we see why David Ortiz did so well in MVP voting. Taking inter-game performance into account, Ortiz moves much more decisively ahead of Rodrigez in winning percentage, 0.620–0.572, and also moves ahead of him in wins over 0.500, 3.8–2.9.

Intra-Game Adjustments:
Performance in Team Wins versus Team Losses

In addition to adjusting for inter-game context, I also adjust for intra-game context. As with inter-game adjustments, I adjust for two factors here: Context and Win Adjustments.

Intra-Game Context

Intra-game context adjusts player wins and losses to normalize the total number of player decisions per game to be equal to exactly three decisions per team per game.

Alex Rodriguez played in an average Intra-Game context of 1.070 about 7.0% above average. This increased Rodriguez's total player decisions by 2.8.

David Ortiz had an average Intra-Game context of 1.012 (1.2% above average), increasing his total player decisions by 0.4.

The intra-game context adjustment basically gives A-Rod as much of an edge in player decisions over Ortiz as the inter-game context adjustment gave to Big Papi. The reason for this is that intra-game context is somewhat negatively correlated to inter-game context. This is because games with lots of high-leverage plays will tend to generate more player decisions than games with relatively few high-leverage plays. But, at the end of the day, all games count exactly the same in the standings: a team can only win a game once no matter how many clutch hits its players managed to get.

Intra-Game Win Adjustment

There is one final adjustment that I make to pW-L records. This adjusts player wins and losses such that the players on a team earn exactly two player wins in any team win and exactly one win in any team loss, and that players earn exactly two player losses in any team loss and exactly one loss in any team win. In this adjustment, positive events which contributed to wins are weighted more heavily than positive events which happened in team losses, while negative events which contributed to team losses get more weight than negative events which happened in team wins.

This final adjustment improves David Ortiz's player winning percentage by 0.008 and Alex Rodriguez's winning percentage by 0.023.

This final adjustment benefits both Rodriguez and Ortiz, as they both tended to perform better in games which their teams won than they did in games which their teams lost. Of course, this is true of most players (that's why their teams win those games after all). Rodriguez and Ortiz were both also helped by the fact that their teams won 95 games apiece.

While this adjustment helped both players, the help to Ortiz was fairly minimal, an extra 0.3 wins (and a reduction of 0.3 losses). Rodriguez, on the other hand, gained more than 3 times as many wins as Ortiz (1.0) by virtue of having produced better in Yankee victories than in Yankee losses.

Does this make sense?

Well, here are A-Rod's numbers.

Alex Rodriguez's Batting Line in 2005

	G	PA	BA	OBP	SLG	Runs	RBI
Yankee Wins	95	437	0.376	0.490	0.736	101	101
Yankee Losses	67	278	0.241	0.313	0.430	23	29

Now, as I said, most players perform better in games that their team wins than in games that their team loses. On aggregate that would have to be true; that's why the winning teams win and the losing teams lose. But, let's compare Rodriguez's numbers to David Ortiz's numbers.

David Ortiz's Batting Line in 2005

	G	PA	BA	OBP	SLG	Runs	RBI
Red Sox Wins	94	431	0.332	0.441	0.685	92	104
Red Sox Losses	65	282	0.253	0.330	0.490	27	44

Now, compare just those top lines. A-Rod outhit Ortiz in victories by 0.044 in batting average, 0.049 in OBP, and 0.051 in slugging (which makes his OPS a full 0.100 higher than Ortiz). He outscored him by 9 runs and had only 3 fewer RBIs. And remember, the Yankees and Red Sox won the same number of games (although Ortiz sat out one Red Sox victory).

So, while Ortiz performed better in situations that were very valuable within the context of a particular game—inter-game context—A-Rod performed better in situations that ended up contributing to Yankee wins—intra-game context. And, in fact, combining batting, baserunning, and fielding, these effects were nearly offsetting: Ortiz gained about 1.3 wins on Rodriguez through inter-game adjustments while Rodriguez got 0.9 of those wins back through intra-game adjustments.

Let me try to illustrate with an example.

On September 29, 2005, David Ortiz went 3-for-5 including a home run leading off the bottom of the 8th inning to tie the score 4–4 and a walk-off RBI single with one out in the bottom of the 9th inning. Baseball-Reference.com credits Ortiz with a WPA of 0.584 for the game. Obviously, those hits were huge for the Red Sox and Ortiz was rightly celebrated as the hero of that game.

On April 26, 2005, the Yankees defeated the Los Angeles Angels of Anaheim (or whatever they were calling themselves that season) 12–4. The Yankees took a 3–0 lead in the bottom of the first inning and led 10–2 by the end of the 4th inning. Obviously, there weren't a lot of "clutch" situations in this game. It was over early.

Do you know why it was over early? Because Alex Rodriguez hit a 2-out, 3-run home run in the bottom of the first inning to give the Yankees that 3–0 lead, he hit a 2-out, 2-run home run in the bottom of the third inning to extend the Yankees' lead to 5–2, and he capped it off with a 2-out grand slam in the bottom of the 4th inning to give the Yankees that aforementioned 10–2 lead. For all of that, Baseball-Reference.com only credits Alex Rodriguez with a WPA of 0.490 for that game.

Take Ortiz's two RBIs off the scoreboard for the Red Sox in that September 29th game, and the Blue Jays would have won that game 4–3. Then again, if Ortiz had struck out in his final at-bat, Manny Ramirez would have come to bat with the potential winning run still in scoring position (albeit with two outs).

Take Rodriguez's ten RBIs off the scoreboard for the Yankees on April 26th and the Angels would have won that game 4–2. Moreover, all three of Rodriguez's home runs came with two outs in the inning. Turn them into outs and the Yankees would have had no further opportunities in any of those innings.

In retrospect, Alex Rodriguez's performance that day was not merely every bit as valuable as Ortiz's, but almost certainly more so, even if it was less "clutch" by a conventional inter-game "win probability" reckoning.

My pW-L records credit David Ortiz with a batting won-lost record that day of 0.48–0.02, good for 0.46 net wins. Alex Rodriguez had a batting won-lost record on his big day of 0.91–0.02, good for 0.89 net wins. That seems like a reasonable reflection of the importance of both of these performances.

#3. Comparing a Third Baseman to a Designated Hitter

Taking everything into account, here is where we stand with Alex Rodriguez and David Ortiz in 2005.

Final pW-L Records: 2005

	pWins	pLosses	pWinPct	Wins Over .500
Alex Rodriguez	25.7	17.5	0.595	4.1
David Ortiz	20.1	11.9	0.628	4.1

So, Alex Rodriguez earned more Player Wins (pWins) than David Ortiz, 25.7–20.1, while Ortiz had a higher winning percentage, 0.628–0.598. A-Rod leads in pWins over .500, by an amount that can only be described as trivial, 4.124–4.095.

BUT IS THIS REALLY A TOTALLY FAIR COMPARISON?

In terms of fielding wins, is an average third baseman worth the same as an average first baseman or, worse, an "average" designated hitter? Clearly, an average third baseman is a better fielder than an average first baseman and is considerably more valuable than an average designated hitter.

Why? Think of it this way. To replace David Ortiz, all the Boston Red Sox would have had to do in 2005 would have been to find the best possible hitter they could find. That hitter would surely be a good deal worse than David Ortiz, but the pool of possible replacements for Ortiz was nevertheless fairly large: the population of major-league caliber hitters.

On the other hand, if the New York Yankees had to replace Alex Rodriguez, they would have not only had to have found a hitter, but they would have had to find a hitter who could also play third base. The pool of possible replacement candidates to replace Rodriguez—major-league caliber third basemen—would clearly be smaller than the pool of possible replacements for Ortiz.

Positional Average

A player who hit (and ran) like an average third baseman given Alex Rodriguez's batting opportunities, and fielded like an average third baseman given A-Rod's fielding opportunities, would have been expected to compile a 0.501 winning percentage. In contrast, a player who hit (and ran) like an average DH/1B given David Ortiz's batting opportunities, and fielded like an average first baseman given Ortiz's fielding opportunities, would have been expected to compile a 0.515 winning percentage.

Using these figures for "average," then, Alex Rodriguez's final won-lost record was 4.1 pWins over Positional Average (pWOPA) while David Ortiz compiled a pWOPA of 3.6, a solid, albeit modest, lead for A-Rod.

Replacement Level

Alex Rodriguez earned 35% more Player decisions than Ortiz because he played so many more innings in the field than Ortiz. If Rodriguez had earned the same number of decisions as Ortiz (if, say, he missed 40 games to injury), is it likely that the Yankees could have found an average player (which, in Rodriguez's case, means a 0.501 player) to make up those extra decisions? No, it is not. Instead, the most likely scenario is that the Yankees would have had to make up those Player decisions with a below-average player. Consider who the Yankees played at third base in April of 2009 while A-Rod recovered from a hip injury: Cody Ransom, who batted a robust .190/.256/.329 for the Yankees.

Hence, instead of comparing A-Rod and Big Papi to average players, a more relevant measure of the relative value contributed by Alex Rodriguez and David Ortiz is to measure how many Wins they contribute over Replacement Level (WORL). As discussed earlier in this chapter, I set Replacement Level one standard deviation below positional average.

In constructing replacement level, I calculate separate standard deviations for four groups of players: position players who play the field, offense-only players (DH, PH, PR), starting pitchers, and relief pitchers. The logic behind the distinction between the first two is that, in replacing a fielder, a team may be able to ameliorate some of the loss of A-Rod's bat by replacing him with a player who was a better defensive third baseman. For a DH, such as Ortiz, however, there is no such opportunity to ameliorate the loss of Ortiz's bat (outside of the ability to find a better baserunner).

The standard deviation applied to Alex Rodriguez's positional average for 2005 was 3.6%, so that the relevant replacement level for Rodriguez is 0.465 (0.501–0.036). For Ortiz, the standard deviation was somewhat wider, 5.9%, so that the relevant replacement level for Ortiz is 0.456 (0.515–0.059).

Wins over Replacement Level for Rodriguez and Ortiz are shown below.

Final pW-L Records: 2005

	pWins	pLosses	pWinPct	Wins Over Positional Average	Repl Level
Alex Rodriguez	25.7	17.5	0.595	4.1	5.6
David Ortiz	20.1	11.9	0.628	3.6	5.5

Alex Rodriguez earned 5.6 pWins over Replacement Level (pWORL) in 2005 for the New York Yankees. David Ortiz earned 5.5 pWins over Replacement Level (pWORL) for the Boston Red Sox. Both Rodriguez and Ortiz had excellent seasons that were extremely valuable to their respective teams. It was close, but, ultimately, I think that the voters got this one right: Alex Rodriguez deserved to be the Most Valuable Player in the American League in 2005.

4. Components of Player Won-Lost Records

Player Wins and Losses are calculated using a nine-step process, each step of which assumes average performance in all subsequent steps. Each step of the process is associated with a Component of Player Decisions (Wins and Losses). These nine components are outlined briefly below. Each of these components is then discussed in detail later in this chapter. There are four basic positions from which a player can contribute toward his baseball team's probability of winning: Batter, Baserunner, Pitcher, and Fielder. Player decisions are allocated to each of these four positions, as appropriate, within each of the following nine components. pW-L records by these four factors are looked at more closely in Chapters 5 (Offense), 6 (Pitching), and 7 (Fielding).

The nine basic components of pW-L records are the following.

Component 1: Base stealing. Player decisions are assessed to baserunners, pitchers, and catchers for stolen bases, caught stealing, pickoffs, and balks.

Component 2: Wild Pitches and Passed Balls. Player decisions are assessed to baserunners, pitchers, and catchers for wild pitches and passed balls.

Component 3: Balls not in Play. Player decisions are assessed to batters and pitchers for plate appearances that do not involve the batter putting the ball in play: i.e., strikeouts, walks, and hit-by-pitches.

Component 4: Balls in Play. Player decisions are assessed to batters and pitchers on balls that are put in play, including home runs, based on how and where the ball is hit.

Component 5: Hits versus Outs on Balls in Play. Player decisions are assessed to batters, pitchers, and fielders on balls in play, based on whether they are converted into outs or not.

Component 6: Singles versus Doubles versus Triples. Player decisions are assessed to batters, pitchers, and fielders on hits in play, on the basis of whether the hit becomes a single, a double, or a triple.

Component 7: Double Plays. Player decisions are assessed to batters, baserunners, pitchers, and fielders on ground-ball outs in double-play situations, based on whether or not the batter grounds into a double play.

Component 8: Baserunner Outs. Player decisions are assessed to batters, baserunners, and fielders on the basis of baserunner outs.

Component 9: Baserunner Advancements. Player decisions are assessed to batters, baserunners, and fielders on the basis of how many bases, if any, baserunners advance on balls in play.

The distribution of Player Wins and Losses by Component varies across seasons and across leagues, depending on the exact distribution of plays. The average distribution of Player decisions by component across all seasons for which I have calculated pW-L records is shown in the table below.

Breakdowns of Player Decisions by Component: 1930–2015
Distribution of Player Decisions

	Pct of Total	Pct of Off/Def Component Decisions Allocated to Player Decisions			
		Batters	*Baserunners*	*Pitchers*	*Fielders*
Component 1	2.2%	0.0%	100.0%	52.2%	47.8%
Component 2	1.3%	0.0%	100.0%	76.3%	23.7%
Component 3	14.8%	100.0%	0.0%	100.0%	0.0%
Component 4	35.3%	100.0%	0.0%	100.0%	0.0%
Component 5	32.7%	100.0%	0.0%	30.2%	69.8%
Component 6	3.5%	100.0%	0.0%	25.6%	74.4%
Component 7	1.6%	79.4%	20.6%	34.7%	65.3%
Component 8	2.3%	41.8%	58.2%	0.0%	100.0%
Component 9	6.2%	44.9%	55.1%	0.0%	100.0%
Total Share of Offense/Defense		91.4%	8.6%	63.6%	36.4%
Total		45.7%	4.3%	31.8%	18.2%

Offensive wins and losses are divided between batters and baserunners. The batter/baserunner breakdown is approximately 91% batters, 9% baserunners. Defensive wins and losses are divided between pitchers and fielders. In general, pitchers are credited with just under two-thirds (65.4 percent) of total defensive wins and losses, including their role in preventing or allowing stolen bases as well as pitcher fielding. Fielders other than pitchers account for the other 34.6 percent of defensive player decisions.

The breakdown of Player decisions by component has changed somewhat over time. Results since 2003 are shown below.

Breakdowns of Player Decisions by Component: 2003–2015
Distribution of Player Decisions

	Pct of Total	Pct of Off/Def Component Decisions Allocated to Player Decisions			
		Batters	*Baserunners*	*Pitchers*	*Fielders*
Component 1	1.8%	0.0%	100.0%	51.8%	48.2%
Component 2	1.4%	0.0%	100.0%	75.5%	24.5%
Component 3	16.5%	100.0%	0.0%	100.0%	0.0%
Component 4	35.6%	100.0%	0.0%	100.0%	0.0%
Component 5	32.3%	100.0%	0.0%	28.6%	71.4%
Component 6	3.1%	100.0%	0.0%	26.4%	73.6%
Component 7	2.1%	84.1%	15.9%	27.4%	72.6%
Component 8	1.7%	40.1%	59.9%	0.0%	100.0%
Component 9	5.5%	43.2%	56.8%	0.0%	100.0%
Total Share of Offense / Defense		92.4%	7.6%	64.7%	35.3%
Total		46.2%	3.8%	32.4%	17.6%

On the offensive side, baserunning has become somewhat less important recently, falling to 7.6% of total offensive decisions. On the defensive side, strikeouts and walks (Component 3) are higher in recent years, which has reduced the importance of fielding to 17.6% of total Player decisions. Overall, though, the results are generally quite similar over the entire 80+ years over which I have calculated pW-L records.

Overall, the breakdown of batting / baserunning / pitching / and fielding (counting pitcher fielding as "pitching") is 45.7% / 4.3% / 32.7% / 17.3%. This creates a breakdown between pitchers (excluding pitcher hitting and baserunning, but including pitcher fielding) and non-pitchers of 32.7% v. 67.3%, or approximately 2-to-1 for position players vis-à-vis pitchers.

The breakdown of fielding player wins and losses (on balls in play) by component and by fielding position are summarized below.

Breakdown of Fielding Decisions by Position: 1930–2015

Percent of Component Decisions by Fielder

Component	P	C	1B	2B	3B	SS	LF	CF	RF
5	5.5%	1.0%	7.1%	15.4%	15.3%	17.6%	12.6%	12.6%	12.9%
6	1.4%	0.0%	1.8%	0.5%	2.3%	0.3%	38.6%	22.7%	32.4%
7	6.8%	2.0%	3.6%	38.9%	4.6%	44.0%	0.0%	0.0%	0.0%
8	2.8%	0.9%	5.4%	7.9%	4.6%	6.8%	24.3%	21.5%	25.8%
9	6.1%	0.8%	5.6%	8.1%	8.2%	9.9%	19.4%	21.0%	20.7%
Total Fielding	5.2%	0.9%	6.2%	13.2%	12.0%	15.0%	16.1%	15.1%	16.2%

Note: Pitcher numbers here represent only the "fielding" portion of the pitcher's credit, not the "pitching" portion of the credit.

Overall, outfielders accumulate just under 50% of fielding player decisions (47.4%). In contrast, Bill James's Win Shares credit only 36% of non-catcher fielding Win Shares to outfielders. As such, my allocation of fielding decisions to outfielders may seem excessive. It is important to remember, however, that (as far as I could tell reading his book, *Win Shares*), while Bill James's fielding allocation is imposed, the fielding allocation here is derived from the actual results.

In 2006, for example, in games played in American League ballparks, 37.7% of all batting outs recorded by somebody other than the pitcher or catcher were recorded by outfielders. This is similar to Bill James's Win Shares allocation and is not terribly different from the 38.1% of Component 5 fielding decisions recorded by outfielders. Of all balls in play that were fielded by somebody other than the pitcher or catcher, however, outfielders were the first fielder to handle 53.5% of all such plays. This is reflected in my work by the large amount of Component 6, 8, and 9 Player decisions accumulated by outfielders. As such, I believe that the distribution of fielding games coming out of my work is reasonable.

Further, it is important to understand that I am not saying that outfield defense is therefore more valuable than infield defense. Outfielders accumulate more fielding wins but they also accumulate more fielding losses. An outstanding defensive outfielder may accumulate more value than a similarly outstanding defensive infielder but only to the extent that the outfielder would be expected to field more balls in play. An outfielder will not accumulate any more value than an infielder simply by virtue of his being an outfielder.

Event Probabilities

The key to properly assessing Player Wins and Losses is to credit each player with the change in Win Probability attributable to him, assuming average performances by all other players. In order to do this, it is necessary to determine what the probability is of certain events occurring, such as the probability of a baserunner advancing from 1st to 3rd on a single, the probability of a particular ball-in-play becoming an out versus a single versus an extra-base hit, and many other similar probabilities.

Wherever possible, the probabilities of relevant events are initially calculated by direct observation—that is, the probability of a baserunner being caught trying to steal second is calculated by simply summing up all of the runners caught stealing second and dividing by the total number of possible runners.

In some cases, however, because of differences in the underlying context in which events occur (e.g., caught stealings may occur in a higher average context than not-caught stealings), direct probabilities may produce more player wins than player losses (or vice versa) for a particular component or sub-component of player decisions. To help to maintain the underlying assumption that the overall winning percentage within a particular season should be 0.500 for every component and sub-component of interest, my results are therefore refined by scaling them back to 0.500 at the aggregate level. The calculations of each specific component are described later in this chapter.

#1. Stolen Bases, Caught Stealing, and Wild Pitches

In the case of stolen bases, caught stealings, wild pitches, and the like, unique probabilities are calculated for each of the 24 base-out states. The probabilities of positive stolen base events—identified below as "stolen bases," but including advancements on errant pickoff attempts, errors on caught stealings, defensive indifference, and balks—caught stealing events (including pickoffs), and wild pitches/passed balls (I make no distinction between wild pitches and passed balls) by base-out state across all seasons for which I have calculated pW-L records are presented below.

The specific probabilities actually used in calculating pW-L records are uniquely determined for each league and each season.

Outs	Baserunners	SB	CS	WP/PB
0	0	0.0%	0.0%	0.0%
0	1	5.6%	3.2%	1.9%
0	2	1.1%	0.5%	2.2%
0	3	0.2%	0.2%	1.7%
0	1–2	1.5%	1.4%	2.1%
0	1–3	4.1%	1.1%	2.1%
0	2–3	0.2%	0.1%	1.5%
0	1–2–3	0.2%	0.1%	1.5%
1	0	0.0%	0.0%	0.1%
1	1	6.0%	3.7%	1.9%
1	2	1.9%	0.9%	2.3%
1	3	0.3%	0.7%	1.6%
1	1–2	1.8%	1.4%	2.2%
1	1–3	4.6%	1.9%	2.1%
1	2–3	0.2%	0.3%	1.4%
1	1–2–3	0.2%	0.3%	1.4%
2	0	0.0%	0.0%	0.1%
2	1	6.7%	3.4%	1.8%
2	2	0.9%	0.2%	2.1%
2	3	0.3%	0.2%	1.6%
2	1–2	0.9%	0.4%	2.0%
2	1–3	6.1%	1.5%	2.0%
2	2–3	0.3%	0.1%	1.5%
2	1–2–3	0.3%	0.2%	1.4%

Except for the case where the bases are initially empty, wild pitches and passed balls are somewhat uniform across base-out states, occurring between 1.4 and 2.3 percent of the time. Wild pitches and/or passed balls with the bases empty represent cases where the batter reached first base safely on a dropped third strike.

In general, wild pitches and passed balls are least common when there is a runner on third base who must score for any runners to advance (i.e., excluding runners on first and third), occurring 1.5% of the time, versus 2.0% of the time otherwise.

Stolen bases and caught stealings are much more dependent on both the position of the baserunners as well as on the number of outs than are wild pitches and passed balls.

Stolen base attempts of second base increase in frequency with the number of outs. With only a runner on first base, stolen base attempts (SB plus CS above) are somewhat less common with nobody out (8.8%) than with one or two outs (9.8%). Stolen base attempts of third base are far more frequent with one out (2.8% for a runner on second base only, 3.1% for runners on first and second) than with either zero (1.7% for a runner on second base only, 2.8% for runners on first and second) or two outs (1.2%, 1.3%). Apparently, baseball players and managers take seriously the old adage, "Don't make the first or last out at third base."

Stolen base success rates are much greater with two outs than with zero or one outs. Overall, over the time period studied here, stolen base success rates were 68.9% with two outs, 62.3% with one out, and 63.7% with no outs.

#2. Balls in Play

In the case of balls in play, the probabilities of many things are dependent on the exact location of the ball and how it was hit. For example, the probability of driving in a runner from third is vastly different on a ground out to the pitcher (17.4% over all of the seasons used here) versus a fly out to center field (84.0% over the same time period). Hence, in theory, ball-in-play probabilities should be calculated for each unique location/hit type combination.

My data source is Retrosheet event files. Some Retrosheet event files provide some data on the location of balls in play and hit types. Retrosheet event locations are described on their website (see, http://www.retrosheet.org/location.htm). For my purposes, I consider there to be 17 locations, defined by the fielder(s) nearest to the play—1, 13, 15, 2, 23, 25, 3, 34, 4, 5, 56, 6, 7, 78, 8, 89, and 9—three possible depths of the hit—shallow (S), medium (M), and deep (D)—and four hit types—bunts (B), ground balls (G), fly balls (F or P), and line drives (L).

The exact level of detail available from Retrosheet with respect to locations and hit types for balls in play varies a great deal over time. Complete (or very nearly complete) location data are only available from Retrosheet from 1989 through 1999. For most balls in play, more recent event files only provide very limited location data. For example, an event file may identify a single as being a single to left field (S7). But there's a big difference between a ground ball through the hole at shortstop and a line drive off the left field wall that the left fielder manages to play well enough to hold the batter at first base.

Hit type data—i.e., bunts vs. ground balls vs. fly balls vs. line drives—are available for virtually all non-outs (i.e., singles, doubles, and triples) from 2003 onward. For other years (except for 1989–1999, where complete hit type data are available), hit type data are mostly limited only to outs (i.e., ground outs are distinguished from fly outs). Unfortunately, as we go farther back in time, Retrosheet play-by-play data tell us less and less. Prior to 1988, it is common (but not universal) for play-by-play data to not even identify the fielder on base hits (i.e., singles to left field are not distinguished from singles to right field). Going still further back, there are even some outs for which the fielder is not identified.

#A. Batted Ball Results

My solution to the lack of location data for most years is to use the 1989–1999 event files to generate weights by location and to impute estimated locations based upon complete location data from 1989 to 1999 and what information is available in other event files. I defend my use of location data in this way later in this chapter.

For calculating Player wins and losses, I divide balls in play based on the end result of the play—out, single, double, triple (batters reaching on fielding errors are treated as "singles" here)—and the first fielder to touch the ball. For outs, that is the player who recorded the first assist/unassisted putout. For hits, it is the fielder occupying the field to which the ball was hit—e.g., the left fielder for a single to left field (S7). If the hit type of the play is identified (bunt, ground ball, fly ball, line drive), this information is also used in determining the appropriate probabilities.

From the 1989–1999 data, I then calculate the expected location of the event. That is, for, say, a single to left field, I look at all singles to left field from 1989 to 1999 and calculate the probability that such a play was in each of the relevant locations. For example, the table below shows the distribution by location of line drive singles to left field. From the expected location, I then calculate the expected probabilities of all relevant events—probability of a base hit, probability of particular players making the out, probability of a runner scoring from second, etc. Data on hit type (ground ball, fly ball, etc.) are used for recent seasons for which hit-type data are available for all, or virtually all, plays (2003 onward). For earlier years (2000–2002 and pre–1989 seasons), data on hit type is generally not available, especially on base hits. Hence, these data are not used in these cases.

Line Drive Single to Left Field, 1989–1999

		Total Balls in Play		Probability of Line Drive Being a _ at given Location			
Location	Depth	Number	Percent	Out	Single	Double	Triple
Unknown	Unknown	292	0.83%				
1	Unknown	5	0.01%	73.14%	26.08%	0.78%	0.00%
34	Unknown	3	0.01%	57.47%	42.07%	0.46%	0.00%
34	Deep	4	0.01%	5.32%	92.74%	1.85%	0.09%
4	Medium	1	0.00%	40.67%	57.23%	0.96%	1.14%
4	Deep	5	0.01%	11.92%	86.42%	1.66%	0.00%
5	Unknown	181	0.52%	77.34%	8.07%	14.59%	0.00%
5	Shallow	7	0.02%	84.08%	7.02%	5.48%	3.42%
5	Deep	731	2.08%	0.80%	38.97%	60.23%	0.00%
56	Unknown	1,093	3.11%	61.11%	38.65%	0.24%	0.00%
56	Shallow	23	0.07%	91.20%	8.50%	0.00%	0.29%
56	Deep	3,684	10.48%	3.33%	95.18%	1.47%	0.02%
6	Unknown	177	0.50%	88.83%	10.82%	0.35%	0.00%
6	Shallow	2	0.01%	38.32%	61.08%	0.60%	0.00%
6	Medium	5	0.01%	40.84%	58.16%	0.60%	0.41%

		Total Balls in Play		Probability of Line Drive Being a _ at given Location			
Location	Depth	Number	Percent	Out	Single	Double	Triple
6	Deep	2,100	5.98%	6.96%	90.64%	1.85%	0.55%
7	Unknown	2,755	7.84%	29.09%	41.85%	28.33%	0.72%
7	Shallow	12,438	35.39%	9.45%	73.37%	16.73%	0.45%
7	Medium	4,735	13.47%	41.63%	34.38%	23.31%	0.67%
7	Deep	574	1.63%	41.49%	7.76%	49.72%	1.02%
78	Unknown	651	1.85%	21.75%	46.59%	30.71%	0.94%
78	Shallow	3,721	10.59%	7.68%	84.46%	6.73%	1.12%
78	Medium	1,661	4.73%	35.13%	44.91%	15.75%	4.21%
78	Deep	230	0.65%	36.61%	6.98%	55.73%	0.69%
8	Unknown	4	0.01%	36.54%	58.08%	3.82%	1.55%
8	Shallow	32	0.09%	8.23%	89.53%	1.43%	0.81%
8	Medium	9	0.03%	42.02%	50.50%	3.84%	3.64%
8	Deep	4	0.01%	71.06%	7.58%	19.77%	1.59%
89	Unknown	1	0.00%	22.87%	50.25%	25.12%	1.75%
89	Shallow	5	0.01%	7.49%	84.83%	4.74%	2.94%
89	Medium	2	0.01%	31.72%	44.13%	12.48%	11.68%
9	Unknown	3	0.01%	32.53%	40.79%	20.63%	6.05%
9	Shallow	3	0.01%	9.24%	73.65%	14.93%	2.18%
9	Deep	1	0.00%	48.02%	8.69%	43.28%	0.00%
	TOTALS	**35,142**	**100.00%**	**18.85%**	**64.20%**	**16.24%**	**0.71%**

As the above example shows, a line drive single to left field had an *a priori* probability of becoming an out of 18.85%. For fly balls, the *a priori* probability of becoming an out was 84.05%. For ground balls, the *a priori* probability of becoming an out was 55.23%. Overall, the *a priori* probability of a single to left field becoming an out, regardless of hit type, was 37.41%.

The individual probabilities of fielders having made an out on a play which becomes a generic single to left field ranged from 46.4% by the left fielder to 26.1% by the shortstop, 23.9% by the third baseman, 3.1% by the center fielder, and 0.4% by other fielders. For ground-ball singles, the relevant probabilities are 55.8% for the third baseman and 43.6% for the shortstop. For fly ball singles, on the other hand, left fielders would be expected to convert 74.9% of all outs (74.3% for line drives) with center fielders expected to convert 9.8% (4.4% for line drives).

For the probabilities of the play becoming an out, single, double, or triple, one further adjustment is made for recent years. For recent years, while these various weights are not known for specific locations, they are, of course, known for the league as a whole. For example, in the 2005 American League, 31.52% of all line drives (excluding home runs) were converted into outs. From 1989 to 1999, however, 33.41% of line drives were converted into outs. The weights used for other leagues are adjusted to tie the aggregate weights to the actual league-wide percentages. This is done through the use of the Matchup Formula, which is described later in this chapter.

#B. BASERUNNER OUTS/ADVANCEMENTS

In addition to the probability of a ball-in-play becoming an out, single, double, or triple, and the probability the ball is played by each of the various fielders, the other events for which weights are needed are the probability of baserunner advancements and/or baserunning outs. Such probabilities are, of course, a function of the specific baserunner—batter, runner on first, runner on second, runner on third; the batting event—

out, single, double, triple; the fielder of the ball, and, where available, the hit type (bunt, ground ball, fly ball, line drive) of the ball. For these events, probabilities are simply calculated by direct observation for the baserunner/bat event/fielder/hit type combinations for which data are available. For earlier years, probabilities are calculated by hit type for outs where possible (i.e., unique probabilities are calculated for a baserunner scoring from third base on a ground out versus a fly out), but not for hits (when hit type data are not recorded for hits).

In the case of baserunner advancements on singles and doubles, separate probabilities are also calculated based on the number of outs (two versus fewer than two).

Dividing Credit Between Batters and Baserunners and Between Pitchers and Fielders

In many cases, it is not clear exactly who should get credit for a particular play. For example, pitchers and catchers share responsibility for Component 1 (base stealing) player decisions. The allocation of player decisions in these cases is done based on the relative skill level apparent by the relevant players.

The technique outlined here is used to divide responsibility between pitchers and catchers for Component 1 (base stealing) and Component 2 (wild pitches and passed balls) player decisions, between pitchers and fielders for Components 5 (hits vs. outs), 6 (single vs. double vs. triple), and 7 (double plays), and between batters and baserunners for Components 7, 8 (baserunner outs), and 9 (baserunner advancements).

The division of Component 1 Player decisions between pitchers and catchers is used here as an illustration of the general technique.

#1. Basic Theory

How does one determine how to divide credit between pitchers and catchers for Component 1 (base stealing) player decisions?

Let's begin by asking, what if somebody deserved no credit for a particular component of Player decisions but we allocated player decisions to them anyway? For example, what if we assigned Component 1 player decisions to the defensive team's right fielder? What would we expect Component 1 player decisions to look like in that case? Essentially, we would expect every right fielder to have a Component 1 winning percentage of 0.500 plus or minus some random variation.

Suppose we were to try to predict a right fielder's Component 1 winning percentage over some time period based on his Component 1 winning percentage over some other time period. We would expect, in such a persistence equation, for there to be no predictive ability of this component.

Alternately, what would we expect Component 1 player decisions to look like if we assigned them to players who had different levels of talent in terms of affecting the opponents' base stealing? In such a case, we would expect a player's Component 1 winning percentage to be equal to his "true" winning percentage (his "true-talent") plus or minus some random variation and for a player's Component 1 winning percentage over some time period to have significant predictive capability over other time periods.

In other words, the extent to which a player's winning percentage at some point in time is predictive of his winning percentage at some other point is suggestive of the extent to which there is a true skill involved in a particular component. Based on this, Player wins and losses are allocated in proportion to the extent to which a player's winning percentage has predictive power.

#2. Mathematics

The basis for dividing shared player decisions is Persistence Equations. I divide the plays that took place in a particular season into two pools: odd and even. To evaluate the persistence of skills, I then fit a simple equation which attempts to explain winning percentage by component on even plays as a function of the same factor for odd plays:

$$(\text{Win \%})_{\text{Even}} = b \cdot (\text{Win \%})_{\text{Odd}} + (1-b) \cdot (\text{Win \%})_{\text{Baseline}}$$

where $(\text{Win \%})_{\text{Baseline}}$ represents a baseline toward which Component winning percentage regresses over time.

The coefficient b in the persistence equation measures the persistence of Component winning percentage between the two samples (even plays v. odd plays) and, hence, the extent to which Component winning percentage is a true "skill" for the relevant set of players being evaluated.

This equation is estimated using a Weighted Least Squares technique which weights observations by the harmonic mean of the number of games over which the even and odd winning percentages have been compiled squared.

#3. Complication: Controlling for the Talent of the Other Players Involved

Earlier, I identified a defensive team's right fielder as an example of a player for whom we would expect his Component 1 winning percentage to simply be randomly distributed. In fact, however, some of you might have seen a flaw in my example.

In 2004, the Montreal Expos allowed only 58 stolen bases on the season, while catching 41 opposing baserunners attempting to steal. Based on this, the Montreal Expos compiled a team-wide Component 1.1 (base stealing by runners on first base) winning percentage of 0.645. Of course, this means that Expos right-fielders would have a combined Component 1.1 winning percentage of 0.645, not 0.500, not because Expos right fielders had some innate ability to prevent the other team from stealing bases, but because they had the good fortune to be teammates with Brian Schneider, who amassed an unadjusted Component 1.1 winning percentage of 0.660 at catcher.

On the other hand, the 2002 New York Mets allowed 151 stolen bases against only 53 caught stealing, leading to a team-wide context-neutral Component 1.1 winning percentage of 0.431, due, in part, to the notorious problems of their catcher, Mike Piazza, who allowed 125 stolen bases (which led the National League) against 27 caught stealing in 121 games caught, for a context-neutral Component 1.1 winning percentage of 0.320.

Unfortunately, this problem with attempting to measure "true-talent" Component

1 winning percentage is not limited to outfielders, where we know that no such talent exists. In fact, on average, the context-neutral Component 1.1 winning percentage for Montreal Expos pitchers in 2004 was 0.645, not necessarily because Expos pitchers were particularly adept at holding runners on base, but, in large part, because Brian Schneider was their catcher. Yet, pitchers do have some ability here. The key is to separate the ability of Montreal Expos pitchers from the ability of Montreal Expos catchers.

The first step before one can accurately assess "true-talent" Component 1 winning percentages is to adjust player winning percentages for the context in which these percentages were amassed. Specifically, pitchers' Component 1 winning percentages are adjusted to control for the Component 1 winning percentages of their catchers, and catchers' Component 1 winning percentages are adjusted to control for the Component 1 winning percentages of their pitchers. Similar adjustments are done for all Components for which Player Decisions are to be shared.

This is done iteratively. First, pitchers' Component 1 winning percentages are adjusted to control for the Component 1 winning percentages of their catchers. This is done using the Matchup Formula.

The Matchup Formula

One of the coolest formulas I have come across in sabermetrics is the Matchup Formula, sometimes called the Log5 Matchup Formula, which I learned from Bill James.

- If a team with a 0.667 winning percentage faces a team with a 0.450 winning percentage, how often would you expect the 0.667 team to win?
- If a 0.300 hitter faces a pitcher with a 0.290 batting average against, in a league with a 0.250 batting average, how well do we expect the batter to hit?
- If 49.0% of a particular type of ball were turned into outs in a league when 70.2% of all balls-in-play were turned into outs, what percentage of these would be outs in a league where only 69.4% of all balls-in-play were converted into outs?

The answers to all of these questions can be solved with the Matchup Formula. I'll begin with the simplest version. Let W_1 be the winning percentage of Team 1 and W_2 be the winning percentage of Team 2. The probability of Team 1 beating Team 2 is given by the following formula:

$$\text{Probability of Team 1 Winning} = W_1 \cdot (1 - W_2) / [W_1 \cdot (1 - W_2) + W_2 \cdot (1 - W_1)]$$

So, for example, a team with a 0.667 winning percentage will beat a team with a 0.450 winning percentage approximately 71.0% of the time.

The formula implicitly assumes that both of these teams faced average (or at least equivalent) opposition in compiling those winning percentages. So, what if Team 1 has a 0.667 winning percentage, but the average record of their opponents was only 0.440, while Team 2's 0.450 winning percentage was amassed against opponents with an average winning percentage of 0.520?

Let W_1 be Team 1's winning percentage, O_1 be the average record of Team 1's opponents, W_2 be Team 2's winning percentage, and O_2 be the average record of Team 2's opponents. In this case, the probability of Team 1 beating Team 2 follows the same basic formula, but with a twist:

$$\text{Probability of Team 1 Winning} = W'_1 \cdot (1-W'_2) / [W'_1 \cdot (1-W'_2) + W'_2 \cdot (1-W'_1)]$$
$$\text{where}$$
$$W'_1 = W_1 \cdot O_1 / [W_1 \cdot O_1 + (1-W_1) \cdot (1-O_1)]$$
$$W'_2 = W_2 \cdot O_2 / [W_2 \cdot O_2 + (1-W_2) \cdot (1-O_2)]$$

Plugging in the numbers from above (0.667 against 0.440 opponents versus 0.450 against 0.520 opponents), we find that Team 1 has a 64.0% chance of defeating Team 2.

There is still one more additional piece of information. The formula so far assumes that all of the numbers within the formula are relative to a 0.500 context. What about the batting average example? If a 0.300 hitter faces a pitcher with a 0.290 batting average against in a league with a 0.250 batting average, how well do we expect the batter to hit? Relating this to our earlier formulae, the 0.300 corresponds to W_1, the 0.290 actually equals $(1-W_2)$ (W_2 would be the pitcher's success rate, which is 0.710 in this case). Let's complicate this further and assume that the 0.300 hitter has faced pitchers with an average batting average against of 0.265—so, O_1 equals 0.735 here (1−0.265)—and the pitcher has faced opponents with an average batting average of 0.270 (which will equal O_2). Now, we have one more new piece of information—we'll call it L—the league batting average, which is 0.250 in this example.

Let P_1 equal the probability that Batter 1 gets a hit against Pitcher 2. Here, the Matchup Formula, in its entirety, becomes the following:

$$P_0 = W'_1 \cdot (1-W'_2) / [W'_1 \cdot (1-W'_2) + W'_2 \cdot (1-W'_1)]$$
$$\text{where}$$
$$W'_1 = W_1 \cdot O_1 / [W_1 \cdot O_1 + (1-W_1) \cdot (1-O_1)]$$
$$W'_2 = W_2 \cdot O_2 / [W_2 \cdot O_2 + (1-W_2) \cdot (1-O_2)]$$
$$\text{and}$$
$$P_1 = P_0 \cdot (1-L) / [P_0 \cdot (1-L) + L \cdot (1-P_0)]$$

And, in our example, our 0.300 hitter would be expected to bat 0.304 against this particular pitcher in this particular league.

Use of Matchup Formula in Allocating Credit for Player Decisions

For those components where multiple players share credit for player decisions, such as pitchers and catchers with respect to stolen bases, the relative credit is divided between the relevant players through a set of persistence equations that are described next in this chapter.

The major drawback to pW-L records that are tied to team records as developed here is that, for a particular play, the pitcher and catcher are assumed to bear equal responsibility—not in terms of equivalent player decisions, but in terms of the fact that wins are credited to both pitchers and catchers for plays in which the defensive team earns wins and losses are debited to both pitchers and catchers for plays in which the defensive team earns losses. In reality, it is perfectly reasonable to envision a scenario whereby, for example, a pitcher does a terrible job of holding a baserunner on and is only saved by a perfect throw from the catcher to catch the runner stealing. In such a case, it may be more reasonable to credit the pitcher with a loss for his role in preventing stolen bases while crediting the catcher with more wins than he currently receives. Another example of this would be a catcher who, while normally excellent at preventing wild pitches and avoiding passed balls, has the misfortune of regularly catching a knuckleball pitcher.

In terms of pWins and pLosses, where the object is to ensure that player wins and losses relate perfectly to team wins and losses, such a situation is largely unavoidable. If one wants to neutralize individual player records in order to move beyond team records, however, then, at a seasonal level, one can use the Matchup Formula to adjust for the performance of the other players with whom a particular player shared credits.

Suppose, for example, that a pitcher compiled a Component 1 (base stealing) winning percentage of 0.515 but that the catchers with whom he shared that Component 1 credit compiled an average winning percentage (weighted by the number of Component 1 points which they shared with this particular pitcher) of 0.535.

In such a case, the Matchup Formula can be used to adjust the pitcher's Component 1 winning percentage. Here, the pitcher's winning percentage (0.515) would correspond to W_1 in the Matchup Formula above. The average winning percentage of his catchers (0.535) would correspond to O_1, the context in which the pitcher performed. Plugging these values into the Matchup Formula would produce an adjusted Component 1 winning percentage for this pitcher of 0.480.

BACK TO OUR PERSISTENCE EQUATIONS

After pitchers' winning percentages are adjusted based on catcher winning percentages, catcher winning percentages are then adjusted based on these newly-adjusted pitcher winning percentages. Ideally, one might prefer to continue the iterative process until all Component 1 winning percentages do not change between iterations. For computational simplicity, I simply repeat this process three more times for both pitchers and catchers.

Returning to the earlier examples, the adjusted Component 1.1 winning percentages for Montreal Expos pitchers was 0.577 in 2004 (versus 0.645 unadjusted), while Montreal Expos catchers put up a combined adjusted Component 1.1 winning percentage of 0.560 (versus 0.645 unadjusted). Here, because Expos pitchers and catchers were both above-average in this component in 2004, their combined winning percentage ends up being greater than either of their individual winning percentages. The whole is greater than the sum of the parts.

For the 2002 New York Mets, their pitchers' adjusted winning percentage was 0.519 (versus 0.431 unadjusted) while Mets' catchers had an adjusted winning percentage of 0.415 (0.320 for Mike Piazza and 0.689 for other Mets' catchers). Mets pitchers weren't bad at preventing stolen bases in 2002; they simply had the misfortune of pitching to one of the worst catchers in modern times at stopping an opponent's running game.

The Persistence Equations by which shared Player Wins and Losses are calculated are estimated using component winning percentages which have been adjusted in this way for the winning percentages of players' teammates.

#4. Example Persistence Equations

Persistence equations are estimated using all of the seasons for which I have estimated pW-L records, which model player winning percentage for the Component of interest on even-numbered plays as a function of player winning percentage for the Component of interest on odd-numbered plays:

$$(\text{Component Win Pct})_{\text{Even}} = b \cdot (\text{Component Win Pct})_{\text{Odd}} + (1-b) \cdot (\text{WinPct})_{\text{Baseline}}$$

where (WinPct)$_{Baseline}$ represents a baseline winning percentage toward which Component winning percentages regress over time.

The results for Component 1.1, Component 1 (base stealing) for the baserunner on first base, are shown below.

Persistence of Component 1 Winning Percentage: Baserunner on First Base

Pitchers: n = 35,396
WinPct$_{Even}$ = (26.96%) • WinPct$_{Odd}$ + (73.04%) • 0.5000
(53.14)

Catchers: n = 7,485
WinPct$_{Even}$ = (23.71%) • WinPct$_{Odd}$ + (76.29%) • 0.5000
(20.926)

The number n is the number of players over whom the equation was estimated, that is, who accumulated any Player wins and/or losses on both odd- and even-numbered plays within a particular season. The numbers in parentheses below the equation are t-statistics. T-statistics measure the significance of the regression coefficients, that is, the confidence we have that these coefficients are greater than zero. The greater the t-statistic, the more confident we are that the true value of a particular coefficient is greater than zero. Roughly, if the t-statistic is greater than 2, then we can be at least 95% certain that the true value of b is greater than zero (given that certain statistical assumptions underlying our model hold).

For baserunners on first base, Component 1 win percentage is significantly persistent for both pitchers and catchers with t-statistics far greater than two for both sets of players. The persistence is somewhat weaker for catchers (23.7%) than for pitchers (27.0%), although the two numbers are very close. The percentage of Component 1 Player decisions with a runner on first base (Component 1.1) which are attributed to pitchers is set equal to the pitcher persistence coefficient (27.0%) divided by the sum of the persistence coefficients for pitchers and catchers (27.0% + 23.7%). This leads to 53.2% of Component 1.1 decisions being allocated to pitchers and 46.8% of Component 1.1 decisions allocated to catchers.

#5. *Changes in Component Splits Over Time*

There is no reason to believe that the split of credit between positions should be constant over time. On the other hand, if a distinct persistence equation is estimated every year, this could well produce significant year-to-year shifts because of statistical quirks from small sample sizes. Ideally, what we would like to do is allow for gradual changes in component splits over time, but do so in a way that reduces the likelihood of flukish year-to-year changes.

To accomplish this, I estimate unique Persistence Equations for every season, but I use all of my data in all of these equations. I simply weight the data based on how close to the season of interest it is. Each observation is multiplied by a Year$_{Weight}$, which is equal to the following:

$$Year_{Weight} = 1 - abs(Year - Year_{Target}) / 100$$

where "Year" is the year in which the observation occurred, and Year$_{Target}$ is the year for which shares are being estimated. So observations in the target year get a Year$_{Weight}$ of 1.0, observations one year before or after the target year get a Year$_{Weight}$ of 0.99, observations two years removed from the target year get a Year$_{Weight}$ of 0.98, etc.

The result is a set of share weights that vary by year but do so fairly gradually. For example, the share of credit for Component 1.1 (base stealing by runners on first base) attributed to pitchers varies by season within a range of 51.4% to 56.0%.

#6. Final Proportions of Shared Player Decisions

Separate persistence equations and, hence, separate share weights, are calculated for specific fielders and by specific baserunners, so that, for example, Component 5 shares for first basemen and third basemen will differ. Also, as noted above, these share weights vary by season.

Average breakdowns of shared components across all seasons for which I have calculated pW-L records are summarized in the table below. The numbers below are averages across all fielders/baserunners and across all seasons, so do not necessarily apply precisely for any specific players or seasons.

Shared Components Based on Persistence Equations

Component	Pitcher	Fielder
Component 1	52.2%	47.8%
Component 2	76.3%	23.7%
Component 5	31.4%	68.6%
Component 6	25.9%	74.1%
Component 7	36.3%	63.7%
Component	*Batter*	*Baserunner*
Component 7	79.4%	20.6%
Component 8	53.3%	46.7%
Component 9	48.9%	51.1%

Component 1: Base Stealing

In the first step of calculating Player Wins and Losses, baserunners, pitchers, and catchers are given credit and blame for either advancing (allowing) or failing to advance by (preventing) stolen bases (or defensive indifference) and for being caught stealing or picked off and failing to be caught stealing or picked off.

Overall, 2.2% of raw Player Decisions were accrued in this step across all seasons for which I have calculated pW-L records. Because stolen bases are an elective strategy, however, the share of total Player decisions earned in this Component has tended to vary more over time than other components. In the 1950s, for example, base stealing was fairly rare until the pennant-winning 1959 "Go-Go" Chicago White Sox; hence, Component 1 made up only 1.7% of total Player decisions during this decade. In the 1960s, spurred by the base stealing of players such as Luis Aparicio, Maury Wills, and Lou Brock, as well as the increased importance of one-run strategies due to the lower offensive levels, Component 1 grew to 2.0% of all Player decisions. Base stealing grew still more in importance in the 1970s (2.6% of total Player decisions) and peaked in the 1980s at 2.9%, thanks to a new generation of base stealers including Rickey Henderson, Tim Raines, Willie Wilson, and others. Base stealing lessened somewhat in importance in the 1990s (2.4% of total player decisions for the decade), especially the late 1990s, as offensive levels increased, making one-run strategies relatively less important. The lessening of the importance of base stealing continued into the 21st century, with Component 1 accounting for 1.9% of total Player decisions since 2000.

CALCULATION OF COMPONENT 1 PLAYER DECISIONS

Credits for actual stolen bases, caught stealings, and the like are calculated simply as the change in win probability resulting from the change in the base/out situation (and the score, if appropriate).

The probability of a stolen base is calculated based on the league-wide percentage of times a base was stolen given this particular baserunner/out state—that is, 24 probabilities are calculated, one for each base-out state (of course, the three bases-empty scenarios have no chance of a stolen base). Unique probabilities are calculated for each league-season. As an example, average probabilities across all seasons for which I have calculated pW-L records are shown below.

Outs	Baserunners	SB	CS	Success Rate
0	1	5.6%	3.2%	63.5%
0	2	1.1%	0.5%	69.5%
0	3	0.2%	0.2%	57.4%
0	1–2	1.5%	1.4%	52.4%
0	1–3	4.1%	1.1%	78.4%
0	2–3	0.2%	0.1%	62.3%
0	1–2–3	0.2%	0.1%	62.1%
1	1	6.0%	3.7%	61.8%
1	2	1.9%	0.9%	69.0%
1	3	0.3%	0.7%	29.9%
1	1–2	1.8%	1.4%	56.7%
1	1–3	4.6%	1.9%	70.8%
1	2–3	0.2%	0.3%	38.5%
1	1–2–3	0.2%	0.3%	45.6%
2	1	6.7%	3.4%	66.5%
2	2	0.9%	0.2%	80.2%
2	3	0.3%	0.2%	62.5%
2	1–2	0.9%	0.4%	68.3%
2	1–3	6.1%	1.5%	80.2%
2	2–3	0.3%	0.1%	68.1%
2	1–2–3	0.3%	0.2%	65.3%

In addition to wins and losses for actually stealing bases, baserunners, pitchers, and catchers are also credited or debited with their failure to steal or be caught stealing. The win probability at the beginning of a play is calculated based on the probability of each possible event which could subsequently occur. This includes, of course, some possibility that a baserunner may steal one or more bases as well as the possibility that some baserunner may be picked off or caught stealing.

The net win probability in the absence of any stolen bases is calculated as follows. The overall win probability is equal to the weighted average of the win probability with and without base-stealing, i.e.,

$$\text{WinProb} = \text{Prob(SB)} \cdot \text{WinProb}_{SB} + (1-\text{Prob(SB)}) \cdot \text{WinProb}_{noSB}$$

where Prob(SB) is the probability of a stolen base, which, as noted above, is base-out dependent. If no stolen base occurs, then the resulting Win Probability will be WinProb$_{noSB}$ above, which can be calculated as follows:

$$\text{WinProb}_{\text{noSB}} = [1/(1-\text{Prob(SB)})] \cdot (\text{WinProb} - \text{Prob(SB)} \cdot \text{WinProb}_{\text{SB}})$$

The net effect on Win Probability, then, of not stealing a base will simply be the difference: $\text{WinProb}_{\text{noSB}} - \text{WinProb}$.

Balks are included in Component 1 under the assumption that balks tend to be the result of pitchers worrying about possible stolen bases. Of course, balks are relatively rare, so it makes little difference whether they are lumped together with stolen bases or with wild pitches and passed balls in Component 2. In fact, mathematically, it makes literally no difference. The only difference is whether player decisions due to balks are called Component 1 or Component 2.

One way in which stolen bases are unique among the nine components of Player Decisions is that stolen base attempts are purely elective. That is, the offensive team chooses whether or not to attempt to steal a base, unlike, say, balls in play or wild pitches, which just happen. Because of this, the value of a stolen base is intrinsically dependent on the context in which it takes place. To acknowledge this, I do not calculate a "context-neutral" version of Component 1 player decisions. All Component 1 player decisions are tied to the context in which they occurred, so that "context-neutral" Component 1 player decisions are exactly equal to "context-dependent" Component 1 player decisions. An example of how context affects the value of a player's stolen bases is discussed later in this chapter, where I compare Ichiro Suzuki's and Mike Cameron's Component 1 player decisions for the 2002 Seattle Mariners.

Offensively, stolen bases, caught stealings, and the lack thereof, are credited to baserunners. Defensively, the credit for these things is shared by pitchers and catchers. This is one of several cases where credit may be shared by different players. The basic process whereby this credit is divided was described earlier in this chapter. The specific division of defensive Component 1 player decisions is presented next.

DIVISION OF COMPONENT 1 GAME POINTS
BETWEEN PITCHERS AND CATCHERS

One measure of the extent to which a particular factor is a skill is the extent to which a player's winning percentage persists over time. To evaluate the persistence of skills, I fit a simple persistence equation which modeled Component 1 winning percentage on even-numbered plays as a function of Component 1 winning percentage on odd-numbered plays:

$$(\text{Component 1 Win Pct})_{\text{Even}} = b \cdot (\text{Component 1 Win Pct})_{\text{Odd}} + (1-b) \cdot (\text{WinPct})_{\text{Baseline}}$$

where $(\text{WinPct})_{\text{Baseline}}$ represents a baseline winning percentage toward which Component 1 winning percentages regress over time.

Equations of this type were fit for Component 1 player decisions for pitchers and catchers as described earlier in this chapter. Separate equations were estimated for each base. Separate equations were estimated for each season as described earlier in this chapter.

The average division of Component 1 player decisions by base, across all seasons for which I have calculated pW-L records, are as follows.

Component 1	Pitcher	Catcher
First Base	53.2%	46.8%
Second Base	75.2%	24.8%
Third Base	39.4%	60.6%
Total	**52.2%**	**47.8%**

LEVEL OF CREDIT FOR NOT ATTEMPTING STOLEN BASES

Player decisions are awarded not only for stolen bases and caught stealing, but also for a lack of stolen bases and caught stealings when given the opportunity. For most of the seasons for which I have calculated pW-L records, the failure to attempt a stolen base was actually a net positive for a base runner. That is, the expected gain in win percentage to an offensive team from a stolen base times the number of actual stolen bases, defensive indifferences, and balks was less than the expected loss in win percentage to an offensive team from being caught stealing times the number of actual caught stealings, including pickoffs. This has not been true every season, and, in fact, this tendency has reversed itself for seasons since 2007.

Regardless of whether a net positive or net negative, it is worth noting that very few player decisions are actually earned by failing to attempt a stolen base. With a runner on first base and second base open, the failure to steal second base cost an average of 0.000292 losses per plate appearance in 2009, for example. Avoiding being caught stealing (or picked off), on the other hand, earned an average of 0.000266 wins per plate appearance.

An interesting contrast can be made between the most prolific base stealer in the Major Leagues from 2000 to 2006, Juan Pierre, who stole 325 bases and was caught stealing 116 times, and perhaps the least prolific base stealer during this time period, Tony Clark, who reached base approximately 580 times over this time period (excluding home runs) and was credited with no stolen bases and a single caught stealing over this time period.

Juan Pierre, from 2000 to 2006, earned a total of 6.42 stolen base wins, the most stolen base wins earned by any baserunner over this time period. He also led all players in stolen base losses, however, with 6.28, for a Component 1 winning percentage of 0.506 and 0.15 net wins.

Tony Clark, on the other hand, because he never ran, amassed a mere 0.24 stolen base wins, but, because he was only caught stealing once, he also amassed only 0.15 stolen base losses, for a Component 1 winning percentage of 0.614 and 0.09 net wins.

In other words, Juan Pierre's 441 stolen base attempts generated 0.06 more net wins for his teams than Tony Clark's one (unsuccessful) stolen base attempt did over these seven years. To be fair to Juan Pierre, he earned a total of 1.89 net Component 1 wins over his career.

BASERUNNERS VERSUS PITCHERS VERSUS CATCHERS

Overall, Component 1 player decisions account for 2.2% of total player decisions. The relative importance of base stealing as a component of total player value is quite different, however, for baserunners, pitchers, and catchers.

Because of the perfect symmetry between offensive and defensive player decisions, base stealing accounts for a total of 2.2% of total offensive player decisions. The importance of base stealing varies considerably, however, across players. Returning to my earlier examples, Juan Pierre accumulated 7.1% of his total player decisions in Component 1 over the course of his career, while Tony Clark's base stealing accounted for only 0.6% of his total player decisions.

The highest percentage of total offensive player decisions within Component 1 for a single season for a player that played regularly (min. 100 games played, 10 player decisions) was probably Otis Nixon for the 1990 Montreal Expos who had 50 stolen bases and

13 caught stealing in 119 games (263 plate appearances and 26 pinch-running appearances), for a Component 1 won-lost record of 1.45–1.12. Base stealing accounted for a total of 20.7% of Nixon's total offensive player decisions and 16.0% of his total player decisions that year.

In contrast, base stealing is a more minor aspect of overall pitching, with Component 1 player decisions accounting for only 1.8% of total pitching player decisions (not including fielding, batting, and baserunning decisions earned by pitchers). For catchers, on the other hand, Component 1 player decisions are a huge percentage of overall catcher fielding, accounting for 62.6% of total fielding value for catchers (catchers are given no credit for game calling or pitch framing in pW-L records).

The top 25 baserunners, pitchers, and catchers in net Component 1 wins (wins minus losses) are presented in the next three tables.

Component 1: Baserunning Wins
Top 25 Players (Sorted by Net Wins)

		Wins	Losses	Win Pct	Net Wins
1	Rickey Henderson	32.1	20.1	0.615	**12.0**
2	Tim Raines	18.7	9.4	0.665	**9.3**
3	Willie Wilson	14.8	7.1	0.675	**7.7**
4	Joe Morgan	17.3	10.3	0.627	**7.0**
5	Lou Brock	23.1	16.5	0.583	**6.6**
6	Vince Coleman	17.8	11.3	0.612	**6.5**
7	Bert Campaneris	20.1	13.7	0.595	**6.4**
8	Davey Lopes	13.0	7.0	0.650	**6.0**
9	Paul Molitor	12.1	6.2	0.660	**5.8**
10	Luis Aparicio	12.8	7.7	0.624	**5.1**
11	Ozzie Smith	13.9	9.2	0.602	**4.7**
12	Eric Davis	8.8	4.6	0.657	**4.2**
13	Ron LeFlore	11.7	7.5	0.609	**4.2**
14	Cesar Cedeno	13.5	9.7	0.583	**3.9**
15	Otis Nixon	14.1	10.4	0.576	**3.7**
16	Amos Otis	8.1	4.3	0.650	**3.7**
17	Marquis Grissom	10.4	6.8	0.606	**3.7**
18	Tommy Harper	10.5	6.9	0.603	**3.6**
19	Kenny Lofton	12.2	8.7	0.584	**3.5**
20	Jimmy Rollins	9.2	5.8	0.615	**3.5**
21	Johnny Damon	8.2	4.8	0.631	**3.4**
22	Barry Larkin	8.2	4.8	0.631	**3.4**
23	Stan Javier	5.7	2.4	0.707	**3.3**
24	Jose Reyes	10.5	7.3	0.590	**3.2**
25	Carl Crawford	9.3	6.1	0.605	**3.2**

Component 1: Pitching Wins
Top 25 Players (Sorted by Net Wins)

		Wins	Losses	Win Pct	Net Wins
1	Gaylord Perry	6.1	3.9	0.609	**2.2**
2	Steve Carlton	8.3	6.2	0.572	**2.1**
3	Kenny Rogers	3.5	1.6	0.693	**2.0**
4	Tom Glavine	4.7	2.9	0.617	**1.8**
5	Frank Viola	4.0	2.2	0.644	**1.8**
6	Sam McDowell	3.2	1.5	0.681	**1.7**
7	Mark Buehrle	2.8	1.2	0.707	**1.6**
8	*Bobo Newsom*	4.8	3.2	*0.600*	**1.6**
9	Claude Osteen	3.5	1.9	0.645	**1.6**
10	Jim Perry	3.4	1.8	0.653	**1.6**
11	*Max Lanier*	2.5	0.9	0.732	**1.6**

		Wins	Losses	Win Pct	Net Wins
12	Andy Pettitte	3.6	2.1	0.634	1.5
13	*Warren Spahn*	*5.0*	*3.5*	*0.588*	*1.5*
14	Mickey Lolich	4.6	3.2	0.590	1.4
15	Mark Langston	4.7	3.3	0.588	1.4
16	Bret Saberhagen	3.3	1.9	0.637	1.4
17	Fernando Valenzuela	5.1	3.7	0.578	1.4
18	John Tudor	3.1	1.7	0.644	1.4
19	*Mel Harder*	*3.6*	*2.3*	*0.611*	*1.3*
20	Phil Niekro	7.7	6.4	0.545	1.3
21	*Vern Kennedy*	*3.2*	*2.0*	*0.620*	*1.3*
22	Mike Morgan	4.1	2.8	0.591	1.3
23	Geoff Zahn	2.5	1.3	0.663	1.2
24	Mike Moore	3.8	2.6	0.595	1.2
25	*Dolf Luque*	*2.8*	*1.6*	*0.639*	*1.2*

Component 1: Catcher Wins
Top 25 Players (Sorted by Net Wins)

		Wins	Losses	Win Pct	Net Wins
1	Ivan Rodriguez	18.2	13.0	0.583	5.2
2	Gary Carter	24.5	20.2	0.548	4.3
3	Yadier Molina	9.8	6.0	0.619	3.8
4	Bob Boone	20.8	17.1	0.549	3.7
5	Jim Sundberg	17.7	14.5	0.549	3.1
6	Lance Parrish	16.9	14.0	0.546	2.9
7	Tony Pena	20.0	17.2	0.538	2.9
8	*Al Lopez*	*13.5*	*10.9*	*0.554*	*2.6*
9	Rick Dempsey	14.8	12.6	0.540	2.2
10	*Gabby Hartnett*	*11.2*	*9.0*	*0.554*	*2.2*
11	*Bill Dickey*	*11.6*	*9.4*	*0.552*	*2.2*
12	Steve Yeager	11.2	9.1	0.553	2.1
13	Thurman Munson	11.3	9.2	0.552	2.1
14	Johnny Bench	13.3	11.1	0.543	2.1
15	Henry Blanco	7.1	5.1	0.583	2.0
16	*Mike Tresh*	*9.2*	*7.2*	*0.560*	*2.0*
17	*Buddy Rosar*	*8.1*	*6.1*	*0.569*	*2.0*
18	Ron Karkovice	7.4	5.5	0.574	1.9
19	Charles Johnson	8.9	7.2	0.554	1.7
20	Del Crandall	9.9	8.2	0.547	1.7
21	Buck Rodgers	6.7	5.1	0.570	1.6
22	Tom Pagnozzi	7.1	5.5	0.565	1.6
23	Jody Davis	12.6	10.9	0.534	1.6
24	Earl Battey	6.4	5.0	0.564	1.5
25	Brian Schneider	6.8	5.4	0.556	1.4

BASE STEALING CONTEXT

Unlike most other events in baseball, stolen bases are purely elective plays by the offensive team (or player). To recognize this, I do not believe that it makes sense to talk about "context-neutral" base stealing, as one factor that can distinguish between good and bad base stealers is their ability to evaluate context in making the decision whether or not to attempt a stolen base.

Because of context, then, not all stolen bases are created equally, nor are all caught stealings. A terrific example of this was two teammates on the 2002 Seattle Mariners: Mike Cameron and Ichiro Suzuki. In 2002, Cameron and Ichiro each stole 31 bases for the Seattle Mariners; Cameron was caught stealing 8 times while Ichiro was caught stealing

15 times. Based on this, a casual observer would likely conclude that Mike Cameron had a better season than Ichiro in terms of base stealing.

In fact, however, Mike Cameron's Component 1 record in 2002 was 0.5 wins and 0.7 losses (0.409 winning percentage; –0.2 net wins, i.e., wins minus losses) while Ichiro's record was 0.9–0.9 (0.497, –0.0). Why was this? Basically, because Ichiro was smarter about when he attempted to steal bases, so that his successful steals were worth more and his caught stealings cost less than Mike Cameron's attempts.

Here is how many wins and losses Cameron and Ichiro's stolen bases and caught stealings were worth, on average.

Component 1 Decisions Per SB Attempt

	Ichiro Suzuki		*Mike Cameron*	
Runner on	SB	CS/PO	SB	CS/PO
1st base	0.020	–0.047	0.015	–0.063
2nd base	0.026	–0.026	0.015	–0.028

Ichiro's stolen bases were about 50% more valuable than Cameron's and his caught stealings cost less. Also working in Ichiro's favor was the fact that while Cameron was only charged with 8 official caught stealings, he was also picked off 3 times (Ichiro was picked off once). Put it all together, along with the Component 1 decisions earned by the players for not stealing and being caught stealing, and the end result is that Ichiro Suzuki was about 0.2 net wins better (or, perhaps, "less bad" given that both players were sub-0.500 Component 1 players in 2002) than Mike Cameron (relative to 0.500) as a base stealer in 2002.

While 2002 was a bad Component 1 season for both players, the fact that Ichiro produced a better Component 1 record relative to raw stolen base and caught stealing than Mike Cameron is consistent with their careers. Ichiro Suzuki, in his career through 2015 (2001–2015), compiled a Component 1 record of 9.8–7.0 (0.582 winning percentage, 2.8 net wins) on the strength of 498 stolen bases against 125 caught stealings and/or pickoffs. Overall, Ichiro's rank in Component 1 net wins across all seasons for which I have calculated pW-L records is 37th. This works out to about 0.0047 net Component 1 wins per stolen base attempt for his career.

Mike Cameron's career stolen base numbers (1995–2011) are somewhat worse—297 SB, 97 CS/PO—although not necessarily too much so, but his Component 1 record is more notably worse than Ichiro's, 5.2–4.7 (0.524, 0.5, 336th-best across all seasons for which I have calculated pW-L records). This works out to only 0.0012 net wins per stolen base attempt. (In both cases, here, the net wins per stolen base attempt are calculated by simply dividing Component 1 decisions by official SB/CS/PO data. Component 1 decisions are also accumulated on plays in which baserunners do not pick up an SB or CS.)

Some players are much better base stealers than others; and one way in which some players are better is in knowing when to attempt their stolen bases. By incorporating context into the results, Component 1 Player wins and losses provide a deeper insight into which players are the best base stealers than raw stolen base and caught stealing totals.

Component 2: Wild Pitches and Passed Balls

In the second step of calculating Player Wins and Losses, baserunners, pitchers, and catchers are given credit and blame for either advancing (allowing) or failing to advance by (preventing) wild pitches or passed balls.

Credits and debits for wild pitches and passed balls (and the occasional case of a baserunner being thrown out trying to advance on a wild pitch or passed ball) are calculated simply as the change in win probability resulting from the change in the base/out situation (and the score, if appropriate). Component 2 is also where credit is given to batters for successfully reaching base on a dropped third strike.

The probability of a wild pitch or passed ball is calculated based on the league-wide percentage of times such an event occurred given a particular baserunner/out state—that is, 24 probabilities are calculated, one for each base-out state (in this case, non-zero probabilities in bases-empty situations refer to incidences of the batter reaching base safely on a dropped third strike). Unique probabilities are calculated for each league-season. As an example, average probabilities across all seasons for which I have calculated pW-L records are shown below.

Outs	Baserunners	WP/PB
0	0	0.0%
0	1	1.9%
0	2	2.2%
0	3	1.7%
0	1–2	2.1%
0	1–3	2.1%
0	2–3	1.5%
0	1–2–3	1.5%
1	0	0.1%
1	1	1.9%
1	2	2.3%
1	3	1.6%
1	1–2	2.2%
1	1–3	2.1%
1	2–3	1.4%
1	1–2–3	1.4%
2	0	0.1%
2	1	1.8%
2	2	2.1%
2	3	1.6%
2	1–2	2.0%
2	1–3	2.0%
2	2–3	1.5%
2	1–2–3	1.4%

As with stolen bases, credit is also given for not throwing wild pitches or committing passed balls. The net win probability in the absence of any wild pitch or passed ball is calculated as follows. The overall win probability is equal to the weighted average of the win probability with and without wild pitches, i.e.,

$$\text{WinProb} = \text{Prob(WP)} \cdot \text{WinProb}_{WP} + (1-\text{Prob(WP)}) \cdot \text{WinProb}_{noWP}$$

where Prob(WP) is the probability of a wild pitch (or passed ball), which, as noted above, is base-out dependent. The win probability in the absence of a wild pitch (or passed ball), WinProb_{noWP}, can then be calculated as follows:

$$\text{WinProb}_{noWP} = [1/(1-\text{Prob(WP)})] \cdot (\text{WinProb} - \text{Prob(WP)} \cdot \text{WinProb}_{WP})$$

The net effect on win probability, then, of no wild pitch or passed ball during a plate appearance will simply be the difference: WinProb_{noWP} – WinProb.

Offensively, wild pitches, passed balls, and the lack thereof, are credited to baserunners. Defensively, the credit for these things are shared by pitchers and catchers. This is one of several cases where credit may be shared by different players. The basic process whereby this credit is divided was described earlier in this chapter.

Equations of this type were fit for Component 2 player decisions for pitchers and catchers as described earlier in this chapter. Separate equations were estimated for each base. Separate equations were estimated for each season as described earlier in this chapter.

The average division of Component 2 player decisions by base, across all seasons for which I have calculated pW-L records, are as follows.

Component 1	*Pitcher*	*Catcher*
Batter	70.4%	29.6%
First Base	69.4%	30.6%
Second Base	76.3%	23.7%
Third Base	79.6%	20.4%
Total	**76.3%**	**23.7%**

The top 25 baserunners, pitchers, and catchers in net Component 2 wins (wins minus losses) are presented in the next three tables.

Component 2: Baserunning Wins
Top 25 Players (Sorted by Net Wins)

		Wins	*Losses*	*Win Pct*	*Net Wins*
1	Carl Yastrzemski	5.8	4.4	0.571	**1.5**
2	Willie Mays	5.0	3.9	0.562	**1.1**
3	Miguel Tejada	3.2	2.3	0.587	**1.0**
4	Bobby Bonds	3.7	2.7	0.575	**1.0**
5	Ozzie Guillen	2.8	1.8	0.601	**0.9**
6	Billy Williams	4.4	3.5	0.555	**0.9**
7	Lee Maye	2.4	1.6	0.607	**0.9**
8	Barry Larkin	3.7	2.9	0.565	**0.9**
9	Alan Trammell	3.5	2.6	0.569	**0.8**
10	Yogi Berra	2.4	1.6	0.606	**0.8**
11	Manny Sanguillen	2.4	1.6	0.604	**0.8**
12	Bert Campaneris	4.2	3.4	0.553	**0.8**
13	Craig Biggio	4.7	3.9	0.547	**0.8**
14	*Ted Williams*	*3.1*	*2.3*	*0.573*	***0.8***
15	Ken Landreaux	2.0	1.2	0.622	**0.8**
16	Vic Davalillo	2.5	1.8	0.588	**0.8**
17	Don Buford	3.1	2.4	0.569	**0.8**
18	Richie Hebner	2.8	2.0	0.578	**0.8**
19	Jose Valentin	2.2	1.5	0.600	**0.7**
20	Lou Whitaker	3.7	3.0	0.555	**0.7**
21	Felipe Alou	3.5	2.7	0.558	**0.7**
22	Luis Aparicio	4.5	3.8	0.542	**0.7**
23	Roy Howell	1.6	0.9	0.634	**0.7**
24	Dave Parker	3.3	2.6	0.556	**0.7**
25	Al Kaline	4.2	3.5	0.542	**0.6**

Component 2: Pitching Wins
Top 25 Players (Sorted by Net Wins)

		Wins	*Losses*	*Win Pct*	*Net Wins*
1	Luis Tiant	2.8	0.9	0.763	**2.0**
2	Greg Maddux	3.7	1.8	0.672	**1.9**
3	Tom Glavine	3.4	1.8	0.661	**1.7**
4	Bob Friend	2.8	1.2	0.698	**1.6**
5	Dennis Eckersley	2.4	0.8	0.747	**1.6**
6	Jamie Moyer	2.9	1.3	0.690	**1.6**

		Wins	Losses	Win Pct	Net Wins
7	Mark Buehrle	2.3	0.7	0.753	**1.5**
8	Livan Hernandez	2.5	1.0	0.711	**1.5**
9	Robin Roberts	2.9	1.5	0.657	**1.4**
10	Lew Burdette	2.1	0.8	0.735	**1.3**
11	Curt Simmons	2.6	1.3	0.672	**1.3**
12	Juan Marichal	3.1	1.8	0.632	**1.3**
13	John Burkett	2.1	0.8	0.715	**1.2**
14	Jim Bunning	3.2	2.0	0.620	**1.2**
15	Catfish Hunter	2.7	1.5	0.641	**1.2**
16	Bartolo Colon	2.2	1.0	0.683	**1.2**
17	Bill Monbouquette	1.6	0.5	0.760	**1.1**
18	Fergie Jenkins	3.5	2.4	0.595	**1.1**
19	Claude Osteen	3.1	2.0	0.606	**1.1**
20	Greg Swindell	1.7	0.7	0.719	**1.1**
21	Jim Barr	1.7	0.7	0.715	**1.0**
22	Randy Wolf	1.9	0.9	0.682	**1.0**
23	John Candelaria	1.9	0.9	0.676	**1.0**
24	Dick Hall	1.1	0.1	0.919	**1.0**
25	Randy Jones	1.5	0.5	0.748	**1.0**

Component 2: Catcher Wins
Top 25 Players (Sorted by Net Wins)

		Wins	Losses	Win Pct	Net Wins
1	Yogi Berra	2.9	2.0	0.585	**0.8**
2	Bill Freehan	4.3	3.6	0.548	**0.8**
3	Jason Varitek	2.9	2.2	0.568	**0.7**
4	Carlton Fisk	4.4	3.8	0.542	**0.7**
5	Jake Gibbs	1.3	0.6	0.673	**0.7**
6	Mike Piazza	3.5	2.9	0.550	**0.6**
7	Brad Ausmus	4.0	3.3	0.544	**0.6**
8	Matt Wieters	1.7	1.1	0.612	**0.6**
9	Del Crandall	2.7	2.1	0.562	**0.6**
10	Bruce Benedict	2.1	1.5	0.583	**0.6**
11	Ramon Hernandez	3.3	2.7	0.549	**0.6**
12	Dan Wilson	2.6	2.0	0.562	**0.6**
13	Terry Kennedy	3.0	2.4	0.553	**0.6**
14	*Buddy Rosar*	*1.4*	*0.9*	*0.618*	**0.6**
15	Sandy Alomar, Jr.	2.8	2.2	0.553	**0.5**
16	Charlie O'Brien	1.6	1.1	0.600	**0.5**
17	Darrin Fletcher	2.3	1.8	0.564	**0.5**
18	Charles Johnson	2.8	2.3	0.551	**0.5**
19	Manny Sanguillen	2.9	2.4	0.548	**0.5**
20	Carlos Ruiz	2.3	1.8	0.560	**0.5**
21	Gary Carter	4.3	3.8	0.530	**0.5**
22	Sherm Lollar	2.6	2.1	0.551	**0.5**
23	Kurt Suzuki	2.5	2.1	0.551	**0.5**
24	Randy Hundley	2.6	2.2	0.548	**0.5**
25	Don Slaught	2.7	2.3	0.545	**0.4**

An example of how teammate performance can affect a player's won-lost records, using Component 2 as the example, is presented next.

Example of Teammate Effects on Shared Components: Doug Mirabelli

In 2000, Doug Mirabelli committed 5 passed balls in 80 games for the San Francisco Giants, good for a (teammate-unadjusted) context-neutral Component 2 winning percentage of 0.604.

In 2003, Doug Mirabelli committed 14 passed balls in only 55 games for the Boston Red Sox, posting a (teammate-unadjusted) context-neutral Component 2 winning percentage of 0.482.

Did Doug Mirabelli really get that much worse in just three years? Well, he did age from 29 in 2000 to 32 in 2003, so some of that could be age-related decline. But, more significantly for Mirabelli, in 2003, he was the personal catcher for knuckleballer Tim Wakefield, who had a career (context-neutral, teammate-adjusted) Component 2 winning percentage of 0.254.

In order to make pW-L records meaningful as measures of player talent, it is necessary to control for the ability of one's teammates. This is done using the Matchup Formula as described earlier in this chapter.

The case of Doug Mirabelli, sometime personal catcher for knuckleballer Tim Wakefield, is instructive in this regard.

Doug Mirabelli's teammate-unadjusted context-neutral Component 2 won-lost records over his career were as follows:

Year	Team	Wins	Losses	Win Pct
1996	SFN	0.02	0.04	0.337
1997	SFN	0.00	0.00	1.000
1998	SFN	0.01	0.01	0.530
1999	SFN	0.06	0.02	0.800
2000	SFN	0.16	0.10	0.604
2001	TEX	0.05	0.05	0.483
2001	BOS	0.11	0.13	0.446
2002	BOS	0.10	0.10	0.506
2003	BOS	0.10	0.10	0.482
2004	BOS	0.10	0.17	0.359
2005	BOS	0.06	0.07	0.474
2006	SDN	0.01	0.01	0.602
2006	BOS	0.11	0.17	0.395
2007	BOS	0.07	0.14	0.339
CAREER		**0.97**	**1.12**	**0.463**

Outside of Boston over these years, Mirabelli's Component 2 winning percentage was over 0.500 in five of seven seasons, with an overall winning percentage of 0.582. In contrast, Mirabelli's Component 2 winning percentage was below 0.500 in six of his seven seasons in Boston, with an overall Component 2 winning percentage in Boston of 0.421. Overall, Mirabelli rates as a fairly poor catcher at preventing wild pitches and passed balls, with an overall Component 2 winning percentage of 0.463.

When Mirabelli's Component 2 won-lost record is adjusted to control for the pitchers who Mirabelli caught, however, the results are the following:

Year	Team	Wins	Losses	Win Pct
1996	SFN	0.02	0.04	0.325
1997	SFN	0.00	0.00	1.000
1998	SFN	0.01	0.01	0.528
1999	SFN	0.06	0.02	0.788
2000	SFN	0.16	0.11	0.602
2001	TEX	0.05	0.05	0.484
2001	BOS	0.12	0.13	0.477
2002	BOS	0.11	0.09	0.540
2003	BOS	0.10	0.09	0.524
2004	BOS	0.12	0.15	0.460
2005	BOS	0.08	0.05	0.597
2006	SDN	0.01	0.01	0.587

Year	Team	Wins	Losses	Win Pct
2006	BOS	0.13	0.15	0.460
2007	BOS	0.10	0.12	0.454
CAREER		**1.07**	**1.01**	**0.514**

Adjusting for the pitchers he caught, Doug Mirabelli turns out to have been slightly above average at preventing wild pitches and passed balls through his career. Outside of Boston over these years, Mirabelli's Component 2 winning percentage remains fairly consistent after adjusting for his teammates, at 0.578. With Boston, on the other hand, Mirabelli's combined Component 2 winning percentage improves dramatically from 0.421 unadjusted to 0.492 adjusted.

In words, adjusting for Mirabelli's teammates brings his Component 2 winning percentages closer together over time. Mathematically, the standard deviation of Mirabelli's winning percentages falls from 0.109 unadjusted—i.e., Mirabelli's Component 2 winning percentages fell mostly in a range of 0.463 +/- 0.109 (0.354–0.572)—to 0.084 adjusted—i.e., Mirabelli's Component 2 winning percentages range from 0.430 to 0.598 (0.514 +/- 0.084).

Mirabelli was still a bit worse in Boston than elsewhere. Of course, outside of one month in 2006 in San Diego, his career outside of Boston came at ages 25–30, while his Boston career was from ages 30–36. So based on age alone, we would have expected him to probably be a little less agile at blocking would-be wild pitches in Boston than in San Francisco and Texas.

It seems clear to me that the latter set of numbers more accurately reflect Doug Mirabelli's ability to prevent wild pitches and passed balls.

Component 3: Balls Not in Play

In the third step of calculating Player Wins and Losses, batters and pitchers are given credit and blame for plate appearances that do not result in the ball being put into play: i.e., strikeouts, walks, and hit batsmen. Unlike Components 1, 2, 5, 6, 7, 8, and 9; Components 3 and 4 are not constrained to be 0.500 Components by construction. Instead, the combined winning percentage of Components 3 and 4 is equal to 0.500.

CALCULATION OF COMPONENT 3 PLAYER DECISIONS

Components 3 and 4 are calculated together. After Components 1 (stolen bases) and 2 (wild pitches) are accounted for, Components 3 and 4 are determined by calculating the expected value of the plate appearance, based purely on the basic result—walk, strikeout, or ball in play—assuming average results following the play. If the batter does not put the ball in play, the results are credited to Component 3. If the batter does put the ball in play (including hitting a home run), the results are credited to Component 4.

For strikeouts and walks, any baserunner advancement beyond normal—e.g., a batter reaching base on a dropped third strike or a baserunner going from first to third on a walk and a wild pitch—is attributed to Component 2. Like Component 1, where baserunners earn Component 1 decisions for not stealing as well as for stealing, batters are credited/debited with Component 2 decisions on strikeouts both for successfully reaching first base on a dropped third strike as well as for failing to reach first base safely. Component

3 decisions for strikeouts are calculated given an average probability of the batter successfully reaching first base on strike three.

Intentional walks are issued at the discretion of the pitching team. To acknowledge this, I do not calculate a "context-neutral" version of Component 3 decisions for intentional walks. Instead, intentional walks are tied to the context in which they occurred, so that "context-neutral" Component 3 intentional walks are exactly equal to their "context-dependent" Component 3 value.

Relative Values of Strikeouts and Walks

On average, across all seasons for which I have calculated pW-L records, a strikeout had a net win value (for the batter) of −0.0214 while unintentional walks and hit batsmen have had an average net win value of 0.0316.

These values have varied somewhat over time due to differences in the run-scoring environment, although not by as much as most other offensive events. A strikeout-to-walk ratio (including hit-by-pitches, but excluding intentional walks) for a pitcher greater than 1.47 will produce a Component 3 winning percentage over 0.500, while a strikeout-to-walk ratio for a batter less than 1.47 will produce a Component 3 winning percentage over 0.500.

The strikeout-to-walk ratio in major league baseball has increased in recent years, as the number of strikeouts has increased. Since 2000, the strikeout-to (unintentional)-walk ratio (including hit-by-pitches) in major league baseball was 2.07 with pitchers having a Component 3 winning percentage of 0.594 over this time period.

Across all seasons for which I have calculated pW-L records, Component 3 accounted for 14.8% of total Player decisions. That share has grown over time as strikeouts have increased. Since 2000, Component 3 has accounted for 16.7% of total Player decisions. Component 3 Player decisions are assigned entirely to batters and pitchers.

The top 25 batters and pitchers in net Component 3 wins (wins minus losses) are presented in the next two tables.

Component 3: Batting Wins
Top 25 Players (Sorted by Net Wins)

		Wins	Losses	Win Pct	Net Wins
1	Ted Williams	63.4	15.3	0.805	**48.1**
2	Joe Morgan	61.7	21.1	0.746	**40.7**
3	Mel Ott	54.5	16.2	0.771	**38.3**
4	Eddie Yost	56.8	19.7	0.742	**37.0**
5	Barry Bonds	67.9	33.3	0.671	**34.6**
6	Stan Musial	48.3	14.7	0.767	**33.7**
7	Stan Hack	41.6	8.5	0.830	**33.1**
8	Luke Appling	43.6	10.9	0.800	**32.7**
9	Rickey Henderson	68.3	36.5	0.652	**31.8**
10	Augie Galan	36.7	7.3	0.834	**29.4**
11	Pete Rose	53.2	23.9	0.690	**29.3**
12	Eddie Stanky	36.4	7.4	0.831	**29.0**
13	Lou Gehrig	40.0	11.9	0.771	**28.1**
14	Charlie Gehringer	34.4	6.6	0.838	**27.7**
15	Carl Yastrzemski	57.0	29.7	0.657	**27.2**
16	Arky Vaughan	33.1	6.3	0.841	**26.8**
17	Richie Ashburn	38.8	12.0	0.764	**26.8**
18	Elmer Valo	32.0	6.1	0.841	**25.9**
19	Willie Randolph	40.2	14.4	0.736	**25.8**

		Wins	Losses	Win Pct	Net Wins
20	Ferris Fain	30.9	5.6	0.846	25.2
21	Rick Ferrell	31.2	6.0	0.838	25.2
22	Paul Waner	31.9	6.7	0.826	25.1
23	Jim Gilliam	33.1	8.8	0.790	24.4
24	Wade Boggs	39.8	16.0	0.713	23.8
25	Nellie Fox	28.1	4.7	0.857	23.4

Component 3: Pitching Wins
Top 25 Players (Sorted by Net Wins)

		Wins	Losses	Win Pct	Net Wins
1	Randy Johnson	105.5	48.3	0.686	57.2
2	Roger Clemens	101.1	50.0	0.669	51.1
3	Curt Schilling	66.4	21.8	0.752	44.6
4	Greg Maddux	71.7	30.1	0.704	41.6
5	Pedro Martinez	67.7	26.3	0.720	41.4
6	Mike Mussina	61.1	24.3	0.715	36.8
7	John Smoltz	65.3	29.7	0.688	35.6
8	Fergie Jenkins	67.2	32.8	0.672	34.4
9	Bert Blyleven	78.5	46.1	0.630	32.4
10	Javier Vazquez	54.2	24.3	0.690	29.8
11	Gaylord Perry	74.2	45.1	0.622	29.1
12	Tom Seaver	75.3	46.3	0.619	29.0
13	Don Sutton	73.8	44.9	0.622	28.9
14	Dennis Eckersley	51.2	24.3	0.678	26.9
15	Danny Haren	42.9	16.0	0.729	26.9
16	C.C. Sabathia	55.2	29.1	0.655	26.1
17	Nolan Ryan	120.3	94.4	0.560	25.9
18	Steve Carlton	85.2	59.3	0.589	25.8
19	David Wells	47.9	22.1	0.684	25.8
20	Roy Halladay	45.3	19.8	0.696	25.5
21	Felix Hernandez	46.0	20.6	0.691	25.4
22	Cole Hamels	41.0	15.9	0.721	25.2
23	Juan Marichal	47.5	23.0	0.674	24.5
24	Johan Santana	42.3	18.1	0.700	24.2
25	Zack Greinke	40.4	16.5	0.710	23.9

Component 4: Balls in Play

In the fourth step of calculating Player Wins and Losses, batters and pitchers are given credit and blame for plate appearances that result in the ball being put into play. Wins and losses are assigned in this step based on the expected value of the balls in play. The calculation of these expected values was discussed earlier in this chapter.

CALCULATION OF COMPONENT 4 PLAYER DECISIONS

Components 3 and 4 are calculated together. After Components 1 (stolen bases) and 2 (wild pitches) are accounted for, Components 3 and 4 are evaluated by calculating the expected value of the plate appearance, based purely on the basic result—walk, strikeout, or ball in play—assuming average results following the play. If the batter does not put the ball in play, the results are credited to Component 3. If the batter does put the ball in play (including hitting a home run), the results are credited to Component 4. Component 4 decisions are calculated assuming average results based on where and how the ball is hit. Whether the ball becomes a hit or an out is allocated in Component 5.

As explained in the description of Component 3, Components 3 and 4 are not individually constrained to 0.500 winning percentages. Instead, the combined winning percentage of Components 3 and 4 is equal to 0.500. Overall, recently, putting the ball in play is a net positive event for the offense. Since 2000, the overall Component 4 winning percentage for hitters was 0.544.

Home Runs: Component 3 or Component 4?

In sabermetric circles, it is fairly common to distinguish between home runs and other balls hit into play. In fact, frequently, the term "balls-in-play" or BIP is used to denote those balls that are hit into play excluding home runs. The logic for this distinction is most apparent in the study of Defense-Independent Pitching Statistics, or DIPS. I discuss DIPS and the impact of pitchers on balls-in-play in some detail in Chapter 6.

To my mind, the proper distinction is whether the batter hits the ball or not. Based on this, I have chosen to allocate wins and losses attributable to home runs to Component 4—balls hit by the batter—rather than Component 3. Since Components 3 and 4 are calculated simultaneously, however, this is, in fact, a purely semantic decision. If one were inclined to include home runs as part of Component 3, one could do so by simply re-defining all Component 4 decisions resulting from home runs as Component 3 decisions instead. In fact, I do precisely this in Chapter 6, where I look at what pW-L records have to say about the question of what control pitchers have on balls in play.

Overall, for all seasons for which I have calculated pW-L records, Component 4 decisions account for 35.3% of total Player decisions, 38.6% of all Batting decisions, and 55.4% of total Pitcher decisions.

The top 25 batters and pitchers in net Component 4 wins (wins minus losses) are presented in the next two tables. The top 25 batters and pitchers in combined Component 3 and 4 net wins (wins minus losses) are presented in two tables after that.

Component 4: Batting Wins
Top 25 Players (Sorted by Net Wins)

		Wins	Losses	Win Pct	Net Wins
1	Barry Bonds	149.7	70.8	0.679	**79.0**
2	Hank Aaron	173.7	98.6	0.638	**75.1**
3	Willie Mays	149.0	84.3	0.639	**64.8**
4	Harmon Killebrew	122.2	57.7	0.679	**64.6**
5	Mike Schmidt	116.9	52.9	0.689	**64.0**
6	Jim Thome	112.0	49.2	0.695	**62.9**
7	Alex Rodriguez	130.1	68.1	0.656	**62.0**
8	Willie Stargell	110.6	48.6	0.695	**62.0**
9	Sammy Sosa	115.5	53.6	0.683	**61.9**
10	Frank Robinson	136.3	74.9	0.645	**61.4**
11	Mark McGwire	100.9	39.6	0.718	**61.3**
12	Mickey Mantle	114.1	53.5	0.681	**60.6**
13	Manny Ramirez	110.8	51.6	0.682	**59.2**
14	Reggie Jackson	121.2	62.3	0.661	**58.9**
15	Albert Pujols	119.6	63.9	0.652	**55.8**
16	Willie McCovey	115.2	60.4	0.656	**54.8**
17	*Ted Williams*	*113.3*	*59.5*	*0.656*	**53.8**
18	Ken Griffey, Jr.	124.3	71.8	0.634	**52.5**
19	Adam Dunn	89.6	38.7	0.698	**50.9**
20	Fred McGriff	107.9	57.7	0.652	**50.2**
21	Duke Snider	102.6	53.4	0.657	**49.1**

		Wins	Losses	Win Pct	Net Wins
22	Frank Thomas	105.9	57.9	0.647	**48.0**
23	Miguel Cabrera	93.8	46.0	0.671	**47.8**
24	Dave Kingman	89.8	42.7	0.677	**47.0**
25	Frank Howard	90.6	43.9	0.674	**46.7**

Component 4: Pitching Wins
Top 25 Players (Sorted by Net Wins)

		Wins	Losses	Win Pct	Net Wins
1	Mel Harder	109.2	78.5	0.582	**30.8**
2	Bob Feller	114.4	83.9	0.577	**30.5**
3	Red Ruffing	116.6	87.5	0.571	**29.1**
4	Lefty Grove	94.4	65.9	0.589	**28.5**
5	Dutch Leonard	108.4	81.4	0.571	**27.0**
6	Bob Lemon	94.2	67.2	0.584	**27.0**
7	Ted Lyons	106.1	79.4	0.572	**26.7**
8	Dizzy Trout	89.4	62.8	0.587	**26.6**
9	Warren Spahn	168.9	143.1	0.541	**25.8**
10	Tommy John	144.1	120.2	0.545	**23.9**
11	Early Wynn	142.4	119.0	0.545	**23.4**
12	Lefty Gomez	76.4	53.2	0.589	**23.2**
13	Allie Reynolds	79.3	57.7	0.579	**21.6**
14	Big Bill Lee	91.6	70.6	0.565	**21.0**
15	Claude Passeau	86.6	66.5	0.565	**20.1**
16	Wes Ferrell	77.2	57.3	0.574	**20.0**
17	Jim Palmer	120.8	101.9	0.543	**19.0**
18	Bump Hadley	78.3	59.4	0.568	**18.8**
19	Willis Hudlin	71.0	52.2	0.576	**18.8**
20	Bucky Walters	95.6	77.0	0.554	**18.6**
21	Mike Garcia	70.4	52.2	0.574	**18.2**
22	Max Lanier	50.5	33.1	0.604	**17.4**
23	Bob Rush	78.2	61.2	0.561	**17.0**
24	Thornton Lee	69.8	52.8	0.569	**16.9**
25	Joe Dobson	68.4	51.5	0.570	**16.9**

Components 3 & 4: Batting Wins
Top 25 Players (Sorted by Net Wins)

		Wins	Losses	Win Pct	Net Wins
1	Barry Bonds	217.6	104.1	0.677	**113.6**
2	Ted Williams	176.7	74.8	0.702	***101.9***
3	Hank Aaron	213.8	127.8	0.626	**86.0**
4	Mel Ott	163.1	80.1	0.671	**83.0**
5	Mickey Mantle	168.3	90.1	0.651	**78.2**
6	Harmon Killebrew	171.4	94.1	0.646	**77.4**
7	Willie Mays	193.5	116.2	0.625	**77.3**
8	Frank Robinson	184.0	107.2	0.632	**76.8**
9	Mike Schmidt	164.9	91.8	0.642	**73.1**
10	Stan Musial	172.8	105.6	0.621	**67.2**
11	Albert Pujols	151.7	85.3	0.640	**66.4**
12	Frank Thomas	154.1	88.3	0.636	**65.8**
13	Mark McGwire	138.5	74.3	0.651	**64.2**
14	Carl Yastrzemski	188.4	124.9	0.601	**63.5**
15	Willie McCovey	155.8	92.7	0.627	**63.1**
16	Lou Gehrig	121.0	58.2	0.675	**62.8**
17	Gary Sheffield	156.2	94.2	0.624	**62.0**
18	Jimmie Foxx	134.3	73.8	0.645	**60.5**
19	Manny Ramirez	149.0	90.9	0.621	**58.0**
20	Jim Thome	162.3	104.5	0.608	**57.8**
21	Eddie Mathews	153.8	96.4	0.615	**57.4**

		Wins	Losses	Win Pct	Net Wins
22	Alex Rodriguez	172.8	116.1	0.598	**56.8**
23	Jeff Bagwell	138.8	84.0	0.623	**54.7**
24	*Babe Ruth*	*90.9*	*36.7*	*0.713*	**54.3**
25	Todd Helton	134.2	81.9	0.621	**52.4**

Note that pW-L records have only been calculated for 9 seasons of Babe Ruth's 22-year career.

Components 3 & 4: Pitching Wins
Top 25 Players (Sorted by Net Wins)

		Wins	Losses	Win Pct	Net Wins
1	Roger Clemens	224.8	166.5	0.574	**58.3**
2	Greg Maddux	210.3	159.0	0.569	**51.3**
3	Randy Johnson	196.6	155.1	0.559	**41.5**
4	Pedro Martinez	134.3	93.4	0.590	**40.8**
5	Kevin Brown	141.7	103.8	0.577	**37.9**
6	Nolan Ryan	244.8	209.3	0.539	**35.5**
7	Gaylord Perry	225.9	191.3	0.541	**34.6**
8	*Warren Spahn*	*222.5*	*188.5*	*0.541*	**34.1**
9	Mike Mussina	159.7	127.0	0.557	**32.7**
10	*Lefty Grove*	*129.6*	*97.0*	*0.572*	**32.6**
11	Tommy John	191.4	161.9	0.542	**29.5**
12	John Smoltz	152.7	123.9	0.552	**28.8**
13	Tom Seaver	202.1	174.2	0.537	**27.9**
14	Curt Schilling	146.4	118.6	0.552	**27.7**
15	Don Sutton	222.0	194.6	0.533	**27.4**
16	Mariano Rivera	61.0	33.7	0.644	**27.3**
17	Roy Halladay	120.5	94.5	0.560	**26.0**
18	Bob Gibson	169.4	144.6	0.539	**24.8**
19	*Dutch Leonard*	*131.9*	*107.6*	*0.551*	**24.3**
20	Tim Hudson	132.9	108.6	0.550	**24.3**
21	Bret Saberhagen	108.6	85.2	0.560	**23.3**
22	Jim Palmer	168.1	144.8	0.537	**23.3**
23	Juan Marichal	150.2	127.1	0.542	**23.1**
24	Hoyt Wilhelm	99.8	76.8	0.565	**23.0**
25	*Bob Feller*	*168.6*	*145.7*	*0.536*	**22.8**

Component 5: Hits vs. Outs

In the fifth step of calculating Player Wins and Losses, batters, pitchers, and fielders are given credit and blame for balls in play becoming hits or outs.

Calculation of Component 5 Player Decisions

Credits and debits for whether balls in play become hits or outs are assigned in Component 5. The average value of the ball in play, based on the location and hit type of the ball, was assigned to batters and pitchers in Component 4. Component 5 player wins and losses are calculated based on an average result of the play, given that it is either a hit or an out. For hits, debits and credits based on the type of hit—single, double, or triple—are assigned in Component 6. Credits for double plays, baserunner outs, and baserunner advancements are assigned in Components 7, 8, and 9, respectively. For fielders, Component 5 player decisions are the portion of pW-L records that are most comparable to other play-by-play measures of fielding, such as UZR, PMR, +/-, and TotalZone.

Division of Component 5 Game Points Between Pitchers and Fielders

Component 5 Player decisions are shared between pitchers and fielders based on the extent to which player winning percentages persist across different sample periods. The mathematics underlying this division was described earlier in this chapter.

Persistence equations were fit for Component 5 player decisions for pitchers and fielders as described earlier in this chapter. Separate equations were estimated for each fielding position. Separate equations were estimated for each season as described earlier in this chapter.

The average division of Component 5 player decisions by fielding position, across all seasons for which I have calculated pW-L records, are as follows.

Component 5	Pitcher	Fielder
Catcher	33.8%	66.2%
First Baseman	35.2%	64.8%
Second Baseman	30.8%	69.2%
Third Baseman	27.1%	72.9%
Shortstop	27.4%	72.6%
Left Fielder	36.8%	63.2%
Center Fielder	30.5%	69.5%
Right Fielder	34.2%	65.8%
Total	**31.4%**	**68.6%**

Overall, pitchers earn about 34.0% of defensive Component 5 Player decisions, including 3.8% of Component 5 player decisions which are compiled on balls-in-play that are fielded by the pitcher. Excluding pitchers and catchers, infielders are allocated about 69.7% of Component 5 Player decisions involving them, while outfielders are allocated 65.0% of relevant Component 5 Player decisions.

Component 5 Player Decisions by Fielding Position

The breakdown of Component 5 Player decisions by fielding position is as follows:

Position	1930–2015	Since 2003
Pitcher	5.5%	4.9%
Catcher	1.0%	0.9%
First Base	7.1%	7.8%
Second Base	15.4%	15.4%
Third Base	15.3%	16.0%
Shortstop	17.6%	16.6%
Left Field	12.6%	12.3%
Center Field	12.7%	13.1%
Right Field	12.9%	13.0%

For older years (typically, pre–1974), there is less information on the first fielder to field hits and, in some cases, there is even uncertainty on the fielder(s) involved in some outs on balls-in-play. These will lead to less reliable fielding records in general, although it is not clear to me that this would affect the distribution of fielding plays for those plays which can be identified.

Excluding pitchers and catchers, the numbers look like this:

Position	1930–2015	Since 2003
First Base	7.6%	8.2%
Second Base	16.5%	16.4%

Position	1930–2015	Since 2003
Third Base	16.3%	17.0%
Shortstop	18.8%	17.6%
Left Field	13.5%	13.1%
Center Field	13.5%	13.9%
Right Field	13.8%	13.8%

The top 25 players in net Component 5 wins (wins minus losses) are presented in the next eleven tables: batters, pitchers, and each of the nine fielding positions (including pitchers).

Component 5: Batting Wins
Top 25 Players (Sorted by Net Wins)

		Wins	Losses	Win Pct	Net Wins
1	Roberto Clemente	87.3	63.2	0.580	24.1
2	Rod Carew	90.0	68.8	0.567	21.2
3	Lou Brock	87.3	66.4	0.568	20.9
4	*Stan Musial*	*94.7*	*75.7*	*0.556*	*19.0*
5	Derek Jeter	99.2	81.3	0.549	17.8
6	Willie McGee	70.8	54.1	0.567	16.6
7	Tony Gwynn	91.1	74.8	0.549	16.3
8	Willie Mays	78.2	62.6	0.555	15.5
9	Kirby Puckett	65.5	50.1	0.567	15.4
10	Ichiro Suzuki	88.1	73.3	0.546	14.8
11	Vada Pinson	80.5	65.9	0.550	14.6
12	*Enos Slaughter*	*70.9*	*56.8*	*0.555*	*14.1*
13	Mickey Rivers	52.0	38.4	0.575	13.6
14	Paul Molitor	93.9	80.7	0.538	13.2
15	Willie Wilson	66.2	54.0	0.551	12.3
16	Jose Cruz, Sr.	64.8	52.9	0.551	11.9
17	Larry Walker	54.5	42.8	0.561	11.8
18	Ken Griffey, Sr.	60.8	49.1	0.553	11.7
19	Matty Alou	54.1	42.4	0.561	11.7
20	Richie Ashburn	76.3	64.7	0.541	11.6
21	*Joe Medwick*	*69.6*	*58.0*	*0.545*	*11.5*
22	Andres Galarraga	59.6	48.3	0.553	11.3
23	*Ted Williams*	*62.2*	*51.0*	*0.549*	*11.2*
24	Craig Biggio	87.9	77.3	0.532	10.6
25	Brett Butler	72.9	62.4	0.539	10.6

Component 5: Pitching Wins
Top 25 Players (Sorted by Net Wins)

		Wins	Losses	Win Pct	Net Wins
1	Tom Seaver	38.1	34.3	0.526	3.8
2	Don Sutton	43.3	39.8	0.521	3.5
3	Catfish Hunter	28.8	25.6	0.529	3.2
4	*Warren Spahn*	*43.2*	*40.0*	*0.519*	*3.2*
5	Charlie Hough	30.7	27.6	0.527	3.2
6	Robin Roberts	41.1	38.0	0.520	3.1
7	*Ted Lyons*	*31.1*	*28.2*	*0.524*	*2.9*
8	Don Newcombe	18.7	16.1	0.538	2.6
9	*Lon Warneke*	*26.5*	*24.1*	*0.524*	*2.4*
10	Bob Buhl	22.7	20.4	0.527	2.3
11	Dave Stieb	24.1	21.8	0.525	2.3
12	Sid Fernandez	13.8	11.5	0.545	2.3
13	Fergie Jenkins	37.0	34.8	0.516	2.2
14	Roger Clemens	35.9	33.7	0.516	2.2
15	Ralph Terry	16.8	14.7	0.533	2.1
16	Whitey Ford	26.3	24.2	0.521	2.1

		Wins	Losses	Win Pct	Net Wins
17	Milt Pappas	27.9	25.8	0.519	2.1
18	Vida Blue	27.9	25.8	0.519	2.1
19	Bronson Arroyo	19.8	17.7	0.527	2.0
20	Jack Morris	31.6	29.5	0.517	2.0
21	Tom Glavine	37.3	35.3	0.514	2.0
22	Luis Tiant	27.6	25.6	0.519	2.0
23	Jim Palmer	30.5	28.5	0.517	2.0
24	*Ralph Branca*	*12.7*	*10.7*	*0.542*	**2.0**
25	Johnny Podres	19.8	17.9	0.526	2.0

Component 5: Fielder Wins, P
Top 25 Players (Sorted by Net Wins)

		Wins	Losses	Win Pct	Net Wins
1	Tom Glavine	5.6	3.2	0.633	2.3
2	Phil Niekro	6.1	3.8	0.615	2.3
3	Dennis Martinez	4.9	3.0	0.617	1.9
4	Greg Maddux	8.2	6.4	0.560	1.8
5	Kenny Rogers	5.0	3.3	0.603	1.7
6	Tom Seaver	5.1	3.4	0.599	1.7
7	Dave Stieb	3.4	1.9	0.647	1.5
8	Kirk Rueter	2.9	1.4	0.669	1.5
9	*Lon Warneke*	*3.9*	*2.4*	*0.615*	**1.5**
10	Zack Greinke	2.4	1.0	0.712	1.4
11	Stu Miller	2.8	1.4	0.671	1.4
12	*Harry Gumbert*	*4.5*	*3.2*	*0.589*	**1.4**
13	Mike Marshall	2.7	1.4	0.666	1.3
14	Javier Vazquez	3.1	1.8	0.636	1.3
15	Mike Mussina	3.5	2.1	0.619	1.3
16	Jamie Moyer	4.1	2.8	0.596	1.3
17	*Freddie Fitzsimmons*	*4.8*	*3.5*	*0.579*	**1.3**
18	Paul Splittorff	3.1	1.8	0.632	1.3
19	Bobby Shantz	3.2	2.0	0.621	1.2
20	Randy Jones	3.2	2.0	0.619	1.2
21	Livan Hernandez	4.0	2.8	0.589	1.2
22	*Hal Schumacher*	*4.4*	*3.2*	*0.579*	**1.2**
23	Jim Palmer	3.9	2.8	0.588	1.2
24	Bret Saberhagen	2.9	1.7	0.627	1.2
25	*Guy Bush*	*3.2*	*2.1*	*0.610*	**1.2**

Component 5: Fielder Wins, C
Top 25 Players (Sorted by Net Wins)

		Wins	Losses	Win Pct	Net Wins
1	*Bill Dickey*	*3.6*	*2.8*	*0.566*	**0.8**
2	Brad Ausmus	2.7	1.9	0.591	0.8
3	Johnny Bench	3.0	2.2	0.574	0.8
4	*Rick Ferrell*	*4.4*	*3.7*	*0.546*	**0.7**
5	Bill Freehan	2.6	1.9	0.584	0.7
6	*Al Lopez*	*4.8*	*4.1*	*0.542*	**0.7**
7	*Jimmie Wilson*	*2.0*	*1.3*	*0.602*	**0.7**
8	Tom Haller	1.9	1.3	0.593	0.6
9	Jerry Grote	2.5	1.9	0.567	0.6
10	Carlton Fisk	3.2	2.7	0.546	0.5
11	*Ray Schalk*	*1.0*	*0.5*	*0.672*	**0.5**
12	*Mickey Cochrane*	*2.4*	*1.9*	*0.555*	**0.5**
13	Del Rice	2.8	2.4	0.545	0.5
14	Brian McCann	2.1	1.6	0.562	0.5
15	Ted Simmons	2.4	1.9	0.553	0.5
16	Rick Dempsey	2.4	1.9	0.553	0.5

		Wins	Losses	Win Pct	Net Wins
17	Johnny Edwards	2.5	2.1	0.548	**0.4**
18	Elston Howard	2.1	1.6	0.556	**0.4**
19	Brent Mayne	1.4	1.0	0.585	**0.4**
20	*Mike Tresh*	*2.7*	*2.3*	*0.540*	**0.4**
21	Jerry McNertney	0.9	0.5	0.642	**0.4**
22	Greg Myers	1.1	0.8	0.597	**0.4**
23	*Phil Masi*	*2.8*	*2.4*	*0.536*	**0.4**
24	Roy Campanella	2.6	2.2	0.538	**0.4**
25	Charlie Moore	1.3	0.9	0.581	**0.4**

Component 5: Fielder Wins, 1B
Top 25 Players (Sorted by Net Wins)

		Wins	Losses	Win Pct	Net Wins
1	John Olerud	26.2	22.5	0.538	**3.7**
2	Mark Grace	30.5	27.0	0.530	**3.5**
3	Albert Pujols	24.3	21.4	0.533	**3.0**
4	Mark Teixeira	23.7	21.0	0.531	**2.8**
5	Adrian Gonzalez	21.0	18.5	0.533	**2.6**
6	*Bill Terry*	*15.3*	*12.8*	*0.544*	**2.5**
7	Steve Garvey	22.6	20.2	0.528	**2.4**
8	Vic Power	13.6	11.3	0.547	**2.4**
9	Tino Martinez	22.7	20.4	0.526	**2.3**
10	*Frank McCormick*	*17.1*	*15.0*	*0.532*	**2.1**
11	Todd Helton	28.8	26.8	0.518	**2.0**
12	Gil Hodges	19.2	17.3	0.527	**2.0**
13	Will Clark	26.2	24.3	0.519	**2.0**
14	*George McQuinn*	*18.8*	*16.9*	*0.527*	**1.9**
15	Keith Hernandez	25.2	23.3	0.520	**1.9**
16	Kevin Youkilis	7.4	5.5	0.572	**1.8**
17	Mark McGwire	21.6	19.7	0.522	**1.8**
18	Sid Bream	11.7	9.9	0.541	**1.8**
19	Wes Parker	10.9	9.1	0.544	**1.7**
20	Pete O'Brien	16.7	15.1	0.525	**1.6**
21	Derrek Lee	23.2	21.8	0.516	**1.5**
22	Justin Morneau	16.9	15.5	0.522	**1.4**
23	Kevin Young	12.5	11.1	0.531	**1.4**
24	Jeff King	6.9	5.5	0.557	**1.4**
25	George Scott	22.0	20.6	0.516	**1.3**

Component 5: Fielder Wins, 2B
Top 25 Players (Sorted by Net Wins)

		Wins	Losses	Win Pct	Net Wins
1	Nellie Fox	58.5	52.3	0.528	**6.2**
2	Lou Whitaker	57.8	52.3	0.525	**5.4**
3	Mark Ellis	36.2	31.2	0.537	**5.0**
4	Ryne Sandberg	57.4	52.5	0.522	**4.9**
5	Frank White	54.0	49.4	0.522	**4.6**
6	Dustin Pedroia	32.0	27.8	0.535	**4.2**
7	*Hughie Critz*	*29.6*	*25.8*	*0.534*	**3.8**
8	Chase Utley	39.6	35.9	0.524	**3.7**
9	Orlando Hudson	36.2	32.8	0.525	**3.4**
10	*Lonny Frey*	*27.5*	*24.3*	*0.531*	**3.2**
11	Rennie Stennett	27.4	24.5	0.528	**3.0**
12	Craig Counsell	14.1	11.4	0.552	**2.6**
13	Adam Kennedy	33.6	31.0	0.520	**2.6**
14	Pokey Reese	13.2	10.6	0.554	**2.6**
15	Ian Kinsler	37.5	35.0	0.518	**2.6**
16	Glenn Hubbard	37.5	34.9	0.518	**2.5**

		Wins	Losses	Win Pct	Net Wins
17	Joe Gordon	40.4	38.0	0.516	2.5
18	Placido Polanco	25.3	23.0	0.524	2.4
19	Jackie Robinson	17.4	15.1	0.536	2.3
20	Julio Cruz	29.0	26.8	0.520	2.2
21	Jose Oquendo	16.2	14.0	0.537	2.2
22	Mark Lemke	23.1	20.9	0.525	2.2
23	*Max Bishop*	*21.1*	*18.9*	*0.527*	2.2
24	Jim Gilliam	23.3	21.2	0.524	2.1
25	Bobby Grich	44.1	42.0	0.512	2.1

Component 5: Fielder Wins, 3B
Top 25 Players (Sorted by Net Wins)

		Wins	Losses	Win Pct	Net Wins
1	Brooks Robinson	71.9	59.2	0.548	12.7
2	Buddy Bell	58.1	51.2	0.531	6.8
3	Scott Rolen	55.2	48.6	0.532	6.7
4	Adrian Beltre	65.8	59.2	0.526	6.6
5	Terry Pendleton	55.1	48.6	0.531	6.5
6	Tim Wallach	55.6	49.2	0.531	6.5
7	Mike Schmidt	60.6	54.3	0.528	6.4
8	Robin Ventura	49.7	43.5	0.533	6.2
9	Evan Longoria	28.8	23.5	0.551	5.4
10	Matt Williams	47.5	42.1	0.530	5.4
11	Aurelio Rodriguez	47.1	42.2	0.527	4.9
12	*George Kell*	*39.6*	*35.0*	*0.531*	4.6
13	Eric Chavez	36.4	31.8	0.534	4.6
14	*Ken Keltner*	*38.8*	*34.2*	*0.531*	4.6
15	Brandon Inge	32.2	27.9	0.536	4.4
16	Vinny Castilla	44.3	40.1	0.525	4.3
17	Gary Gaetti	60.4	56.1	0.518	4.2
18	Clete Boyer	37.8	34.1	0.526	3.7
19	Jeff Cirillo	34.1	30.4	0.529	3.7
20	Don Wert	23.5	19.9	0.542	3.7
21	Jim Davenport	21.0	17.7	0.543	3.4
22	Mike Lowell	36.8	33.5	0.524	3.4
23	*Red Rolfe*	*26.8*	*23.7*	*0.530*	3.1
24	Juan Uribe	15.2	12.3	0.553	2.9
25	Pedro Feliz	24.6	21.7	0.531	2.9

Component 5: Fielder Wins, SS
Top 25 Players (Sorted by Net Wins)

		Wins	Losses	Win Pct	Net Wins
1	Ozzie Smith	83.1	73.5	0.531	9.7
2	Mark Belanger	53.5	45.3	0.541	8.2
3	Pee Wee Reese	60.7	52.9	0.534	7.7
4	*Lou Boudreau*	*48.6*	*40.9*	*0.543*	7.7
5	Omar Vizquel	74.7	68.7	0.521	6.1
6	Cal Ripken	68.4	62.5	0.522	5.9
7	Ozzie Guillen	53.3	48.0	0.526	5.3
8	*Eddie Miller*	*47.9*	*43.3*	*0.525*	4.6
9	Garry Templeton	59.7	55.5	0.518	4.2
10	Bud Harrelson	38.4	34.4	0.528	4.0
11	Bill Russell	52.2	48.2	0.520	4.0
12	Rey Sanchez	27.0	23.0	0.539	3.9
13	Alan Trammell	59.0	55.2	0.517	3.8
14	Luis Aparicio	77.8	74.0	0.512	3.8
15	Larry Bowa	64.9	61.2	0.514	3.7
16	Roy McMillan	58.9	55.3	0.516	3.6

		Wins	Losses	Win Pct	Net Wins
17	*Marty Marion*	*50.1*	*46.7*	*0.518*	**3.4**
18	Ed Brinkman	52.4	49.0	0.517	**3.4**
19	Ernie Banks	33.5	30.2	0.527	**3.4**
20	Maury Wills	46.5	43.3	0.518	**3.2**
21	Adam Everett	22.5	19.5	0.536	**3.0**
22	J.J. Hardy	38.3	35.3	0.520	**3.0**
23	Jack Wilson	37.8	34.9	0.520	**2.9**
24	Greg Gagne	48.1	45.3	0.515	**2.8**
25	Bucky Dent	39.9	37.1	0.518	**2.8**

Component 5: Fielder Wins, LF
Top 25 Players (Sorted by Net Wins)

		Wins	Losses	Win Pct	Net Wins
1	Roy White	37.0	30.2	0.551	**6.9**
2	Barry Bonds	58.1	52.3	0.526	**5.8**
3	Willie Wilson	19.5	14.3	0.578	**5.2**
4	Rickey Henderson	52.2	47.1	0.526	**5.1**
5	Carl Crawford	35.7	31.2	0.534	**4.5**
6	Joe Rudi	25.7	21.3	0.546	**4.3**
7	Johnny Damon	14.8	11.3	0.566	**3.5**
8	Geoff Jenkins	19.8	16.6	0.545	**3.3**
9	Gary Ward	20.8	17.9	0.539	**3.0**
10	Charlie Maxwell	18.1	15.5	0.539	**2.6**
11	*Al Simmons*	*25.0*	*22.6*	*0.525*	***2.4***
12	Bernard Gilkey	20.5	18.1	0.531	**2.4**
13	Luis Gonzalez	47.5	45.2	0.513	**2.3**
14	Ron Gant	23.3	21.0	0.526	**2.3**
15	Brett Gardner	11.0	8.9	0.554	**2.1**
16	Alex Gordon	18.5	16.6	0.528	**1.9**
17	Darin Erstad	7.0	5.1	0.580	**1.9**
18	*Charlie Keller*	*19.1*	*17.2*	*0.527*	***1.9***
19	B.J. Surhoff	18.1	16.3	0.527	**1.8**
20	George Foster	31.9	30.1	0.515	**1.8**
21	*Ethan Allen*	*6.7*	*5.0*	*0.573*	***1.7***
22	Sandy Amoros	6.6	4.9	0.574	**1.7**
23	Tony Gonzalez	8.8	7.2	0.552	**1.7**
24	*Bibb Falk*	*11.8*	*10.2*	*0.538*	***1.7***
25	Coco Crisp	6.5	4.8	0.572	**1.6**

Component 5: Fielder Wins, CF
Top 25 Players (Sorted by Net Wins)

		Wins	Losses	Win Pct	Net Wins
1	Amos Otis	43.3	35.1	0.553	**8.2**
2	Duke Snider	31.2	23.3	0.572	**7.9**
3	Willie Davis	46.1	38.4	0.545	**7.7**
4	Curt Flood	34.9	29.5	0.542	**5.4**
5	Andruw Jones	40.7	35.5	0.534	**5.1**
6	Mike Cameron	41.2	36.9	0.527	**4.2**
7	Gary Pettis	23.6	20.2	0.538	**3.4**
8	*Mike Kreevich*	*27.0*	*23.7*	*0.533*	***3.3***
9	Franklin Gutierrez	11.5	8.4	0.577	**3.1**
10	Mickey Mantle	34.8	31.7	0.523	**3.1**
11	*Lloyd Waner*	*34.2*	*31.2*	*0.523*	***3.1***
12	Lenny Dykstra	25.4	22.6	0.530	**2.9**
13	Lance Johnson	27.7	25.2	0.524	**2.5**
14	Jim Piersall	25.0	22.4	0.527	**2.5**
15	Carlos Beltran	35.6	33.1	0.518	**2.5**
16	Darin Erstad	13.1	10.6	0.552	**2.5**

		Wins	Losses	Win Pct	Net Wins
17	Devon White	34.4	32.0	0.518	2.4
18	Billy North	21.7	19.2	0.530	2.4
19	B.J. Upton	24.3	21.9	0.526	2.4
20	Darrin Jackson	10.0	7.8	0.562	2.2
21	Coco Crisp	23.7	21.5	0.524	2.2
22	Dave Henderson	23.3	21.1	0.524	2.2
23	Jim Edmonds	37.4	35.2	0.515	2.2
24	Carl Furillo	6.9	4.8	0.589	2.1
25	*Vince DiMaggio*	*25.8*	*23.8*	*0.520*	*2.0*

Component 5: Fielder Wins, RF
Top 25 Players (Sorted by Net Wins)

		Wins	Losses	Win Pct	Net Wins
1	Carl Furillo	32.9	24.0	0.578	8.9
2	Ichiro Suzuki	44.6	35.8	0.554	8.7
3	Brian Jordan	22.6	17.3	0.567	5.3
4	Al Kaline	40.9	36.1	0.531	4.8
5	Tony Oliva	25.6	20.9	0.550	4.7
6	*Mel Ott*	*45.1*	*40.5*	*0.527*	*4.6*
7	Roger Maris	23.8	19.9	0.545	3.9
8	Johnny Callison	35.9	32.0	0.529	3.9
9	Sammy Sosa	47.0	43.1	0.522	3.9
10	Jay Bruce	25.8	22.3	0.536	3.5
11	Austin Kearns	19.9	16.6	0.546	3.3
12	Alexis Rios	28.7	25.4	0.531	3.3
13	*Gene Moore*	*21.3*	*18.0*	*0.542*	*3.3*
14	*Wally Moses*	*40.1*	*36.9*	*0.521*	*3.2*
15	Paul O'Neill	37.8	34.8	0.521	3.0
16	Jesse Barfield	30.0	27.0	0.526	3.0
17	Reggie Sanders	25.5	22.6	0.530	2.9
18	Josh Reddick	13.3	10.5	0.560	2.9
19	*Paul Waner*	*49.0*	*46.6*	*0.512*	*2.4*
20	*Carl Reynolds*	*11.6*	*9.2*	*0.557*	*2.4*
21	Tony Armas	13.9	11.7	0.543	2.2
22	Giancarlo Stanton	17.7	15.6	0.532	2.2
23	Tony Gwynn	42.3	40.3	0.512	2.1
24	*Kiki Cuyler*	*15.6*	*13.6*	*0.535*	*2.1*
25	*Sam Rice*	*15.4*	*13.3*	*0.535*	*2.0*

The next section takes a brief sidebar to look more closely at my use of location data in calculating pW-L records.

USE OF LOCATION DATA IN CALCULATING pW-L RECORDS

For balls in play, there are three pieces of information that are potentially useful in determining the value of a particular play and to whom that value should be credited (or debited): (i) the first fielder to make a play on the ball, (ii) the type of hit (bunt, ground ball, fly ball, line drive), and (iii) the location of the ball. The extent to which these three pieces of information are available in Retrosheet play-by-play data varies considerably through the years.

(i) First Fielder

The first fielder to touch the ball is the most important consideration for determining credit. The first fielder to touch the ball is identified for virtually all plays for the last 30 years of Retrosheet data. For earlier years, the first fielder to touch base hits is frequently unknown. As data goes back even further, there are even some outs for which the fielder of record is unknown.

For my work, the identity of the first fielder is used for assigning credit whenever this information is available. When this information is not available, credit is allocated across all fielders in the proportion to which fielders get credit across similar plays for which the fielder is known.

(ii) Hit Type

The second level of detail on balls in play is the type of hit: bunt, ground ball, fly ball (or pop up), line drive. This information is available from Retrosheet for all balls in play for the years 1989–1999 and for seasons since 2003. For other years, hit types are generally only available on outs-in-play, not hits.

As with first-fielder information, hit-type information is used in calculating pW-L records whenever this information is available. When this information is not available, credit is allocated based on the expected distribution of hit type based on the final play result.

(iii) Location

For the years 1989–1999, the location of all balls-in-play are identified in Retrosheet's play-by-play data. I do not use this location data directly in calculating pW-L records, however. Instead, I use location data for these seasons to calculate expected *ex ante* probabilities for ball-in-play events. That is, based on 1989–1999 location data, I calculate what the probability of an out would have been on a play that ended up as, say, a line drive double to the left fielder. The calculation of these *ex ante* probabilities was described earlier in this chapter.

After a great deal of research and consideration, I decided to use location data only in this indirect way even for those seasons for which Retrosheet provides location data (i.e., 1989–1999). I made this decision for several reasons. For one thing, using location data only indirectly leads to a more consistent methodology across all seasons for which I estimate pW-L records. But also, it was not clear to me, in looking at results from those years for which location data are available, that the location data actually improved the results.

Location data is fundamentally subjective, by its very nature. Relying on individual pieces of subjective data will inevitably introduce errors and possible biases into the valuation of these individual plays. Relying on location data only indirectly, however, and by relying on all of the location data—11 years' worth—in assessing every play, should allow these individual errors to balance out and offset in such a way as to vastly reduce any potential biases or errors.

Consider, for example, an article at the website, Hardballtimes.com, titled "Ghosts in the Outfield," which looked at the impact of using STATS data versus BIS data for calculating UZR fielding statistics. This article found that simply changing the data source leads to wildly different stories about some players' defense: was Andruw Jones the best fielder in baseball from 2003 to 2008 (+112 runs in UZR using BIS data) or a slightly below-average center fielder (–5 using STATS)? If the results are that unstable across different location measurements of the same plays, then it's hard to see exactly how much information location data is bringing to the party at all. I discuss this specific article in more detail in Chapter 7 where I compare my fielding won-lost records to alternate fielding measures, UZR, DRA, and DRS.

Beyond the question of whether the actual locations being reported are accurate, however, another issue with using location data is that I think that relying too heavily on location data builds on a fundamental assumption that I am not entirely sure is true. This is that balls hit to the same location are more similar than balls that end up with the same end result. That is, a fielding system based on location data treats two fly balls to medium right-center field as equivalent—implicitly assuming that all fly balls to medium right-center field are created equally. My fielding system here treats two fly-ball doubles fielded by the right fielder as equivalent—implicitly assuming that all fly-ball doubles fielded by the right fielder are equivalent.

I am not saying the latter of these implicit assumptions is necessarily right, so much as I wonder whether the former implicit assumption is actually more right. And if our focus is purely on player value rather than player talent (as it is in my system), then, in fact, in many ways it makes more sense to me to view one fly-ball double to right field as being equal in value to any other fly-ball double to right field than to view a fly-ball double to medium right-center field as being equal in value to a fly out to the same location.

The Impact of Location Data on My Fielding System

The problem with evaluating fielding systems, in general, is that we do not really know what the "right" answer is—after all, if we knew the right answer, we would just use that.

One thing that I can compare, however, is how my results compare to what they would have been had I used location data for those years for which it is available, 1989–1999. For those seasons, I calculated pW-L records both ways. I then calculated a weighted correlation of winning percentages by fielding position between the two methods. I calculated correlations two ways: for overall (context-neutral, teammate-adjusted) fielding win percentage and for Component 5 win percentage, which is based purely on whether a ball in play becomes a hit or an out and corresponds most directly to other location-based fielding systems. The results were as follows:

**Weighted Correlation, Fielding Winning Percentages:
Location Data v. No Location Data**

	Total	*Component 5*
Pitcher	82.6%	82.1%
Catcher	75.6%	72.7%
First Base	86.1%	84.2%
Second Base	77.1%	71.5%
Third Base	89.8%	89.0%
Shortstop	80.1%	75.5%
Left Field	92.7%	89.0%
Center Field	88.7%	83.5%
Right Field	93.2%	88.6%

Note: Catcher figures exclude SB, WP; Totals calculated using the same pitcher-fielder splits for both sets of numbers.

These correlations are extremely high, which is quite encouraging.

It occurs to me that one way in which fielding records based on location data (e.g., fly balls to medium right field) can be compared to fielding records based on event data (e.g., fly-ball doubles fielded by the right fielder) is by comparing the extent to which player win percentages persist.

As I explained earlier in this chapter, I divide credit on balls in play between pitchers and fielders based on "persistence equations" which measure the extent to which player winning percentages on even-numbered plays can be explained as a function of player winning percentage on odd-numbered plays within the same season: i.e.,

$$\text{WinPct}_{Even} = 0.500 + b \cdot (\text{WinPct}_{Odd} - 0.500)$$

The coefficient b in the Persistence Equation measures the persistence of fielding winning percentage between the two samples (even plays v. odd plays). Broadly speaking, a higher value of b in a persistence equation suggests that more of a real skill is being measured. Hence, if the values of b in persistence equations based on location data were consistently higher than the values of b in persistence equations based on event data, this could suggest that location-based data were capturing more fielding skill than event-based data.

The next three tables, then, compares the values of b from persistence equations for Components 5, 6, and 7, for both pitchers and fielders based on location-based and event-based data.

Persistence Coefficients, Location Data v. No Location Data
Component 5

	Pitcher		Fielder	
	Location	Event	Location	Event
Catcher	22.9%	23.8%	33.1%	6.4%
First Base	9.4%	8.7%	46.6%	42.9%
Second Base	9.3%	14.0%	41.4%	28.7%
Third Base	3.6%	5.9%	35.4%	41.1%
Shortstop	19.0%	12.0%	49.0%	31.6%
Left Field	14.5%	16.2%	37.9%	38.9%
Center Field	3.2%	12.2%	37.2%	39.5%
Right Field	15.9%	18.6%	39.2%	36.8%

Persistence Coefficients, Location Data v. No Location Data
Component 6

	Pitcher		Fielder	
	Location	Event	Location	Event
Catcher	72.1%	−2.9%	25.2%	9.6%
First Base	19.3%	−18.7%	20.8%	19.0%
Second Base	67.0%	80.4%	34.9%	62.7%
Third Base	73.8%	38.7%	23.2%	14.8%
Shortstop	90.4%	90.4%	34.8%	24.4%
Left Field	4.4%	−0.1%	40.4%	24.0%
Center Field	9.9%	11.6%	16.9%	23.3%
Right Field	12.8%	11.0%	36.9%	25.1%

Persistence Coefficients, Location Data v. No Location Data
Component 7

	Pitcher		Fielder	
	Location	Event	Location	Event
Catcher	7.1%	16.1%	7.9%	14.2%
First Base	72.6%	71.0%	34.0%	34.3%

	Pitcher		Fielder	
	Location	Event	Location	Event
Second Base	7.6%	7.8%	29.1%	29.5%
Third Base	91.2%	88.3%	36.2%	33.4%
Shortstop	−2.9%	−2.2%	16.6%	15.4%

There are a lot of numbers there. Let me try to walk through some of the numbers to give an idea of what they are saying. I will then provide some summary data.

Let's start with catchers. For Component 5, which measures whether a ball-in-play is converted into an out or a hit, on plays made by the catcher, the persistence in pitcher win percentages is very similar for location-based data (22.9%) versus event-based data (23.8%). For fielders (i.e., catchers), however, the persistence is much stronger using location-based data (33.1%) than for event-based data (6.4%). This is clearly a vote in support of the superiority of location-based data.

Plays made by the third baseman, on the other hand, suggest that event-based data is superior, with somewhat greater persistence coefficients for both pitchers (5.9% vs. 3.6% using location-based data) and fielders (41.1% vs. 35.4%).

The next table combines the results across fielders. The numbers here are weighted averages, with the total share of fielding decisions by component used for weights (these weights differ slightly between location-based and event-based records; the numbers used here are the average of the two).

Component 5

	Pitcher		Fielder	
	Location	Event	Location	Event
All Positions	*10.9%*	*12.4%*	*40.9%*	*36.1%*
Location—Event	−1.5%		4.9%	

Component 6

	Pitcher		Fielder	
	Location	Event	Location	Event
All Positions	*11.8%*	*8.2%*	*33.2%*	*24.0%*
Location—Event	3.6%		9.2%	

Component 7

	Pitcher		Fielder	
	Location	Event	Location	Event
All Positions	*8.1%*	*8.6%*	*23.9%*	*23.6%*
Location—Event	−0.4%		0.3%	

So, on average, location data do not seem to provide any additional information in evaluating Component 5 performance for pitchers. This makes sense to me. Pitchers have some control over what happens to balls in play, but at a much more generalized level of detail—e.g., fly balls vs. ground balls, perhaps how hard a ball is hit—than by location. That is, I am skeptical that a pitcher can control whether a ground ball is hit in the 56 hole or more directly in the 6 hole. Hence, it makes sense to me that focusing on events rather than locations provides somewhat more information than focusing on location (although the difference here, 1.5%, is not really enough to favor either of these two over the other with any degree of certainty).

In contrast, location-based data does appear to provide some additional information in evaluating Component 5 performance for fielders, although the difference between the two persistence coefficients, on average, is relatively small (less than 5%).

For Component 6–whether hits are converted into singles, doubles, or triples—location data seems to provide more persistent measures for both pitchers and fielders. This makes sense as, for example, the depths of fly ball hits likely makes a big difference as to how many bases they go for. Still, the differences here are not enormous (less than 10% for both pitchers and fielders). For Component 7–whether ground ball outs are converted into double plays—on the other hand, location data appears to add essentially no value.

Overall, the results seem generally supportive of the idea that calculating fielding records based on events rather than locations is probably not much, if any, worse than location-based fielding records. Ultimately, the proof of the pudding is in the eating. I look at fielding pW-L records in detail in Chapter 7. I compare my fielding records to alternate fielding systems (including UZR) at the end of that chapter.

Component 6: Singles vs. Doubles vs. Triples

In the sixth step of calculating Player Wins and Losses, batters, pitchers, and fielders are given credit and blame for the number of bases gained on hits on balls-in-play, i.e., singles versus doubles versus triples.

Calculation of Component 6 Player Decisions

Given that the batter reached base safely on a ball-in-play (via either hit or error), credits and debits are assigned in Component 6 for how many bases the batter gains. Basically, Component 6 credits batters for hitting doubles and triples as opposed to singles. Component 6 decisions are allocated assuming average baserunner advancement. Credits for baserunner outs and advancements are assigned in Components 8 and 9. Overall, Component 6 accounts for approximately 3.5% of total Player decisions across all seasons for which I have calculated pW-L records. This has declined slightly, to 3.2% since 2000.

Component 6 Player decisions are shared between pitchers and fielders based on the extent to which player winning percentages persist across different sample periods. The mathematics underlying this division was described earlier in this chapter.

Persistence equations were fit for Component 6 player decisions for pitchers and fielders as described earlier in this chapter. Separate equations were estimated for each fielding position. Separate equations were estimated for each season as described earlier in this chapter.

The average division of Component 6 player decisions by fielding position, across all seasons for which I have calculated pW-L records, are as follows.

Component 6	Pitcher	Fielder
Catcher	100.0%	0.0%
First Baseman	0.0%	100.0%
Second Baseman	54.7%	45.3%
Third Baseman	53.8%	46.2%
Shortstop	75.5%	24.5%
Left Fielder	15.4%	84.6%
Center Fielder	26.4%	73.6%
Right Fielder	30.5%	69.5%
Total	**25.9%**	**74.1%**

Left fielders receive the largest percentage of Component 6 credit of any fielder (outside of first basemen): 84.6%.

This reflects two things, I believe. First, most extra-base hits are to the outfield, which is reflected in outfielders receiving more credit in general than infielders, and, specific to left-fielders, the range in fielding talent is probably greatest (at least among the outfield positions) at left field, where many teams try to hide some of their worst fielders (Frank Howard, Kevin Reimer, Manny Ramirez) while other teams put players who are very fast if nothing else (Lou Brock, Rickey Henderson, Carl Crawford), which likely helps to cut off would-be extra-base hits to the gaps.

FURTHER THOUGHTS ON COMPONENT 6 PLAYER DECISIONS

On offense, Component 6 is, of course, allocated to batters. This is obvious and, really, there is no other reasonable alternative. It is, however, open to debate whether the ability to stretch singles into doubles and doubles into triples is properly viewed as "batting" as opposed to "baserunning." In general, I classify Component 6 as "batting" to be consistent with most other general batting measures, both traditional (e.g., total bases, slugging percentage) and sabermetric (e.g., runs created, batting wins), which distinguish between extra-base hits and singles. The extent to which Component 6 might be more reasonably viewed as a baserunning skill, however, is explored in Chapter 5.

Overall, Component 6 makes up about 14.9% of total fielding decisions for outfielders. In contrast, most defensive metrics focus exclusively on an outfielder's ability to convert balls-in-play to outs. Attention is also generally paid to outfielders' throwing arms and their ability to throw out baserunners and/or limit baserunner advancement (Components 8 and 9 of pW-L records). The ability of an outfielder to hold batters to singles, preventing extra-base hits, on the other hand, is a bit of a forgotten, but nevertheless important, defensive skill.

The top 25 players in net Component 6 wins (wins minus losses) are presented in the next five tables: batters, pitchers, and each of the three outfield positions (Component 6 is a sufficiently small share of infielder fielding that career leaders in infield Component 6 are not particularly meaningful).

Component 6: Batting Wins
Top 25 Players (Sorted by Net Wins)

		Wins	Losses	Win Pct	Net Wins
1	Stan Musial	15.6	10.6	0.596	5.0
2	George Brett	13.3	8.5	0.608	4.7
3	Roberto Clemente	12.8	9.2	0.581	3.6
4	Joe Medwick	10.9	7.4	0.595	3.5
5	Enos Slaughter	10.6	7.3	0.592	3.3
6	Dick Allen	7.5	4.4	0.632	3.1
7	Mickey Vernon	10.7	7.7	0.582	3.0
8	Vada Pinson	11.4	8.4	0.575	3.0
9	Jeff Heath	6.9	4.0	0.632	2.9
10	Juan Samuel	7.1	4.2	0.626	2.9
11	Willie Mays	12.0	9.2	0.566	2.8
12	Johnny Callison	7.7	4.9	0.611	2.8
13	Joe DiMaggio	8.7	5.9	0.595	2.8
14	Dolph Camilli	7.0	4.3	0.621	2.7
15	Arky Vaughan	9.3	6.6	0.584	2.7
16	Hal McRae	8.8	6.2	0.586	2.6

		Wins	Losses	Win Pct	Net Wins
17	Hank Greenberg	6.4	3.9	0.625	**2.6**
18	Carl Crawford	7.1	4.5	0.610	**2.6**
19	Babe Herman	6.0	3.4	0.634	**2.5**
20	Gus Suhr	6.9	4.4	0.611	**2.5**
21	Lou Brock	12.1	9.6	0.557	**2.5**
22	Barry Bonds	9.1	6.6	0.579	**2.5**
23	Dwight Evans	8.9	6.4	0.581	**2.5**
24	Larry Walker	7.1	4.7	0.601	**2.4**
25	Cesar Cedeno	8.5	6.2	0.581	**2.4**

Component 6: Pitching Wins
Top 25 Players (Sorted by Net Wins)

		Wins	Losses	Win Pct	Net Wins
1	Jerry Reuss	3.3	2.5	0.562	**0.7**
2	Greg Maddux	3.6	2.9	0.553	**0.7**
3	Juan Marichal	2.8	2.2	0.567	**0.7**
4	Kevin Brown	2.3	1.7	0.574	**0.6**
5	*Ted Lyons*	2.6	2.1	*0.558*	**0.5**
6	Tom Glavine	3.3	2.8	0.544	**0.5**
7	*Claude Passeau*	2.6	2.1	*0.555*	**0.5**
8	Mike Garcia	1.7	1.2	0.586	**0.5**
9	Claude Osteen	2.9	2.5	0.544	**0.5**
10	*Mel Harder*	2.8	2.4	*0.546*	**0.5**
11	*Warren Spahn*	4.0	3.5	*0.531*	**0.5**
12	Tommy John	4.0	3.6	0.530	**0.5**
13	*Hal Schumacher*	2.1	1.7	*0.559*	**0.4**
14	*Harry Gumbert*	1.9	1.5	*0.562*	**0.4**
15	Don Drysdale	2.6	2.1	0.545	**0.4**
16	Bob Gibson	2.9	2.5	0.539	**0.4**
17	Bob Friend	3.3	2.9	0.533	**0.4**
18	Phil Niekro	4.3	3.9	0.525	**0.4**
19	*Tommy Bridges*	2.1	1.7	*0.554*	**0.4**
20	*Hal Newhouser*	2.4	2.0	*0.545*	**0.4**
21	*Big Bill Lee*	2.5	2.1	*0.543*	**0.4**
22	*Cliff Melton*	1.2	0.8	*0.595*	**0.4**
23	*Spud Chandler*	1.2	0.8	*0.594*	**0.4**
24	Jim Abbott	1.2	0.9	0.587	**0.4**
25	Ned Garver	2.0	1.6	0.550	**0.4**

Component 6: Fielder Wins, LF
Top 25 Players (Sorted by Net Wins)

		Wins	Losses	Win Pct	Net Wins
1	Jo-Jo Moore	10.9	8.2	0.571	**2.7**
2	Dusty Baker	8.8	6.5	0.578	**2.4**
3	Minnie Minoso	12.4	10.5	0.540	**1.8**
4	Barry Bonds	17.6	15.8	0.527	**1.8**
5	Rickey Henderson	16.0	14.8	0.519	**1.2**
6	Garret Anderson	8.8	7.7	0.533	**1.1**
7	Jose Cruz, Sr.	10.3	9.2	0.527	**1.1**
8	Rocky Colavito	4.5	3.4	0.567	**1.1**
9	*Chet Laabs*	2.9	1.9	*0.607*	**1.0**
10	Joe Rudi	8.3	7.3	0.532	**1.0**
11	Willie Horton	9.2	8.2	0.528	**1.0**
12	B.J. Surhoff	5.4	4.5	0.545	**0.9**
13	Bernard Gilkey	6.4	5.6	0.532	**0.8**
14	Ben Oglivie	9.5	8.8	0.520	**0.7**
15	Tim Raines	12.7	12.0	0.514	**0.7**
16	Mike Felder	2.0	1.3	0.606	**0.7**

		Wins	Losses	Win Pct	Net Wins
17	Johnny Damon	3.8	3.2	0.545	0.6
18	*Sid Gordon*	*6.3*	*5.7*	*0.526*	*0.6*
19	Ralph Garr	7.1	6.5	0.523	0.6
20	Gene Stephens	2.6	2.0	0.567	0.6
21	Jeffrey Leonard	6.6	6.0	0.524	0.6
22	Geoff Jenkins	6.2	5.6	0.525	0.6
23	Roy White	12.2	11.6	0.512	0.6
24	*Ethan Allen*	*2.2*	*1.7*	*0.574*	*0.6*
25	Joe Orsulak	2.6	2.0	0.560	0.6

Component 6: Fielder Wins, CF
Top 25 Players (Sorted by Net Wins)

		Wins	Losses	Win Pct	Net Wins
1	Curt Flood	7.7	5.6	0.579	2.1
2	*Joe DiMaggio*	*9.1*	*7.2*	*0.557*	*1.9*
3	Bill Bruton	7.2	5.9	0.551	1.3
4	Carlos Beltran	6.6	5.3	0.556	1.3
5	Devon White	6.3	5.0	0.556	1.3
6	Willie Davis	8.8	7.7	0.536	1.2
7	Willie Mays	13.8	12.7	0.521	1.1
8	Larry Doby	6.4	5.3	0.544	1.0
9	Gorman Thomas	3.9	2.9	0.571	1.0
10	Mike Cameron	6.7	5.7	0.538	0.9
11	Ron LeFlore	4.0	3.1	0.561	0.9
12	Vic Davalillo	3.1	2.3	0.578	0.8
13	Ken Berry	4.2	3.3	0.556	0.8
14	Paul Blair	6.4	5.5	0.535	0.8
15	Cesar Cedeno	6.6	5.9	0.531	0.8
16	Mickey Stanley	4.4	3.7	0.546	0.7
17	Brett Butler	7.8	7.1	0.525	0.7
18	John Shelby	2.7	2.1	0.568	0.7
19	Lenny Green	2.7	2.1	0.564	0.6
20	Bake McBride	1.3	0.7	0.654	0.6
21	Andrew McCutchen	3.9	3.3	0.542	0.6
22	Grady Sizemore	3.2	2.7	0.549	0.6
23	Hal Jeffcoat	1.9	1.4	0.585	0.6
24	Al Bumbry	3.3	2.7	0.545	0.6
25	Rowland Office	2.5	1.9	0.562	0.6

Component 6: Fielder Wins, RF
Top 25 Players (Sorted by Net Wins)

		Wins	Losses	Win Pct	Net Wins
1	*Mel Ott*	*14.4*	*10.7*	*0.574*	*3.7*
2	Roberto Clemente	16.5	14.4	0.535	2.2
3	*Chuck Klein*	*10.4*	*8.5*	*0.549*	*1.9*
4	Tony Gwynn	11.8	10.3	0.534	1.5
5	Al Kaline	11.4	10.0	0.533	1.4
6	*Bill Nicholson*	*10.3*	*9.0*	*0.535*	*1.3*
7	Raul Mondesi	8.7	7.4	0.540	1.3
8	*Tommy Henrich*	*6.1*	*5.0*	*0.553*	*1.2*
9	Jackie Jensen	7.5	6.4	0.541	1.1
10	Reggie Sanders	6.3	5.2	0.545	1.0
11	*Pete Fox*	*8.2*	*7.2*	*0.532*	*1.0*
12	Ellis Valentine	5.1	4.1	0.553	1.0
13	Reggie Smith	6.0	5.1	0.543	1.0
14	Claudell Washington	6.9	5.9	0.536	0.9
15	Hank Bauer	6.0	5.1	0.541	0.9
16	*Bruce Campbell*	*9.2*	*8.3*	*0.526*	*0.9*

		Wins	Losses	Win Pct	Net Wins
17	Dwight Evans	12.9	12.0	0.518	**0.9**
18	Brian Jordan	5.2	4.3	0.547	**0.9**
19	Sixto Lezcano	7.2	6.3	0.532	**0.9**
20	Tony Armas	3.9	3.0	0.562	**0.9**
21	Dave Winfield	11.8	11.0	0.518	**0.8**
22	Andre Ethier	5.3	4.5	0.542	**0.8**
23	*Earl Webb*	*4.0*	*3.3*	*0.549*	**0.7**
24	Roger Maris	5.7	5.0	0.533	**0.7**
25	Jeremy Hermida	2.7	2.0	0.573	**0.7**

Component 7: Double Plays

In the seventh step of calculating Player Wins and Losses, batters, baserunners, pitchers, and fielders are given credit and blame for whether or not ground-ball outs become double plays in potential double-play situations.

Calculation of Component 7 Player Decisions

Component 7 comes into play when ground-ball outs are recorded in double-play situations—defined as a runner on first base and fewer than two outs. Offensive Component 7 games are split between the batter and the baserunner on first base. Defensive Component 7 games are split between pitchers and fielders. Fielding Component 7 games are split between the fielder who starts the initial play and the potential pivot man on the double play.

Division of Component 7 Decisions Between Pitchers and Fielders

Component 7 Player decisions are shared between batters and baserunners, and between pitchers and fielders based on the extent to which player winning percentages persist across different sample periods. The mathematics underlying this division were described earlier in this Chapter.

For Component 7, decisions allocated to fielders are split evenly between the fielder who starts the initial play and the pivot man. In the latter case (the pivot man), such a fielder only receives Component 7 credit or blame if he is involved in the play. That is, on a ground ball to the shortstop, if the baserunner on first is forced out, 6–4, then the second baseman would be considered the pivot man in this case and would share some Component 7 credit or blame based on whether he was able to complete the 6–4–3 double play. If, however, the shortstop simply threw directly to first for the 6–3 out, then all blame for failing to turn the double play in that case would fall on the shortstop.

Persistence equations were fit for Component 7 player decisions for pitchers and fielders as described earlier in this chapter. Separate equations were estimated for each fielding position. Separate equations were estimated for each season as described earlier in this chapter.

The average division of Component 7 player decisions by fielding position, across all seasons for which I have calculated pW-L records, are as follows.

Component 7	Pitcher	Fielder
Catcher	68.4%	31.6%
First Baseman	64.9%	35.1%
Second Baseman	35.6%	64.4%
Third Baseman	67.0%	33.0%
Shortstop	23.9%	76.1%
Total	**36.3%**	**63.7%**

Player decisions are credited significantly more heavily to middle infielders than to corner infielders and catchers. Component 7 accounts for 8.9% of fielding decisions by second basemen and shortstops.

Impact of the Baserunner on First Base on Double Play Ground Balls

Component 7 Player decisions are divided between pitchers and fielders based on the extent to which player winning percentages persist across different sample periods as described earlier in this chapter. A similar analysis was undertaken to see if the baserunner on first base had any apparent influence on Component 7. Persistence equations were estimated for batters and baserunners.

The results were as follows.

Persistence of Component 7 Winning Percentage

Batters: n = 36,998
$WinPct_{Even}$ = (20.65%) • $WinPct_{Odd}$ + (79.35%) • 0.5000
(39.51)

Baserunners: n = 34,179
$WinPct_{Even}$ = (4.97%) • $WinPct_{Odd}$ + (95.03%) • 0.5000
(9.384)

The persistence coefficient is much stronger for batters (20.6%) than for baserunners (5.0%). Nevertheless, the persistence coefficient in the baserunner equation is significant with a t-statistic greater than 2. Based on this, I divide offensive credit and blame for Component 7 decisions between batters and baserunners. Batters are given 80.6% of the credit here, which is equal to the batter persistence coefficient, 20.6%, divided by the sum of the two coefficients (20.6% + 5.0%). Baserunners are credited with the other 19.4% of offensive Component 7 player decisions.

The top 25 players in net Component 7 wins (wins minus losses) are presented in the next nine tables: batters, baserunners, pitchers, and each of the four primary infield positions (excluding pitchers and catchers).

Component 7: Batting Wins
Top 25 Players (Sorted by Net Wins)

		Wins	Losses	Win Pct	Net Wins
1	Ichiro Suzuki	5.5	1.5	0.782	**4.0**
2	Johnny Damon	4.8	1.4	0.771	**3.4**
3	Carl Crawford	4.0	1.3	0.753	**2.7**
4	Steve Finley	4.9	2.6	0.655	**2.3**
5	Brett Butler	3.2	1.0	0.759	**2.2**
6	Randy Winn	3.4	1.3	0.728	**2.1**
7	Craig Biggio	4.0	2.1	0.651	**1.9**
8	*Luke Appling*	*3.9*	*2.0*	*0.656*	***1.8***

		Wins	Losses	Win Pct	Net Wins
9	Juan Pierre	3.3	1.4	0.695	**1.8**
10	Luis Castillo	3.7	1.9	0.657	**1.8**
11	*Mike Tresh*	*2.2*	*0.5*	*0.830*	***1.8***
12	Jose Reyes	2.8	1.2	0.700	**1.6**
13	Ozzie Guillen	3.4	1.8	0.658	**1.6**
14	Chase Utley	3.2	1.6	0.665	**1.6**
15	Cristian Guzman	2.9	1.4	0.681	**1.6**
16	Willie Wilson	2.8	1.4	0.673	**1.5**
17	Michael Bourn	2.0	0.6	0.777	**1.4**
18	Jason Heyward	2.2	0.7	0.742	**1.4**
19	Darin Erstad	2.7	1.3	0.672	**1.4**
20	Corey Patterson	2.0	0.7	0.749	**1.3**
21	Jack Wilson	2.6	1.3	0.668	**1.3**
22	Devon White	3.0	1.7	0.640	**1.3**
23	Kenny Lofton	3.2	1.9	0.627	**1.3**
24	*Stan Hack*	*1.9*	*0.8*	*0.715*	***1.2***
25	Tim Foli	2.5	1.3	0.651	**1.2**

Component 7: Baserunning Wins
Top 25 Players (Sorted by Net Wins)

		Wins	Losses	Win Pct	Net Wins
1	*Joe Kuhel*	*1.3*	*0.7*	*0.634*	***0.5***
2	Lou Brock	0.9	0.5	0.653	**0.4**
3	*Thurman Tucker*	*0.6*	*0.2*	*0.758*	***0.4***
4	*Frankie Crosetti*	*0.8*	*0.4*	*0.658*	***0.4***
5	Jim Gilliam	0.9	0.6	0.621	**0.4**
6	*Taffy Wright*	*0.7*	*0.3*	*0.672*	***0.4***
7	Richie Ashburn	1.3	0.9	0.580	**0.4**
8	*Joe Stripp*	*0.6*	*0.3*	*0.691*	***0.3***
9	*Lonny Frey*	*0.8*	*0.5*	*0.627*	***0.3***
10	*Buddy Myer*	*0.8*	*0.4*	*0.641*	***0.3***
11	*Ralph Hodgin*	*0.5*	*0.2*	*0.732*	***0.3***
12	Julian Javier	0.6	0.3	0.667	**0.3**
13	*Augie Galan*	*1.0*	*0.7*	*0.594*	***0.3***
14	*Phil Cavarretta*	*0.7*	*0.4*	*0.631*	***0.3***
15	*Chet Laabs*	*0.5*	*0.2*	*0.694*	***0.3***
16	Paul Molitor	1.1	0.8	0.576	**0.3**
17	Eddie Yost	1.0	0.7	0.581	**0.3**
18	Sam Rice	0.5	0.3	0.680	**0.3**
19	*Barney McCosky*	*0.6*	*0.3*	*0.645*	***0.3***
20	*Phil Rizzuto*	*0.7*	*0.4*	*0.618*	***0.3***
21	Don Blasingame	0.7	0.4	0.625	**0.3**
22	*Dom DiMaggio*	*0.9*	*0.6*	*0.593*	***0.3***
23	*Arky Vaughan*	*0.8*	*0.6*	*0.594*	***0.3***
24	*Pepper Martin*	*0.5*	*0.2*	*0.684*	***0.3***
25	*Stan Hack*	*1.2*	*0.9*	*0.564*	***0.3***

Component 7: Pitching Wins
Top 25 Players (Sorted by Net Wins)

		Wins	Losses	Win Pct	Net Wins
1	Chuck Finley	2.2	1.4	0.606	**0.8**
2	*Alvin Crowder*	*1.4*	*0.6*	*0.687*	***0.7***
3	Steve Carlton	2.1	1.4	0.601	**0.7**
4	Bob Knepper	1.7	1.0	0.627	**0.7**
5	Whitey Ford	1.9	1.3	0.603	**0.6**
6	Kenny Rogers	2.1	1.5	0.589	**0.6**
7	*Warren Spahn*	*2.4*	*1.7*	*0.574*	***0.6***
8	*Bob Weiland*	*1.3*	*0.7*	*0.651*	***0.6***

		Wins	Losses	Win Pct	Net Wins
9	Andy Pettitte	2.3	1.7	0.571	**0.6**
10	Shawn Estes	1.4	0.8	0.631	**0.6**
11	Brian Anderson	1.0	0.4	0.708	**0.6**
12	*Hal Newhouser*	*1.9*	*1.4*	*0.583*	***0.5***
13	Jake Westbrook	1.5	1.0	0.601	**0.5**
14	Zane Smith	1.6	1.1	0.584	**0.5**
15	*Johnny Broaca*	*0.7*	*0.3*	*0.712*	***0.4***
16	Mike Caldwell	1.5	1.1	0.584	**0.4**
17	Al Leiter	1.6	1.1	0.581	**0.4**
18	*Bobo Newsom*	*1.8*	*1.4*	*0.569*	***0.4***
19	Mike Hampton	1.7	1.3	0.568	**0.4**
20	*Monte Weaver*	*0.9*	*0.5*	*0.655*	***0.4***
21	Bobby Witt	1.4	1.0	0.584	**0.4**
22	Dan Schatzeder	0.8	0.4	0.674	**0.4**
23	*Walt Masterson*	*1.1*	*0.7*	*0.608*	***0.4***
24	John Lannan	0.9	0.5	0.634	**0.4**
25	Jason Marquis	1.2	0.8	0.596	**0.4**

Component 7: Fielder Wins, 1B
Top 25 Players (Sorted by Net Wins)

		Wins	Losses	Win Pct	Net Wins
1	Wally Joyner	1.0	0.5	0.663	**0.5**
2	Todd Helton	1.1	0.7	0.623	**0.4**
3	Pete O'Brien	0.7	0.4	0.660	**0.3**
4	*Hal Trosky*	*0.7*	*0.4*	*0.654*	***0.3***
5	Tino Martinez	0.8	0.5	0.611	**0.3**
6	Adrian Gonzalez	0.7	0.4	0.618	**0.3**
7	Gil Hodges	0.8	0.6	0.594	**0.3**
8	Will Clark	0.8	0.5	0.594	**0.3**
9	Albert Pujols	0.7	0.4	0.603	**0.2**
10	Steve Garvey	1.0	0.7	0.564	**0.2**
11	*Gus Suhr*	*0.7*	*0.4*	*0.598*	***0.2***
12	Willie Montanez	0.5	0.3	0.639	**0.2**
13	Norm Cash	0.7	0.5	0.579	**0.2**
14	Bill Skowron	0.6	0.4	0.602	**0.2**
15	Dee Fondy	0.4	0.2	0.637	**0.2**
16	*Babe Young*	*0.3*	*0.1*	*0.677*	***0.1***
17	James Loney	0.5	0.3	0.595	**0.1**
18	Dick Allen	0.4	0.2	0.632	**0.1**
19	Mike Hargrove	0.5	0.3	0.592	**0.1**
20	John Mayberry	0.5	0.4	0.580	**0.1**
21	Dan Johnson	0.3	0.1	0.679	**0.1**
22	Hal Morris	0.4	0.2	0.619	**0.1**
23	Wes Parker	0.3	0.2	0.620	**0.1**
24	Jack Clark	0.3	0.2	0.647	**0.1**
25	*George Kelly*	*0.2*	*0.1*	*0.678*	***0.1***

Component 7: Fielder Wins, 2B
Top 25 Players (Sorted by Net Wins)

		Wins	Losses	Win Pct	Net Wins
1	Fernando Vina	5.0	2.9	0.632	**2.1**
2	Tom Herr	5.2	3.8	0.580	**1.4**
3	Robby Thompson	5.6	4.3	0.563	**1.3**
4	Willie Randolph	7.5	6.3	0.544	**1.2**
5	Red Schoendienst	3.9	2.9	0.578	**1.1**
6	Bobby Richardson	3.0	2.1	0.592	**0.9**
7	Carlos Baerga	5.4	4.5	0.545	**0.9**
8	*Billy Herman*	*4.4*	*3.5*	*0.554*	***0.9***

		Wins	Losses	Win Pct	Net Wins
9	Bill Mazeroski	5.0	4.2	0.546	**0.8**
10	Jim Gantner	4.8	4.0	0.543	**0.8**
11	Damion Easley	4.8	4.0	0.543	**0.8**
12	Billy Ripken	3.2	2.5	0.566	**0.8**
13	Miguel Cairo	3.0	2.2	0.572	**0.8**
14	Kelly Johnson	3.9	3.1	0.553	**0.7**
15	Alex Cora	2.2	1.5	0.595	**0.7**
16	Ted Sizemore	2.8	2.1	0.573	**0.7**
17	Scott Fletcher	3.4	2.8	0.554	**0.7**
18	*Lonny Frey*	*2.5*	*1.8*	*0.579*	***0.7***
19	Mark McLemore	5.2	4.6	0.534	**0.7**
20	Glenn Hubbard	4.1	3.5	0.538	**0.6**
21	Luis Alicea	3.8	3.2	0.542	**0.6**
22	Mark Grudzielanek	4.4	3.8	0.536	**0.6**
23	*Joe Gordon*	*3.4*	*2.8*	*0.547*	***0.6***
24	Danny Espinosa	2.2	1.7	0.573	**0.6**
25	*Charlie Gehringer*	*4.2*	*3.7*	*0.534*	***0.5***

Component 7: Fielder Wins, 3B
Top 25 Players (Sorted by Net Wins)

		Wins	Losses	Win Pct	Net Wins
1	*Jimmie Dykes*	*0.8*	*0.5*	*0.633*	***0.4***
2	Joe Randa	0.8	0.4	0.639	**0.3**
3	*Mark Christman*	*0.5*	*0.1*	*0.759*	***0.3***
4	Gary Gaetti	1.2	0.9	0.576	**0.3**
5	Clete Boyer	0.7	0.4	0.621	**0.3**
6	Aurelio Rodriguez	0.9	0.6	0.595	**0.3**
7	Ken Caminiti	0.9	0.6	0.592	**0.3**
8	Robin Ventura	0.9	0.7	0.584	**0.3**
9	Evan Longoria	0.7	0.5	0.606	**0.3**
10	*Pie Traynor*	*0.7*	*0.5*	*0.609*	***0.3***
11	*Bob Elliott*	*0.8*	*0.5*	*0.591*	***0.2***
12	Doug DeCinces	0.7	0.5	0.595	**0.2**
13	Paul Molitor	0.5	0.2	0.660	**0.2**
14	Owen Friend	0.2	0.0	0.960	**0.2**
15	Jeff Cirillo	0.6	0.4	0.593	**0.2**
16	*Jim Tabor*	*0.7*	*0.5*	*0.584*	***0.2***
17	Fernando Tatis	0.4	0.2	0.644	**0.2**
18	*Whitey Kurowski*	*0.5*	*0.3*	*0.626*	***0.2***
19	Andy Carey	0.5	0.3	0.619	**0.2**
20	*Sibby Sisti*	*0.3*	*0.1*	*0.746*	***0.2***
21	Bubba Phillips	0.5	0.3	0.609	**0.2**
22	*Cookie Lavagetto*	*0.4*	*0.2*	*0.637*	***0.2***
23	Ken Boyer	0.8	0.6	0.568	**0.2**
24	Kevin Seitzer	0.5	0.3	0.613	**0.2**
25	Chipper Jones	0.9	0.7	0.555	**0.2**

Component 7: Fielder Wins, SS
Top 25 Players (Sorted by Net Wins)

		Wins	Losses	Win Pct	Net Wins
1	Cal Ripken	10.7	8.7	0.553	**2.1**
2	Mike Bordick	8.5	6.6	0.562	**1.9**
3	Neifi Perez	6.2	4.8	0.566	**1.5**
4	Tim Foli	4.5	3.1	0.592	**1.4**
5	Troy Tulowitzki	7.0	5.8	0.549	**1.3**
6	Jose Valentin	6.0	4.8	0.555	**1.2**
7	Alan Trammell	7.6	6.4	0.542	**1.2**
8	Andrelton Simmons	3.0	1.8	0.621	**1.2**

		Wins	Losses	Win Pct	Net Wins
9	Phil Rizzuto	3.5	2.4	0.591	**1.1**
10	Jose Uribe	4.0	3.0	0.572	**1.0**
11	Jimmy Rollins	9.9	8.9	0.526	**1.0**
12	Cliff Pennington	3.5	2.5	0.578	**0.9**
13	Brendan Ryan	4.4	3.4	0.559	**0.9**
14	Ozzie Smith	9.9	9.0	0.522	**0.8**
15	Alvaro Espinoza	3.5	2.7	0.566	**0.8**
16	*Eddie Miller*	*3.3*	*2.5*	*0.568*	***0.8***
17	Rey Ordonez	4.1	3.3	0.552	**0.8**
18	Alvin Dark	2.7	2.0	0.580	**0.7**
19	Alex Cora	2.7	2.0	0.575	**0.7**
20	Elvis Andrus	6.4	5.7	0.529	**0.7**
21	Bobby Wine	2.3	1.6	0.587	**0.7**
22	Ron Hansen	2.7	2.0	0.574	**0.7**
23	Pee Wee Reese	3.7	3.0	0.550	**0.7**
24	Rey Quinones	1.7	1.0	0.626	**0.7**
25	Scott Fletcher	3.1	2.5	0.559	**0.7**

Component 8: Baserunner Outs

In the eighth step of calculating Player Wins and Losses, batters, baserunners, and fielders are given credit and blame for baserunning outs. Components 8 and 9 are the only two components for which pitchers receive no credit. Instead, the ability to throw out baserunners and/or allow/prevent baserunner advancement (Component 9) are attributed entirely to the fielders responsible for the play(s).

CALCULATION OF COMPONENT 8 PLAYER DECISIONS

Component 8 doles out credits and debits for whether any baserunners (including the batter) are thrown out on the bases. Ground-ball double plays are not included here—those are measured in Component 7. As with most other components, players are credited for baserunner outs as well as for avoiding (failing to make) baserunner outs, so that the overall Component 8 winning percentage is 0.500. Component 8 Player decisions are first allocated to any baserunner on third base, followed by any baserunner on second, followed by any baserunner on first, then, finally by the batter.

IMPACT OF THE BATTER ON BASERUNNER OUTS

Component 8 Player decisions are shared between batters and baserunners based on the extent to which player winning percentages persist across different sample periods. The mathematics underlying this division were described earlier in this chapter. Separate equations were estimated for each base. Separate equations were estimated for each season as described earlier in this chapter.

The average division of Component 8 player decisions by base, across all seasons for which I have calculated pW-L records, are as follows.

Component 8	*Batter*	*Baserunner*
First Base	48.7%	51.3%
Second Base	59.9%	40.1%
Third Base	52.0%	48.0%
Total	**53.3%**	**46.7%**

The top 25 players in net Component 8 wins (wins minus losses) are presented in the next eleven tables: batters, baserunners, and each of the nine fielding positions (including pitchers).

Component 8: Batting Wins
Top 25 Players (Sorted by Net Wins)

		Wins	Losses	Win Pct	Net Wins
1	Joe Kuhel	2.3	1.4	0.609	**0.8**
2	Mel Ott	2.4	1.6	0.597	**0.8**
3	Bill Nicholson	1.7	1.0	0.637	**0.7**
4	Eddie Murray	2.6	1.9	0.581	**0.7**
5	Walker Cooper	1.5	0.7	0.664	**0.7**
6	John Milner	1.0	0.3	0.764	**0.7**
7	Arky Vaughan	2.0	1.3	0.603	**0.7**
8	Harry Danning	0.9	0.2	0.820	**0.7**
9	Frank Robinson	2.4	1.8	0.578	**0.7**
10	Cecil Travis	1.5	0.8	0.641	**0.7**
11	Rogers Hornsby	1.1	0.5	0.699	**0.6**
12	Shawn Green	1.3	0.7	0.661	**0.6**
13	Gary Sheffield	1.8	1.1	0.609	**0.6**
14	Babe Dahlgren	1.1	0.5	0.689	**0.6**
15	Joe L. Morgan	2.2	1.5	0.584	**0.6**
16	Jose Cardenal	1.7	1.1	0.608	**0.6**
17	Jimmie Foxx	1.7	1.1	0.608	**0.6**
18	Tony Clark	0.8	0.2	0.814	**0.6**
19	Vic Wertz	1.9	1.3	0.596	**0.6**
20	Hank Aaron	3.0	2.4	0.556	**0.6**
21	Billy Rogell	1.3	0.7	0.649	**0.6**
22	Rico Carty	1.5	0.9	0.620	**0.6**
23	Johnny Edwards	1.2	0.6	0.665	**0.6**
24	Joe Adcock	1.7	1.1	0.604	**0.6**
25	Dale Mitchell	1.0	0.5	0.687	**0.6**

Component 8: Baserunning Wins
Top 25 Players (Sorted by Net Wins)

		Wins	Losses	Win Pct	Net Wins
1	Mel Ott	3.4	1.7	0.671	**1.7**
2	Ted Williams	3.5	1.9	0.645	**1.6**
3	Mickey Mantle	3.1	1.7	0.646	**1.4**
4	Garret Anderson	2.1	0.8	0.735	**1.3**
5	Red Schoendienst	3.7	2.4	0.609	**1.3**
6	Wade Boggs	3.6	2.3	0.610	**1.3**
7	Willie Randolph	3.0	1.7	0.636	**1.3**
8	John Olerud	2.3	1.1	0.680	**1.2**
9	Robin Yount	3.5	2.3	0.605	**1.2**
10	Tim Raines	3.0	1.9	0.616	**1.1**
11	Derek Jeter	3.1	2.0	0.608	**1.1**
12	Lloyd Waner	2.8	1.7	0.620	**1.1**
13	Hank Aaron	4.2	3.1	0.573	**1.1**
14	Paul Waner	3.5	2.5	0.588	**1.0**
15	Al Simmons	2.4	1.3	0.640	**1.0**
16	Charlie Gehringer	2.8	1.8	0.609	**1.0**
17	Ichiro Suzuki	2.6	1.6	0.621	**1.0**
18	Eddie Mathews	3.0	2.0	0.600	**1.0**
19	Bernie Williams	2.4	1.4	0.628	**1.0**
20	Paul Molitor	3.7	2.8	0.573	**0.9**
21	Dixie Walker	3.0	2.0	0.594	**0.9**
22	Darin Erstad	1.6	0.7	0.700	**0.9**
23	Barry Larkin	2.4	1.4	0.623	**0.9**

		Wins	Losses	Win Pct	Net Wins
24	Jimmie Foxx	2.7	1.8	0.603	**0.9**
25	Alan Trammell	2.6	1.7	0.602	**0.9**

Component 8: Fielder Wins, P
Top 25 Players (Sorted by Net Wins)

		Wins	Losses	Win Pct	Net Wins
1	Joe Niekro	0.7	0.2	0.740	**0.4**
2	*Tex Hughson*	*0.5*	*0.1*	*0.786*	***0.4***
3	*Elden Auker*	*0.5*	*0.2*	*0.753*	***0.3***
4	*Mort Cooper*	*0.4*	*0.1*	*0.791*	***0.3***
5	*Tex Carleton*	*0.4*	*0.1*	*0.841*	***0.3***
6	Juan Marichal	0.5	0.2	0.719	**0.3**
7	Jamie Moyer	0.4	0.1	0.768	**0.3**
8	Livan Hernandez	0.4	0.1	0.749	**0.3**
9	Larry McWilliams	0.4	0.1	0.788	**0.3**
10	*Clay Bryant*	*0.3*	*0.0*	*0.893*	***0.3***
11	Larry Gura	0.4	0.1	0.765	**0.3**
12	*Wes Ferrell*	*0.4*	*0.2*	*0.720*	***0.3***
13	*Pete Appleton*	*0.4*	*0.1*	*0.798*	***0.3***
14	Jim Palmer	0.5	0.2	0.678	**0.2**
15	Gary Peters	0.4	0.1	0.747	**0.2**
16	*Dizzy Trout*	*0.6*	*0.3*	*0.632*	***0.2***
17	Jim Bunning	0.4	0.1	0.739	**0.2**
18	Dan Petry	0.3	0.1	0.768	**0.2**
19	Bob Purkey	0.4	0.2	0.686	**0.2**
20	*Claude Passeau*	*0.4*	*0.2*	*0.683*	***0.2***
21	Juan Pizarro	0.4	0.1	0.732	**0.2**
22	*Nels Potter*	*0.4*	*0.1*	*0.725*	***0.2***
23	Chuck Stobbs	0.3	0.1	0.730	**0.2**
24	*Bill Bailey*	*0.2*	*0.0*	*0.952*	***0.2***
25	*Bob Chipman*	*0.3*	*0.1*	*0.774*	***0.2***

Component 8: Fielder Wins, C
Top 25 Players (Sorted by Net Wins)

		Wins	Losses	Win Pct	Net Wins
1	*Mickey Cochrane*	*0.6*	*0.2*	*0.780*	***0.5***
2	*Rick Ferrell*	*0.8*	*0.5*	*0.639*	***0.4***
3	*Al Todd*	*0.5*	*0.2*	*0.721*	***0.3***
4	*Tony Giuliani*	*0.3*	*0.0*	*0.892*	***0.3***
5	Brad Ausmus	0.4	0.1	0.762	**0.2**
6	Jim Sundberg	0.4	0.2	0.670	**0.2**
7	Bobby Estalella	0.2	0.0	0.997	**0.2**
8	*Mickey Owen*	*0.6*	*0.4*	*0.608*	***0.2***
9	Yogi Berra	0.5	0.3	0.620	**0.2**
10	*Johnny Gooch*	*0.3*	*0.1*	*0.711*	***0.2***
11	*Frankie Hayes*	*0.7*	*0.5*	*0.590*	***0.2***
12	*Roy Partee*	*0.4*	*0.2*	*0.664*	***0.2***
13	Carlton Fisk	0.4	0.3	0.620	**0.2**
14	Mike Ryan	0.2	0.1	0.753	**0.2**
15	*Mickey Livingston*	*0.3*	*0.1*	*0.716*	***0.2***
16	Wiki Gonzalez	0.2	−0.0	1.016	**0.2**
17	Bengie Molina	0.2	0.1	0.758	**0.2**
18	*Earl Grace*	*0.2*	*0.1*	*0.732*	***0.2***
19	Joe Torre	0.4	0.2	0.645	**0.2**
20	Josh Paul	0.2	−0.0	1.036	**0.2**
21	Buddy Rosar	0.4	0.2	0.623	**0.2**
22	Joe Azcue	0.3	0.1	0.698	**0.1**
23	*Cy Perkins*	*0.2*	*0.1*	*0.764*	***0.1***

		Wins	Losses	Win Pct	Net Wins
24	Ernie Lombardi	0.5	0.3	0.590	**0.1**
25	Dave Rader	0.3	0.1	0.674	**0.1**

Component 8: Fielder Wins, 1B
Top 25 Players (Sorted by Net Wins)

		Wins	Losses	Win Pct	Net Wins
1	Gil Hodges	2.7	2.0	0.580	**0.8**
2	Todd Helton	2.1	1.5	0.592	**0.7**
3	Joe Adcock	2.1	1.5	0.584	**0.6**
4	Vic Power	2.1	1.5	0.579	**0.6**
5	Keith Hernandez	2.5	2.0	0.557	**0.5**
6	*Jim Bottomley*	*2.2*	*1.7*	*0.564*	***0.5***
7	Ferris Fain	2.2	1.7	0.556	**0.4**
8	Eddie Murray	2.5	2.0	0.547	**0.4**
9	Wally Joyner	1.6	1.2	0.574	**0.4**
10	Andres Galarraga	1.8	1.4	0.566	**0.4**
11	Ernie Banks	1.7	1.3	0.567	**0.4**
12	*Rudy York*	*2.2*	*1.8*	*0.550*	***0.4***
13	Jeff Bagwell	1.9	1.5	0.559	**0.4**
14	*Johnny Mize*	*2.2*	*1.9*	*0.546*	***0.4***
15	*Eddie Robinson*	*1.7*	*1.3*	*0.560*	***0.4***
16	Greg Brock	1.1	0.8	0.595	**0.4**
17	*Jimmy Wasdell*	*0.7*	*0.4*	*0.648*	***0.3***
18	*Don Kolloway*	*0.7*	*0.4*	*0.661*	***0.3***
19	*Dick Siebert*	*1.8*	*1.5*	*0.550*	***0.3***
20	Fred McGriff	1.8	1.5	0.549	**0.3**
21	Nate Colbert	1.3	1.0	0.565	**0.3**
22	*Babe Young*	*1.0*	*0.7*	*0.586*	***0.3***
23	Willie Aikens	0.8	0.5	0.617	**0.3**
24	Steve Garvey	1.9	1.6	0.542	**0.3**
25	*Frank McCormick*	*2.2*	*1.9*	*0.535*	***0.3***

Component 8: Fielder Wins, 2B
Top 25 Players (Sorted by Net Wins)

		Wins	Losses	Win Pct	Net Wins
1	*Emil Verban*	*2.3*	*1.4*	*0.615*	***0.9***
2	*Ski Melillo*	*3.1*	*2.2*	*0.576*	***0.8***
3	Bobby Grich	3.3	2.6	0.566	**0.8**
4	Eric Young	2.2	1.5	0.602	**0.8**
5	Don Blasingame	2.5	1.9	0.573	**0.7**
6	*Charlie Gehringer*	*4.1*	*3.5*	*0.540*	***0.6***
7	Robinson Cano	2.0	1.4	0.582	**0.6**
8	Jackie Robinson	1.5	1.0	0.608	**0.6**
9	Lou Whitaker	3.0	2.4	0.551	**0.6**
10	Chase Utley	1.8	1.3	0.586	**0.5**
11	Carlos Baerga	1.6	1.1	0.593	**0.5**
12	Delino DeShields	2.1	1.6	0.569	**0.5**
13	Jerry Coleman	1.6	1.1	0.591	**0.5**
14	*Lou Chiozza*	*1.1*	*0.6*	*0.640*	***0.5***
15	Pete Suder	2.0	1.5	0.564	**0.5**
16	Whitey Wietelmann	0.7	0.2	0.744	**0.5**
17	*Sparky Adams*	*1.1*	*0.6*	*0.635*	***0.4***
18	Tony Cuccinello	2.7	2.3	0.543	**0.4**
19	Julian Javier	2.8	2.3	0.542	**0.4**
20	Ron Belliard	1.5	1.1	0.579	**0.4**
21	Felix Millan	2.2	1.8	0.549	**0.4**
22	*Johnny Hudson*	*0.7*	*0.3*	*0.679*	***0.4***
23	Pete Rose	1.3	0.9	0.582	**0.4**

		Wins	Losses	Win Pct	Net Wins
24	*Rip Russell*	*0.4*	*0.1*	*0.883*	**0.3**
25	John Donaldson	0.9	0.5	0.616	**0.3**

Component 8: Fielder Wins, 3B
Top 25 Players (Sorted by Net Wins)

		Wins	Losses	Win Pct	Net Wins
1	*Billy Werber*	2.0	1.2	0.622	**0.8**
2	Aurelio Rodriguez	2.3	1.6	0.589	**0.7**
3	Ron Santo	2.6	2.0	0.565	**0.6**
4	Graig Nettles	2.8	2.2	0.558	**0.6**
5	*Jim Tabor*	*1.7*	*1.2*	*0.600*	**0.6**
6	Gary Gaetti	2.1	1.6	0.578	**0.6**
7	Eddie Mathews	2.5	2.0	0.562	**0.6**
8	Darrell Evans	2.0	1.5	0.577	**0.5**
9	Mike Schmidt	2.6	2.1	0.552	**0.5**
10	*Ken Keltner*	*2.0*	*1.6*	*0.561*	**0.4**
11	Ryan Zimmerman	0.9	0.4	0.662	**0.4**
12	Eric Chavez	1.0	0.6	0.634	**0.4**
13	Jeff King	0.8	0.4	0.676	**0.4**
14	Vinny Castilla	1.3	0.9	0.591	**0.4**
15	Ed Charles	1.2	0.8	0.604	**0.4**
16	Paul Molitor	1.0	0.6	0.622	**0.4**
17	Wade Boggs	1.7	1.3	0.565	**0.4**
18	Chase Headley	0.7	0.4	0.670	**0.4**
19	Fernando Tatis	0.8	0.4	0.646	**0.4**
20	Bobby Bonilla	1.0	0.6	0.606	**0.3**
21	Joe Torre	0.8	0.4	0.638	**0.3**
22	Juan Uribe	0.5	0.2	0.709	**0.3**
23	Jim Morrison	0.9	0.6	0.610	**0.3**
24	Edgardo Alfonzo	0.7	0.4	0.627	**0.3**
25	Scott Brosius	0.7	0.4	0.629	**0.3**

Component 8: Fielder Wins, SS
Top 25 Players (Sorted by Net Wins)

		Wins	Losses	Win Pct	Net Wins
1	*Lou Boudreau*	4.0	2.2	0.642	**1.8**
2	Jack Wilson	1.9	1.0	0.661	**0.9**
3	Ozzie Smith	3.8	3.1	0.552	**0.7**
4	Luis Aparicio	4.0	3.3	0.548	**0.7**
5	*John Paul Sullivan*	*1.5*	*0.9*	*0.636*	**0.6**
6	*Marty Marion*	*3.2*	*2.6*	*0.552*	**0.6**
7	Leo Cardenas	2.8	2.2	0.560	**0.6**
8	Ron Hansen	1.9	1.4	0.585	**0.6**
9	Frank Taveras	1.9	1.4	0.580	**0.5**
10	Joe Millette	0.5	0.0	0.980	**0.5**
11	Toby Harrah	1.6	1.1	0.591	**0.5**
12	*Red Kress*	*1.4*	*1.0*	*0.597*	**0.5**
13	*Rabbit Warstler*	*1.7*	*1.2*	*0.577*	**0.5**
14	Hal Lanier	1.2	0.8	0.610	**0.4**
15	Roy McMillan	3.3	2.8	0.534	**0.4**
16	*Travis Jackson*	*1.8*	*1.4*	*0.563*	**0.4**
17	Ed Brinkman	2.5	2.1	0.544	**0.4**
18	Travis Fryman	0.8	0.4	0.676	**0.4**
19	*Joe Hoover*	*1.1*	*0.7*	*0.603*	**0.4**
20	Cal Ripken	2.5	2.1	0.539	**0.4**
21	*Glenn Wright*	*1.5*	*1.2*	*0.564*	**0.3**
22	Gary DiSarcina	1.2	0.8	0.589	**0.3**
23	Ron Gardenhire	0.6	0.3	0.686	**0.3**

		Wins	Losses	Win Pct	Net Wins
24	Felix Fermin	1.1	0.7	0.592	0.3
25	Zoilo Versalles	1.9	1.6	0.547	0.3

Component 8: Fielder Wins, LF
Top 25 Players (Sorted by Net Wins)

		Wins	Losses	Win Pct	Net Wins
1	*Indian Bob Johnson*	11.9	8.1	0.595	**3.8**
2	Carl Yastrzemski	11.9	9.0	0.571	**3.0**
3	Bernard Gilkey	6.8	4.4	0.606	**2.4**
4	Bobby Higginson	5.2	3.0	0.629	**2.1**
5	Minnie Minoso	7.5	5.9	0.561	**1.7**
6	Yoenis Cespedes	2.9	1.4	0.683	**1.6**
7	Willie Stargell	6.3	4.8	0.570	**1.6**
8	B.J. Surhoff	4.4	3.0	0.599	**1.5**
9	Billy Williams	8.0	6.6	0.548	**1.4**
10	*Jo-Jo Moore*	5.6	4.3	*0.565*	**1.3**
11	Hank Sauer	5.8	4.5	0.562	**1.3**
12	*Goose Goslin*	7.6	6.4	*0.544*	**1.2**
13	Alfonso Soriano	4.5	3.2	0.579	**1.2**
14	Geoff Jenkins	4.3	3.2	0.576	**1.1**
15	Jim Rice	8.7	7.5	0.534	**1.1**
16	Pat Burrell	5.6	4.5	0.553	**1.1**
17	Mike Greenwell	5.4	4.3	0.555	**1.1**
18	Carson Bigbee	2.9	1.9	0.602	**1.0**
19	Lonnie Smith	6.0	5.0	0.544	**1.0**
20	*Ed Levy*	1.3	0.3	*0.792*	**1.0**
21	Del Ennis	6.8	5.9	0.537	**0.9**
22	Gene Richards	4.0	3.1	0.565	**0.9**
23	Alex Gordon	3.9	2.9	0.568	**0.9**
24	Warren Cromartie	3.5	2.6	0.574	**0.9**
25	*Smead Jolley*	2.3	1.4	0.620	**0.9**

Component 8: Fielder Wins, CF
Top 25 Players (Sorted by Net Wins)

		Wins	Losses	Win Pct	Net Wins
1	*Dom DiMaggio*	9.6	6.8	0.587	**2.9**
2	*Terry Moore*	7.0	4.8	0.593	**2.2**
3	Kirby Puckett	6.7	4.5	0.597	**2.2**
4	Jim Edmonds	7.3	5.3	0.579	**2.0**
5	Kenny Lofton	8.1	6.1	0.569	**2.0**
6	Adam Jones	4.9	3.0	0.623	**1.9**
7	Willie Davis	9.2	7.5	0.551	**1.7**
8	Bill Tuttle	5.6	3.9	0.589	**1.7**
9	Ken Griffey, Jr.	8.7	7.1	0.550	**1.6**
10	Andy Van Slyke	5.3	3.7	0.586	**1.6**
11	Carlos Beltran	6.3	4.8	0.567	**1.5**
12	Paul Blair	6.8	5.3	0.560	**1.4**
13	Brian L. Hunter	3.7	2.3	0.620	**1.4**
14	Leonys Martin	2.6	1.2	0.679	**1.4**
15	Hal Jeffcoat	3.3	2.0	0.620	**1.3**
16	Gary Pettis	4.4	3.3	0.572	**1.1**
17	Mark Kotsay	4.1	3.1	0.575	**1.1**
18	Cesar Geronimo	4.7	3.7	0.561	**1.0**
19	Andruw Jones	6.7	5.7	0.541	**1.0**
20	*Sam Chapman*	6.4	5.4	*0.543*	**1.0**
21	Del Unser	5.7	4.7	0.548	**1.0**
22	Joe DiMaggio	7.9	6.9	0.533	**1.0**

		Wins	Losses	Win Pct	Net Wins
23	Myril Hoag	2.3	1.4	0.628	**0.9**
24	Dave Philley	4.0	3.1	0.566	**0.9**
25	Elliott Maddox	2.9	2.0	0.595	**0.9**

Component 8: Fielder Wins, RF
Top 25 Players (Sorted by Net Wins)

		Wins	Losses	Win Pct	Net Wins
1	Jesse Barfield	9.3	5.4	0.630	**3.8**
2	Roberto Clemente	15.0	12.1	0.554	**2.9**
3	Jeff Francoeur	7.3	4.3	0.626	**2.9**
4	*Roy Cullenbine*	*5.6*	*3.3*	*0.626*	***2.3***
5	Johnny Callison	9.8	7.6	0.565	**2.3**
6	Rusty Staub	9.4	7.7	0.551	**1.7**
7	Ellis Valentine	5.4	3.7	0.593	**1.7**
8	*Buddy Lewis*	*5.2*	*3.6*	*0.587*	***1.5***
9	Larry Walker	8.5	7.0	0.548	**1.5**
10	Mike Hershberger	4.1	2.6	0.609	**1.5**
11	Cory Snyder	4.8	3.4	0.584	**1.4**
12	Orlando Merced	3.7	2.5	0.601	**1.2**
13	Jose Guillen	5.5	4.3	0.561	**1.2**
14	Greg Gross	3.1	1.9	0.616	**1.2**
15	Jack Clark	5.9	4.8	0.554	**1.2**
16	Glenn Wilson	5.3	4.1	0.561	**1.1**
17	*Willard Marshall*	*6.0*	*4.9*	*0.552*	***1.1***
18	Reggie Sanders	5.2	4.1	0.561	**1.1**
19	*Joe Grace*	*2.5*	*1.4*	*0.645*	***1.1***
20	Ron Fairly	3.5	2.4	0.594	**1.1**
21	Bobby Abreu	7.9	6.8	0.538	**1.1**
22	*Roy Johnson*	*3.4*	*2.4*	*0.588*	***1.0***
23	Ollie Brown	4.9	3.9	0.556	**1.0**
24	*Chuck Hostetler*	*1.1*	*0.2*	*0.849*	***0.9***
25	Mike Cuddyer	3.8	2.8	0.570	**0.9**

Component 9: Baserunner Advancements

In the ninth step of calculating Player Wins and Losses, batters, baserunners, and fielders are given credit and blame for baserunner advancements.

Calculation of Component 9 Player Decisions

Component 9 doles out credits and debits for whether any baserunners (including the batter) advance above or below expectations given the type of play (hit, out) and the location and hit type (if available). Component 9 player decisions are allocated to any baserunner on third base first, followed by any baserunner on second, followed by any baserunner on first, then, finally by the batter. Component 9 accounts for 6.2% of total player decisions, making it the fourth-largest component behind Components 3, 4, and 5. Component 9 is the largest component of baserunner player decisions, accounting for 39.4% of total baserunner decisions. Component 9 is the second-largest component of fielding decisions for both infielders and outfielders, behind only Component 5. Component 9 accounts for 12.1% of total fielding decisions for infielders (excluding pitchers and catchers) and 22.7% of total fielding decisions for outfielders.

IMPACT OF THE BATTER ON BASERUNNER ADVANCEMENTS

Component 9 Player decisions are shared between batters and baserunners based on the extent to which player winning percentages persist across different sample periods. The mathematics underlying this division were described earlier in this chapter. Separate equations were estimated for each base. Separate equations were estimated for each season as described earlier in this chapter.

The average division of Component 9 player decisions by base, across all seasons for which I have calculated pW-L records, are as follows.

Component 9	Batter	Baserunner
First Base	29.3%	70.7%
Second Base	39.3%	60.7%
Third Base	100.0%	0.0%
Total	**48.9%**	**51.1%**

The most surprising result, here, is that no positive persistence of Component 9 winning percentage was found for baserunners on third base. Hence, these player decisions are allocated entirely to batters. I guess the ability to score from third base on a sacrifice fly, for example, is much more a function of how far the fly ball was hit than of how fast the baserunner is.

The top 25 players in net Component 9 wins (wins minus losses) are presented in the next eleven tables: batters, baserunners, and each of the nine fielding positions (including pitchers).

Component 9: Batting Wins
Top 25 Players (Sorted by Net Wins)

		Wins	Losses	Win Pct	Net Wins
1	Willie McCovey	7.5	4.5	0.625	**3.0**
2	*Luke Appling*	8.3	5.6	*0.596*	**2.7**
3	Rusty Staub	9.1	6.7	0.577	**2.4**
4	Boog Powell	5.8	3.7	0.615	**2.2**
5	*Ted Williams*	7.2	5.0	*0.589*	**2.2**
6	Kent Hrbek	5.1	3.0	0.627	**2.1**
7	George Brett	7.8	5.8	0.574	**2.0**
8	Fred Lynn	5.4	3.5	0.608	**1.9**
9	*Bob Elliott*	6.7	4.8	*0.582*	**1.9**
10	Harold Baines	6.7	4.9	0.579	**1.8**
11	*Babe Ruth*	3.2	1.4	*0.694*	**1.8**
12	Larry Doby	4.6	2.9	0.617	**1.8**
13	Billy Williams	7.5	5.8	0.565	**1.7**
14	Carl Yastrzemski	9.3	7.6	0.551	**1.7**
15	*Joe Medwick*	7.5	5.8	*0.563*	**1.7**
16	Ryan Howard	3.3	1.7	0.661	**1.6**
17	Norm Siebern	4.1	2.5	0.621	**1.6**
18	*Lou Gehrig*	5.1	3.6	*0.590*	**1.6**
19	Eddie Murray	7.6	6.1	0.557	**1.6**
20	Willie Stargell	6.1	4.5	0.573	**1.5**
21	Reggie Jackson	6.3	4.8	0.570	**1.5**
22	*Ernie Lombardi*	4.8	3.3	*0.593*	**1.5**
23	Fred McGriff	5.4	3.9	0.581	**1.5**
24	Tito Francona	4.4	2.9	0.603	**1.5**
25	*Dixie Walker*	7.2	5.7	*0.557*	**1.5**

Component 9: Baserunning Wins
Top 25 Players (Sorted by Net Wins)

		Wins	Losses	Win Pct	Net Wins
1	Willie Davis	8.9	5.1	0.633	**3.7**
2	Rod Carew	10.6	7.2	0.594	**3.4**
3	Bert Campaneris	8.3	5.1	0.620	**3.2**
4	Vada Pinson	8.9	5.7	0.609	**3.2**
5	Willie Wilson	7.6	4.5	0.629	**3.1**
6	Robin Yount	10.3	7.1	0.590	**3.1**
7	Kenny Lofton	8.2	5.1	0.617	**3.1**
8	Minnie Minoso	6.7	3.8	0.639	**2.9**
9	Brett Butler	9.5	6.9	0.579	**2.6**
10	Toby Harrah	7.7	5.1	0.601	**2.6**
11	Frank Robinson	9.8	7.2	0.576	**2.6**
12	Ryne Sandberg	8.2	5.7	0.591	**2.5**
13	Bobby Bonds	7.1	4.7	0.604	**2.4**
14	Tim Raines	8.8	6.5	0.578	**2.4**
15	Lou Brock	10.5	8.2	0.563	**2.4**
16	Rickey Henderson	11.0	8.6	0.560	**2.4**
17	Al Smith	5.8	3.4	0.629	**2.4**
18	*Augie Galan*	*7.4*	*5.1*	*0.592*	**2.3**
19	Pee Wee Reese	8.5	6.2	0.578	**2.3**
20	Luis Aparicio	9.8	7.6	0.565	**2.3**
21	Tommy Harper	6.6	4.4	0.602	**2.3**
22	*Billy Herman*	*7.9*	*5.7*	*0.581*	**2.2**
23	*Johnny Pesky*	*5.5*	*3.4*	*0.622*	**2.2**
24	Dick McAuliffe	6.2	4.0	0.606	**2.2**
25	Lonnie Smith	5.9	3.7	0.612	**2.1**

Component 9: Fielder Wins, P
Top 25 Players (Sorted by Net Wins)

		Wins	Losses	Win Pct	Net Wins
1	*Jack Russell*	*1.8*	*0.7*	*0.710*	**1.0**
2	Don Drysdale	1.6	0.7	0.693	**0.9**
3	Tug McGraw	1.1	0.4	0.731	**0.7**
4	*Hal Newhouser*	*1.2*	*0.5*	*0.688*	**0.7**
5	Danny Jackson	1.2	0.6	0.683	**0.7**
6	Charlie Hough	1.2	0.6	0.671	**0.6**
7	Jack Billingham	1.3	0.7	0.657	**0.6**
8	Clay Carroll	1.3	0.7	0.645	**0.6**
9	Jerry Koosman	1.5	0.9	0.622	**0.6**
10	*Mickey Haefner*	*0.9*	*0.3*	*0.736*	**0.6**
11	Roger McDowell	1.0	0.4	0.695	**0.6**
12	*Alex Carrasquel*	*0.7*	*0.1*	*0.846*	**0.5**
13	Jimmy Key	1.2	0.7	0.644	**0.5**
14	Livan Hernandez	1.3	0.7	0.632	**0.5**
15	Rollie Fingers	0.9	0.4	0.709	**0.5**
16	*Johnny Humphries*	*0.7*	*0.2*	*0.812*	**0.5**
17	John Candelaria	0.9	0.4	0.703	**0.5**
18	John Franco	1.0	0.5	0.680	**0.5**
19	Ray Burris	1.2	0.7	0.635	**0.5**
20	Kirk Rueter	0.8	0.3	0.750	**0.5**
21	*Jesse Petty*	*0.7*	*0.2*	*0.800*	**0.5**
22	Don Stanhouse	0.7	0.2	0.802	**0.5**
23	*Virgil Trucks*	*1.1*	*0.6*	*0.639*	**0.5**
24	Camilo Pascual	1.2	0.7	0.626	**0.5**
25	*Larry French*	*1.5*	*1.1*	*0.592*	**0.5**

Component 9: Fielder Wins, C
Top 25 Players (Sorted by Net Wins)

	Player	Wins	Losses	Win Pct	Net Wins
1	*Rollie Hemsley*	0.9	0.6	0.606	**0.3**
2	Roy Campanella	0.7	0.4	0.650	**0.3**
3	*Shanty Hogan*	0.5	0.2	0.715	**0.3**
4	Gabby Hartnett	0.8	0.5	0.604	**0.3**
5	Ivan Rodriguez	1.2	0.9	0.564	**0.3**
6	*Mike Guerra*	0.4	0.1	0.741	**0.3**
7	Greg Myers	0.4	0.2	0.691	**0.2**
8	Damian Miller	0.4	0.2	0.676	**0.2**
9	Chris Snyder	0.5	0.2	0.653	**0.2**
10	*Mickey Cochrane*	0.6	0.4	0.610	**0.2**
11	Elston Howard	0.5	0.3	0.629	**0.2**
12	Yogi Berra	0.6	0.4	0.592	**0.2**
13	Joe Astroth	0.3	0.1	0.713	**0.2**
14	Yadier Molina	1.1	0.9	0.546	**0.2**
15	Thurman Munson	0.6	0.4	0.598	**0.2**
16	Hank Foiles	0.3	0.1	0.741	**0.2**
17	Miguel Montero	0.6	0.4	0.586	**0.2**
18	Mike Piazza	0.7	0.5	0.570	**0.2**
19	*Al Todd*	0.7	0.5	0.573	**0.2**
20	Chad Kreuter	0.4	0.2	0.636	**0.2**
21	*Johnny Gooch*	0.3	0.2	0.672	**0.2**
22	*Frankie Pytlak*	0.4	0.3	0.618	**0.2**
23	Joe Nolan	0.2	0.1	0.760	**0.2**
24	Welington Castillo	0.2	0.1	0.761	**0.2**
25	Caleb Joseph	0.2	0.0	0.907	**0.2**

Component 9: Fielder Wins, 1B
Top 25 Players (Sorted by Net Wins)

	Player	Wins	Losses	Win Pct	Net Wins
1	Derrek Lee	5.2	3.9	0.574	**1.3**
2	Albert Pujols	5.0	3.8	0.570	**1.2**
3	Will Clark	5.6	4.5	0.555	**1.1**
4	Don Mattingly	4.4	3.3	0.571	**1.1**
5	Mark Grace	6.7	5.6	0.544	**1.1**
6	*Mickey Rocco*	2.1	1.2	0.626	**0.8**
7	Vic Power	3.1	2.3	0.574	**0.8**
8	Kevin Young	2.7	1.9	0.587	**0.8**
9	Adrian Gonzalez	4.2	3.4	0.550	**0.8**
10	*Lou Gehrig*	4.2	3.4	0.549	**0.7**
11	Jason Thompson	3.8	3.1	0.554	**0.7**
12	Ron Fairly	3.5	2.8	0.555	**0.7**
13	Wally Joyner	5.0	4.3	0.535	**0.7**
14	George C. Scott	5.0	4.3	0.536	**0.7**
15	Chris Chambliss	4.9	4.2	0.534	**0.6**
16	Deron Johnson	2.0	1.4	0.587	**0.6**
17	Keith Hernandez	5.4	4.8	0.529	**0.6**
18	Dan Driessen	3.2	2.6	0.550	**0.6**
19	*George McQuinn*	4.3	3.7	0.535	**0.6**
20	Earl Torgeson	3.6	3.0	0.543	**0.6**
21	*Gus Suhr*	3.7	3.1	0.540	**0.5**
22	Ed Kranepool	2.9	2.3	0.552	**0.5**
23	Greg Brock	2.4	1.8	0.563	**0.5**
24	John Olerud	5.2	4.7	0.525	**0.5**
25	Dale Long	2.4	1.9	0.555	**0.5**

Component 9: Fielder Wins, 2B
Top 25 Players (Sorted by Net Wins)

		Wins	Losses	Win Pct	Net Wins
1	Dave Cash	6.3	4.9	0.564	**1.4**
2	Ted Sizemore	5.4	4.1	0.571	**1.4**
3	Willie Randolph	8.4	7.1	0.542	**1.3**
4	Felix Millan	6.4	5.4	0.543	**1.0**
5	*Ski Melillo*	*4.8*	*3.9*	*0.554*	***0.9***
6	Bobby Knoop	5.3	4.4	0.547	**0.9**
7	*Tony Lazzeri*	*5.4*	*4.5*	*0.545*	***0.9***
8	Joe Gordon	5.9	5.0	0.541	**0.9**
9	*Lou Stringer*	*2.3*	*1.4*	*0.618*	***0.9***
10	Ron Hunt	5.9	5.1	0.539	**0.8**
11	Cookie Rojas	5.6	4.7	0.540	**0.8**
12	Sandy Alomar, Sr.	4.3	3.4	0.554	**0.8**
13	Dick Green	4.3	3.5	0.552	**0.8**
14	*Jerry Priddy*	*5.7*	*4.9*	*0.538*	***0.8***
15	Jose Lind	4.2	3.5	0.544	**0.7**
16	Tom Herr	5.3	4.6	0.535	**0.7**
17	*Del Young*	*1.6*	*1.0*	*0.611*	***0.6***
18	Julian Javier	6.0	5.4	0.525	**0.6**
19	Delino DeShields	5.6	5.0	0.526	**0.6**
20	*Pete Coscarart*	*3.5*	*2.9*	*0.543*	***0.6***
21	Rich Dauer	3.0	2.4	0.549	**0.5**
22	Bobby Richardson	4.4	3.9	0.532	**0.5**
23	Don Blasingame	5.1	4.6	0.527	**0.5**
24	Eddie Miksis	2.2	1.6	0.567	**0.5**
25	*Billy Herman*	*9.3*	*8.8*	*0.514*	***0.5***

Component 9: Fielder Wins, 3B
Top 25 Players (Sorted by Net Wins)

		Wins	Losses	Win Pct	Net Wins
1	Wayne Garrett	3.4	1.8	0.647	**1.5**
2	*Stan Hack*	*7.3*	*5.9*	*0.552*	***1.4***
3	Scott Spiezio	1.9	0.6	0.761	**1.3**
4	Doug Rader	6.3	5.1	0.553	**1.2**
5	Ken Reitz	5.0	3.8	0.566	**1.2**
6	Robin Ventura	6.7	5.6	0.547	**1.2**
7	*George Kell*	*5.8*	*4.7*	*0.553*	***1.1***
8	Aurelio Rodriguez	7.2	6.1	0.541	**1.1**
9	Terry Pendleton	7.3	6.2	0.540	**1.1**
10	Kevin Seitzer	4.1	3.1	0.569	**1.0**
11	Matt Dominguez	2.0	1.0	0.666	**1.0**
12	Edwin Encarnacion	3.3	2.3	0.587	**1.0**
13	Toby Harrah	3.9	2.9	0.569	**0.9**
14	Casey McGehee	2.3	1.3	0.628	**0.9**
15	Doug DeCinces	4.9	4.0	0.552	**0.9**
16	Tim Wallach	8.2	7.3	0.530	**0.9**
17	Mike Lowell	4.4	3.5	0.554	**0.9**
18	Bill Rigney	1.4	0.6	0.716	**0.9**
19	Chone Figgins	2.4	1.6	0.605	**0.8**
20	Ron Cey	7.9	7.1	0.528	**0.8**
21	*Harlond Clift*	*7.0*	*6.2*	*0.532*	***0.8***
22	George Brett	6.6	5.8	0.532	**0.8**
23	Pete Rose	2.7	1.9	0.583	**0.8**
24	Danny Ainge	0.9	0.2	0.849	**0.8**
25	Bobby Adams	3.0	2.2	0.572	**0.8**

Component 9: Fielder Wins, SS
Top 25 Players (Sorted by Net Wins)

		Wins	Losses	Win Pct	Net Wins
1	Dave Concepcion	11.0	9.2	0.545	**1.8**
2	*Lou Boudreau*	*7.4*	*5.8*	*0.561*	***1.6***
3	Don Kessinger	11.7	10.3	0.532	**1.4**
4	*Lyn Lary*	*7.1*	*5.8*	*0.551*	***1.3***
5	Tim Foli	8.2	6.8	0.544	**1.3**
6	Tony Fernandez	8.0	6.7	0.544	**1.3**
7	Luis Aparicio	12.0	10.7	0.529	**1.3**
8	*Lennie Merullo*	*4.8*	*3.6*	*0.574*	***1.2***
9	Mark Belanger	8.1	6.9	0.540	**1.2**
10	Ozzie Smith	13.9	12.7	0.521	**1.1**
11	*Dick Bartell*	*8.5*	*7.4*	*0.535*	***1.1***
12	Jose Uribe	4.5	3.4	0.571	**1.1**
13	*Billy Urbanski*	*4.4*	*3.3*	*0.571*	***1.1***
14	*Granny Hamner*	*5.0*	*4.0*	*0.558*	***1.0***
15	Dick Schofield, Jr.	6.0	5.1	0.541	**0.9**
16	Bert Campaneris	10.0	9.1	0.524	**0.9**
17	Mike Bordick	5.3	4.5	0.545	**0.9**
18	Frank Taveras	5.6	4.8	0.542	**0.9**
19	*Jim Levey*	*2.6*	*1.8*	*0.593*	***0.8***
20	Rey Ordonez	3.5	2.7	0.565	**0.8**
21	Julio Lugo	4.4	3.6	0.550	**0.8**
22	Jose Valentin	4.7	3.9	0.545	**0.8**
23	Royce Clayton	8.2	7.5	0.524	**0.8**
24	Freddie Patek	7.1	6.4	0.526	**0.7**
25	Zoilo Versalles	6.5	5.8	0.528	**0.7**

Component 9: Fielder Wins, LF
Top 25 Players (Sorted by Net Wins)

		Wins	Losses	Win Pct	Net Wins
1	Carl Yastrzemski	21.6	18.3	0.541	**3.3**
2	Joe Rudi	10.4	7.7	0.576	**2.7**
3	Tom Grieve	4.4	1.9	0.702	**2.5**
4	*George Case*	*8.0*	*5.7*	*0.586*	***2.4***
5	*Goose Goslin*	*13.3*	*11.1*	*0.546*	***2.3***
6	Al Woods	7.3	5.3	0.579	**2.0**
7	Andres Mora	2.9	1.1	0.730	**1.9**
8	Alex Gordon	7.4	5.7	0.568	**1.8**
9	B.J. Surhoff	7.2	5.5	0.568	**1.7**
10	Steve Braun	5.8	4.1	0.585	**1.7**
11	*Hal Lee*	*7.3*	*5.9*	*0.553*	***1.4***
12	Bubba Morton	1.7	0.3	0.862	**1.4**
13	Ryan Church	3.0	1.7	0.648	**1.4**
14	Pete Rose	7.2	5.8	0.553	**1.4**
15	Rickey Henderson	19.5	18.3	0.517	**1.3**
16	*Guy Curtright*	*3.1*	*2.0*	*0.609*	***1.1***
17	Juan Rivera	4.6	3.5	0.568	**1.1**
18	*Hoot Evers*	*4.6*	*3.5*	*0.570*	***1.1***
19	Carl Crawford	12.3	11.2	0.523	**1.1**
20	*Indian Bob Johnson*	*15.8*	*14.8*	*0.518*	***1.1***
21	*Dave Harris*	*2.3*	*1.3*	*0.643*	***1.0***
22	*Jo-Jo Moore*	*11.8*	*10.8*	*0.522*	***1.0***
23	Henry Cotto	2.5	1.5	0.625	**1.0**
24	Johnny Grubb	4.1	3.1	0.569	**1.0**
25	George Bell	10.5	9.5	0.525	**1.0**

Component 9: Fielder Wins, CF
Top 25 Players (Sorted by Net Wins)

		Wins	Losses	Win Pct	Net Wins
1	Willie Mays	32.9	29.1	0.531	3.8
2	*Joe DiMaggio*	*16.1*	*13.3*	*0.546*	*2.7*
3	Andy Van Slyke	11.8	9.1	0.564	2.7
4	Cesar Geronimo	10.9	8.4	0.567	2.6
5	Cesar Cedeno	17.8	15.4	0.536	2.4
6	*Vince DiMaggio*	*14.4*	*12.2*	*0.542*	*2.2*
7	Andre Dawson	12.1	9.9	0.550	2.2
8	Vic Davalillo	8.2	6.1	0.574	2.1
9	Adam Jones	11.6	9.5	0.548	2.0
10	Andruw Jones	16.6	14.6	0.531	1.9
11	Paul Blair	14.0	12.1	0.536	1.9
12	*Hank Edwards*	*2.6*	*0.7*	*0.781*	*1.9*
13	Vada Pinson	19.4	17.5	0.526	1.9
14	Doug Glanville	8.6	6.7	0.561	1.9
15	Gary Geiger	6.5	4.7	0.579	1.8
16	Matty Alou	10.3	8.6	0.544	1.6
17	Jim Piersall	12.0	10.4	0.536	1.6
18	Mickey Stanley	11.1	9.5	0.538	1.6
19	*Catfish Metkovich*	*5.8*	*4.2*	*0.576*	*1.5*
20	Rob Ducey	2.1	0.5	0.793	1.5
21	Dave Henderson	10.1	8.6	0.540	1.5
22	Dwayne Murphy	12.0	10.7	0.530	1.4
23	Shane Victorino	6.8	5.4	0.555	1.3
24	Dale Murphy	12.0	10.7	0.527	1.2
25	Ken Griffey, Jr.	19.7	18.5	0.516	1.2

Component 9: Fielder Wins, RF
Top 25 Players (Sorted by Net Wins)

		Wins	Losses	Win Pct	Net Wins
1	Roberto Clemente	26.0	22.5	0.536	3.5
2	Ellis Valentine	9.5	6.6	0.588	2.9
3	Al Kaline	18.6	15.8	0.541	2.8
4	Jose Bautista	8.5	5.8	0.596	2.7
5	Raul Mondesi	13.5	10.9	0.554	2.6
6	Dwight Evans	20.7	18.4	0.529	2.3
7	Jesse Barfield	12.6	10.4	0.547	2.2
8	Tony Oliva	12.0	9.9	0.549	2.1
9	Larry Walker	16.3	14.4	0.532	1.9
10	Jeff Francoeur	13.1	11.2	0.538	1.9
11	*Pete Fox*	*12.3*	*10.6*	*0.538*	*1.8*
12	Jack Clark	11.5	9.8	0.539	1.7
13	*Ethan Allen*	*2.6*	*1.0*	*0.729*	*1.6*
14	Tim Salmon	12.5	10.9	0.533	1.6
15	Bobby Abreu	18.0	16.4	0.523	1.5
16	Ichiro Suzuki	16.4	14.9	0.524	1.5
17	Will Venable	5.3	3.9	0.576	1.4
18	Rusty Staub	17.7	16.3	0.521	1.4
19	Willie Kirkland	8.4	7.0	0.545	1.4
20	Johnny Callison	16.5	15.2	0.522	1.4
21	Jim Piersall	3.6	2.2	0.617	1.4
22	Felipe Alou	7.3	6.0	0.550	1.3
23	Hank Aaron	20.8	19.5	0.516	1.3
24	*George Case*	*5.1*	*3.8*	*0.574*	*1.3*
25	Al Cowens	12.2	10.9	0.528	1.3

Relationship of Components 8 and 9

Component 8, baserunner outs, and Component 9, baserunner advancements, are very closely related. From the perspective of the baserunner, there is a school of thought that more aggressive baserunning has as its upside greater than average baserunner advancement (Component 9) with a downside of increased baserunner outs (Component 8).

For fielders (mostly outfielders), conventional wisdom suggests a similar negative relationship as the outfielders with the strongest arms will simply deter baserunners from trying to advance (Component 9), leading to relatively fewer baserunner outs (Component 8).

Basic Correlation Between Component 8 and Component 9 Winning Percentages

Looking at Components 8 and 9, how do players' Component 8 winning percentages compare with their Component 9 winning percentages? I calculated weighted correlations for Component 8 and 9 winning percentages across all of the years over which I have calculated pW-L records. Correlations range in value from –100% to +100%. A correlation of +100% would mean that Component 8 and Component 9 winning percentages were perfectly proportional. A correlation of –100% would mean that Component 8 and 9 winning percentages moved in precisely opposite directions. A correlation of 0% would mean that Component 8 and 9 winning percentages are entirely unrelated.

The results are as follows:

Batters: –2.13%
Baserunners: –0.45%
Fielders: 2.00%

In general, all of these correlations are extremely small, suggesting—somewhat surprisingly, perhaps—that Component 8 and Component 9 are essentially uncorrelated, and are, therefore, likely measuring distinct skills.

Alternately, this apparent lack of correlation could be the result of offsetting correlations.

On the one hand, good baserunners tend to be good at all aspects of baserunning, and it makes sense that outfielders with good throwing arms would be good at everything which involves throwing. This would suggest a strong *positive* correlation between Components 8 and 9.

On the other hand, the logic which I laid out above—(1) that fielders who have the best throwing arms deter base advancement and therefore have less opportunity to throw out baserunners, or (2) that aggressive baserunning may lead to higher-than-average Component 8 losses and Component 9 wins—would suggest a *negative* correlation between Components 8 and 9.

If, in fact, both hypotheses are true, perhaps that explains the apparent lack of correlation—the positive and negative factors essentially cancel one another out.

The top 25 players in net combined Component 8 and 9 wins (wins minus losses) are presented in the final eleven tables of this chapter: batters, baserunners, and each of the nine fielding positions (including pitchers).

Components 8 & 9: Batting Wins
Top 25 Players (Sorted by Net Wins)

		Wins	Losses	Win Pct	Net Wins
1	Willie McCovey	9.6	6.8	0.584	2.8
2	Rusty Staub	11.9	9.2	0.563	2.7
3	Kent Hrbek	6.4	3.9	0.622	2.5
4	*Ted Williams*	*9.5*	*7.1*	*0.571*	2.4
5	George Brett	10.3	7.9	0.565	2.4
6	Eddie Murray	10.2	7.9	0.563	2.3
7	Boog Powell	7.6	5.3	0.587	2.2
8	Carl Yastrzemski	12.3	10.2	0.547	2.1
9	*Bob Elliott*	*8.9*	*6.8*	*0.566*	*2.1*
10	Harold Baines	8.9	6.8	0.567	2.1
11	Rico Carty	6.3	4.2	0.596	2.0
12	*Ernie Lombardi*	*6.6*	*4.6*	*0.589*	*2.0*
13	*Babe Ruth*	*4.1*	*2.2*	*0.655*	*1.9*
14	Frank Howard	5.8	3.9	0.597	1.9
15	Norm Siebern	5.3	3.4	0.609	1.9
16	Duke Snider	7.3	5.5	0.572	1.8
17	Fred McGriff	7.1	5.2	0.575	1.8
18	Tito Francona	5.6	3.8	0.598	1.8
19	Larry Doby	6.1	4.3	0.589	1.8
20	Ted Kluszewski	6.8	5.0	0.578	1.8
21	*Bill Nicholson*	*6.5*	*4.7*	*0.580*	*1.8*
22	Dave Winfield	10.6	8.8	0.546	1.8
23	Reggie Jackson	8.4	6.7	0.559	1.8
24	Billy Williams	9.8	8.0	0.549	1.7
25	*Al Simmons*	*7.9*	*6.1*	*0.561*	*1.7*

Components 8 & 9: Baserunning Wins
Top 25 Players (Sorted by Net Wins)

		Wins	Losses	Win Pct	Net Wins
1	Robin Yount	13.7	9.4	0.594	4.3
2	Willie Wilson	10.1	6.3	0.617	3.8
3	Willie Davis	11.8	8.2	0.590	3.6
4	Tim Raines	11.9	8.3	0.587	3.5
5	Bert Campaneris	11.1	7.7	0.592	3.5
6	Kenny Lofton	10.7	7.6	0.587	3.2
7	Tommy Harper	8.9	5.7	0.607	3.1
8	Paul Molitor	14.3	11.3	0.559	3.0
9	Frank Robinson	13.5	10.5	0.562	3.0
10	Brett Butler	12.4	9.5	0.567	2.9
11	Toby Harrah	10.5	7.6	0.580	2.9
12	Ryne Sandberg	11.0	8.1	0.575	2.9
13	Rickey Henderson	14.9	12.1	0.552	2.8
14	*Billy Herman*	*11.1*	*8.3*	*0.572*	*2.8*
15	Pee Wee Reese	11.8	9.0	0.567	2.8
16	Red Schoendienst	11.5	8.8	0.568	2.7
17	Davey Lopes	8.6	5.9	0.593	2.7
18	Bill Bruton	8.2	5.4	0.599	2.7
19	Maury Wills	10.6	7.9	0.573	2.7
20	*Johnny Pesky*	*7.8*	*5.1*	*0.605*	*2.7*
21	Rod Carew	14.6	11.9	0.551	2.7
22	Richie Ashburn	13.6	10.9	0.555	2.7
23	Dick McAuliffe	8.3	5.7	0.591	2.5
24	Hank Aaron	15.3	12.8	0.545	2.5
25	Vada Pinson	12.5	10.0	0.555	2.5

Components 8 & 9: Fielder Wins, P
Top 25 Players (Sorted by Net Wins)

		Wins	Losses	Win Pct	Net Wins
1	Jack Russell	2.1	0.9	0.700	1.2
2	Don Drysdale	1.8	1.0	0.659	0.9
3	Tug McGraw	1.4	0.5	0.720	0.8
4	Livan Hernandez	1.7	0.9	0.659	0.8
5	Jerry Koosman	1.9	1.2	0.620	0.7
6	Larry McWilliams	1.2	0.5	0.697	0.7
7	Kirk Rueter	1.0	0.4	0.735	0.6
8	Mickey Haefner	1.0	0.5	0.691	0.6
9	Danny Jackson	1.2	0.7	0.649	0.6
10	Johnny Humphries	0.8	0.2	0.779	0.6
11	Ray Burris	1.4	0.8	0.628	0.6
12	Clay Carroll	1.4	0.9	0.618	0.6
13	Charlie Leibrandt	1.6	1.0	0.604	0.5
14	Jack Billingham	1.3	0.8	0.625	0.5
15	Roger McDowell	1.1	0.5	0.664	0.5
16	Hal Newhouser	1.3	0.8	0.625	0.5
17	John Candelaria	1.0	0.5	0.673	0.5
18	Gary Peters	1.1	0.5	0.662	0.5
19	Don Stanhouse	0.7	0.2	0.764	0.5
20	Ellis Kinder	0.9	0.4	0.693	0.5
21	Mike Caldwell	1.3	0.8	0.619	0.5
22	Dave Freisleben	0.7	0.2	0.788	0.5
23	Camilo Pascual	1.4	0.9	0.604	0.5
24	Joe Niekro	1.6	1.1	0.590	0.5
25	Bob Shawkey	0.7	0.3	0.735	0.5

Components 8 & 9: Fielder Wins, C
Top 25 Players (Sorted by Net Wins)

		Wins	Losses	Win Pct	Net Wins
1	Mickey Cochrane	1.2	0.5	0.689	0.7
2	Rollie Hemsley	1.5	1.0	0.593	0.5
3	Al Todd	1.2	0.7	0.626	0.5
4	Yogi Berra	1.2	0.8	0.604	0.4
5	Rick Ferrell	1.5	1.1	0.571	0.4
6	Johnny Gooch	0.7	0.3	0.691	0.4
7	Roy Campanella	0.9	0.6	0.610	0.3
8	Shanty Hogan	0.7	0.3	0.670	0.3
9	Damian Miller	0.6	0.3	0.650	0.3
10	Thurman Munson	0.8	0.5	0.603	0.3
11	Elston Howard	0.7	0.5	0.611	0.3
12	Ernie Lombardi	1.1	0.8	0.568	0.3
13	Mike Ryan	0.4	0.2	0.680	0.2
14	Clay Dalrymple	0.8	0.5	0.588	0.2
15	Tony Giuliani	0.3	0.1	0.755	0.2
16	Ivan Rodriguez	1.3	1.1	0.546	0.2
17	Frankie Pytlak	0.6	0.4	0.606	0.2
18	Joe Azcue	0.5	0.3	0.637	0.2
19	Mickey Livingston	0.4	0.2	0.678	0.2
20	Greg Myers	0.4	0.2	0.658	0.2
21	Jim Sundberg	0.9	0.7	0.562	0.2
22	Welington Castillo	0.3	0.1	0.762	0.2
23	Randy Hundley	0.5	0.3	0.621	0.2
24	Don Slaught	0.7	0.5	0.586	0.2
25	Mickey Owen	1.1	0.9	0.547	0.2

Components 8 & 9: Fielder Wins, 1B
Top 25 Players (Sorted by Net Wins)

		Wins	Losses	Win Pct	Net Wins
1	Albert Pujols	6.3	4.9	0.562	1.4
2	Vic Power	5.2	3.8	0.576	1.4
3	Don Mattingly	5.8	4.6	0.557	1.2
4	Will Clark	6.9	5.7	0.545	1.1
5	Keith Hernandez	7.9	6.8	0.537	1.1
6	Wally Joyner	6.6	5.5	0.544	1.1
7	Mark Grace	8.1	7.0	0.535	1.1
8	Derrek Lee	6.1	5.1	0.545	1.0
9	Gil Hodges	7.1	6.2	0.534	0.9
10	Kevin Young	3.4	2.5	0.577	0.9
11	Greg Brock	3.5	2.6	0.573	0.9
12	Jason Thompson	5.1	4.3	0.544	0.8
13	*Rudy York*	*5.7*	*4.9*	*0.539*	*0.8*
14	*Gus Suhr*	*5.5*	*4.7*	*0.537*	*0.8*
15	Ed Kranepool	4.2	3.4	0.550	0.8
16	Eddie Murray	8.7	7.9	0.523	0.8
17	*Lou Gehrig*	*6.2*	*5.5*	*0.532*	*0.7*
18	Adrian Gonzalez	5.0	4.3	0.539	0.7
19	Jeff Bagwell	8.1	7.4	0.523	0.7
20	*Mickey Rocco*	*2.7*	*2.0*	*0.575*	*0.7*
21	Deron Johnson	2.8	2.1	0.571	0.7
22	John Olerud	6.6	5.9	0.527	0.7
23	*George McQuinn*	*6.4*	*5.7*	*0.527*	*0.7*
24	Dale Long	3.5	2.9	0.551	0.7
25	Whitey Lockman	3.1	2.4	0.558	0.6

Components 8 & 9: Fielder Wins, 2B
Top 25 Players (Sorted by Net Wins)

		Wins	Losses	Win Pct	Net Wins
1	*Ski Melillo*	*7.9*	*6.2*	*0.562*	*1.7*
2	Dave Cash	8.1	6.5	0.556	1.6
3	Ted Sizemore	7.2	5.8	0.554	1.4
4	Felix Millan	8.6	7.2	0.544	1.4
5	Willie Randolph	11.1	9.8	0.533	1.4
6	Don Blasingame	7.7	6.5	0.541	1.2
7	Delino DeShields	7.6	6.6	0.537	1.1
8	Bobby Knoop	7.0	6.0	0.540	1.0
9	Julian Javier	8.8	7.8	0.530	1.0
10	*Joe Gordon*	*8.5*	*7.6*	*0.530*	*1.0*
11	Cookie Rojas	7.6	6.7	0.532	0.9
12	Robinson Cano	5.9	5.0	0.538	0.8
13	*Billy Herman*	*13.1*	*12.3*	*0.515*	*0.8*
14	Sandy Alomar, Sr.	5.7	4.9	0.535	0.7
15	*Lou Stringer*	*2.7*	*2.0*	*0.578*	*0.7*
16	Tom Herr	7.0	6.2	0.528	0.7
17	*Tony Lazzeri*	*7.3*	*6.6*	*0.526*	*0.7*
18	Jackie Robinson	3.9	3.1	0.551	0.7
19	Pete Rose	4.3	3.6	0.545	0.7
20	Jerry Adair	4.2	3.5	0.546	0.7
21	Marty Perez	2.9	2.2	0.567	0.7
22	Dick Green	5.7	5.0	0.531	0.7
23	Carlos Baerga	4.9	4.3	0.535	0.6
24	*Sparky Adams*	*2.5*	*1.9*	*0.573*	*0.6*
25	Keith Lockhart	2.1	1.5	0.587	0.6

Components 8 & 9: Fielder Wins, 3B
Top 25 Players (Sorted by Net Wins)

		Wins	Losses	Win Pct	Net Wins
1	Aurelio Rodriguez	9.6	7.8	0.552	1.8
2	Wayne Garrett	4.1	2.5	0.624	1.6
3	Doug Rader	7.9	6.6	0.546	1.3
4	Scott Spiezio	2.0	0.7	0.742	1.3
5	Ken Reitz	6.0	4.7	0.559	1.3
6	Tim Wallach	9.9	8.8	0.530	1.1
7	*George Kell*	*7.7*	*6.6*	*0.540*	*1.1*
8	Robin Ventura	7.7	6.5	0.540	1.1
9	Doug DeCinces	6.4	5.4	0.544	1.0
10	Matt Dominguez	2.2	1.1	0.653	1.0
11	*Ken Keltner*	*7.5*	*6.6*	*0.535*	*1.0*
12	Kevin Seitzer	4.7	3.7	0.558	1.0
13	*Stan Hack*	*8.6*	*7.6*	*0.529*	*0.9*
14	*Harlond Clift*	*8.7*	*7.8*	*0.527*	*0.9*
15	Edwin Encarnacion	3.4	2.6	0.574	0.9
16	Joe Torre	2.8	1.9	0.595	0.9
17	Clete Boyer	6.7	5.8	0.533	0.8
18	Casey McGehee	2.4	1.5	0.607	0.8
19	Bill Rigney	1.5	0.7	0.684	0.8
20	*Wally Gilbert*	*2.5*	*1.7*	*0.597*	*0.8*
21	*Doc Prothro*	*1.2*	*0.4*	*0.751*	*0.8*
22	Troy Glaus	5.0	4.2	0.543	0.8
23	Ron Cey	9.5	8.7	0.522	0.8
24	Toby Harrah	4.6	3.8	0.546	0.8
25	Danny Ainge	1.0	0.2	0.815	0.8

Components 8 & 9: Fielder Wins, SS
Top 25 Players (Sorted by Net Wins)

		Wins	Losses	Win Pct	Net Wins
1	*Lou Boudreau*	*11.3*	*8.0*	*0.587*	*3.4*
2	Luis Aparicio	15.9	13.9	0.533	2.0
3	Ozzie Smith	17.7	15.9	0.528	1.8
4	Dave Concepcion	13.7	11.9	0.535	1.8
5	Tim Foli	10.3	8.8	0.541	1.6
6	Don Kessinger	14.4	12.9	0.528	1.5
7	Tony Fernandez	9.8	8.3	0.542	1.5
8	Frank Taveras	7.6	6.2	0.551	1.4
9	*Dick Bartell*	*11.0*	*9.7*	*0.533*	*1.4*
10	Jose Uribe	5.7	4.4	0.567	1.4
11	Mark Belanger	10.2	8.9	0.535	1.4
12	*Lennie Merullo*	*5.8*	*4.6*	*0.559*	*1.2*
13	Jack Wilson	6.4	5.2	0.552	1.2
14	Rey Ordonez	4.5	3.4	0.569	1.1
15	Toby Harrah	5.8	4.7	0.551	1.1
16	Zoilo Versalles	8.4	7.4	0.532	1.0
17	*Granny Hamner*	*6.7*	*5.7*	*0.541*	*1.0*
18	*Lyn Lary*	*9.0*	*7.9*	*0.530*	*1.0*
19	Royce Clayton	10.0	9.0	0.527	1.0
20	*Billy Urbanski*	*5.3*	*4.3*	*0.553*	*1.0*
21	Ron Hansen	7.8	6.8	0.535	1.0
22	Mike Bordick	6.6	5.6	0.541	1.0
23	*Skeeter Newsome*	*6.5*	*5.5*	*0.540*	*1.0*
24	Julio Lugo	5.4	4.4	0.547	0.9
25	Johnny Logan	9.6	8.7	0.523	0.9

Components 8 & 9: Fielder Wins, LF
Top 25 Players (Sorted by Net Wins)

		Wins	Losses	Win Pct	Net Wins
1	Carl Yastrzemski	33.6	27.3	0.552	6.3
2	*Indian Bob Johnson*	*27.7*	*22.8*	*0.548*	**4.9**
3	Goose Goslin	20.9	17.5	0.546	3.5
4	B.J. Surhoff	11.7	8.5	0.580	3.2
5	Tom Grieve	5.8	2.9	0.671	3.0
6	Alex Gordon	11.3	8.6	0.568	2.7
7	Bobby Higginson	11.4	8.9	0.561	2.5
8	Willie Stargell	18.1	15.6	0.537	2.5
9	Bernard Gilkey	14.9	12.5	0.544	2.4
10	*Jo-Jo Moore*	*17.4*	*15.1*	*0.535*	**2.3**
11	Joe Rudi	14.1	12.0	0.540	2.1
12	Andres Mora	3.6	1.6	0.694	2.0
13	Steve Braun	8.0	6.1	0.569	1.9
14	Yoenis Cespedes	5.7	3.8	0.599	1.9
15	*George Case*	*10.5*	*8.7*	*0.546*	**1.8**
16	Juan Rivera	6.9	5.2	0.571	1.7
17	Ryan Church	3.8	2.1	0.641	1.7
18	Barry Bonds	32.5	30.9	0.512	1.6
19	Pete Rose	10.3	8.8	0.540	1.5
20	*Hoot Evers*	*7.0*	*5.5*	*0.560*	**1.5**
21	George Bell	15.1	13.6	0.526	1.5
22	Vince Coleman	15.7	14.2	0.525	1.5
23	Bubba Morton	1.8	0.4	0.832	1.5
24	Al Woods	9.2	7.8	0.542	1.4
25	Jeffrey Leonard	13.3	11.9	0.528	1.4

Components 8 & 9: Fielder Wins, CF
Top 25 Players (Sorted by Net Wins)

		Wins	Losses	Win Pct	Net Wins
1	Willie Mays	45.0	40.7	0.525	4.3
2	Andy Van Slyke	17.0	12.8	0.571	4.2
3	Adam Jones	16.4	12.5	0.568	4.0
4	*Joe DiMaggio*	*23.9*	*20.2*	*0.542*	**3.7**
5	Cesar Geronimo	15.6	12.0	0.565	3.6
6	*Dom DiMaggio*	*24.4*	*21.0*	*0.537*	**3.4**
7	Paul Blair	20.8	17.4	0.544	3.3
8	Jim Edmonds	21.6	18.5	0.538	3.1
9	Andruw Jones	23.2	20.3	0.534	3.0
10	*Vince DiMaggio*	*19.9*	*17.0*	*0.539*	**2.9**
11	Andre Dawson	16.8	13.9	0.546	2.8
12	Ken Griffey, Jr.	28.4	25.6	0.526	2.8
13	Vada Pinson	27.0	24.3	0.527	2.7
14	Bill Tuttle	16.5	13.8	0.545	2.7
15	Gary Geiger	9.0	6.5	0.581	2.5
16	Brian L. Hunter	10.2	7.8	0.568	2.4
17	Dave Henderson	14.5	12.2	0.545	2.4
18	Kenny Lofton	24.3	21.9	0.526	2.4
19	Vic Davalillo	10.7	8.3	0.562	2.3
20	*Terry Moore*	*19.2*	*16.9*	*0.532*	**2.3**
21	Matty Alou	13.7	11.5	0.544	2.2
22	Dwayne Murphy	17.4	15.2	0.534	2.2
23	Hal Jeffcoat	7.7	5.7	0.572	1.9
24	Cesar Cedeno	23.2	21.2	0.521	1.9
25	Shane Victorino	9.1	7.3	0.554	1.8

Retrosheet has not released complete play-by-play data for the early parts of their careers, so that some of the results here are extrapolated. But, based on the data we do have, the three DiMaggio brothers were all among the top 10 centerfielders at controlling baserunner advancement among all players for whom I have calculated pW-L records.

Components 8 & 9: Fielder Wins, RF
Top 25 Players (Sorted by Net Wins)

		Wins	Losses	Win Pct	Net Wins
1	Roberto Clemente	41.0	34.6	0.542	**6.4**
2	Jesse Barfield	21.9	15.9	0.579	**6.0**
3	Jeff Francoeur	20.3	15.6	0.567	**4.8**
4	Ellis Valentine	14.9	10.3	0.590	**4.5**
5	Johnny Callison	26.4	22.8	0.537	**3.6**
6	Jose Bautista	11.8	8.2	0.590	**3.6**
7	Al Kaline	27.5	24.1	0.534	**3.5**
8	Larry Walker	24.8	21.4	0.537	**3.4**
9	Rusty Staub	27.1	23.9	0.531	**3.1**
10	*Roy Cullenbine*	*11.8*	*8.8*	*0.572*	*2.9*
11	Dwight Evans	30.4	27.4	0.525	**2.9**
12	Jack Clark	17.4	14.6	0.544	**2.8**
13	Raul Mondesi	19.2	16.4	0.540	**2.8**
14	Bobby Abreu	25.8	23.2	0.527	**2.6**
15	Glenn Wilson	14.6	12.2	0.545	**2.4**
16	Hank Aaron	31.5	29.4	0.518	**2.2**
17	Willie Kirkland	12.4	10.3	0.547	**2.1**
18	Tony Oliva	16.5	14.4	0.534	**2.1**
19	*Chuck Klein*	*23.8*	*21.9*	*0.521*	*1.9*
20	Al Cowens	18.5	16.7	0.526	**1.8**
21	Alexis Rios	15.6	13.8	0.531	**1.8**
22	*Tommy Henrich*	*12.9*	*11.1*	*0.537*	*1.8*
23	*Bob Kennedy*	*8.7*	*7.0*	*0.557*	*1.8*
24	Tim Salmon	18.1	16.4	0.526	**1.8**
25	Richard Hidalgo	7.7	5.9	0.564	**1.7**

5. Offensive Player Won-Lost Records

This chapter takes a somewhat closer look at offensive pW-L records. Offensive pW-L records can be earned by players as either a batter or a baserunner.

Batting

Batting accounts for approximately 45.7% of total Player decisions. Batting decisions are accumulated in seven Components:

- Component 3: Balls not in Play
- Component 4: Balls in Play
- Component 5: Hits vs. Outs
- Component 6: Singles v. Doubles v. Triples
- Component 7: Double Plays
- Component 8: Baserunning Outs, and
- Component 9: Baserunner Advancements

Offensive Player decisions in Components 7, 8, and 9 are shared between Batters and Baserunners.

The average breakdown of these components is as follows:

	1930–2015	*2000–2015*
Component 3: Balls not in Play	16.2%	18.1%
Component 4: Balls in Play	38.6%	38.7%
Component 5: Hits vs. Outs	35.8%	34.6%
Component 6: Singles v. Doubles v. Triples	3.9%	3.5%
Component 7: Double Plays	1.4%	1.7%
Component 8: Baserunning Outs	1.1%	0.8%
Component 9: Baserunner Advancements	3.0%	2.6%

Comparing Offensive pW-L Records

There is one minor complication when it comes to comparing offensive won-lost records across players. pW-L records are constructed so that they will produce an overall winning percentage of 0.500 at every level. So, overall, batters will compile a 0.500 batting winning percentage, baserunners will compile a 0.500 baserunning winning percentage, etc. That 0.500 will include all of the batters in a particular league.

In the National League (and in both leagues prior to 1973), the pool of "batters" who combine to produce that 0.500 winning percentage includes pitchers. In the American League since 1973, however, the pool of "batters" who combine to produce a 0.500 winning percentage will not include pitchers but will include designated hitters.

Because of this, the average non-pitcher will be an above-average hitter in the National League while the average non-pitcher will be an average hitter in the American League (since 1973) by construction. In order to compare American League and National League hitters, therefore, one has to compare them to different baselines. Specifically, I calculate separate positional averages for hitters in DH and non–DH leagues. I call this term PosAvg_b, the positional average for non-pitcher batters (and baserunners).

Batting prowess, relative to average, can then be calculated by comparing a players batting (or baserunning) wins (call it eWins_b) to the number of wins an average non-pitcher would have been expected to accumulate in that player's total decisions, which is equal to PosAvg_b*(eWins_b + eLosses_b). I call this difference WOPA_b: batting (or baserunning) wins over positional average for non-pitchers.

Batting Leaders of the Retrosheet Era

The top 50 players in career batting wins over non-pitcher average (WOPA_b) are shown in the table below.

		eWins	eLosses	eWOPA_b
1	Ted Williams	260.2	142.7	54.8
2	Barry Bonds	303.5	186.3	54.0
3	Hank Aaron	332.4	233.7	44.1
4	Mickey Mantle	241.9	149.7	42.4
5	Willie Mays	294.1	199.7	42.4
6	Stan Musial	298.7	206.7	41.2
7	Mel Ott	244.4	154.7	41.1
8	Frank Robinson	277.5	191.0	39.1
9	Lou Gehrig	186.8	109.9	35.7
10	Mike Schmidt	234.2	160.2	33.4
11	Jimmie Foxx	200.9	128.0	33.3
12	Alex Rodriguez	263.0	197.2	32.3
13	Frank Thomas	222.2	158.2	31.7
14	Harmon Killebrew	232.1	162.0	31.6
15	Jim Thome	225.0	160.4	31.5
16	Willie McCovey	224.8	155.7	30.9
17	Carl Yastrzemski	304.3	236.7	30.7
18	Manny Ramirez	219.6	157.7	30.4
19	Albert Pujols	230.2	165.7	29.6
20	Reggie Jackson	248.2	186.9	29.4
21	Mark McGwire	176.1	118.3	28.0
22	Babe Ruth	123.2	64.8	27.6
23	Eddie Mathews	224.8	162.7	27.3
24	Willie Stargell	209.2	148.6	26.8
25	Jeff Bagwell	211.6	151.7	26.6
26	Johnny Mize	176.0	118.5	26.0
27	Gary Sheffield	237.1	180.3	25.7
28	Todd Helton	209.5	152.5	25.4
29	Chipper Jones	233.1	175.4	25.3
30	Duke Snider	194.4	138.3	24.8
31	Al Kaline	255.3	198.2	24.5
32	Larry Walker	183.3	128.9	24.3

		eWins	eLosses	eWOPA_b
33	Billy Williams	235.5	179.8	24.1
34	Dick Allen	172.1	119.1	24.0
35	Joe Morgan	233.9	178.8	23.8
36	Ken Griffey, Jr.	240.1	190.7	23.3
37	Miguel Cabrera	188.5	139.4	23.3
38	*Joe DiMaggio*	*179.0*	*126.8*	*23.1*
39	Rafael Palmeiro	250.8	203.6	23.1
40	David Ortiz	207.0	160.4	22.8
41	Rickey Henderson	256.0	209.4	22.5
42	Fred McGriff	216.4	167.8	22.3
43	Jason Giambi	187.8	142.2	22.3
44	Dwight Evans	220.8	176.1	22.3
45	*Dolph Camilli*	*145.0*	*97.0*	*21.8*
46	Norm Cash	179.9	130.7	21.8
47	*Hank Greenberg*	*144.8*	*96.7*	*21.7*
48	Ralph Kiner	146.0	98.3	21.4
49	Edgar Martinez	181.0	137.9	21.4
50	Lance Berkman	171.5	124.9	20.9

Baserunning

Baserunning accounts for approximately 4.3% percent of total Player decisions. Baserunning decisions are accumulated in five Components:

- Component 1: Stolen Bases
- Component 2: Wild Pitches and Passed Balls
- Component 7: Double Plays
- Component 8: Baserunning Outs, and
- Component 9: Baserunner Advancements

Offensive Player decisions in Components 7, 8, and 9 are shared between Batters and Baserunners.

Baserunning decisions can be broken down in two ways: by component and by the starting base of the baserunner. The table below shows both of these breakdowns over the full time period over which I have estimated Player decisions.

		Starting Base			
Component	*Batter*	*First*	*Second*	*Third*	*Total by Component*
Component 1		19.6%	3.9%	2.2%	**25.7%**
Component 2	1.1%	6.0%	4.3%	3.9%	**15.3%**
Component 7		3.9%			**3.9%**
Component 8	5.9%	5.5%	3.4%	0.9%	**15.7%**
Component 9	5.9%	17.0%	16.5%	0.0%	**39.4%**
Total by Baserunner	**12.9%**	**52.1%**	**28.1%**	**7.0%**	

The only one of these five components that is tracked with traditional baseball statistics, Component 1, accounts for only one-quarter of total baserunning.

The numbers identified by me as "baserunning" are limited to those which are completely divorced from a player's batting. There are, however, aspects of batting which have a strong baserunning component, such as the ability to stretch extra-base hits or the ability to avoid hitting into a double play. The relationship between batting and baserunning is explored later in this chapter.

Baserunning Leaders of the Retrosheet Era

The top 50 players in career baserunning wins over non-pitcher average (WOPA_b) are shown in the table below.

		eWins	eLosses	eWOPA_b
1	Rickey Henderson	53.3	37.3	7.8
2	Tim Raines	35.6	21.6	6.6
3	Willie Wilson	29.0	16.1	6.4
4	Bert Campaneris	36.5	24.5	5.6
5	Paul Molitor	30.9	21.9	4.5
6	Davey Lopes	24.7	15.6	4.2
7	Vince Coleman	27.0	17.9	4.2
8	Joe Morgan	37.3	27.7	4.2
9	Luis Aparicio	31.5	23.0	3.7
10	Lou Brock	42.7	33.9	3.6
11	Kenny Lofton	26.8	19.4	3.6
12	Otis Nixon	24.4	17.6	3.2
13	Barry Larkin	22.6	15.5	3.2
14	Tommy Harper	22.7	15.8	3.1
15	Johnny Damon	23.0	16.8	3.1
16	Ron LeFlore	20.0	13.9	3.0
17	Willie Davis	24.6	17.9	2.9
18	Robin Yount	24.6	18.8	2.9
19	Jimmy Rollins	23.3	16.9	2.9
20	Amos Otis	20.0	14.3	2.8
21	Mookie Wilson	18.4	12.5	2.7
22	Ozzie Smith	31.1	24.7	2.7
23	Eric Davis	16.7	10.8	2.7
24	Cesar Cedeno	27.7	21.5	2.6
25	Carl Crawford	18.7	13.3	2.6
26	Juan Pierre	25.9	20.2	2.5
27	Marquis Grissom	22.2	16.7	2.4
28	Devon White	18.9	13.9	2.4
29	Roberto Alomar	24.5	19.4	2.4
30	Rajai Davis	12.3	7.5	2.4
31	Maury Wills	29.0	23.3	2.3
32	Mickey Mantle	19.5	14.3	2.3
33	Ichiro Suzuki	23.5	18.9	2.3
34	Gary Redus	14.2	9.4	2.3
35	Tony Womack	15.3	10.3	2.2
36	Jacoby Ellsbury	12.1	7.6	2.2
37	Willie Mays	29.8	24.3	2.2
38	Hank Aaron	27.4	22.0	2.2
39	Alex Rodriguez	20.6	16.2	2.2
40	Derek Jeter	24.6	20.1	2.2
41	Carlos Beltran	18.1	13.5	2.2
42	Bobby Bonds	24.8	20.0	2.2
43	Jose Reyes	21.1	16.4	2.1
44	Mickey Rivers	17.6	13.4	2.1
45	Lou Whitaker	20.8	16.8	2.0
46	Lonnie Smith	20.3	15.7	2.0
47	Toby Harrah	19.5	15.4	2.0
48	Delino DeShields	19.9	15.4	2.0
49	Ryne Sandberg	22.4	17.7	2.0
50	Lance Johnson	15.4	11.4	1.9

Batting vs. Baserunning: The Impact of Speed on pW-L Records

The distinction between Batting and Baserunning is arguably more subjective than I make it sound in some of my work. In particular, there is a baserunning component to several batting components: Component 5—e.g., the ability to beat out infield hits, Component 6—e.g., the ability to stretch doubles into triples, and Component 7—the ability to beat out relay throws on would-be double plays.

Setting aside Components 5, 6, and 7, the other batting components (3, 4, 8, and 9) can be thought of as "Pure Batting" components.

Weighted correlations of player winning percentages by component can help to provide some insight into the extent to which these mixed components can best be classified as Batting or Baserunning. Correlations range in value from −1 (−100%) to +1 (100%). A correlation of 100% would mean that the two winning percentages move perfectly in sync; a correlation of −100% would mean that, as a player's pure batting winning percentage increases, his mixed winning percentage decreases proportionally; a correlation of zero would suggest no relation at all between the two winning percentages for players.

	Weighted Correlation with	
Component	*Pure Batting*	*Baserunning*
Component 5	28.3%	11.4%
Component 6	12.6%	10.3%
Component 7	−3.2%	9.4%

Overall, the correlation between the winning percentage of Pure Batting components and Component 5 winning percentage is 28.3%, suggesting a fairly significant positive relationship between these two sets of winning percentages. The correlation between Baserunning winning percentages and Component 5 winning percentages, on the other hand, is 11.4%, not quite as strong as the correlation with Pure Batting but somewhat significant nonetheless. One could use these two correlations to separate Component 5 into a "batting" versus a "baserunning" skill. Setting the "batting" share equal to the batting correlation (28.3%) divided by the sum of the two correlations (28.3% + 11.4%) suggests that Component 5 offensive player decisions could be characterized as 71.2% batting vs. 28.8% baserunning.

Doing the same thing with Component 6, the correlations are 12.6% with Pure Batting and 10.3% with Baserunning. Using this to divide Component 6 would lead to a split of 55.0% batting, 45.0% baserunning.

The most interesting result comes from the Component 7 decisions allocated to batters. The correlation between Component 7 winning percentages and Pure Batting components is −3.2%, suggesting, at best, *no* correlation between batting ability and the ability to avoid hitting into double plays. The correlation between Component 7 winning percentage and baserunning winning percentage, on the other hand, is 9.4%, small, but positive. In other words, one might perhaps better characterize Component 7 as a pure baserunning component rather than as a batting component at all.

If one divides Components 5 and 6 between batting and baserunning as suggested above, and considers Component 7 as purely baserunning, the split between batting and baserunning changes from 91.4% batting—8.6% baserunning to 79.1% batting—20.9% baserunning. This latter split is perhaps a more accurate reflection of the extent to which speed and/or baserunning ability really affects a player's offensive value.

Offensive Leaders of the Retrosheet Era

The top 50 players in career offensive wins, batting plus baserunning, over non-pitcher average (WOPA_b) are shown in the table below.

		eWins	*eLosses*	*eWOPA_b*
1	Barry Bonds	332.4	210.4	55.9
2	*Ted Williams*	*277.4*	*157.2*	*55.9*
3	Hank Aaron	359.7	255.7	46.3
4	Mickey Mantle	261.4	164.0	44.7
5	Willie Mays	323.9	224.1	44.6
6	*Mel Ott*	*261.0*	*169.6*	*41.8*
7	*Stan Musial*	*322.8*	*229.4*	*41.4*
8	Frank Robinson	301.7	212.1	40.3
9	Alex Rodriguez	283.7	213.4	34.5
10	*Lou Gehrig*	*199.9*	*125.0*	*34.5*
11	*Jimmie Foxx*	*213.9*	*141.4*	*32.8*
12	Mike Schmidt	253.1	181.3	31.9
13	Jim Thome	237.3	173.9	30.9
14	Frank Thomas	234.3	172.1	30.9
15	Harmon Killebrew	243.8	175.0	30.7
16	Albert Pujols	246.6	180.0	30.5
17	Rickey Henderson	309.3	246.8	30.4
18	Willie McCovey	237.8	170.1	29.9
19	Carl Yastrzemski	331.3	264.6	29.9
20	Manny Ramirez	232.1	172.1	29.4
21	Reggie Jackson	268.8	209.2	28.4
22	Jeff Bagwell	229.9	166.7	27.9
23	Joe L. Morgan	271.2	206.6	27.9
24	Eddie Mathews	241.1	177.1	27.9
25	*Babe Ruth*	*129.9*	*71.5*	*27.5*
26	Willie Stargell	222.5	161.7	26.7
27	Gary Sheffield	256.8	197.8	26.6
28	Mark McGwire	184.2	129.3	26.5
29	Al Kaline	277.6	217.6	25.5
30	Chipper Jones	249.5	190.8	25.5
31	Larry Walker	200.7	143.5	25.4
32	*Johnny Mize*	*186.6*	*130.5*	*25.1*
33	Billy Williams	254.3	197.4	24.4
34	Todd Helton	223.1	167.7	24.4
35	Dick Allen	186.8	132.9	24.2
36	*Joe DiMaggio*	*192.8*	*138.0*	*24.1*
37	Duke Snider	208.6	153.5	24.0
38	Ken Griffey, Jr.	256.3	206.0	23.8
39	Dwight Evans	238.8	192.1	23.3
40	Miguel Cabrera	199.7	151.5	22.8
41	Rafael Palmeiro	266.1	220.4	22.3
42	George Brett	263.9	220.2	21.8
43	*Hank Greenberg*	*155.1*	*106.7*	*21.6*
44	Jason Giambi	197.5	153.3	21.6
45	Fred McGriff	230.0	182.5	21.6
46	Ralph Kiner	155.3	107.4	21.3
47	David Ortiz	216.7	173.0	21.3
48	Norm Cash	191.6	144.3	20.6
49	Lance Berkman	183.8	138.0	20.4
50	Edgar Martinez	192.4	151.4	20.4

Net Win Values for Offensive Events

One of the byproducts of calculating pW-L records is the ability to calculate context-neutral win values for various events. The next section of this chapter looks at these win values. In all cases, the values shown here are net offensive win values (i.e., wins minus losses, expressed in terms of the offensive team during the event) and are summed across all components. So, for example, the win value for triples is equal to the Component 4 win value for balls in play plus the Component 5 win value for hits (as opposed to outs) on balls in play plus the Component 6 win value for triples (as opposed to singles or doubles) on hits in play. Context-neutral wins and losses are normalized in my work such that total context-neutral player decisions in a season are equal to three times the number of team games played. (Basic Player wins and losses are normalized so that the players on a team earn exactly three decisions in every team game. Context-neutral decisions are normalized to equal basic decisions at the season level, but not necessarily at the game level.)

Positive Offensive Events

The first set of numbers are for positive offensive events: singles, doubles, triples, home runs, and walks. The numbers for "singles" here include ROE (reached on error) and "walks" include hit-by-pitches:

	RpG	HR	T	D	S/ROE	W/HBP	IW
1930–2015	4.71	0.144	0.080	0.060	0.036	0.032	0.006
1968 AL	3.41	0.173	0.099	0.074	0.042	0.033	0.004
2000 AL	5.31	0.127	0.069	0.051	0.035	0.031	0.007

RpG are runs per 27 outs for games used in calculating pW-L records.

Average numbers are shown across all seasons for which I have calculated pW-L records as well as for the two most extreme run-scoring leagues for which I have estimated pW-L records.

Offensive events were more valuable than average in 1968 and less valuable than average in 2000. Runs were 55.7% more plentiful in the 2000 AL than in 1968. Home runs were 36.2% more valuable in 1968 than in 2000. Extra-base hits are similarly more valuable: 42.3% more valuable for triples, 45.6% more valuable for doubles. The difference in win values is a fair bit less for simply reaching first base, however, and virtually identical for a walk.

Why?

Because runs were much rarer in 1968, the value of a guaranteed run—a home run—was huge, as was the value of getting into scoring position. The additional value of simply getting on first base in a low run-scoring environment, on the other hand, is relatively slight because, in 1968, if you walked, the odds were very strong that you weren't going to get much farther than first base anyway.

The one offensive event here that was less valuable (to the hitting team) in 1968 than in 2000 was the intentional walk. When hits are at a premium, there's less downside risk to the pitching team of walking a batter because, as with an unintentional walk, the odds are very high that the next batter isn't going to do anything to put any runs on the scoreboard.

Outs

Different types of outs have different win values. Ground balls, fly balls, and especially bunts, can lead to baserunner advancements, but ground balls can also lead to double plays. Net win values for batting out by the type of out are shown in the next table.

Batting Outs

	All	K	BIP
1930–2015	−0.023	−0.021	−0.024
1968 AL	−0.023	−0.022	−0.024
2000 AL	−0.025	−0.022	−0.025

The average win value of an out is surprisingly constant across run-scoring environments. This is because the number of outs in a game does not change with the run environment—there are 27 outs in a 9-inning baseball game, no matter how many hits, walks, and runs are accumulated in those nine innings.

A strikeout is actually slightly less costly on average than an out on a ball-in-play, although the difference is fairly minor.

The next table decomposes outs on BIP by hit type.

	Bunt	Groundball	Fly Ball	Line Drive
1930–2015	−0.016	−0.025	−0.023	−0.027
1968 AL	−0.015	−0.025	−0.023	−0.026
2000 AL	−0.021	−0.026	−0.024	−0.032

The most costly type of out is actually a line-drive out, since these practically never result in base advancement and can frequently lead to double plays.

The least costly type of out, on the other hand, is a bunt out. Bunt outs are also the ones whose value varies the most over time. Some of this difference could, however, be due to the level of data reported by Retrosheet. For many earlier seasons, the only plays that are identified as bunts are sacrifice bunts. Sacrifice bunts will be less costly than other types of bunt outs (e.g., failed sacrifice bunts, double plays on sacrifice attempts), however. Hence, the true win value of bunts may be understated in early years (including, perhaps, 1968).

Wins vs. Runs

Baseball events are more typically valued in terms of runs as opposed to wins. The next table compares win values from my work with linear-weights run values. The linear-weights run values here are taken from the *2006 Hardball Times Baseball Annual* ("What's a Batted Ball Worth?" by Dave Studenmund, pp. 142–143), which, in turn, cites an article by Tom Ruane. These run values are for 2002–2004. To make the comparison consistent, the net win values in the next table are also for 2002–2004. The average runs scored per 9 innings over these three years was 5.01.

Event	HR	T	D	S	W	IW	Out
Net Win Value	0.135	0.074	0.056	0.036	0.030	0.007	−0.024
Linear Weight Value	1.394	1.055	0.772	0.465	0.315	0.176	−0.278
Runs per Win	10.3	14.2	13.8	13.0	10.5	24.7	11.7

Two numbers seem particularly worthy of comment here.

First, home runs are somewhat more valuable in terms of wins than in terms of runs. For example, the linear-weights run values suggest that a single and a triple are worth more (1.52 runs) than a home run (1.39 runs), whereas the win values suggest just the opposite: the home run (0.135 wins) is worth more than the combined win value of a single and a triple (0.036 + 0.074 = 0.110 wins). The same is true of a home run vis-à-vis two doubles (run value of 1.54 runs vs. win value of 0.112).

Why might this be? Well, first, I should acknowledge that it could just be a fluke of the data (although these specific relationships are true, as far as I can tell, for every league and for every season for which I have calculated pW-L records). More likely, I think there is something to this result. Specifically, I think the key is that a home run always generates at least one run, whereas, while, for example, a triple produces more than one run on average, there are cases where a team will fail to score any runs in an inning despite hitting a triple.

The key to winning baseball games is to score runs (and prevent the other team from scoring—this argument works exactly the same in that respect from a defensive standpoint). There are two factors which affect the number of runs scored: the expected number of runs scored, which is measured by the linear-weights run value, and the probability of scoring one or more runs. A home run produces a higher probability of scoring (100%) than other types of hits and, hence, has a greater impact on winning, even controlling for the expected number of runs scored.

The other event which has markedly different run and win values is the intentional walk. Based on linear weights, an intentional walk is worth approximately 55% of an unintentional walk. The win value of an intentional walk, on the other hand, is only 24% of the value of an unintentional walk. While I should again acknowledge the possibility that this is a data fluke, I think that this suggests that major-league managers generally do a pretty decent job of issuing intentional walks appropriately and that linear-weights run values likely overstate the true cost of intentional walks (and understate the strategic abilities of major-league managers).

Balls in Play by Hit Type

The next table looks at all balls-in-play by hit type, regardless of what the final outcome of the play was. Information on the hit type of non-outs is not given for most years of Retrosheet play-by-play data. Hence, these figures are only shown here since 2003. For this table, all home runs are considered "Fly Balls"; in truth, some home runs may be more properly characterized as line drives.

	All BIP	*Bunt*	*GB*	*FB*	*LD*
since 2003: Incl Home Runs	0.0016	−0.0038	−0.0096	0.0036	0.0257
since 2003: Excl Home Runs	−0.0036	−0.0038	−0.0096	−0.0133	0.0257

If one includes home runs, then putting the ball in play is a net positive offensive event. If the ball stays in the ballpark, however, then a ball-in-play is a net positive for the defense. The same is true of fly balls.

Ground balls and bunts are net negative offensive events, much more so for ground balls. In contrast, the linear-weight run values calculated by Studenmund in the *2006 Hardball Times Annual* article referenced earlier, were virtually identical for bunts (−0.103) and ground balls (−0.101). For my work, I treat bunts as context-dependent events, since the decision to bunt is purely elective based on the context of the situation. It turns out that, as with intentional walks, major-league teams are pretty smart about knowing when to bunt, so that the win value of bunts is much greater than the simple run value would suggest.

Finally, the old Little League saying, "A walk's as good as a hit" isn't true (a walk is about half as valuable as an average hit). But, it turns out that a walk (win value of 0.029 since 2003) is about as good as a line drive (win value of 0.026).

Baserunning

The next table shows net offensive values for stolen bases, caught stealings, and advancements on wild pitches and passed balls.

Stolen base numbers here include all baserunner advancements on stolen-base attempts, including defensive indifference, balks, and errors on pickoffs. Caught stealing figures include successful pickoffs as well.

	SB	CS	WP
1930–2015	0.018	−0.039	0.027
1968 AL	0.027	−0.045	0.034
2000 AL	0.015	−0.038	0.022

Event	SB	CS	WP
Net Win Value (2002–04)	0.016	−0.036	0.025
Linear Weight Value	0.178	−0.440	*0.25*
Runs per Win	10.9	12.2	9.9

Tom Ruane's work did not report a linear weight value for wild pitches and I had a good bit of difficulty finding a reasonable value.

There are a few interesting results here. First, the ratio of win value and run value for stolen bases and caught stealing is similar to those for other events. This is in sharp contrast to intentional walks, the other events that I treat as purely contextual, and suggests that stolen base attempts are not particularly high-context, in general.

The average win value of a wild pitch is around 50% greater than the average win value of a successful stolen base. While this may seem wrong at first blush—both of these events simply advance a baserunner by one base—the reason is actually pretty simple. Wild pitches and passed balls are much more evenly distributed across bases, whereas the vast majority of stolen bases are by baserunners on first base.

From 2000 to 2008, for example, there were a total of 206 stolen bases with either a runner on third base, runners on second and third, or the bases loaded (i.e., situations where the runner on third would have to advance for anybody else to advance). In contrast, there were 1,871 wild pitches and passed balls in these same base-states.

As with earlier offensive events, the increased value of the positive offensive events—stolen bases and wild pitches—are greater than the increased negative value of negative offensive events—caught stealing—in lower run-scoring environments. The win values of stolen bases and caught stealings can be combined to calculate the break-even rate at which the net win value of stolen base attempts is exactly equal to zero. These values are shown in the table below.

Stolen Base Success Rates

	Break-even	*Actual*
1930–2015	68.0%	64.5%
1968 AL	62.9%	64.4%
2000 AL	72.3%	68.7%

The break-even success rate for stolen base attempts is generally lower the lower the run-scoring environment: 62.9% in 1968 vs. 72.3% in 2000. The stolen base success rate was actually four percentage points higher in the American League in 2000 than in 1968. Yet, because of the difference in run-scoring environment, stolen bases were a net positive offensive event in 1968 but a net negative offensive event in 2000.

As indicated in the table, across all seasons for which I have calculated pW-L records, the actual success rate for stolen bases has tended to be fairly close to, but slightly below, breakeven.

More recently, however, stolen base attempts have been a net positive event since 2007 or so. Over the past decade, the actual stolen base success rate, 68.8% has been extremely close to (and slightly better than) the breakeven rate, 67.7%. Major league baseball teams and players appear to be getting smarter about the timing of their stolen base attempts.

Marginal Win Values of Bases

Going back to the first table, with walks, singles, doubles, triples, and home runs, one can calculate the net win value of advancing an additional base. Note that these differences should be greater than the value of stolen bases or wild pitches, since these would involve additional baserunner advancement as well (that is, part of the added value of a double over a single is that a runner on second is practically guaranteed to score on a double but is less likely to score on a single).

	1st	2nd	3rd	Home
1930–2015	0.032	0.024	0.019	0.064
1968 AL	0.033	0.032	0.025	0.074
2000 AL	0.031	0.016	0.019	0.058

Not all bases are created equal; nor are all bases affected the same by the run-scoring environment.

In most run-scoring environments, reaching first base (via walk) is more valuable than moving from first base to second base (the difference in value between a single and a double). But the value of reaching first base is very similar across run-scoring environment while the value of advancing into scoring position increases dramatically as the average number of runs scored declines.

In most run-scoring environments, moving from first base to second base is more valuable than moving from second base to third base. The exception, somewhat curiously to me, is the high-scoring 2000 American League. It could be the case that teams were more likely to play station-to-station baseball in 2000, partly because the cost of a baserunning out was higher and perhaps partly because players were slower in 2000 because of a preponderance of sluggers.

Moving from second base to third base was far more valuable in the extremely low run-scoring environment of 1968 than in either 2000 or on average. With fewer hits in 1968, the ability to score on an out or a wild pitch was more valuable.

Finally, moving from third base to home plate is by far the most valuable base advancement.

Why?

Because moving from third base to home plate puts a run on the scoreboard. As I noted above, in observing that the win value for home runs is greater than the run value, increasing the probability of a run scoring—to 100% in this case—is crucial to increasing the team's odds of winning the game.

Best Hitters: 1968 vs. 2000

The best hitter in the 1968 American League (as measured by batting wins over non-pitcher average) was Carl Yastrzemski of the Boston Red Sox, who amassed a batting line of .301/.426/.495 with 23 home runs, 74 RBI, and 90 runs scored. The .301 batting average and .426 OBP led the American League that year, as did Yastrzemski's .922 OPS, 170 park-adjusted OPS+, and 119 walks. To really drive home how low the offensive levels were in 1968, Yastrzemski's .495 slugging percentage average was 4th in the American League and his 90 runs scored were good for 2nd. In fact, his 74 RBIs were good for 8th in the AL that year.

The best hitter in the 2000 American League was Carlos Delgado of the Toronto Blue Jays, who put up a batting line of .344/.470/.664 with 41 HR, 137 RBI, and 115 runs scored. Delgado led the American League in times on base, total bases, and runs created; finished 2nd in batting average, OBP, SLG, and walks; was 3rd in park-adjusted OPS+; and placed 4th in home runs and RBIs.

Superficially, Carlos Delgado's 2000 season was vastly superior to Carl Yastrzemski's 1968 season. Delgado out-hit Yaz .344–.301; he out-homered Yaz 41–23; he had more RBI 137–74.

Delgado's context-neutral batting won-lost record was an impressive 17.1–10.3, 3.4 batting wins over non-pitcher average. In context, however, Carl Yastrzemski's 1968 was quite similar: 16.8–10.2, 3.1 batting wins over non-pitcher average.

Pinch Hitting and Designated Hitting: Is There a DH/PH Penalty?

In *The Book*, Tango, Lichtman, and Dolphin studied player performances pinch hitting and DHing. Their conclusions were as follows:

> A player is significantly less effective as a pinch hitter than he is as a starter.... Players also lose effectiveness when being used as a designated hitter; the DH penalty is about half that of the PH penalty [Tango, Lichtman, and Dolphin, *The Book: Playing the Percentages in Baseball*, page 113].

I decided to undertake a similar analysis using pW-L records. Across all of the seasons for which I have estimated pW-L records, 36,209 players earned offensive Player decisions as a pinch hitter as well as while playing a fielding position (i.e., excluding DH and pinch-running appearances as well as PH appearances). Using the harmonic mean of the players' offensive Player decisions as a PH and as a position player for weights, the weighted average winning percentage of these players as pinch hitters was 0.476. The weighted average offensive winning percentage for the same players when playing the field was 0.484. So, on average, a player's offensive winning percentage is 0.009 less as a pinch-hitter than as a non–PH. Overall, 59.0% of these players (21,346) had a worse offensive winning percentage as pinch hitters than as position players. So, I generally find the same result as *The Book*: players hit somewhat worse as pinch hitters than when they are playing a regular fielding position.

Doing the same thing for designated hitters (DHs), I find a weighted average offensive winning percentage as a DH of 0.512 and as position players (again, excluding PH and PR appearances) of 0.521 for the players who have done both in a single season. This works out to a DH "penalty" of 0.010. Overall, 59.2% of these players (3,731) had a worse offensive winning percentage as designated hitters than as position players, very similar to the PH penalty that I found above. This differs somewhat from *The Book*, which found a much smaller "DH penalty" than "PH penalty."

Out of curiosity, I did the same thing for pinch runners, comparing baserunning winning percentages for pinch runners as pinch runners versus when they reached base as a batter. Pinch runners have a weighted average baserunning winning percentage of 0.495 as pinch runners versus 0.521 for the same players otherwise, for the 17,779 players who did both in a single season. This works out to a PR penalty of 0.026. Overall, 53.5% of these players (9,514) had a worse baserunning winning percentage as pinch runners.

Finally, I looked at players who earned player decisions as both a DH and a pinch hitter in the same season. There were a total of 6,011 such players. The weighted average of their winning percentage as a DH was 0.509 vs. 0.456 as a pinch hitter, implying a "PH penalty" of 0.053.

In calculating positional averages (which serve as the baseline from which I calculate positional replacement levels), I use the actual average winning percentage for these positions, as outlined in Chapter 3. Hence, these positional penalties are implicitly adjusted for in the calculation of these positional averages and replacement levels.

6. Pitching Player Won-Lost Records

Pitching accounts for approximately 32.7% of total Player decisions, including Pitcher fielding, almost exactly one-third of total Player decisions. Since three Player decisions are allocated per team game, this means that total Player wins earned by pitchers approximately equal the traditional measure of total Pitcher wins, at least on an aggregate level.

Twelve pitchers earned 300 or more traditional pitcher wins during the seasons for which I have calculated pW-L records: Warren Spahn (363)*, Greg Maddux (355), Roger Clemens (354), Steve Carlton (329), Nolan Ryan (324), Don Sutton (324), Phil Niekro (318), Gaylord Perry (314), Tom Seaver (311), Tom Glavine (305), Randy Johnson (303), and Early Wynn (300)*. (*Retrosheet is missing play-by-play data for 3 games of Warren Spahn's career and 91 games of Early Wynn's career.)

In contrast, there have been ten pitchers to amass 300 or more pWins: Warren Spahn (361), Nolan Ryan (360), Steve Carlton (345), Phil Niekro (337), Greg Maddux (331), Gaylord Perry (326), Don Sutton (325), Roger Clemens (319), Tom Seaver (313), and Robin Roberts (302).

Including position players, there are a total of 72 major-league players who have accumulated 300 or more pWins over the seasons for which I have calculated pW-L records (extrapolating to incorporate missing games). A table of these players was shown earlier in Chapter 1.

Pitching decisions (excluding pitcher fielding) are accumulated in seven components:

Component 1: Stolen Bases

Component 2: Wild Pitches and Passed Balls

Component 3: Balls not in Play

Component 4: Balls in Play

Component 5: Hits vs. Outs

Component 6: Singles v. Doubles v. Triples

Component 7: Double Plays

The average breakdown of these components for pitchers (excluding pitcher fielding) is as follows:

	1930–2015	*2000–2015*
Component 1: Stolen Bases	1.8%	1.5%
Component 2: Wild Pitches	1.6%	1.6%
Component 3: Balls not in Play	23.3%	25.6%

	1930–2015	*2000–2015*
Component 4: Balls in Play	55.4%	55.0%
Component 5: Hits vs. Outs	15.5%	14.2%
Component 6: Singles v. Doubles v. Triples	1.4%	1.3%
Component 7: Double Plays	0.9%	0.8%

By far the most significant component for pitchers is Component 4—the expected value of balls in play, which accounts for over half of all pitcher decisions. Component 4 includes home runs in addition to what are sometimes referred to as "balls-in-play." There is a school of thought, expounded in the theory of DIPS, that pitchers have relatively little control over balls in play outside of home runs, and that pitcher talent primarily manifests itself through the ability to control strikeouts, walks, and home runs. Combining home runs with Component 3 produces a "DIPS" subset of pitching player decisions. Taken together, these account for 35.9% of all Pitcher decisions across all seasons for which I have calculated pW-L records. This percentage has increased in recent years, with increases in the numbers of strikeouts and home runs, to 40.2% since 2000. Even since 2000, however, the non-home run subset of Component 4 actually contributes a slightly larger share of Pitcher value: 40.5% (42.8% across all seasons for which I have calculated pW-L records).

Pitchers share credit with fielders for all of these components except for Components 3 and 4. The percentage of the credit given to pitchers in these components (excluding plays where the pitcher is also the fielder) is shown in the next table. The shares shown here are averages across all seasons for which I have calculated pW-L records. The actual share of credit assigned to pitchers varies by sub-component (i.e., by which fielder(s) are involved in a play) and by year.

Component 1	52.2%
Component 2	76.3%
Component 5	31.4%
Component 6	25.9%
Component 7	36.3%

The extent to which pitchers can affect hits on balls in play has been a controversial issue in recent years. My research suggests that, in general, pitchers bear about one-third of the responsibility for what happens to batted balls which stay in the field of play. Pitchers are more responsible for stolen bases than catchers and bear about three-quarters of the responsibility for wild pitches and passed balls.

Starting Pitchers vs. Relief Pitchers

Differences between starting pitchers and relief pitchers are explored next. In evaluating pW-L records, I consider starting pitcher and relief pitcher to be two separate positions. Some differences between starting pitchers and relief pitchers are explored here.

Pitcher Contexts

Across all seasons for which I have calculated pW-L records, the overall pW-L records of starting pitchers and relief pitchers were as follows:

Pitcher Context, 1930–2015

Pitcher–Role	Context-Neutral Decisions	Win Pct.
Starting Pitcher	203,889	0.499
Relief Pitcher	*86,746*	*0.502*
Non-Save Situations	55,587	0.500
Save Situations*	18,050	0.510
Tie Games	13,109	0.499

*Save situations are defined here as situations in which the winning or tying run is either on base, at bat, or on deck. This excludes saves earned by pitching at least three innings in a win, regardless of situation, or by pitching at least one inning with a 3-run lead. This also includes what would be classified as "holds" instead of saves.

Pitcher–Role	Context		
	Inter-Game	Intra-Game	Combined
Starting Pitcher	1.002	1.076	1.078
Relief Pitcher	*0.995*	*0.821*	*0.816*
Non-Save Situations	0.437	1.018	0.445
Save Situations*	2.027	0.810	1.641
Tie Games	1.939	0.649	1.257

Pitcher–Role	Win Adjustments	
	Inter-Game	Intra-Game
Starting Pitcher	−0.002	0.003
Relief Pitcher	*0.004*	*0.005*
Non-Save Situations	0.001	−0.031
Save Situations*	−0.001	0.065
Tie Games	0.007	−0.045

There are several comparisons that I find interesting here. The first one is that relief pitchers compiled a slightly higher overall winning percentage than starting pitchers: 0.502 to 0.499. As a general rule, pitchers tend to perform better—lower ERA, more strikeouts, better context-neutral winning percentage—as relief pitchers than as starters. In fact, however, the difference in context-neutral winning percentages actually understates the impact of this. This is because, in general (with many exceptions, of course), starters tend to be better pitchers than relievers, especially non-closers. To some extent, many, if not most, relief pitchers are failed starters.

A better way to determine the extent to which pitching in relief would be expected to improve one's player winning percentage, then, is to focus on pitchers who both started and relieved within the same season and compare these player's winning percentages. Among all seasons for which I have calculated pW-L records, a total of 14,849 player-seasons included both starting pitching and relief pitching. Weighting each of these players' performances by the harmonic mean of their starting and relief pitching Player Decisions, these pitchers compiled a weighted average winning percentage of 0.476 as starting pitchers and 0.496 as relief pitchers. Using the Matchup Formula to re-center these winning percentages around 0.500, the average winning percentage for these pitchers as starters was 0.493 and for these pitchers as relievers was 0.517. Looked at in this way, the positional average for starting pitchers appears to be about 2.4% (0.024) lower than for relief pitchers. This difference forms the basis for calculating positional averages and positional replacement levels as described in Chapter 3.

The second comparison above is the difference in contexts. Inter-game context is comparable for relief pitchers, 0.995, and for starting pitchers, 1.002. This virtual equality masks large differences, however, depending on situation. Relief pitchers in hold and save situations (excluding saves earned by closers for pitching the ninth inning with a 3-run lead), 2.027, and tie games, 1.939, have an extremely high inter-game context. Relief appearances in non-save situations have an average inter-game context less than half as big as that of starting pitchers (0.437).

The story is quite different, however, for intra-game context. Starting pitchers have an average intra-game context of 1.076 versus 0.821 for relief pitchers. This is because average intra-game context is highest in the early innings of games. The relationship of inter-game and intra-game context across innings was discussed in Chapter 2.

Combining inter-game and intra-game context, starting pitchers have a combined average context of 1.078 vs. 0.816 for relief pitchers. This difference in combined overall context is taken account of in my construction of final context-neutral won-lost records, eWins and eLosses, through the inclusion of an expected context. The calculation of expected context was discussed in Chapter 2.

The use of relief pitchers has changed considerably over the 80+ years over which I have estimated pW-L records. The same results since 2000 are shown in the next table.

Pitcher Context, 2000–2015

Pitcher—Role	Context-Neutral Decisions	Win Pct.
Starting Pitcher	50,698	0.496
Relief Pitcher	*26,136*	*0.507*
Non-Save Situations	16,620	0.506
Save Situations*	5,555	0.517
Tie Games	3,962	0.501

*Save situations are defined here as situations in which the winning or tying run is either on base, at bat, or on deck. This excludes saves earned by pitching at least three innings in a win, regardless of situation, or by pitching at least one inning with a 3-run lead. This also includes what would be classified as "holds" instead of saves.

Pitcher-Role	Context		
	Inter-Game	Intra-Game	Combined
Starting Pitcher	0.988	1.093	1.080
Relief Pitcher	*1.023*	*0.826*	*0.845*
Non-Save Situations	0.416	1.034	0.430
Save Situations*	2.137	0.819	1.750
Tie Games	2.011	0.657	1.320

Pitcher—Role	Win Adjustments	
	Inter-Game	Intra-Game
Starting Pitcher	−0.002	−0.001
Relief Pitcher	*0.003*	*0.012*
Non-Save Situations	−0.000	−0.017
Save Situations*	−0.001	0.068
Tie Games	0.006	−0.050

The general relationships identified above are all still true. More recently, however, there has been a somewhat greater spread in winning percentages between starting pitchers and relief pitchers. Relief pitchers have also seen a somewhat higher average inter-game context in recent years than in earlier seasons.

Changes in Relief Pitcher Roles Over Time

The next table shows a breakdown of context-neutral pitching decisions by pitcher role by decade from the 1950s to the 2000s (2000–2015).

Breakdown of Context-Neutral Pitching Decisions by Role

Role	1950s	1960s	1970s	1980s	1990s	2000s
Starter	72.7%	71.3%	72.3%	69.7%	67.3%	66.0%
Reliever	27.3%	28.7%	27.7%	30.3%	32.7%	34.0%
Non-Save	18.6%	18.5%	17.4%	18.3%	20.4%	21.6%
Save / Hold	4.9%	5.7%	5.9%	7.1%	7.4%	7.2%
Tie Games	3.8%	4.6%	4.4%	4.9%	4.9%	5.2%

From the 1950s through the 1970s, the overall percentage of (context-neutral) pitching decisions earned by relief pitchers was relatively constant. This relatively constant overall usage masked underlying changes in relief pitcher usage, however. Specifically, over this time period, the use of relief pitchers declined by 1.2% in non-save situations, but rose 1.0% in save situations.

The 1980s saw the greatest increase in overall relief pitcher decisions of any decade (2.6%). This increase in relief-pitcher usage spanned all three roles shown here, with the use of relief pitchers in non-save situations returning to 1960s levels, while the share of total pitcher decisions earned by relief pitchers in save situations and tie games increased by a combined 1.7%.

The 1990s and 2000s have seen a continuing increase in overall relief pitcher usage. Interestingly (to me), however, the increase in relief pitcher usage over the past 20 years appears to be almost entirely centered on increased relief pitcher usage in non-save situations.

To get a better feel for how the changing roles of relief pitchers have interacted with changing usage, the final table here shows a breakdown of context-dependent pitching decisions, pWins and pLosses, by pitcher role by decade from the 1950s to the 2000s (2000–2015).

Breakdown of Context-Dependent Pitching Decisions by Role

Role	1950s	1960s	1970s	1980s	1990s	2000s
Starter	79.2%	77.1%	77.6%	74.4%	72.2%	71.2%
Reliever	20.8%	22.9%	22.4%	25.6%	27.8%	28.8%
Non-Save	8.9%	8.4%	7.7%	8.1%	9.0%	9.3%
Save / Hold	7.3%	8.9%	9.3%	11.4%	12.4%	12.7%
Tie Games	4.6%	5.6%	5.4%	6.1%	6.3%	6.8%

Pitching Leaders of the Retrosheet Era

The top 50 players in net career pitching wins, i.e., eWins minus eLosses, are shown in the table below.

		eWins	eLosses	Net Wins
1	Roger Clemens	274.5	213.5	33.9
2	Greg Maddux	264.9	211.1	33.0
3	Pedro Martinez	159.3	117.3	23.5
4	*Warren Spahn*	280.4	239.4	23.5
5	Randy Johnson	235.0	193.0	23.2
6	Kevin Brown	177.3	139.3	22.1
7	Mike Mussina	195.3	160.3	21.1
8	Gaylord Perry	285.1	250.1	20.8
9	Tom Seaver	254.4	222.5	20.4
10	Don Sutton	279.6	249.8	19.6
11	Nolan Ryan	298.9	267.4	18.7
12	Curt Schilling	178.7	148.0	17.8

		eWins	eLosses	Net Wins
13	John Smoltz	188.5	158.7	17.8
14	Tim Hudson	167.3	140.4	17.0
15	Jim Palmer	209.7	183.5	16.7
16	*Lefty Grove*	*164.7*	*130.3*	*16.5*
17	Bert Blyleven	268.2	243.1	16.4
18	Roy Halladay	148.6	121.4	16.4
19	Tommy John	247.4	221.1	15.9
20	Whitey Ford	172.3	146.9	15.8
21	Tom Glavine	233.3	213.9	15.4
22	Bret Saberhagen	137.4	111.8	15.2
23	Bob Gibson	209.8	184.1	15.1
24	Andy Pettitte	182.1	157.7	14.9
25	*Bob Feller*	*208.6*	*183.1*	*14.1*
26	Juan Marichal	186.8	161.9	14.1
27	Clayton Kershaw	88.5	64.1	14.0
28	Robin Roberts	251.6	228.1	13.9
29	C.C. Sabathia	163.5	142.0	13.5
30	Felix Hernandez	123.4	102.5	13.4
31	*Ted Lyons*	*163.8*	*141.3*	*12.4*
32	*Red Ruffing*	*191.9*	*168.8*	*12.3*
33	Roy Oswalt	121.8	101.3	12.3
34	Mariano Rivera	73.4	45.4	12.3
35	Johan Santana	112.6	91.8	12.2
36	Steve Carlton	279.0	260.0	12.1
37	Bob Friend	193.3	171.3	11.6
38	Billy Pierce	178.2	159.6	11.3
39	*Carl Hubbell*	*157.7*	*137.3*	*11.3*
40	*Mel Harder*	*175.0*	*152.4*	*11.3*
41	Ron Guidry	129.4	109.8	11.3
42	Orel Hershiser	164.6	146.0	11.2
43	Kevin Appier	142.7	124.4	11.0
44	Steve Rogers	147.0	130.8	10.9
45	Don Drysdale	186.1	172.3	10.4
46	Jim Bunning	206.9	190.5	10.4
47	Cliff Lee	117.5	101.6	10.4
48	Fergie Jenkins	241.1	225.9	10.4
49	Jake Peavy	124.5	109.2	10.3
50	David Cone	160.2	144.1	10.3

Pitching vs. Fielding

The most challenging part of constructing any player valuation system—and pW-L records are no exception—is figuring out how to divide defensive value between pitchers and fielders.

For the most part, figuring out who to credit on offense is fairly straightforward. There are some plays where it may be debatable whether a batter or baserunner is responsible for something that happens on the bases (e.g., batters who hit longer doubles will score more runners from first; faster baserunners will score more often from first on a double). And there may be semantic debates about whether some piece of a player's value is batting or baserunning, but not which player gets the value (e.g., is the ability to beat out large numbers of infield hits a batting skill or a baserunning one?).

But defense is a different story. Even in the modern game with strikeouts reaching record levels and ever-climbing, the majority of plays still involve the pitcher pitching the ball and a fielder fielding the ball. How, then, does one divide credit between pitchers and fielders on balls in play?

Pitching vs. Fielding by Component

pW-L records are calculated sequentially through a series of nine components. The first two components involve plays that do not involve the batter—stolen bases, wild pitches, et al. Components 3 through 9 then walk sequentially through a plate appearance.

Components 3 and 4 are calculated simultaneously and evaluate the basic result of the play before fielders get involved. Component 3 applies to plate appearances which do not end in the batter putting the ball in play (i.e., strikeouts, walks, and hit-by-pitches). Component 4 applies to plate appearances on which the batter makes contact—including home runs—taking into account the type of ball hit (e.g., ground ball, fly ball, line drive).

Components 3 and 4 are awarded entirely to the pitcher. In other words, with respect to balls in play, the pitcher gets credit for inducing a pop up or blame for allowing a line drive, before considering the final result (i.e., whether the ball became an out or the batter reached base).

In sabermetric circles, it is fairly common to distinguish between home runs and other balls hit into play. In fact, the term "balls-in-play" or BIP is generally used to denote those balls that are hit into play excluding home runs. The logic for this distinction is most apparent in the study of Defense-Independent Pitching Statistics, or DIPS.

Several years ago, Voros McCracken developed a theory (called DIPS) that said that the ability to prevent hits on balls in play (excluding home runs) was the same, or virtually the same, for all major-league pitchers. His key conclusion was that one could predict a pitcher's earned run average (ERA) for the next season looking only at that pitcher's strikeouts, walks, and home runs allowed and that this predicted (or DIPS) ERA was, on average, a better predictor of future ERA than actual ERA. In other words, pitchers who had actual ERAs better than their DIPS ERAs would expect to see their ERAs get worse the next season (move toward their DIPS ERAs), while pitchers who had actual ERAs worse than their DIPS ERAs would expect to see their ERAs get better the next season (again, moving them toward their DIPS ERAs). McCracken's conclusion that DIPS ERA was a better predictor than actual ERA was, and almost certainly still is, fundamentally true.

So, how much control do pitchers have over balls in play? A nice write-up of the issue of how much control pitchers have over balls that batters hit is an article by Mike Fast (who now works for the Houston Astros), "Confessions of a DIPS Apostate," that can be found online at the website Hardballtimes.com (http://www.hardballtimes.com/main/article/confessions-of-a-dips-apostate/). One way in which Fast's article is particularly useful is that it provides links to several other studies of the issue in its concluding section (References and Resources).

Some baseball fans have taken McCracken's DIPS theory to what might be viewed as its logical conclusion and argued that pitchers have no effect on balls in play. With all due respect, anybody who has watched baseball for any length of time knows that this argument is simply not true as I have just stated it.

Some pitchers are "groundball pitchers." That is, the balls which are hit off of them tend to be ground balls, not fly balls. In the recent past, well-known groundball pitchers have included, for example, Brandon Webb, whose ground-ball percentages (percentage of total balls-in-play allowed that were ground balls) ranged from 61% to 66% from 2004 to 2007; and Chien-Ming Wang, whose ground-ball percentages ranged from 59% to 64% from 2005 through 2007. On the other hand, Barry Zito's ground-ball percentages over this same time period ranged from 37% to 42% and Curt Schilling's ranged from 34%

to 42%. Suffice it to say that I am not aware of anybody who would seriously argue that Webb, Wang, Zito, and Schilling's ground-ball percentages are entirely the product of luck over this time period. So pitchers clearly have some impact over balls-in-play, right?

In his original DIPS formulation, Voros McCracken put it this way: "Aside from walks, there are two basic outcomes for a pitcher: batter hits the ball or batter strikes out. With the latter, the result is almost always an out. With the former, all sorts of things can happen, including a base hit." Note that one of the "things that can happen" when the batter hits the ball is that he could hit a home run. My distinction between Component 3 and Component 4 follows the logic, then, of McCracken's dichotomy—batter fails to hit the ball (Component 3, McCracken's "batter strikes out") or "batter hits the ball" (Component 4).

The remaining components deal with what happens after the batter hits a ball that stays in the field of play.

Component 5 allocates credit and blame based on whether a ball-in-play was turned into an out or not. This, then, becomes the point at which fielders enter the picture. Component 5 credit and blame is shared between pitchers and fielders on the basis of the extent to which Component 5 winning percentages persist for pitchers and fielders. The process whereby I divide credit and blame between players was described in detail in Chapter 4.

Component 6 is applied on hits-in-play and allocates credit and blame on the basis of how far the batter advances—i.e., singles vs. doubles vs. triples. Like Component 5, Component 6 credit and blame is shared between pitchers and fielders on the basis of the extent to which Component 6 winning percentages persist for pitchers and fielders.

Component 7 is applied on ground ball outs in double-play situations (runner on first, less than two outs) and allocates credit and blame on the basis of whether the defensive team turns a double play or not. Like Components 5 and 6, Component 7 credit and blame is shared between pitchers and fielders on the basis of the extent to which Component 7 winning percentages persist for pitchers and fielders. For fielders, Component 7 decisions are shared between the first fielder to touch the ball and the potential pivot man on the double play (if the initial force out is made on the play).

Finally, Components 8 and 9 assign credit and blame for baserunner outs and baserunner advancement, respectively. In my system, Components 8 and 9 are assigned entirely to fielders.

What do pW-L records have to say about DIPS, balls-in-play, and the relative value of pitchers vs. fielders? The next three tables attempt to answer that question.

Defensive pW-L Records by the Numbers

The first table below breaks down player decisions between pitchers and fielders by component.

Breakdowns of Player Decisions by Component: 1930–2015
Distribution of Player Decisions

		% of Decisions Allocated to	
	Pct. of Total	Pitchers	Fielders
Component 1	2.2%	52.2%	47.8%
Component 2	1.3%	76.3%	23.7%

	Pct. of Total	% of Decisions Allocated to	
		Pitchers	Fielders
Component 3	14.8%	100.0%	0.0%
Component 4	35.3%	100.0%	0.0%
Component 5	32.7%	30.2%	69.8%
Component 6	3.5%	25.6%	74.4%
Component 7	1.6%	34.7%	65.3%
Component 8	2.3%	0.0%	100.0%
Component 9	6.2%	0.0%	100.0%
Total Player Decisions			
Pitching vs. Fielding		**63.6%**	**36.4%**
Pitchers vs. Other Fielders		**65.4%**	**34.6%**

The next-to-last row breaks down pitching vs. fielding. The final row compares pitchers to other fielders. The difference between the two rows is that pitcher fielding is counted as fielding in the former but is attributed to pitchers in the latter. Counting pitcher fielding, pitchers are responsible for approximately two-thirds of defensive player decisions.

The next table separates Components 3 and 4 into the four basic events that can result from a plate appearance: strikeouts, walks (or hit-by-pitch), home runs, and balls in play.

Breakdowns of Player Decisions by Component: Non-BIP vs. BIP
Distribution of Player Decisions

	Percent of Total Events	Decisions	% of Decisions Allocated to	
			Pitchers	Fielders
Component 3		14.8%	100.0%	0.0%
Strikeouts	14.0%	7.8%		
Walks/HBP	9.0%	7.1%		
Component 4		35.3%	100.0%	0.0%
Home Runs	2.1%	8.0%		
Balls-in-Play	74.8%	27.2%		
Component 5		32.7%	30.2%	69.8%
Component 6		3.5%	25.6%	74.4%
Component 7		1.6%	34.7%	65.3%
Component 8		2.3%	0.0%	100.0%
Component 9		6.2%	0.0%	100.0%
BIP Only	74.8%	73.6%		
Pitching vs. Fielding			52.4%	47.6%
Pitchers vs. Other Fielders			54.9%	45.1%

For balls in play (BIP) only (which account for about three-quarters of all Player decisions), pitchers are responsible for about five-ninths of total defensive Player decisions.

The final table, then, breaks down the distribution of components on balls in play.

Breakdowns of Player Decisions by Component: Balls in Play
Distribution of Player Decisions

	% of Total	% of Decisions Allocated to	
		Pitchers	Fielders
Component 4	37.0%	100.0%	0.0%
Component 5	44.4%	30.2%	69.8%
Component 6	4.8%	25.6%	74.4%
Component 7	2.2%	34.7%	65.3%
Component 8	3.2%	0.0%	100.0%
Component 9	8.4%	0.0%	100.0%

In summary, then

1. One-fourth of player decisions occur on plate appearances that do not involve any fielders: walks, strikeouts, home runs
2. One-third of Player decisions on balls in play are awarded directly to pitchers based on how and where the ball is hit: pop-ups vs. ground balls vs. fly balls vs. line drives
3. These two factors combine to account for half of defensive Player decisions: (¼) + (⅓)*(¾) = (½)
4. Of the remaining Player decisions on balls in play, player responsibility is split approximately (⅓) to the pitcher and (⅔) to the fielder
5. This results in an overall breakdown in defensive responsibility of (⅔) to the pitcher and (⅓) to the fielder

Analysis of Individual Pitchers

This chapter concludes with two analyses comparing pitchers.

Roger Clemens vs. Greg Maddux

Probably without question, the two greatest pitchers of the last generation were Roger Clemens and Greg Maddux. Pedro Martinez and Randy Johnson likely have their supporters, but both Clemens and Maddux have the combined peaks, primes, and career length that put them into the conversation as the greatest pitcher in major-league history.

Roger Clemens had 354 traditional pitcher wins in his 24-year career. He led the league in wins 4 times, in ERA 7 times, strikeouts 5 times, and won a record 7 Cy Young Awards. Baseball-Reference.com credits Clemens with 140.3 wins above replacement (WAR).

Greg Maddux had 355 traditional pitcher wins, led his league in ERA 4 times, in innings pitched 5 times, won a record (at any position) 18 Gold Gloves, and 4 (consecutive) Cy Young Awards. Baseball-Reference.com doesn't think quite as highly of Maddux as of Clemens, but his 106.8 career WAR is still 7th all-time among pitchers.

For a time in the early 2000s, debating whether Clemens or Maddux was better made for a good baseball debate. The debate sort of fizzled, as Clemens had a late-career renaissance that seemed to push him definitively ahead of Maddux. Of course, then Clemens was named by Brian McNamee in the Mitchell Report. Nowadays, the debate between Clemens and Maddux seems to rest largely on your opinion of performance-enhancing drugs. If you penalize for them, you probably put Maddux ahead of Clemens. If you don't adjust for them, you probably put Clemens ahead of Maddux.

My pW-L records (which are not adjusted for performance-enhancing drugs) actually show Maddux and Clemens as having been much closer to each other in value over the course of their careers than Baseball-Reference.com and others (e.g., Fangraphs) seem to view them.

My pW-L records for Roger Clemens and Greg Maddux are shown in the table below.

Roger Clemens

Season	Games	pWins	pLosses	pWOPA	pWORL
1984	21	7.1	5.5	0.9	1.4
1985	15	5.9	4.5	0.8	1.3
1986	33	17.3	9.8	4.0	5.3
1987	36	18.4	12.0	3.5	5.1
1988	35	18.1	12.0	3.2	4.7
1989	35	14.9	12.7	1.3	2.6
1990	31	16.6	8.8	4.2	5.4
1991	35	16.6	11.0	3.0	4.3
1992	32	15.6	10.0	3.0	4.4
1993	29	12.8	12.6	0.2	1.4
1994	24	10.6	8.0	1.4	2.5
1995	23	8.8	6.7	1.2	2.1
1996	34	13.4	11.1	1.4	2.8
1997	34	18.3	9.5	4.7	6.3
1998	33	15.8	9.3	3.5	4.9
1999	30	13.0	12.3	0.6	1.9
2000	32	14.1	12.1	1.2	2.6
2001	33	14.3	9.0	2.9	4.2
2002	29	11.6	9.3	1.4	2.5
2003	33	13.6	11.1	1.5	2.9
2004	33	15.0	10.7	3.0	4.3
2005	32	14.1	9.9	2.7	3.8
2006	19	7.1	4.8	1.4	2.0
2007	18	6.0	5.6	0.3	1.0
CAREER RECORDS (Regular Season)	**709**	**318.9**	**228.4**	**51.3**	**79.9**
Postseason	35	12.5	11.2	1.0	2.2
CAREER RECORDS	**744**	**331.4**	**239.6**	**52.3**	**82.0**

Greg Maddux

Season	Games	pWins	pLosses	pWOPA	pWORL
1986	6	1.6	2.3	−0.2	−0.0
1987	34	10.1	13.9	−1.3	−0.2
1988	37	17.8	12.8	3.3	4.6
1989	35	16.1	14.1	1.7	3.0
1990	35	16.0	14.8	1.5	2.8
1991	39	15.6	13.6	1.7	3.0
1992	35	17.6	12.3	3.5	5.0
1993	36	18.1	13.5	2.9	4.3
1994	25	14.5	8.2	3.7	4.9
1995	28	16.6	7.7	5.2	6.4
1996	35	16.3	11.7	3.1	4.5
1997	33	14.5	9.2	3.3	4.6
1998	34	17.2	11.9	3.5	4.9
1999	33	16.0	12.9	2.3	3.7
2000	35	17.1	12.6	3.1	4.5
2001	35	16.2	11.8	3.0	4.4
2002	35	13.3	10.5	2.0	3.1
2003	37	13.6	13.8	0.6	2.0
2004	34	14.7	13.1	1.7	3.1
2005	35	12.6	14.8	−0.3	0.9
2006	34	13.4	12.4	1.2	2.5
2007	35	11.8	11.2	0.9	2.1
2008	34	10.2	13.9	−1.2	−0.0
CAREER RECORDS (Regular Season)	**759**	**330.9**	**273.1**	**45.2**	**74.1**
Postseason	37	12.6	12.4	0.8	2.0
CAREER RECORDS	**796**	**343.5**	**285.5**	**46.0**	**76.1**

In terms of bottom-line career wins over replacement level (pWORL), Clemens beats Maddux, 82.0–76.1, but they're close enough that the little things are liable to matter, and it is worth taking a closer look.

I will begin by looking at a few relatively minor factors: pitcher hitting, postseason performance, and fielding. I then look at how contextual factors affected Clemens's and Maddux's career value. From there, I move to the core of both players' value: their pitching. I end with a minor factor that actually has a fairly big impact on our assessment of whether Clemens or Maddux had the better career: the impact of the 1994–95 strike on their value.

Pitcher Offense

Greg Maddux pitched his entire career in the National League. Hence, outside of interleague games in American League parks, Maddux had to bat in the vast majority of his 740 games started. Overall, for his career, Maddux had 1,812 plate appearances, over which he hit like a fairly typical pitcher–.171/.191/.205. He did manage to hit 5 career home runs and even stole 11 bases (and was caught stealing only 3 times).

Roger Clemens, on the other hand, pitched almost all of his career in the American League. Because of the DH rule, he had a mere 213 plate appearances in his career. His career rate stats were actually slightly better than Maddux's: .173/.236/.207 (OPS+ of 16 v. an OPS+ of 5 for Maddux), although Clemens had no career home runs or stolen bases.

Their context-neutral offensive won-lost records are compared below. The column headed WOPA (wins over positional average) compares their records to the average offensive performance for pitchers.

Roger Clemens				Greg Maddux			
Wins	Losses	Win Pct.	WOPA	Wins	Losses	Win Pct.	WOPA
2.1	4.1	0.342	0.2	19.3	37.8	0.338	1.3

Both Clemens and Maddux actually had slightly better offensive performances than an average pitcher—which, considering both of them had offensive winning percentages under 0.350, tells you just how bad a hitter an average pitcher is. Clemens had a slightly higher winning percentage, but Maddux had nearly ten times as many decisions, and hence had more wins above average. Overall, Maddux picks up about 1 win on Clemens relative to average (and perhaps a bit more than that relative to replacement level).

Postseason Performance

Roger Clemens pitched in 35 postseason games in his career, while Greg Maddux pitched in 37 postseason games. Neither Clemens nor Maddux really had much of a reputation as a particularly good postseason pitcher. Maddux actually had a losing (traditional) record in the postseason over his career, 11–14, although his ERA was fairly respectable (3.27 in 198 IP). Clemens had a winning (traditional) record (12–8), but with a somewhat higher ERA than Maddux (3.75) in almost the exact same number of innings (199).

In terms of pW-L records, both pitchers had lower winning percentages in the postseason than in the regular season, although both pitchers did have winning percentages over 0.500. Their overall postseason records are summarized below.

Roger Clemens				Greg Maddux			
Wins	Losses	Win Pct.	WORL	Wins	Losses	Win Pct.	WORL
12.5	11.2	0.526	2.2	12.6	12.4	0.504	2.0

Clemens had a somewhat higher winning percentage (0.526–0.504), but this is a bit misleading. Clemens pitched most of his postseason games in the AL, with the DH rule, while Maddux pitched most of his postseason games in the NL, with pitchers batting. Maddux's winning percentage here is dragged down, therefore, by his own hitting, which was quite a bit worse than his regular-season batting: .073/.105/.109 over 64 PAs. Overall, taking pitcher hitting into account, Roger Clemens amassed slightly more postseason value than Greg Maddux (as measured by pWORL): 2.2 vs. 2.0.

Fielding

As I noted earlier, Greg Maddux won a record 18 Gold Gloves. Not only is that a record for a pitcher, but it is, in fact, a record at any position. In contrast, Roger Clemens never won a Gold Glove over his 24-year career.

Generally speaking, any pitcher valuation system that starts by considering the runs allowed by a pitcher will already implicitly incorporate pitcher fielding into that value. My system doesn't explicitly begin with runs allowed but rather measures value play by play. I am able, therefore, to distinguish between a pitcher's pitching value and a pitcher's fielding value.

Career fielding value for Roger Clemens and Greg Maddux are shown in the next table.

	Roger Clemens			Greg Maddux	
Wins	Losses	Wins Over 0.500	Wins	Losses	Wins Over 0.500
4.7	4.7	–0.0	12.0	9.6	1.2

Not surprisingly, given their reputations, Maddux earned about 1.2 more wins over 0.500 as a fielder than Clemens. Not only did Maddux have a better winning percentage (0.554–0.499), but he also amassed 7.3 more raw fielding wins than Clemens (although he also amassed 4.9 more raw fielding losses).

Context

So far, the small things generally work slightly in Maddux's favor in the comparison with Clemens. Of course, these were already reflected in the comparison of pWins shown earlier. There is, however, one such factor which works in Clemens's favor: context.

The numbers shown in the first table in this Chapter use pWins and pLosses. These are constructed to tie player wins to team wins. As such, they are calculated reflecting the context in which the events being valued took place.

I also calculate a set of context-neutral pW-L records, eWins and eLosses. A comparison of Roger Clemens and Greg Maddux, as measured by eWins and eLosses is shown next.

Roger Clemens

Season	Games	eWins	eLosses	eWOPA	eWORL
1984	21	7.8	6.9	0.6	1.3
1985	15	5.8	4.2	0.9	1.4
1986	33	16.4	10.6	3.1	4.4
1987	36	18.4	12.2	3.4	5.0
1988	35	16.9	11.0	3.1	4.4
1989	35	15.7	12.6	1.7	3.1
1990	31	14.5	8.8	3.1	4.2
1991	35	16.5	11.2	2.8	4.2

Season	Games	eWins	eLosses	eWOPA	eWORL
1992	32	15.3	10.0	2.9	4.3
1993	29	11.5	10.0	0.9	1.9
1994	24	10.9	7.9	1.6	2.7
1995	23	8.6	8.3	0.4	1.3
1996	34	15.5	11.3	2.5	4.0
1997	34	17.6	8.3	4.9	6.4
1998	33	15.2	9.6	3.1	4.4
1999	30	11.9	10.7	0.8	2.0
2000	32	13.3	11.5	1.1	2.4
2001	33	13.8	11.2	1.6	3.0
2002	29	11.5	9.7	1.1	2.2
2003	33	13.3	11.3	1.2	2.6
2004	33	14.2	11.2	2.3	3.6
2005	32	14.0	9.0	3.1	4.2
2006	19	7.2	5.1	1.3	1.9
2007	18	5.9	5.6	0.3	0.9
CAREER RECORDS (Regular Season)	709	311.9	228.2	47.9	76.0
Postseason	35	12.8	10.5	1.5	2.7
CAREER RECORDS	**744**	**324.6**	**238.7**	**49.3**	**78.7**

Greg Maddux

Season	Games	eWins	eLosses	eWOPA	eWORL
1986	6	1.9	2.5	−0.2	0.0
1987	34	9.4	12.4	−1.0	0.0
1988	37	15.7	14.2	1.5	2.7
1989	35	15.1	13.9	1.3	2.6
1990	35	15.3	13.5	1.7	3.0
1991	39	16.6	15.2	1.5	2.9
1992	35	17.2	12.1	3.5	4.8
1993	36	17.0	12.9	2.7	4.0
1994	25	13.6	7.4	3.6	4.7
1995	28	14.1	7.2	4.2	5.2
1996	35	16.3	10.3	3.8	5.1
1997	33	14.8	9.0	3.6	4.9
1998	34	16.7	10.5	3.9	5.2
1999	33	15.1	12.1	2.2	3.5
2000	35	16.4	12.1	2.9	4.3
2001	35	15.4	11.9	.6	3.9
2002	35	13.6	10.7	2.1	3.3
2003	37	13.9	12.7	1.3	2.7
2004	34	14.1	13.2	1.3	2.7
2005	35	14.3	14.3	0.8	2.1
2006	34	13.0	11.8	1.4	2.6
2007	35	12.3	11.3	1.1	2.3
2008	34	11.7	12.3	0.3	1.5
CAREER RECORDS (Regular Season)	759	323.6	263.2	46.0	74.1
Postseason	37	13.1	10.9	1.8	2.9
CAREER RECORDS	**796**	**336.6**	**274.1**	**47.8**	**77.0**

Neutralizing the context in which Clemens and Maddux performed pulls their records even closer than they already were based on pWins and pLosses. The difference between their regular-season career values of eWORL (expected wins over replacement level) is a mere 1.9 wins. Adding in postseason decisions, Maddux moves within 1.7 eWORL of Clemens, 78.7–77.0.

Adjusting for context has relatively little impact on Greg Maddux's career. In fact,

Maddux's career regular-season eWORL and pWORL are identical (74.1). Maddux loses a bit, however, in the postseason, when his strong context-neutral performance(s) didn't translate into postseason victories like one might have expected (see, for example, his traditional career postseason record of 11–14).

Roger Clemens, however, gains a combined 3.4 regular- and post-season wins over replacement level.

Pitching

Having disposed of (almost) all of the little stuff, then, we're left with the meat of the comparison of Roger Clemens and Greg Maddux: their pitching. Context-neutral pitching records for Roger Clemens and Greg Maddux are shown in the next table.

Roger Clemens

Season	Games	Wins	Losses	Win Pct.	WOPA
1984	21	7.1	6.3	0.528	0.4
1985	15	5.2	4.0	0.565	0.7
1986	33	14.3	10.1	0.586	2.3
1987	36	16.2	11.9	0.576	2.4
1988	35	15.0	10.9	0.579	2.2
1989	35	14.0	11.9	0.540	1.2
1990	31	12.8	8.6	0.598	2.1
1991	35	14.6	10.7	0.578	2.2
1992	32	13.5	9.8	0.579	2.0
1993	29	10.4	9.4	0.525	0.6
1994	24	9.6	7.4	0.565	1.1
1995	23	7.7	7.6	0.503	0.3
1996	34	13.8	10.7	0.563	1.7
1997	34	14.9	8.6	0.634	3.4
1998	33	13.3	9.0	0.597	2.4
1999	30	10.6	9.7	0.522	0.5
2000	32	12.0	10.6	0.529	0.9
2001	33	12.4	10.7	0.538	1.1
2002	29	10.3	9.1	0.531	0.7
2003	33	11.7	10.3	0.532	0.8
2004	33	12.1	9.1	0.570	1.7
2005	32	11.5	7.6	0.600	2.1
2006	19	6.2	4.2	0.596	1.1
2007	18	5.3	5.1	0.508	0.1
CAREER RECORDS (Regular Season)	744	274.5	213.5	0.562	33.9

Greg Maddux

Season	Games	Wins	Losses	Win Pct.	WOPA
1986	6	1.6	2.0	0.097	−0.2
1987	34	8.4	9.9	0.321	−0.6
1988	37	13.1	11.5	0.493	0.9
1989	35	12.3	11.2	0.490	0.8
1990	35	12.6	10.8	0.536	1.0
1991	39	13.6	12.3	0.504	0.9
1992	35	13.8	9.8	0.592	2.4
1993	36	14.0	10.2	0.677	2.1
1994	25	10.8	5.7	0.706	2.7
1995	28	11.2	5.7	0.830	3.0
1996	35	13.1	8.2	0.593	2.6
1997	33	12.2	7.2	0.552	2.6
1998	34	13.4	8.4	0.620	2.8
1999	33	11.9	9.8	0.582	1.2

Season	Games	Wins	Losses	Win Pct.	WOPA
2000	35	13.6	9.8	0.625	2.2
2001	35	12.6	9.7	0.570	1.9
2002	35	10.8	8.7	0.565	1.3
2003	37	11.6	10.1	0.532	1.0
2004	34	11.6	10.6	0.514	0.8
2005	35	11.8	11.3	0.520	0.5
2006	34	10.7	9.5	0.685	0.8
2007	35	10.4	8.8	0.734	0.9
2008	34	9.8	9.8	0.993	0.2
CAREER RECORDS (Regular Season)	796	264.9	211.1	0.556	31.8

Roger Clemens amassed a slightly higher winning percentage over slightly more decisions than Greg Maddux. The two pitchers are, nevertheless, extremely close. If we remove the first two seasons of Maddux's career, when he was a below-average pitcher, he almost catches up to Clemens in winning percentage (0.561–0.562) and wins over positional average (32.6–33.9). Of course, those two seasons really happened for Maddux, and it is certainly to Clemens's credit that he never had a single season of his career when he was a below average pitcher.

The 1994–95 Player Strike

One factor that can come into play when trying to compare players is season lengths. Players from earlier generations who played in 154-game seasons simply had less time available to them to accumulate value than players who played in 162-game seasons. Of course, that doesn't matter in this case, since Maddux's and Clemens's careers spanned almost the exact same seasons and took place entirely in the era of 162-game seasons.

Actually, that last sentence is not entirely accurate. Roger Clemens and Greg Maddux both played in 1994 and 1995, both of which were shortened due to a nasty labor strike that ultimately cost major league baseball the 1994 World Series.

In theory, the 1994–95 strike affected Clemens and Maddux the same. They both missed the same time period to the strike. The reality was not necessarily the same, though.

Roger Clemens missed parts of one pretty good season (1994) and one fairly mediocre season by Roger Clemens's standards (1995). For those two seasons combined, Clemens amassed a pWin–pLoss record of 19.4–14.7, good for a total of 4.6 pWORL.

If Clemens's records in these two seasons are blown up to 162-game equivalents, his record becomes 24.8–18.8, and his pWORL increases to 5.9. This suggests that Roger Clemens lost perhaps 1.3 Player wins to the 1994–95 strike.

The strike could not have come at a worse time for Greg Maddux. Those two seasons, 1994 and 1995, were the years in which Greg Maddux made his case for possibly being the greatest pitcher in major-league history. Maddux's record over those two seasons was a jaw-dropping pWin–pLoss record of 31.1–16.0, good for a total of 11.3 pWORL.

If those records are blown up to 162-game equivalents, Maddux's record becomes 39.3–20.4, and his pWORL increases to 14.1. This would imply that Greg Maddux might have lost 2.9 Player wins to the 1994–95 strike.

In other words, normalizing for the 1994–95 strike in this way gives Greg Maddux 1.6 more wins than Roger Clemens. Replacing their actual records with records projected over a 162-game season for 1994 and 1995 produces the following career comparison.

Roger Clemens

Season	Games	pWins	pLosses	pWOPA	pWORL
1984	21	7.1	5.5	0.9	1.4
1985	15	5.9	4.5	0.8	1.3
1986	33	17.3	9.8	4.0	5.3
1987	36	18.4	12.0	3.5	5.1
1988	35	18.1	12.0	3.2	4.7
1989	35	14.9	12.7	1.3	2.6
1990	31	16.6	8.8	4.2	5.4
1991	35	16.6	11.0	3.0	4.3
1992	32	15.6	10.0	3.0	4.4
1993	29	12.8	12.6	0.2	1.4
1994	*34*	*14.9*	*11.2*	*2.0*	*3.5*
1995	*26*	*9.9*	*7.5*	*1.4*	*2.4*
1996	34	13.4	11.1	1.4	2.8
1997	34	18.3	9.5	4.7	6.3
1998	33	15.8	9.3	3.5	4.9
1999	30	13.0	12.3	0.6	1.9
2000	32	14.1	12.1	1.2	2.6
2001	33	14.3	9.0	2.9	4.2
2002	29	11.6	9.3	1.4	2.5
2003	33	13.6	11.1	1.5	2.9
2004	33	15.0	10.7	3.0	4.3
2005	32	14.1	9.9	2.7	3.8
2006	19	7.1	4.8	1.4	2.0
2007	18	6.0	5.6	0.3	1.0
CAREER RECORDS (Regular Season)	**722**	**324.3**	**232.5**	**52.1**	**81.1**
Postseason	35	12.5	11.2	1.0	2.2
CAREER RECORDS	**757**	**336.8**	**243.7**	**53.0**	**83.3**

Greg Maddux

Season	Games	pWins	pLosses	pWOPA	pWORL
1986	6	1.6	2.3	−0.2	−0.0
1987	34	10.1	13.9	−1.3	−0.2
1988	37	17.8	12.8	3.3	4.6
1989	35	16.1	14.1	1.7	3.0
1990	35	16.0	14.8	1.5	2.8
1991	39	15.6	13.6	1.7	3.0
1992	35	17.6	12.3	3.5	5.0
1993	36	18.1	13.5	2.9	4.3
1994	*35*	*20.5*	*11.6*	*5.2*	*6.8*
1995	*32*	*18.7*	*8.7*	*5.9*	*7.2*
1996	35	16.3	11.7	3.1	4.5
1997	33	14.5	9.2	3.3	4.6
1998	34	17.2	11.9	3.5	4.9
1999	33	16.0	12.9	2.3	3.7
2000	35	17.1	12.6	3.1	4.5
2001	35	16.2	11.8	3.0	4.4
2002	35	13.3	10.5	2.0	3.1
2003	37	13.6	13.8	0.6	2.0
2004	34	14.7	13.1	1.7	3.1
2005	35	12.6	14.8	−0.3	0.9
2006	34	13.4	12.4	1.2	2.5
2007	35	11.8	11.2	0.9	2.1
2008	34	10.2	13.9	−1.2	−0.0
CAREER RECORDS (Regular Season)	**773**	**338.9**	**277.4**	**47.4**	**76.9**
Postseason	37	12.6	12.4	0.8	2.0
CAREER RECORDS	**810**	**351.5**	**289.8**	**48.2**	**78.9**

So Who Was Better? Roger Clemens or Greg Maddux

So, after all of that, who was better, Roger Clemens or Greg Maddux? The best answer is that it was too close to call and/or that a case could be made for either one of them. After adjusting for the 1994–95 strike, the postseason, and everything else, Clemens still leads Maddux in career pWORL, 83.3 to 78.9, and pWOPA, 53.0 to 48.2. Maddux does lead in pWins, 351.5 to 336.8.

At the season level, adjusting 1994 and 1995 up to 162-game equivalents, gives Maddux more pWOPA and more pWORL in both of those seasons than Roger Clemens managed in any season. Outside of those two seasons, though, Clemens holds his own with Maddux in terms of peak and prime. Clemens leads Maddux 4–3 in seasons of pWORL of 5.0 or higher, and they each have 10 seasons with 4+ pWORL.

It's a tough call. If push came to shove, I guess I would pick Clemens, but I probably would not argue the case too hard.

Mariano Rivera vs. Andy Pettitte: How Valuable Can a Relief Pitcher Be?

Earlier in this chapter, I looked at starting pitchers versus relief pitchers generally. I thought it might be illuminating to look at a specific starting pitcher versus a specific relief pitcher, to get a better sense of just how valuable a relief pitcher can be.

For my comparison, I chose almost certainly the best relief pitcher in major-league history, Mariano Rivera, and his longtime teammate, Andy Pettitte.

Mariano Rivera is widely viewed as a future Hall-of-Famer, almost certainly on his first ballot of eligibility. Andy Pettitte is viewed, at best, as something of a marginal Hall-of-Fame candidate (even setting aside his connection to Brian McNamee), although he has his supporters.

The Yankees signed both Rivera and Pettitte as free agents within a week of each other in December of 2007.

- Rivera made $15 million in 2008.
- Pettitte made $16 million.

So Who Was More Valuable in His Career: Mariano Rivera or Andy Pettitte?

My pW-L records for Andy Pettitte and Mariano Rivera are shown in the table below.

Andy Pettitte

Season	Games	pWins	pLosses	pWOPA	pWORL
1995	31	10.7	9.8	0.7	1.8
1996	35	15.0	10.7	2.4	3.9
1997	35	13.9	8.1	3.1	4.4
1998	33	13.7	12.0	1.1	2.5
1999	31	11.8	11.5	0.4	1.6
2000	32	13.3	10.8	1.5	2.7
2001	31	13.4	10.8	1.6	2.9
2002	22	9.6	6.1	1.9	2.8
2003	33	14.4	11.8	1.6	3.1
2004	15	5.6	4.9	0.7	1.2
2005	33	14.0	9.8	2.7	3.8
2006	38	15.0	14.7	0.9	2.4

Season	Games	pWins	pLosses	pWOPA	pWORL
2007	36	12.5	10.7	1.1	2.4
2008	33	13.1	13.5	0.1	1.5
2009	32	12.9	10.5	1.6	2.8
2010	21	8.6	6.2	1.3	2.1
2011	0	0.0	0.0	0.0	0.0
2012	12	4.1	3.9	0.2	0.6
2013	30	10.8	10.0	0.6	1.7
CAREER RECORDS (Regular Season)	**533**	**212.3**	**175.8**	**23.4**	**44.3**
Postseason	44	17.4	14.1	2.0	3.7
CAREER RECORDS	**577**	**229.7**	**189.9**	**25.5**	**48.1**

Mariano Rivera

Season	Games	pWins	pLosses	pWOPA	pWORL
1995	19	4.0	4.1	−0.0	0.4
1996	61	9.7	3.6	2.7	3.6
1997	66	7.3	3.5	1.7	2.4
1998	54	6.5	1.9	2.1	2.6
1999	66	6.5	2.5	1.9	2.5
2000	66	7.4	4.0	1.5	2.3
2001	71	8.8	4.2	2.0	2.9
2002	45	5.3	4.0	0.5	1.2
2003	64	7.3	3.0	2.0	2.7
2004	74	9.3	3.7	2.5	3.4
2005	71	7.6	3.3	2.0	2.7
2006	63	7.1	3.4	1.7	2.4
2007	67	6.4	3.9	1.1	1.8
2008	64	7.7	2.6	2.3	3.0
2009	66	6.2	3.1	1.3	2.0
2010	61	5.7	3.4	1.0	1.7
2011	64	6.3	2.8	1.6	2.2
2012	9	0.7	0.3	0.2	0.3
2013	64	6.9	3.8	1.4	2.1
CAREER RECORDS (Regular Season)	**1,115**	**126.7**	**61.1**	**29.5**	**42.2**
Postseason	96	12.8	3.6	4.3	5.4
CAREER RECORDS	**1,211**	**139.5**	**64.7**	**33.8**	**47.6**

If your stat of choice is pWORL and you include postseason games, Pettitte and Rivera, were about as close in value as two players could be, 48.1–47.6. But they got there in fairly different ways.

Mariano Rivera beats Andy Pettitte handily in regular-season career winning percentage, 0.675–0.547. But Rivera's advantage there is offset by two factors. First, Andy Pettitte amassed 200.4 more regular-season player decisions than Rivera in his career, due to Pettitte having pitched 2,032 more regular-season innings than Rivera. Also, because relief pitchers have higher player winning percentages, on average, than starting pitchers, Rivera's record is compared against a higher positional average (0.518) than Pettitte's (0.487).

Even with the higher positional average, however, Rivera beats Pettitte fairly easily in regular-season wins over positional average (WOPA), 29.5 to 23.4, and extends his lead in pWOPA by another 2.3 wins when the postseason is added.

Moving the comparison from average to replacement level allows Pettitte to gain all of the advantage back, with Pettitte beating Rivera in "replacement wins" (pWORL minus pWOPA) by 8.2 in the regular season and another 0.6 in the postseason.

So, how valuable can a relief pitcher be? Under current usage patterns, it would appear that perhaps an elite relief pitcher can be as valuable as a very good starting pitcher.

7. Fielding Player Won-Lost Records

Fielding, including pitcher fielding, accounted for 18.2% of all Player decisions across all seasons for which I calculate pW-L records. An increase in the numbers of strikeouts and home runs in recent seasons has made fielding slightly less important; since 2000, fielding has accounted for only 17.5% of all player decisions.

Fielding decisions are accumulated in seven components:

- Component 1: Stolen Bases
- Component 2: Wild Pitches and Passed Balls
- Component 5: Hits vs. Outs
- Component 6: Singles v. Doubles v. Triples
- Component 7: Double Plays
- Component 8: Baserunner Outs
- Component 9: Baserunner Advancement

The table below shows how fielding decisions break down by component and by position across all seasons for which I have calculated pW-L records.

Breakdown of Fielding Decisions by Component by Position

Pos	1	2	5	6	7	8	9	All	Total (ex. P, C)
P			3.5%	0.1%	0.2%	0.2%	1.0%	5.0%	
C	2.9%	0.9%	0.6%	0.0%	0.1%	0.1%	0.1%	4.6%	
1B			4.5%	0.1%	0.1%	0.3%	1.0%	6.0%	6.6%
2B			9.7%	0.0%	1.1%	0.5%	1.4%	12.7%	14.1%
3B			9.6%	0.2%	0.1%	0.3%	1.4%	11.6%	12.8%
SS			11.0%	0.0%	1.3%	0.4%	1.7%	14.4%	16.0%
LF			7.9%	2.8%		1.6%	3.3%	15.5%	17.2%
CF			7.9%	1.6%		1.4%	3.6%	14.5%	16.1%
RF			8.1%	2.3%		1.7%	3.5%	15.6%	17.3%
Total	2.9%	0.9%	62.7%	7.2%	2.9%	6.4%	16.9%		

The numbers in the bottom row show the percentage of total fielding decisions accumulated by component. The numbers in the two right-most columns show the distribution of total fielding decisions accumulated by position (the latter column excluding pitchers and catchers).

Component 5, which measures whether a ball is a hit or an out, given where and how it is hit, accounts for just over 60% of all fielding decisions. Most defensive metrics based on play-by-play data—e.g., UZR, PMR, +/−, TotalZone—match up with this measure;

that is, they only look at whether balls-in-play become hits or outs. Of course, by my estimate, this means that such measures miss nearly 40% of all defensive value.

For most of the components for which fielding player decisions are awarded, fielders share these decisions with their pitchers. The exact extent to which fielders and pitchers share these decisions varies by fielding position, by component, and by season. The average percentage of defensive player decisions assigned to fielders by position and component across all seasons for which I have calculated pW-L records are shown in the next table.

Percentage of Total Defensive Decisions Assigned to Fielders

Pos.	1	2	5	Component 6	7	8	9
C	47.8%	23.7%	100.0%	0.0%	16.0%	100.0%	100.0%
1B			60.4%	94.4%	34.5%	100.0%	100.0%
2B			66.8%	45.5%	60.3%	100.0%	100.0%
3B			69.5%	53.2%	35.3%	100.0%	100.0%
SS			72.5%	27.2%	56.9%	100.0%	100.0%
LF			61.2%	86.5%		100.0%	100.0%
CF			67.7%	74.6%		100.0%	100.0%
RF			64.0%	69.1%		100.0%	100.0%

Combining the results from the above two tables, fielders' overall share of responsibility on Components 1–2 and 5–9 is as follows.

Pitcher	100%*
Catcher	42.7%
First Base	65.7%
Second Base	69.5%
Third Base	71.6%
Shortstop	73.5%
Left Field	74.1%
Center Field	76.9%
Right Field	73.5%

*Obviously, pitchers as pitchers can't really "share" decisions with pitchers as fielders. Defensive player decisions associated with plays in which the pitcher is the fielder of record are all counted as "fielding" decisions. This distinction is purely semantic.

Fielding pW-L Records: Best and Worst

Before getting into too much boring detail about the math underlying fielding won-lost records, let's look at some fielding records for major-league players.

Here are the top and bottom 10 fielders by position for their careers as measured by net fielding wins (fielding wins minus fielding losses) over the seasons for which I have calculated pW-L records.

PITCHER

Net Fielding Wins, Pitcher
Top 10 Players

		Wins	Losses	Net Wins
1	Greg Maddux	12.0	9.6	2.3
2	Tom Glavine	7.3	5.0	2.2

		Wins	Losses	Net Wins
3	*Jim Winford*	2.5	0.4	2.1
4	*Hal Newhouser*	6.4	4.4	2.0
5	Bret Saberhagen	4.8	2.8	2.0
6	Ken Dayley	2.6	0.7	1.9
7	Phil Niekro	8.0	6.2	1.8
8	Livan Hernandez	5.8	4.1	1.7
9	*Ed Brandt*	5.0	3.3	1.7
10	*Rene Monteagudo*	2.0	0.3	1.7

Net Fielding Losses, Pitcher
Top 10 Players

		Wins	Losses	Net Wins
1	Sam McDowell	3.4	5.7	−2.3
2	Nolan Ryan	4.9	7.2	−2.3
3	Johnny Vander Meer	3.9	5.8	−1.9
4	Chuck Finley	2.8	4.6	−1.8
5	Hank Aguirre	1.6	3.4	−1.7
6	Matt Garza	1.6	3.3	−1.6
7	Steve D. Barber	3.5	5.1	−1.6
8	*Luke Hamlin*	1.9	3.4	−1.6
9	*Joe Heving*	2.2	3.7	−1.5
10	*Bill Walker*	2.3	3.8	−1.5

The top player on the above list, Greg Maddux, holds the major-league record for most Gold Gloves with 18. So that's encouraging. On the other hand, 16-time Gold Glove winner Jim Kaat does not make my top 10 list.

In fact, Jim Kaat actually scores as very slightly below average for his career, with a career fielding winning percentage of 0.495. Kaat was brilliant when he was young, leading the major leagues in net fielding wins (among pitchers) in 1962 (the year he won his first Gold Glove), and amassing 1.0 net fielding wins through age 29. His fielding slipped as he got older, however, and was mostly below 0.500 after he reached the age of 30 with an overall fielding winning percentage over this time period of 0.426.

Catcher

Net Fielding Wins, Catcher
Top 10 Players

		Wins	Losses	Net Wins
1	Ivan Rodriguez	29.2	23.7	5.5
2	Gary Carter	33.2	28.1	5.2
3	Yadier Molina	16.8	12.9	4.0
4	Jim Sundberg	25.6	21.7	3.9
5	*Al Lopez*	22.5	18.9	3.6
6	Bob Boone	29.6	26.2	3.4
7	*Bill Dickey*	18.5	15.4	3.2
8	Johnny Bench	21.3	18.2	3.1
9	Tony Pena	28.4	25.3	3.1
10	Rick Dempsey	20.9	18.0	3.0

Net Fielding Losses, Catcher
Top 10 Players

		Wins	Losses	Net Wins
1	Mike Piazza	18.1	22.0	−3.9
2	*Frankie Hayes*	15.2	18.4	−3.2

		Wins	Losses	Net Wins
3	Dave Duncan	9.7	11.8	−2.1
4	Dick Dietz	5.1	6.9	−1.8
5	*Babe Phelps*	5.7	7.4	−1.7
6	Bob Tillman	7.0	8.6	−1.6
7	Todd Hundley	11.5	13.1	−1.6
8	Ozzie Virgil	9.4	11.0	−1.6
9	*Hal Wagner*	6.0	7.6	−1.6
10	Alan Ashby	18.0	19.5	−1.5

The numbers shown here for catchers only include traditional fielding measures: stolen bases, wild pitches, and catchers' ability to field balls-in-play. These numbers do not attempt to measure play-calling ability or pitch-framing.

The top six catchers listed here who played since Gold Gloves began to be awarded won 13, 3, 8, 6, 7, and 10 Gold Gloves, respectively. Perhaps the biggest surprise here is that Johnny Bench, winner of 10 Gold Gloves only ranks 8th. A comparison between Gary Carter and Johnny Bench is interesting, I think, in this regard. The vast majority of catcher fielding decisions (about two-thirds) are what I call Component 1, stolen bases and caught stealings.

Johnny Bench caught 14,488.1 (regular-season) innings in his career. For his career, Bench allowed 610 stolen bases, caught 469 baserunners stealing, and picked off an additional 62 men. Gary Carter caught about 20% more innings in his career, 17,369.0. He caught would-be base stealers at a considerably lower rate than Bench (35% vs. 43%), but at a rate that was better than league-average (32% during Carter's career). But Gary Carter caught 62% more would-be base stealers than Johnny Bench (810 CS, 51 PO). Why? Because Carter faced more than twice as many base stealing attempts as Bench (2,359 vs. 1,141). Bench's arm was so good and so well-respected that teams mostly didn't try running on him nearly as often as they ran on other catchers.

For most seasons for which I have calculated pW-L records, the actual stolen base success rate has tended to be very close to the break-even success rate. This means that, on average, never stealing a base is very close in net value to stealing bases at a league-average success rate. The same, then, is true for catchers as well: never having anybody attempt a stolen base has roughly the same net value as throwing out baserunners at a league-average rate. In other words, shutting down the opponents' running game doesn't really show up as that big of a positive in Johnny Bench's fielding record—not that having the 8th-best fielding record of the past 80+ years is at all negative, of course. There could also be ancillary benefits to completely shutting down an opponents' running game; but in my system, any such benefits aren't necessarily going to show up directly in Bench's fielding record, but could instead be showing up in the pitching and/or fielding records of his teammates.

First Base

Net Fielding Wins, First Base
Top 10 Players

		Wins	Losses	Net Wins
1	Albert Pujols	31.7	27.3	4.5
2	John Olerud	33.8	29.5	4.3
3	Mark Grace	40.0	35.7	4.2

		Wins	Losses	Net Wins
4	Vic Power	19.5	15.7	3.8
5	Will Clark	34.9	31.4	3.5
6	Adrian Gonzalez	27.1	23.6	3.5
7	Gil Hodges	27.7	24.3	3.4
8	Keith Hernandez	34.0	30.9	3.1
9	*Frank McCormick*	*24.0*	*21.3*	*2.7*
10	Tino Martinez	29.1	26.4	2.7

Net Fielding Losses, First Base
Top 10 Players

		Wins	Losses	Net Wins
1	Prince Fielder	20.2	23.6	−3.4
2	Fred McGriff	33.7	36.8	−3.1
3	Jason Giambi	19.0	21.4	−2.4
4	Frank Thomas	14.1	16.5	−2.4
5	Dick Stuart	14.8	17.1	−2.3
6	*Mickey Vernon*	*32.6*	*34.8*	*−2.3*
7	Willie McCovey	27.1	29.4	−2.3
8	Cecil Fielder	14.0	16.1	−2.2
9	Pedro Guerrero	9.4	11.5	−2.1
10	Carlos Delgado	29.5	31.6	−2.1

Fielding won-lost records for first basemen do not include any attempt to estimate the ability of first basemen to reach errant throws from other infielders.

Comparing the above list to a list of Gold Glove winners shows a few misses: 9-time winner Don Mattingly and 7-time winner Bill White, among others, don't make the list. Perhaps more surprising, 11-time winner Keith Hernandez, who is considered by many to be the finest defensive first baseman ever, is only 8th on the list. In the case of Hernandez, I think there could be a similar phenomenon to what I observed above with respect to Johnny Bench: Hernandez was such a good fielder that opposing teams avoided testing him, e.g., bunting less often or more toward third base than expected, thereby limiting his opportunities.

Overall, however, the top 10 players generally all had reputations as good fielders during their careers with 7 of the 9 eligible players winning at least two Gold Gloves in their careers (Frank McCormick retired nine years before the first Gold Glove was awarded).

On the other side, the bottom 10 list includes some notoriously bad fielders, such as Frank Thomas, Pedro Guerrero, and Dick "Dr. Strangeglove" Stuart, and several long-career below-average players who make the list more for being fairly bad for a long time (McGriff, McCovey) than for necessarily being truly awful.

SECOND BASE

Net Fielding Wins, Second Base
Top 10 Players

		Wins	Losses	Net Wins
1	Nellie Fox	74.7	69.2	5.5
2	Lou Whitaker	76.1	70.8	5.3
3	Mark Ellis	46.5	41.7	4.7
4	Dustin Pedroia	40.7	36.2	4.5

		Wins	Losses	Net Wins
5	Willie Randolph	73.7	69.3	4.4
6	*Lonny Frey*	*36.7*	*32.3*	*4.4*
7	Chase Utley	51.5	47.3	4.2
8	Ryne Sandberg	74.9	70.7	4.2
9	Frank White	69.9	65.8	4.1
10	*Joe Gordon*	*52.5*	*48.5*	*4.0*

Net Fielding Losses, Second Base
Top 10 Players

		Wins	Losses	Net Wins
1	Rickie Weeks	32.6	38.4	−5.9
2	Steve Sax	57.8	63.6	−5.8
3	Craig Biggio	64.3	68.3	−4.0
4	Juan Samuel	41.8	45.7	−3.9
5	Johnny Temple	39.8	43.2	−3.4
6	Dan Uggla	42.2	45.5	−3.3
7	Jorge Orta	20.1	23.4	−3.3
8	Todd Walker	29.6	32.4	−2.8
9	Alfonso Soriano	25.0	27.8	−2.7
10	Tony Taylor	45.2	47.9	−2.7

Major league baseball began awarding Gold Gloves in 1957, when Nellie Fox was 29 years old and in his 8th season as a starter. Even with the late start, Fox proceeded to win 3 of the first 4 Gold Gloves at second base (including the first one in 1957 when only one Gold Glove was awarded for all of major league baseball). The top 10 list includes five other players who won multiple Gold Gloves.

There are at least a couple of notable omissions, however. Probably the most significant names missing are 10-time Gold Glove winner Roberto Alomar and 8-time Gold Glover Bill Mazeroski.

Mazeroski rates as above average in fielding won-lost records. Mazeroski's record may be understated a bit here, however, because Retrosheet has fairly spotty records (e.g., uncertainty even regarding which fielders made some outs) for several games through Mazeroski's career. If I were to judgmentally create a list of the best fielders for whom I have calculated pW-L records, Bill Mazeroski would likely be a strong candidate to receive a positive judgmental boost.

Roberto Alomar, on the other hand, simply isn't that well-regarded by my system. He scores out as slightly below average overall for his career, with a fielding record of 77.5–77.9. The reason why Alomar scores out as a net negative for his career is because his fielding got distinctly worse starting around 2000 (age 32). Based purely on net wins, he scores as deserving of a Gold Glove in 1994 and close to one in several other seasons. Even before 2000, however, Alomar had several seasons where his fielding record was below 0.500. Outside of Gold Gloves, my assessment of Roberto Alomar's fielding is actually pretty much in line with most other analysts.

The list of worst fielding second basemen for whom I have calculated pW-L records includes Steve Sax, who had infamous throwing issues through much of his career, and several other players who I remember as having good-hit, no-field reputations at second base through their career, including Rickie Weeks, Juan Samuel, Dan Uggla, Jorge Orta, Todd Walker, and Alfonso Soriano. The list also includes 4-time Gold Glove winner Craig Biggio although, like Alomar, my rating of Biggio's second-base defense is not out of line with other statistical measures.

Third Base

Net Fielding Wins, Third Base
Top 10 Players

		Wins	Losses	Net Wins
1	Brooks Robinson	84.6	72.6	12.0
2	Robin Ventura	59.0	51.6	7.4
3	Tim Wallach	67.2	60.0	7.2
4	Terry Pendleton	65.0	57.8	7.2
5	Buddy Bell	69.6	62.5	7.1
6	Aurelio Rodriguez	58.2	51.3	6.9
7	Adrian Beltre	78.4	71.6	6.8
8	Mike Schmidt	74.1	67.4	6.7
9	Evan Longoria	33.7	27.5	6.2
10	Scott Rolen	64.1	57.9	6.1

Net Fielding Losses, Third Base
Top 10 Players

		Wins	Losses	Net Wins
1	*Pinky Higgins*	*51.5*	*58.1*	*−6.6*
2	Todd Zeile	47.3	52.9	−5.6
3	Dean Palmer	33.3	38.6	−5.3
4	Bill Madlock	39.1	44.2	−5.1
5	Aramis Ramirez	58.7	62.7	−3.9
6	Butch Hobson	17.9	21.7	−3.8
7	Jim Presley	26.9	30.6	−3.7
8	Ty Wigginton	19.2	22.8	−3.7
9	*Eddie Yost*	*56.7*	*60.1*	*−3.5*
10	Mark Reynolds	21.7	25.1	−3.4

Brooks Robinson won 16 Gold Gloves and was elected to the Hall of Fame in his first year of eligibility, largely on his reputation as the greatest defensive third baseman in major-league history. My pW-L records agree that Brooks Robinson was the best defensive third baseman of the past 80+ years, and by a substantial margin.

The rest of the top 10 are players with strong defensive reputations. Nine of the 10 won multiple Gold Gloves. The only exception was Aurelio Rodriguez, who spent his fielding prime in the American League during the time when Brooks Robinson held a monopoly on Gold Gloves.

Rodriguez managed to put together a 17-year, 2,017-game major-league career, despite a career batting line of .237/.275/.351 (OPS+ of 76). Rodriguez did finally win one Gold Glove, in 1976, when he had the distinction of being the first American League third baseman not named Brooks Robinson to win the award in 17 years, since Frank Malzone won the first three such awards from 1957 to 1959.

Shortstop

Net Fielding Wins, Shortstop
Top 10 Players

		Wins	Losses	Net Wins
1	Ozzie Smith	110.9	98.6	12.3
2	*Lou Boudreau*	*63.4*	*52.5*	*10.9*
3	Mark Belanger	67.3	57.4	9.9
4	Pee Wee Reese	76.9	67.7	9.2
5	Cal Ripken	90.6	83.3	7.3

		Wins	Losses	Net Wins
6	Alan Trammell	77.4	71.9	5.5
7	Luis Aparicio	98.8	93.4	5.4
8	*Eddie R. Miller*	*60.7*	*55.5*	*5.2*
9	Tim Foli	58.5	53.6	4.9
10	Omar Vizquel	98.7	93.8	4.9

Net Fielding Losses, Shortstop
Top 10 Players

		Wins	Losses	Net Wins
1	Derek Jeter	87.8	96.0	−8.1
2	Ivan DeJesus	47.1	51.3	−4.2
3	Kurt Stillwell	22.7	26.6	−4.0
4	Rafael Ramirez	55.2	59.1	−3.9
5	Ricky Gutierrez	28.9	32.4	−3.5
6	Jeff Blauser	36.7	40.1	−3.4
7	Hanley Ramirez	37.2	40.5	−3.3
8	Mario Guerrero	18.3	21.5	−3.2
9	Jose Reyes	53.7	56.8	−3.1
10	Miguel Tejada	71.9	74.9	−3.0

The seven players on the top 10 list above who played during the Gold Glove era won 13, 8, 2, 4, 9, 0, and 11 Gold Gloves, respectively (Tim Foli is the zero). Of course, Derek Jeter won more Gold Gloves (5) than either Alan Trammell or Cal Ripken. Fielding won-lost records are not the only fielding metric that shows Derek Jeter as having been a poor fielding shortstop.

Left Field

Net Fielding Wins, Left Field
Top 10 Players

		Wins	Losses	Net Wins
1	Barry Bonds	108.1	99.0	9.2
2	Joe Rudi	48.1	40.6	7.4
3	*Jo-Jo Moore*	*54.0*	*47.4*	*6.6*
4	Rickey Henderson	95.4	89.2	6.1
5	*Indian Bob Johnson*	*76.9*	*70.9*	*6.1*
6	Willie Wilson	34.3	28.3	6.0
7	B.J. Surhoff	35.3	29.3	5.9
8	Bernard Gilkey	41.8	36.3	5.5
9	Alex Gordon	34.8	29.8	5.0
10	Geoff Jenkins	37.3	32.4	4.9

Net Fielding Losses, Left Field
Top 10 Players

		Wins	Losses	Net Wins
1	Ralph Kiner	53.1	61.3	−8.2
2	Greg Luzinski	42.0	49.9	−7.9
3	Frank Howard	30.5	38.1	−7.7
4	Gary Matthews, Sr.	56.0	61.8	−5.8
5	Don Baylor	22.2	27.4	−5.1
6	Leon Wagner	33.7	38.7	−5.0
7	Al Martin	30.8	35.8	−5.0
8	Carlos Lee	65.4	70.3	−4.9
9	*Ted Williams*	*84.6*	*88.8*	*−4.3*
10	Jason Bay	45.9	49.9	−4.0

Barry Bonds won 8 Gold Gloves in left field. Greg Luzinski was a comically bad outfielder who became a full-time DH at age 30.

CENTER FIELD

Net Fielding Wins, Center Field
Top 10 Players

		Wins	Losses	Net Wins
1	Amos Otis	73.7	64.6	9.1
2	Willie Davis	84.5	75.5	9.0
3	Andruw Jones	70.8	62.5	8.3
4	Curt Flood	65.2	57.2	8.1
5	Duke Snider	54.3	46.9	7.3
6	*Joe DiMaggio*	*66.5*	*60.3*	*6.2*
7	Paul Blair	57.3	51.2	6.0
8	*Vince DiMaggio*	*51.8*	*46.5*	*5.4*
9	Jim Edmonds	65.0	59.9	5.1
10	Dave Henderson	42.1	37.5	4.7

Net Fielding Losses, Center Field
Top 10 Players

		Wins	Losses	Net Wins
1	Juan Pierre	38.7	44.2	−5.5
2	*Earl Averill*	*54.3*	*59.2*	*−4.9*
3	Dexter Fowler	27.5	32.1	−4.6
4	Bernie Williams	62.9	66.8	−3.9
5	Al Oliver	30.8	34.3	−3.5
6	Gus Bell	30.6	34.1	−3.5
7	Richie Ashburn	82.3	85.5	−3.3
8	*Gee Walker*	*18.9*	*22.0*	*−3.2*
9	Preston Wilson	31.7	34.8	−3.2
10	Ellis Burks	35.0	38.0	-3.0

The players in the top 10 list above generally had strong defensive reputations. Excluding Snider, the DiMaggios, and Henderson, the other six players on the list won 3, 3, 10, 7, 8, and 8 Gold Gloves, respectively. Joe DiMaggio probably would have won a Gold Glove in almost every season of his career had they been awarded while he was playing.

The striking thing about the top 10 list, then, is probably the names it does not include. The most glaring omission here is probably Willie Mays.

Gold Gloves were not awarded until Willie Mays's fifth full season in the major leagues. Because of that, Mays is merely tied (with Roberto Clemente) for the most Gold Gloves by any outfielder in major-league history with twelve. Willie Mays probably made the most famous catch in major-league history in Game 1 of the 1954 World Series. Michael Humphreys ranks Willie Mays as the second-best defensive centerfielder in major-league history in his book, *Wizardry: Baseball's All-Time Greatest Fielders Revealed*. Mays ranks second all-time in career defensive runs saved (DRS) (+176 runs) according to Baseball-Reference.

Not only does Willie Mays not rank among the top 10 defensive centerfielders as measured by pW-L records, but, in fact, pW-L records find Willie Mays to have been merely an average defensive centerfielder. Mays's career fielding record in center field was 109.5–108.3, a 0.503 winning percentage, and 1.3 net wins. To be perfectly honest, I think there is a very good chance that I am under-rating Willie Mays's defense here. Nevertheless, a few points in defense of this number.

First, pW-L records rate Willie Mays as one of the best baseball players in major-league history (at least since 1930). In Chapter 1, Mays ranks third in total pWins and pWins over positional average (pWOPA), and second in pWins over replacement level (pWORL) among all players for whom I have calculated pW-L records. It is not unheard of that a baseball player who was a great overall player may end up being perceived as great at everything, even those things at which he was merely good.

Second, Willie Mays was, in fact, legitimately great at several components of fielding. Center field defense is decomposed into four components, which were discussed in Chapter 4. Willie Mays ranks among the top 10 centerfielders in net fielding wins in 2 of the 4 components: Component 6 (the ability to prevent extra-base hits) and Component 9 (the ability to prevent baserunner advancement). Mays also rates extremely well at Component 8 (the ability to throw out baserunners). The next table shows the top 10 centerfielders in career net fielding wins for these three components among all centerfielders for whom I have calculated pW-L records.

Net Fielding Wins, Center Field
Components 6, 8, and 9
Top 10 Players

		Wins	Losses	Net Wins
1	Joe DiMaggio	33.0	27.5	5.6
2	Willie Mays	58.9	53.4	5.4
3	Adam Jones	21.0	16.5	4.5
4	Paul Blair	27.1	23.0	4.2
5	Andy Van Slyke	21.1	17.1	4.0
6	Dom DiMaggio	31.9	28.2	3.6
7	Cesar Geronimo	19.3	15.9	3.4
8	Vince DiMaggio	26.1	22.7	3.3
9	Vic Davalillo	13.8	10.6	3.2
10	Andruw Jones	30.1	27.0	3.1

As an aside, 3 of the top 8 players here were the DiMaggio brothers. Imagine what kind of outfield they would have been if they'd ever ended up as teammates.

But back to Willie Mays, there is no shame in ranking just behind Joe DiMaggio defensively.

Unfortunately for Willie Mays, the one component of centerfield defense at which he did not excel is also the most important aspect of centerfield defense, Component 5: the ability to convert balls-in-play into outs.

Even at Component 5, however, Willie Mays was solidly above average as a young man. Willie Mays led all major league centerfielders in net fielding wins in 1954 and led all National League centerfielders in 1955. From 1951 to 1956, Willie Mays amassed a fielding won-lost record of 25.9–22.6, a 0.534 winning percentage and 3.3 net wins. Had Willie Mays been able to maintain that pace over his entire career, his career net fielding wins would have totaled 14.9, which would have been more than five wins more than any other player for whom I have calculated pW-L records. Of course, it was never likely that a 35-year-old Willie Mays would be as good a defensive centerfielder as the 25-year-old Mays was. Even the great Willie Mays slowed down with age.

It is certainly not uncommon for a player to acquire a reputation early in his career and hold onto that reputation perhaps longer than he deserves to. Willie Mays was a great defensive centerfielder when he was young. He legitimately made one of the all-time great catches in Game 1 of the 1954 World Series. Willie Mays remained great at many aspects of fielding throughout his career. But maybe he lost a little range as he aged and people just didn't notice (or, at least, say anything about it) because, well, he was Willie Mays. And when a player is as great in all aspects of baseball as Willie Mays was, it's a little unseemly to nitpick about his "flaws" (if, in fact, being an average defensive centerfielder in his mid–30s as pW-L records say he was is even really a flaw).

Or, as I said, I may be under-rating Willie Mays's fielding record.

Another top centerfielder who is, perhaps, notable by his absence here is 8-time Gold Glove winner Garry Maddox. I discuss Maddox's fielding ratings in some detail later in this chapter.

RIGHT FIELD

Net Fielding Wins, Right Field
Top 10 Players

		Wins	Losses	Net Wins
1	Ichiro Suzuki	76.3	66.1	10.2
2	Mel Ott	89.4	79.6	9.9
3	Roberto Clemente	107.1	97.2	9.8
4	Al Kaline	79.8	70.1	9.6
5	Carl Furillo	62.1	52.6	9.5
6	Jesse Barfield	59.5	50.1	9.4
7	Tony Oliva	49.0	41.7	7.3
8	Brian Jordan	39.3	33.0	6.3
9	Johnny Callison	71.7	65.4	6.3
10	Ellis Valentine	35.6	29.4	6.2

Net Fielding Losses, Right Field
Top 10 Players

		Wins	Losses	Net Wins
1	Jeff Burroughs	29.8	36.7	−6.9
2	Ken Singleton	44.3	49.7	−5.5
3	Danny Tartabull	31.7	37.0	−5.3
4	Jay Buhner	48.5	53.1	−4.5
5	Ken Griffey, Sr.	38.9	43.1	−4.2
6	Claudell Washington	39.4	43.4	−4.0
7	Brad Hawpe	28.2	32.1	−3.9
8	Dante Bichette	34.9	38.8	−3.9
9	Shawn Green	59.3	63.1	−3.8
10	Jim Lemon	16.8	20.6	−3.8

Ichiro Suzuki, Roberto Clemente, and Al Kaline each won at least 10 Gold Gloves. Jesse Barfield only won 2 Gold Gloves in his relatively short career (only 6 seasons where he qualified for a batting title) but had the best outfield arm I ever saw (Clemente was a bit before my time). Tony Oliva and Ellis Valentine also each won a Gold Glove in their careers. Carl Furillo's career mostly pre-dated the Gold Glove award, but his nickname was the "Reading Rifle" and he was good enough to play over 300 games in center field in his career, so his appearance on this list is no real surprise, either.

There are, however, a few multiple Gold Glove winners missing from the above list, including Dwight Evans (8), Dave Winfield (7), Larry Walker (7), Tony Gwynn (5), and Hank Aaron (3), although all five of these players rate as above-average rightfielders for their career. The problem, in the cases of at least Evans, Winfield, Gwynn, and Aaron, is that they remained regular right fielders well past their fielding primes—because they were such valuable hitters, giving them many seasons of below-average—but not necessarily *terrible*—fielding.

An alternate measure of career fielding value that doesn't punish players (as much) for below-average fielding is to measure player fielding value against replacement level instead of 0.500. The next table shows the top 25 right fielders in career fielding wins over replacement level (fWORL). Evans, Winfield, Gwynn, and Aaron all make this list, along with the multiple Gold Glove winners seen earlier: Ichiro, Clemente, Kaline, and Barfield.

Fielding Wins Over Replacement Level, Right Field
Top 25 Players

		Wins	Losses	fWORL
1	Mel Ott	89.4	79.6	9.3
2	Ichiro Suzuki	76.3	66.1	9.2
3	Roberto Clemente	107.1	97.2	9.1
4	Carl Furillo	62.1	52.6	8.0
5	Al Kaline	79.8	70.1	8.0
6	Jesse Barfield	59.5	50.1	8.0
7	Dwight Evans	86.7	83.6	6.4
8	Johnny Callison	71.7	65.4	5.9
9	*Wally Moses*	*76.2*	*72.8*	*5.9*
10	Paul O'Neill	69.0	64.7	5.6
11	Alexis Rios	51.1	45.6	5.6
12	*Paul Waner*	*92.9*	*91.6*	*5.5*
13	Sammy Sosa	85.0	81.5	5.5
14	Tony Oliva	49.0	41.7	5.4
15	Hank Aaron	90.3	86.9	5.2
16	Brian Jordan	39.3	33.0	4.8
17	Dave Winfield	76.8	74.8	4.8
18	Reggie Sanders	46.6	41.2	4.6
19	Al Cowens	53.8	50.6	4.6
20	Ellis Valentine	35.6	29.4	4.4
21	Tim Salmon	53.4	50.9	4.4
22	*Gene Moore*	*39.4*	*34.7*	*4.4*
23	Tony Gwynn	79.4	77.0	4.4
24	*Pete Fox*	*51.3*	*48.4*	*4.4*
25	Roger Maris	43.1	37.7	4.3

The top 10 players in career fielding wins over replacement level at the other seven fielding positions are shown next.

Fielding Wins Over Replacement Level, Catcher
Top 10 Players

		Wins	Losses	fWORL
1	Ivan Rodriguez	29.2	23.7	5.8
2	Gary Carter	33.2	28.1	5.2
3	Bob Boone	29.6	26.2	4.4
4	Jim Sundberg	25.6	21.7	4.4
5	Tony Pena, Sr.	28.4	25.3	4.2
6	*Al Lopez*	*22.5*	*18.9*	*4.0*
7	Lance Parrish	24.2	21.9	3.6
8	Rick Dempsey	20.9	18.0	3.5
9	*Bill Dickey*	*18.5*	*15.4*	*3.4*
10	Brad Ausmus	21.0	18.3	3.4

Fielding Wins Over Replacement Level, First Base
Top 10 Players

		Wins	Losses	fWORL
1	John Olerud	33.8	29.5	3.3
2	Albert Pujols	31.7	27.3	3.1

		Wins	Losses	fWORL
3	Gil Hodges	27.7	24.3	2.9
4	Mark Grace	40.0	35.7	2.8
5	Will Clark	34.9	31.4	2.6
6	Vic Power	19.5	15.7	2.6
7	Keith Hernandez	34.0	30.9	2.4
8	Adrian Gonzalez	27.1	23.6	2.4
9	Tino Martinez	29.1	26.4	2.4
10	*George McQuinn*	*26.3*	*23.8*	*2.2*

Fielding Wins Over Replacement Level, Second Base
Top 10 Players

		Wins	Losses	fWORL
1	Nellie Fox	74.7	69.2	10.1
2	Lou Whitaker	76.1	70.8	9.9
3	Willie Randolph	73.7	69.3	9.2
4	Frank White	69.9	65.8	8.9
5	Bill Mazeroski	74.1	72.7	8.6
6	Joe Morgan	81.9	81.9	8.1
7	Ryne Sandberg	74.9	70.7	7.8
8	*Charlie Gehringer*	*63.5*	*61.2*	*7.2*
9	Red Schoendienst	59.7	56.7	7.2
10	Bobby Grich	58.7	56.2	7.1

Fielding Wins Over Replacement Level, Third Base
Top 10 Players

		Wins	Losses	fWORL
1	Brooks Robinson	84.6	72.6	11.2
2	Adrian Beltre	78.4	71.6	8.7
3	Buddy Bell	69.6	62.5	8.2
4	Robin Ventura	59.0	51.6	8.0
5	Gary Gaetti	72.2	67.2	7.5
6	Tim Wallach	67.2	60.0	7.3
7	Mike Schmidt	74.1	67.4	7.3
8	Terry Pendleton	65.0	57.8	7.3
9	Aurelio Rodriguez	58.2	51.3	7.3
10	Scott Rolen	64.1	57.9	7.0

Fielding Wins Over Replacement Level, Shortstop
Top 10 Players

		Wins	Losses	fWORL
1	Ozzie Smith	110.9	98.6	16.9
2	Cal Ripken	90.6	83.3	13.7
3	Luis Aparicio	98.8	93.4	13.7
4	Mark Belanger	67.3	57.4	13.0
5	Omar Vizquel	98.7	93.8	12.6
6	Pee Wee Reese	76.9	67.7	11.8
7	Alan Trammell	77.4	71.9	11.7
8	*Lou Boudreau*	*63.4*	*52.5*	*11.5*
9	Dave Concepcion	82.8	78.2	11.4
10	Larry Bowa	81.5	78.8	10.7

Fielding Wins Over Replacement Level, Left Field
Top 10 Players

		Wins	Losses	fWORL
1	Barry Bonds	108.1	99.0	9.1
2	Rickey Henderson	95.4	89.2	8.3

		Wins	Losses	fWORL
3	Indian Bob Johnson	76.9	70.9	7.1
4	Jo-Jo Moore	54.0	47.4	6.4
5	Joe Rudi	48.1	40.6	5.9
6	Carl Yastrzemski	89.7	86.5	5.5
7	Carl Crawford	60.4	56.8	5.3
8	Roy White	66.4	62.5	5.2
9	B.J. Surhoff	35.3	29.3	5.0
10	Willie Wilson	34.3	28.3	4.9

Fielding Wins Over Replacement Level, Center Field
Top 10 Players

		Wins	Losses	fWORL
1	Amos Otis	73.7	64.6	9.1
2	Willie Davis	84.5	75.5	8.7
3	Andruw Jones	70.8	62.5	8.3
4	Curt Flood	65.2	57.2	7.2
5	Jim Edmonds	65.0	59.9	6.9
6	Joe DiMaggio	66.5	60.3	6.8
7	Kenny Lofton	71.1	68.0	6.7
8	Carlos Beltran	61.9	57.6	6.3
9	Mike Cameron	65.7	62.2	6.2
10	Paul Blair	57.3	51.2	6.2

Replacement level is tied to player position, as explained in Chapter 3. Specifically, replacement level is lower for more difficult fielding positions (e.g., catcher, shortstop) than for less difficult fielding positions (e.g., first base, corner outfield). Because of this, comparing fielding wins against replacement level provides a way to compare fielders across positions, in a way that recognizes that, for example, an average fielding shortstop is a better absolute fielder than an average fielding second baseman.

The next table, then, shows the top 25 players in career fielding wins over replacement level (fWORL), regardless of fielding position.

Fielding Wins Over Replacement Level, All Fielders
Top 25 Players

		Wins	Losses	fWORL
1	Ozzie Smith	111.0	98.5	17.0
2	Cal Ripken	108.8	100.8	15.6
3	Luis Aparicio	98.9	93.3	13.7
4	Omar Vizquel	104.2	99.1	13.2
5	Mark Belanger	67.8	57.7	13.1
6	Pee Wee Reese	80.1	70.6	12.3
7	Dave Concepcion	89.1	84.2	12.1
8	Alan Trammell	79.4	73.9	11.9
9	Lou Boudreau	65.1	54.3	11.6
10	Brooks Robinson	84.8	72.6	11.3
11	Bill Russell	77.8	71.7	11.1
12	Ichiro Suzuki	90.9	78.9	11.0
13	Larry Bowa	81.7	78.9	10.8
14	Bert Campaneris	80.2	78.9	10.5
15	Garry Templeton	80.6	76.3	10.4
16	Carl Furillo	75.7	63.1	10.3
17	Nellie Fox	74.9	69.3	10.2
18	Mel Ott	103.7	93.8	10.2
19	Barry Bonds	115.6	105.0	10.2
20	Lou Whitaker	76.2	70.8	10.0
21	Tony Fernandez	78.4	75.0	9.9

		Wins	Losses	fWORL
22	Don Kessinger	80.1	79.8	9.8
23	Ozzie Guillen	69.5	65.3	9.7
24	Roy McMillan	75.5	71.3	9.7
25	Chris Speier	76.6	74.5	9.6

This chapter concludes with a comparison of fielding pW-L records to some other sabermetric fielding measures.

Fielding pW-L Records vs. Ultimate Zone Rating (UZR)

Perhaps the most prominent modern fielding measure is Ultimate Zone Rating, UZR, which was originally conceived by Mitchel Lichtman and is now reported regularly at Fangraphs.com. I compared my fielding won-lost records to UZR data for ten years, 2003–2012, for all players who played at least 3,000 innings at a given position over those 10 years, for the seven fielding positions other than pitcher and catcher. The total population of players that I compared here was 288 total players (counting some players more than once if they played 3,000 innings at multiple positions), ranging from 30 leftfielders to 49 centerfielders.

I chose 2003 as my cutoff for comparison (Fangraphs reports UZR data starting in 2002) because Retrosheet data since 2003 is very consistent in providing hit-type information (e.g., ground ball, fly ball, line drive), but not detailed location data, for all balls-in-play, hits as well as outs. I stopped in 2012 because that was the last season for which I had data when I first did this comparison several years ago. Overall, 2003–2012 makes for a nice, even ten-year sample period.

Conceptual Difference Between UZR and Fielding pW-L Records

BASIC FIELDING: OUTS VS. HITS ON BALLS-IN-PLAY

UZR is described in great detail on Fangraphs.com's website. The basic concept is that UZR calculates a probability of a ball-in-play being converted into an out, based on the location of the ball, how hard it is hit, the handedness of the batter, the ground-ball tendencies of the pitcher, and various other factors. Fielders are then given credit or blame over and above this said probability, so, for example, for a ball-in-play that had a 75% chance of being an out, if the ball becomes a hit, the responsible fielder(s) are debited with −0.75 "plays made"; if the same ball-in-play became an out, the responsible fielder is credited with 0.25 plays made. Plays are then converted to runs based on the average run value of balls-in-play based on the location, et al.

This aspect of fielding: whether balls-in-play are converted into outs or not corresponds to what I call Component 5.

The key difference between pW-L records and UZR is that while UZR's baseline for evaluating a play is detailed information about the location of a ball-in-play (as well as how hard it was hit, by whom, and against whom), the baseline for evaluating a play in calculating pW-L records is what the final result of the play was—out vs. hit, who fielded it, and what type of hit it was (bunt, ground ball, fly ball, line drive). This is largely because of data limitations with respect to Retrosheet play-by-play data. I discussed this difference and my treatment of location data in general in Chapter 4. In effect, UZR assumes that two hard-hit fly balls to medium center field are created equal. pW-L records assume that two fly-ball doubles fielded by the center fielder are created equal.

Hits vs. Fielding Errors

UZR treats errors somewhat differently from hits. According to the UZR Primer at Fangraphs.com, errors are assumed to have been easy plays with high probabilities of being outs. Hence, UZR penalizes fielders more heavily for errors than for hits on balls-in-play.

In contrast, Fielding pW-L records treat errors the same as base hits. The key distinguishing characteristic of plays in my system is whether the batter reaches base (and, eventually, what base he reaches).

Michael Humphreys discusses the correct treatment of errors in evaluating fielding in his book *Wizardry: Baseball's All-Time Greatest Fielders Revealed* and shows that the true cost to the fielding team of an error or a hit allowed are identical for any given play (see, e.g., *Wizardry*, pp. 77–78). I agree with Humphreys and believe that this is one way in which my pW-L records are clearly superior conceptually to UZR.

Additional Components of Fielding

In addition to the basic "range runs" and "error runs" described above, UZR also calculates run values for fielders based on their ability to turn double plays (infielders) and their ability to control baserunner advancement (outfielders). Fangraphs.com reports these values separately from the UZR estimates based purely on whether balls-in-play are converted to outs or not, but combines them into a single final number which it reports as a player's total UZR.

In addition to Component 5, I also calculate four additional components that are credited (at least partly) to fielders.

Component 6 gives credit or blame on hits-in-play based on how many bases the batter takes. That is, it distinguishes between singles, doubles, and triples among hits-in-play. To the best of my knowledge, there is no parallel to my Component 6 in UZR (or any other fielding metric of which I am aware). UZR uses run values based on the average hit value of a ball, based on its location, hit type, etc., but makes no distinctions between hits which actually end up as singles versus otherwise-identical balls-in-play which actually end up as doubles. Component 6 pW-L records are shared between pitchers and fielders at all fielding positions. Component 6 won-lost records are much more significant, however, for outfielders (for whom they account for approximately 14.9% of Fielding decisions) than for infielders (for whom they account for approximately 0.8% of Fielding decisions).

Component 7 gives credit or blame to infielders (and pitchers) for turning double plays on ground balls in double-play situations. This is essentially comparable to UZR's double-play runs. For pW-L records, Component 7 fielding decisions are shared between the fielder who fields a ground ball and the pivot man on the double play (pivot men only receive fielding losses for plays where they receive the ball in time to record a force out but are unable to complete the double play). So, for example, on a classic 6–4–3 double play, both the shortstop and second baseman will earn Component 7 fielding wins. It was not clear to me in reading the UZR Primer exactly who is credited with double-play runs on a 6-4-3 double play. Component 7 accounts for approximately 6.0% of infielder fielding decisions.

Finally, Components 8 and 9 give credit or blame to fielders for baserunner outs and baserunner advancement, respectively. This is comparable to UZR's Arm runs. The difference here is that Components 8 and 9 are allocated across all fielders, while UZR Arm runs are only allocated to outfielders. Components 8 and 9 combine to account for approximately 15.6% of infielder fielding decisions and 32.7% of outfielder fielding decisions.

Components 5, 6, and 7 are shared between fielders and pitchers, while Components 8 and 9 are allocated entirely to fielders. Because of this, "arm ratings" make up a relatively larger share of fielding won-lost records than they do of total UZR.

Raw Results

I compared two measures of UZR and (context-neutral, teammate-adjusted) net fielding wins (eWins minus eLosses): total UZR runs vs. total net fielding wins, and (Range + Error) UZR runs vs. net Component 5 fielding wins. For outfielders, I also calculated a third measure of net fielding wins which excludes Component 6–since UZR has no counterpart—which I compare to total UZR runs. To be clear, on this last measure, I excluded Component 6 only to allow for an apples-to-apples comparison to UZR. The fact that my fielding records include this measure of the exact value of the hits allowed by fielders while UZR relies only on average hit values across similar plays is, in my opinion, a clear advantage of fielding won-lost records over UZR as an overall measure of player fielding.

The first table summarizes the results for Ultimate Zone Rating (UZR) and net fielding wins (eWins minus eLosses).

UZR Net Fielding Runs (per 1,000 innings)

Position	# of Players	Total UZR		UZR, Range+Error	
		Mean	Std. Dev.	Mean	Std. Dev.
1B	36	−0.12	4.31	−0.09	4.24
2B	41	0.12	4.66	−0.05	4.46
3B	49	0.80	6.24	0.77	6.08
SS	45	0.54	4.90	0.43	4.61
LF	30	−0.46	6.82	−0.21	6.36
CF	49	0.52	6.29	0.27	6.25
RF	38	0.53	6.38	0.23	5.78

Net Fielding eWins (per 1,000 innings)

Position	Total Fielding eWins		Component 5 eWins		Total eWins, excl. Comp. 6	
	Mean	Std. Dev.	Mean	Std. Dev.	Mean	Std. Dev.
1B	0.008	0.209	0.013	0.181		
2B	0.001	0.279	−0.014	0.254		
3B	0.028	0.341	0.018	0.332		
SS	0.044	0.261	0.041	0.197		
LF	−0.002	0.340	−0.002	0.280	−0.007	0.307
CF	0.038	0.373	0.015	0.262	0.032	0.357
RF	0.049	0.405	0.018	0.298	0.052	0.393

The first thing that we have to do before we can compare UZR to net eWins is to put them on the same scale. UZR is expressed in runs while player wins are, of course, expressed in wins. Traditionally, in sabermetric measures, one win is equal to approximately 10 runs. Looking at the standard deviations in the above table, however, the ratio of UZR to player wins is more like 15 to 20. In other words, even if you converted UZR to wins, using a conventional run-to-win translation, the spread of players' net fielding wins is 40–50 percent lower than the spread of UZR.

Why Is the Spread on Player Fielding Wins Lower Than Defensive Runs?

The spread on my net fielding wins is less than the spread of UZR (and other fielding measures) because I assign more credit on balls-in-play to pitchers, whereas stand-alone fielding measures implicitly assign all of the credit on balls-in-play to fielders. The relationship between Pitching and Fielding in my system was explored in some detail in Chapter 6.

Is this reasonable on my part? I believe that it is. Research following up on DIPS theory has consistently found that pitchers have some effect on batting average on balls-in-play (BABIP). The extent to which I allocate such credit to pitchers is based on the extent to which player winning percentages persist for pitchers in these components.

With specific regard to UZR, Mitchel Lichtman, the creator of UZR, looked at how UZR differs for specific pitchers on the same team (specifically, the 2012 Detroit Tigers) and found significant differences across pitchers. While this was a quick-and-dirty analysis that really doesn't even rise to the level of a "study," its results are consistent with the likelihood that there is some pitcher ability being captured within UZR.

More recently, Lichtman wrote an interesting blog post ("How Important is Bayes in Advanced Defensive Metrics?," http://mglbaseball.com/2016/03/04/how-important-is-bayes-in-advanced-defensive-metrics/). In discussing the *a priori* probabilities of a ball-in-play being converted to an out that form the basis for calculating UZR, Lichtman identifies one factor affecting these probabilities that UZR does not include: "whether the player caught the ball or not!" Working through a thought experiment of what UZR might look like taking into account "whether the player caught the ball or not," Lichtman hypothesizes that UZR could be "regressed around 35–40% toward zero." In other words, Lichtman suggests that the true range of player fielding value may be 40% more narrow than UZR.

Fielding pW-L records take account of "whether the player caught the ball or not." In fact, that information is the centerpiece of Component 5 pW-L records. And the range of fielding value, as measured by pW-L records, is, in fact, about 40% narrower than the range as measured by UZR.

In Chapter 8, I compare Fangraphs' measure of WAR (fWAR), which relies upon UZR as its measure of fielding value to eWins, eWOPA, and eWORL. One of my conclusions there is that fielding—i.e., UZR—is over-weighted in Fangraphs' (and Baseball-Reference's) measure of WAR, pW-L records weight fielding appropriately. Lichtman's insight here explains why.

Putting Things on the Same Scale

In order to really compare UZR and what I'll start calling NFW (net fielding wins), it is necessary to put them on the same scale. To do this, I created "z-scores" associated with both statistics. The basic formula for a z-score of variable x is (x—m) / s, where m is the mean of the statistic and s is the standard deviation. I calculated z-scores for each player for UZR and net fielding wins using a value of m equal to zero (since both of these statistics are constructed to be relative to league average by construction) and the standard deviations from the tables shown earlier in the chapter.

For example, Andre Ethier scores at −4.67 total UZR (per 1,000 innings in RF), −2.84 Range+Error UZR (reUZR), −0.422 total NFW, −0.248 Component 5 NFW (NFW5), and −0.515 NFW, excluding Component 6 (NFW589) in right field over the time period being analyzed here. From the earlier tables, the standard deviations associated with these five numbers are 6.38, 5.78, 0.405, 0.298, and 0.393, respectively. This translates, therefore, into z-scores for Andre Ethier in right field of −0.73 for total UZR, −0.49 for reUZR, −1.04 for NFW, −0.83 for NFW5, and −1.31 for NFW589. UZR and pW-L records are in general agreement regarding Andre Ethier's defense in right field: he was generally a below-average defensive right fielder over the seasons considered here.

I did this for every player referenced in the earlier table. I then calculated simple correlations between UZR and NFW by position (UZR to NFW, reUZR to NFW5, and, for the outfield positions, UZR to NFW589).

UZR v. NFW

Position	Total	Comp. 5 only	excl. Comp. 6
1B	0.864	0.886	
2B	0.812	0.826	
3B	0.869	0.873	
SS	0.778	0.793	
LF	0.730	0.721	0.715
CF	0.558	0.494	0.519
RF	0.724	0.698	0.729

Keep in mind that correlations do not tell us which of two measures is more accurate, merely how similar they are to each other.

The correlations associated with the infield positions here are exceptionally high. To the extent that the correlations are somewhat higher for Component 5 only, I believe this is indicative of the extent to which UZR is missing information that I am capturing, particularly via Components 6, 8, and 9. But, to the extent that the difference in correlations is very slight, this is indicative of the fact that this additional information is fairly minimal (and/or that player fielding value is fairly highly correlated across components).

The correlations associated with the corner outfield positions, while not as high as those for the infield, are nevertheless extremely high. The relative correlations with and without Components 6, 8, and 9 differ between leftfield and rightfield such that I'm not inclined to really draw any conclusions in that regard. But overall, the level of correlation between these two systems is very encouraging to me. If UZR is capturing something that I am missing, it does not appear to be a very major factor in the infield or the corner outfield positions.

The lowest correlations are for centerfield. Even here, however, the correlation between overall UZR and total net fielding wins, 0.558, is fairly high. I look more closely at the centerfield numbers and what they might mean below.

The next section looks more closely at how UZR and net fielding wins compare on a position-by-position basis.

Position-by-Position Analysis

First Base

Among the 36 players evaluated here, there are two players for whom the difference in z-scores is greater than one (in absolute value). Looking only at Component 5, there is only one player for whom the (absolute) difference in z-scores is greater than one. These players are shown in the next table.

Fielding Z-Score

		UZR (Fangraphs)		NFW (Thress)	
	Innings	Total	Range+Err	Total	Comp. 5
Mike Jacobs	3,236.1	−2.099	−2.083	−0.890	−1.295
Scott Hatteberg	4,777.0	−0.413	−0.400	0.607	0.800

The only first baseman whose Component 5 z-scores differ by more than one was minor *Moneyball* star Scott "Picking Machine" Hatteberg. My system thinks that Ron Washington did a pretty good job of teaching Hatteberg how to play first base.

Second Base

Among the 41 players evaluated here, there are a total of three players for whom the difference in z-scores is greater than one (in absolute value) for total UZR v. total NFW. For Component 5 vs. Range+Error UZR runs, there are four such players. These players are shown in the next table.

Fielding Z-Score

		UZR (Fangraphs)		NFW (Thress)	
	Innings	Total	Range+Err	Total	Comp. 5
Brandon Phillips	10,043.1	1.313	1.432	−0.389	−0.186
Brian Roberts	9,607.2	0.532	0.607	−0.600	−0.346
Freddy Sanchez	5,413.0	0.666	0.568	−0.146	−0.458
Rickie Weeks	7,703.2	−1.093	−1.055	−2.196	−2.260
Skip Schumaker	3,182.1	−1.997	−2.215	−0.725	−1.261

The difference in z-scores for Roberts and Weeks exceed one for total fielding, but are within one (albeit not by a lot) when only Component 5 is considered. On the other hand, the overall z-scores are within one for Freddy Sanchez but UZR and pW-L records disagree more strongly about Sanchez's basic ability to turn batted balls into outs.

Third Base

Among the 49 players evaluated here, there are a total of four players for whom the difference in z-scores is greater than one (in absolute value). Looking at only Component 5, however, there is only one player with z-scores that differ by more than one. These players are shown in the next table.

Fielding Z-Score

		UZR (Fangraphs)		NFW (Thress)	
	Innings	Total	Range+Err	Total	Comp. 5
David Bell	4,456.0	0.960	0.938	−0.171	0.018
Eric Chavez	6,700.1	0.624	0.633	1.645	1.499

	Innings	UZR (Fangraphs)		NFW (Thress)	
		Total	Range+Err	Total	Comp. 5
Geoff Blum	3,256.0	1.157	1.223	0.144	0.333
Mike Lowell	8,048.0	0.163	0.121	1.337	0.953
Vinny Castilla	4,308.1	0.275	0.206	1.053	1.248

Two of the five players in the above table won Gold Gloves during the decade of interest here: Eric Chavez (who won four) and Mike Lowell (who won one). In both of these cases, my system views their defense more favorably—and, hence, more consistently with Gold Glove voters—than does UZR. Of course, aligning oneself with Gold Glove voters can sometimes be a sketchy proposition historically.

SHORTSTOP

Among the 45 players evaluated here, there are a total of five players for whom the difference in z-scores is greater than one (in absolute value) for total UZR and six players for whom the (absolute) difference exceeds one for (Range+Error) UZR. These players are shown in the next table.

Fielding Z-Score

	Innings	UZR (Fangraphs)		NFW (Thress)	
		Total	Range+Err	Total	Comp. 5
Angel Berroa	5,673.1	−1.163	−1.442	−0.035	−0.769
Asdrubal Cabrera	4,380.0	−1.403	−1.610	−0.129	−0.520
Cliff Pennington	3,971.2	−0.242	−0.568	1.192	0.726
Clint Barmes	4,907.0	1.336	−1.172	1.687	2.242
J.J. Hardy	8,115.0	1.621	1.770	0.505	0.943
Khalil Greene	5,941.2	−0.498	−0.588	0.199	0.687
Marco Scutaro	5,734.2	−0.449	−0.378	0.317	0.776
Michael Young	6,737.1	−1.707	−1.546	−1.078	−0.415
Troy Tulowitzki	6,430.0	0.867	0.658	1.923	1.519

LEFT FIELD

Among the 30 players evaluated here, there are four players for whom the difference in z-scores is greater than one (in absolute value) for total NFW and three players when Component 6 is excluded. Looking only at Component 5, there are five players for whom the (absolute) difference in z-scores is greater than one. All of the players for whom z-scores differ by one or more in at least one of these comparisons are shown in the next table.

Fielding Z-Score

	Innings	UZR (Fangraphs)		NFW (Thress)	
		Total	Range+E	Total	(ex Comp. 6)	Comp. 5 only
A. Soriano	7,680.2	1.375	1.060	0.482	0.456	−0.050
Carlos Lee	10,568.1	−0.222	−0.134	−1.431	−1.333	−1.156
Cliff Floyd	3,757.0	−0.402	−0.690	0.607	0.832	0.603
Jay Payton	3,572.2	0.094	−0.026	1.108	0.872	0.959
Moises Alou	4,007.2	1.003	1.235	−1.225	−1.143	−0.859
Randy Winn	3,084.0	0.528	0.713	1.419	1.235	1.763

Two names that surprised me when I saw them on the above table were Carlos Lee and Moises Alou, not because my ratings surprised me, but because I thought it was a widely-accepted fact that Lee and Alou were below-average, and likely well below-average, defensive leftfielders.

The next table shows their year-by-year ratings in UZR and NFW, expressed as z-scores.

	Carlos Lee			Moises Alou		
Season	Innings	UZR	NFW	Innings	UZR	NFW
2003	1,328.2	0.86	−0.52	1,219.0	1.43	−0.61
2004	1,277.2	1.68	1.11	1,338.1	2.00	−0.99
2005	1,404.0	−0.25	−0.44	576.0	0.61	0.13
2006	1,259.1	−1.69	−2.33	79.0	−3.71	−0.01
2007	1,369.1	−0.32	−1.52	703.0	−0.65	−3.07
2008	915.1	0.02	−3.14	92.1	−0.48	−8.23
2009	1,272.1	−1.08	−2.63			
2010	1,096.1	−2.37	−4.47			
2011	645.1	1.95	1.40			

RIGHT FIELD

Among the 38 players evaluated here, there are a total of seven players for whom the difference in z-scores is greater than one (in absolute value) for total fielding, and eight players for whom the difference in z-scores is greater than one (in absolute value) in the other two comparisons (Component 5 and excluding Component 6). All of the players for whom z-scores differ by one or more in at least one of these comparisons are shown in the next table.

Fielding Z-Score

		UZR (Fangraphs)			NFW (Thress)	
	Innings	Total	Range+E	Total	(ex Comp. 6)	Comp. 5 only
Gary Sheffield	3,925	−1.478	−1.566	−0.226	−0.369	0.068
J.D. Drew	7,805.1	0.922	1.393	0.000	−0.082	0.324
Jason Heyward	3,524.1	1.708	2.166	0.185	0.111	0.850
Jeremy Hermida	3,745	−0.360	−0.180	0.950	0.509	0.466
Jose Bautista	3,450.2	−0.354	−1.280	1.041	1.169	−0.685
K. Fukudome	3,273.2	−0.043	−0.138	1.152	1.161	1.240
Mike Cuddyer	6,064	−0.724	−1.222	−1.144	−1.129	−2.458
Randy Winn	3,622.1	1.874	2.027	0.631	0.615	0.948
Trot Nixon	3,924	1.019	1.129	−0.694	−0.646	−0.633
Xavier Nady	3,579.1	−0.473	−0.145	−1.409	−1.476	−1.176

Randy Winn shows up on the lists for both corner outfield spots. Interestingly, UZR rates Winn as an above-average left fielder and an outstanding right fielder, while pW-L records rate Winn as an outstanding left fielder but merely an above-average right fielder.

Jose Bautista just misses showing up on two lists. He shows up here in right field; at third base, the difference in z-scores for UZR and NFW was 0.995. In both cases, Bautista scores slightly better in terms of converting balls-in-play to outs in net fielding wins, but with a difference in z-score of less than one. But in both cases, Bautista scores especially well in the extra components of fielding pW-L records.

Specifically, Jose Bautista scores extremely well at preventing baserunner advancement, Component 9, at all of the positions which he has played over the years. In fact, he's in the top 5 in career net Component 9 fielding wins among all players for whom I have calculated pW-L records. The next table shows Bautista's career record in Component 9 by position.

Position	eWins	eLoss	Win Pct	Net Wins
3B	1.9	1.3	0.592	0.6
LF	0.4	0.2	0.598	0.1
CF	1.0	0.8	0.549	0.2
RF	8.5	5.8	0.596	2.7
Total	**11.7**	**8.1**	**0.591**	**3.6**

Center Field

Among the 49 players evaluated here, there are a total of fifteen players for whom the difference in z-scores is greater than one (in absolute value) in at least one of the three comparisons made here. This is 30.6% of all of the centerfielders that I evaluated. All of the players for whom z-scores differ by one or more in at least one of these comparisons are shown in the next table.

Fielding Z-Score

		UZR (Fangraphs)			NFW (Thress)	
	Innings	Total	Range+E	Total	(excl Comp. 6)	Comp. 5 only
Adam Jones	6,371.1	−0.487	−1.030	1.110	1.086	−0.272
Andruw Jones	7,327.0	2.223	1.894	0.340	0.250	0.049
B.J. Upton	7,024.2	0.421	0.080	1.420	1.652	1.347
Denard Span	3,712.1	0.617	0.953	−1.638	−1.632	−1.607
Drew Stubbs	4,034.2	0.418	−0.147	0.976	0.754	1.038
Endy Chavez	3,200.0	0.731	0.040	2.167	2.024	1.141
Frank Gutierrez	3,875.1	1.995	1.925	2.344	2.213	3.078
Jacoby Ellsbury	4,030.2	0.746	1.207	−1.579	−1.683	−1.635
Johnny Damon	5,524.0	−1.287	−0.658	−2.027	−1.992	−1.939
Josh Hamilton	3,148.1	−1.132	−1.073	−0.010	0.068	0.173
Juan Pierre	7,316.1	0.387	1.079	−1.418	−1.494	−0.794
Ken Griffey, Jr.	3,198.0	−3.278	−3.269	−2.139	−1.990	−2.316
Mark Kotsay	5,805.1	−0.225	−0.433	0.733	0.787	0.332
Matt Kemp	6,025.0	−1.170	−1.371	0.176	0.320	−0.037
Michael Bourn	6,280.1	1.307	1.096	0.376	0.221	−0.147
Rick Ankiel	3,063.2	−0.306	−0.789	0.563	0.700	−0.003
Rocco Baldelli	3,332.0	0.086	−0.663	1.020	1.153	−0.350
Scott Podsednik	3,326.1	−0.765	−0.669	0.988	1.184	1.507

Of the players in the above table, the fewest z-score differences greater than one were actually found comparing total UZR to total NFW and, interestingly, the most z-score differences greater than one were found when I removed Component 6 decisions from fielding won-lost records. The correlation between the two measures is also strongest (0.558) comparing totals and actually slips just below 50% (0.494) when net Component 5 fielding wins are compared to (Range+Error) UZR.

In other words, fielding won-lost records correlate most strongly to centerfield UZR when Component 6 is included. It appears to me that Component 6—which measures whether a fielder gives up singles, doubles, or triples on hits-in-play—acts as something of a proxy for outfield location data.

Focusing on total UZR vs. total NFW, there are ten players (20.4%) with z-scores which differ by more than one: Adam Jones, Andruw Jones, Denard Span, Endy Chavez, Jacoby Ellsbury, Josh Hamilton, Juan Pierre, Ken Griffey, Jr., Matt Kemp, and Scott Podsednik.

In the case of Griffey, while his two z-scores differ by 1.14, they basically agree that he was an extremely bad defensive centerfielder over the time period in question here.

His UZR z-score is −3.3 versus an NFW z-score of −2.1. In fact, both of these z-scores are the lowest among the 49 centerfielders considered here. Really, UZR and fielding won-lost records agree more than they disagree about Griffey's late-career fielding.

Let me focus, though, on 10-time Gold Glove winner, Andruw Jones. Jones scores significantly better in UZR than in NFW over the sample period considered here. For his career, I actually agree that Andruw Jones was a brilliant defensive centerfielder, among the best of all-time. In fact, he ranks third all-time in career net fielding wins among all centerfielders for whom I have calculated pW-L records. He rates as the best defensive centerfielder in the National League for five consecutive seasons from 1998 through 2002, in most cases by a lot (for example, he led second-place Terry Jones in net wins 1.8–0.5 in 1998). I still think that (Andruw) Jones was pretty good from 2003 to 2006, although not the best in the league anymore, but had fallen to below-average by 2007.

In contrast, the UZR numbers at Fangraphs.com show Jones as remaining an excellent defensive centerfielder through 2007 (average UZR from 2003 to 2007 of 20.8 runs per season).

Except for one little twist. The UZR numbers on Fangraphs aren't the only UZR numbers for Andruw Jones that Mitchel Lichtman has calculated.

Sensitivity of UZR to Data Source

In Chapter 4, I explained how I use location data in calculating fielding won-lost records and defended my decision not to use these data directly even for those seasons where Retrosheet provides location data. There, I cited two studies that were reported on the Internet that looked at differences in UZR calculated using different source data.

In August 2007, Hardball Times published an article by Michael Humphrey (the author of *Wizardry*), titled "Ghosts in the Outfield." In this article, Humphreys reported a comparison of what he called "simplified UZR" ratings using two sets of location data: one from BIS (Baseball Information Systems) and one from STATS. For 2003–05, over a sample of 24 outfielders, the two systems—which should have been identical in all respects except for the firm/person recording the location and hit-type data—had a correlation of only 0.60.

Humphreys' sample included 9 centerfielders. The results for these nine players are shown below. Humphreys' numbers are for 2003–2005 and are presented as runs saved per 1,450 innings played (~162 games).

	Simplified UZR		
Player	*BIS*	*STATS*	*Difference*
Andruw Jones	+19	−2	21
Carlos Beltran	+9	+14	5
Jim Edmonds	+8	−2	10
Johnny Damon	−6	0	6
Juan Pierre	−1	−1	0
Mark Kotsay	+1	−19	20
Marquis Grissom	−18	−6	12
Mike Cameron	+28	+21	7
Vernon Wells	−6	+6	12
Correlation			0.522
Std. Deviation			6.87
Median			10

So, Humphreys is showing a correlation of UZR *with itself* of 0.60 for all outfielders and 0.52 for centerfielders. Suddenly, my correlations of net fielding wins to UZR of 0.66 for all outfielders and 0.56 for centerfielders look pretty good, don't they?

In a more detailed analysis along the same lines, Mitchel Lichtman, the creator of UZR, calculated UZR data for 2003–2008 using data from BIS (bUZR) and again, using the same UZR system, using data from STATS (sUZR) for 240 players. The results were discussed by Lichtman, Tom Tango, and others in an online forum (http://www.insidethe book.com/ee/index.php/site/comments/suzr_v_buzr/). That discussion did not include a correlation between the two, but it was noted that "5 of the top 9" differences in players were for centerfielders. The top two differences were Andruw Jones, +112 runs using BIS data vs. −5 using STATS data, and Carlos Beltran, +9 using BIS data vs. +86 using STATS.

Using the UZR standard deviation (per 1,000 innings) for centerfielders reported above (6.29) and Jones's and Beltran's innings played from 2003 through 2008, the two numbers quoted in the previous paragraph for Jones translate into z-scores of 2.45 (BIS) and −0.11 (STATS), a difference of 2.56. For Beltran, the two z-scores are 0.19 vs. 1.78, a difference of 1.59.

Of the 288 players that I looked at here, the difference in z-scores between UZR and NFW exceeded 1.60 in only eight cases (2.8%): five centerfielders, two corner outfielders, and one infielder (Brandon Phillips). The difference in z-scores between UZR and NFW exceeded 2.0 in only three cases: Moises Alou (LF), Jacoby Ellsbury (CF), and Denard Span (CF). And there were *zero* players for whom the difference in z-scores exceeded the difference in z-scores for Andruw Jones with BIS vs. STATS UZR.

Tom Tango reported that the standard deviation of the difference between bUZR and sUZR in Lichtman's study was 6.0 runs per 150 games with a median difference of 4.0 runs per 150 games and 10% of players having a difference of at least 10 runs per 150 games. I converted my net fielding wins into a UZR-level number (by multiplying my NFW z-scores times the UZR standard deviations by position) and calculated differences between UZR and this UZR-level fielding wins number per 150 games (actually, per 1,350 innings). These results, compared to the results reported by Tango are shown in the next table.

	UZR vs. Net Fielding Wins	*bUZR vs. sUZR*
Std. Deviation of Difference	5.5	6.0
Median Difference	3.5	4.0
Difference > 4	41%	50%
Difference > 10	6%	10%

Or, in words, my results are closer to UZR (using BIS data) than UZR results are to themselves.

Conclusions

Overall, I'm quite pleased with the results here. The total correlation across all seven positions (288 players) investigated here, between UZR and my fielding won-lost records—expressed in terms of z-scores—was 0.745. The z-scores associated with these two systems differed by more than 1.0 in 36 cases (12.5%).

For infielders, the results are even better. The correlation between total UZR and net fielding wins for infielders was 0.835 for the 171 infielders that I evaluated here. The z-scores associated with these two systems differed by more than 1.0 in 15 of 171 cases (8.8%).

As close as these two results are, some of the difference between the two systems is because fielding won-lost records incorporate factors which are not considered in measuring UZR, including fielders' abilities to limit extra-base hits and control baserunner advancement. When only the common factor of simply converting balls-in-play into outs (what I call Component 5) is compared in the two systems, the correlation across all infielders rises to 0.870 and the number of cases where the z-scores differ by more than 1.0 falls to eleven (6.4%).

For corner outfielders, the results are not quite as close as for infielders, but are still very similar. The correlation between total UZR and net fielding wins for corner outfielders was 0.728 and the z-scores differed by more than 1.0 in 11 of 68 cases (16.2%).

The results for centerfielders show the lowest correlation, 0.558, with z-score differences greater than one in 10 of 49 (20.4%) cases. My results for centerfielders are closer to UZR including Component 6–the extent to which hits-in-play are singles, doubles, or triples. This suggests to me that taking explicit account of hits-in-play serves as a useful proxy for more detailed location data.

The lack of correlation between net fielding wins and UZR for centerfielders is not necessarily an indication of a weakness in my fielding wins as a measure of fielding ability. In fact, my results vis-à-vis the UZR numbers presented by Fangraphs.com are comparable to comparisons of UZR calculated using different data sources.

Overall, I am quite pleased how well my fielding pW-L records stack up with UZR.

Fielding pW-L Records vs. DRA and DRS

To the best of my knowledge, there are two other fielding systems which rely on largely the same data source as I do (Retrosheet play-by-play data) and have publicly presented career fielding records. The first of these is Defensive Runs Saved (DRS), which were originally presented by Sean Smith in a Hardball Times article, "Measuring defense for players back to 1956," and are available now online at Baseball-Reference.com. The second system is Defensive Run Average (DRA), which was created by Michael Humphreys, who explained the system in his wonderful book, *Wizardry: Baseball's All-Time Greatest Fielders Revealed*.

In his book, Humphreys presented career fielding numbers (measured in net runs) for all players who played a significant time (typically, more than 3,000 innings) at six defensive positions: second base, third base, shortstop, and each of the three outfield positions. At the time of publication, Humphrey's book included statistics through 2009. Humphreys has subsequently provided his data to *The Baseball Gauge* at Seamheads.com (and apparently revised some of his data somewhat).

Baseball-Reference.com presents DRS values for players from 1953 to the present. To compare my results to Smith's and Humphrey's numbers, therefore, I compared results for the top 150 players in innings played from 1953 through 2009 at each of the six positions discussed by Humphrey.

Raw Results

The first table summarizes the results for DRA (Humphreys), DRS (Smith), and (context-neutral, teammate-adjusted) Net Fielding Wins (eWins minus eLosses).

	Net Fielding Runs (per 1000 innings)				Net Fielding eWins (per 1000 innings)	
	DRA		DRS			
Position	Mean	Std Dev	Mean	Std Dev	Mean	Std Dev
2B	0.63	6.21	0.64	4.82	0.0315	0.2280
3B	−0.39	5.55	−0.05	5.31	0.0107	0.2771
SS	0.46	5.25	0.57	5.29	0.0286	0.2611
LF	−0.30	6.80	−0.25	5.11	−0.0609	0.3706
CF	0.55	6.34	0.93	5.28	0.0473	0.2772
RF	−0.27	5.98	0.16	5.93	0.0285	0.3593

Putting Things on the Same Scale

In order to really compare DRA, DRS, and what I'll start calling NFW (net fielding wins), it is necessary to put them all on the same scale. To do this, I created "z-scores" associated with all three statistics. The basic formula for a z-score of variable x is (x−m) / s, where m is the mean of the statistic and s is the standard deviation. I calculated z-scores for each player for all three fielding stats using a value of m equal to zero (since all three of these statistics are constructed to be relative to league average by construction) and the standard deviations from the above table.

For example, Al Cowens scores at −2.16 DRA (per 1000 innings in RF), 1.22 DRS, and 0.303 NFW. From the previous table, the standard deviations associated with these three numbers are 5.98, 5.93, and 0.359, respectively. This translates, therefore, into z-scores for Al Cowens in right field of −0.36 for DRA, 0.21 for DRS, and 0.84 for NFW.

I did this for every player referenced in the earlier table. I then calculated simple correlations between DRA, DRS, and NFW by position.

Position	DRA v. DRS	DRA v. NFW	DRS v. NFW
2B	0.718	0.703	0.823
3B	0.756	0.596	0.803
SS	0.731	0.733	0.827
LF	0.705	0.595	0.765
CF	0.764	0.514	0.647
RF	0.769	0.624	0.763

I'm not always exactly sure how to interpret correlations. If we thought that one of the other two measures (DRA or DRS) was a very bad measure of fielding, for example, then we probably would prefer a fairly low correlation. On the other hand, if we thought that one of the other two measures was a perfect measure of fielding, then we could view NFW's correlation with it as a measure of how close to perfect pW-L records are at measuring fielding.

Of course, neither of these hypotheticals are true. DRA and DRS are both quite good, but nevertheless imperfect, measures of fielding.

Given that, the correlations here, which are all very high, strike me as very good. I am probably not doing something terribly wrong here and, perhaps, I am even doing something a little more right than some other people.

My pW-L records (NFW) correlate more strongly with DRS (Sean Smith's numbers, as found at Baseball-Reference.com) than with DRA (Michael Humphreys' numbers, as reported at Seamheads.com). This makes sense, since both DRS and NFW are constructed play by play, whereas DRA data are calculated (rather well) at a seasonal level.

Position-by-Position Analysis

Second Base

The next table summarizes differences in z-scores for DRA, DRS, and NFW for the top 150 second basemen in innings played from 1953 through 2009.

	DRA v. DRS	DRA v. NFW	DRS v. NFW
Avg. (abs) Difference	0.56	0.58	0.47
Difference > 1	26	24	13

The first row shows the average (absolute) difference in z-scores. The second row shows the number of players (out of 150) whose z-scores differ by 1.0 or more in the two measures.

There are a total of eight players for whom the difference in z-scores is greater than one (in absolute value) for both DRA vs. NFW and DRS vs. NFW. These players are shown in the next table.

Fielding Z-Score

	Innings	DRA (Humphreys)	DRS (Smith)	NFW (Thress)
Felix Millan	12,666.2	−0.86	−0.28	0.76
Tom Herr	11,890.0	−0.54	−0.24	0.86
Chase Utley	7,195.2	0.12	1.35	2.57
Tony Phillips	5,844.1	1.81	1.31	0.30
Charlie Neal	5,519.2	−0.17	−1.09	0.89
Ken Boswell	4,544.1	−0.62	−0.05	1.09
Aaron Hill	4,350.2	1.77	2.24	0.60
Chuck Schilling	4,286.1	0.86	1.21	−0.32

pW-L records think much more highly of Chase Utley than either DRA or DRS. From 2003 to 2009, Fangraphs reports Chase Utley's UZR at 69.2 runs. Based on the standard error reported earlier in this chapter, this works out to a z-score of 2.06.

On the other hand, DRA and DRS think much more highly of Aaron Hill. From 2005 to 2009, Fangraphs reports Aaron Hill's UZR at 16.9 runs, which works out to a z-score of 0.83.

Of the other players in the table, two of them won Gold Gloves—one apiece: Felix Millan and Charlie Neal. Both Millan and Neal score better in pW-L records than in either DRA or DRS.

Third Base

The next table summarizes differences in z-scores for DRA, DRS, and NFW for the top 150 third basemen in innings played from 1953 through 2009.

	DRA v. DRS	DRA v. NFW	DRS v. NFW
Avg. (abs) Difference	0.56	0.67	0.48
Difference > 1	22	30	19

There are a total of ten players for whom the difference in z-scores is greater than one (in absolute value) for both DRA vs. NFW and DRS vs. NFW. These players are shown in the next table.

Fielding Z-Score

	Innings	DRA (Humphreys)	DRS (Smith)	NFW (Thress)
Ken Reitz	11,216.1	−0.80	−0.30	1.20
Toby Harrah	9,210.1	−2.07	−1.12	−0.08
Don Wert	8,940.0	−0.61	0.36	1.56
Jim Davenport	8,304.1	0.13	0.23	1.53
Tom Brookens	7,925.0	1.79	1.09	0.08
Pete Rose	5,236.1	−1.86	−1.22	−0.03
Joe Torre	4,309.1	−2.81	−1.92	0.39
Hector Lopez	3,840.1	1.26	0.15	−0.99
Shea Hillenbrand	3,839.2	−0.78	−1.18	−2.49
Scott Cooper	3,812.0	0.77	1.33	−0.46

Shea Hillenbrand is the only player on this list who played recently enough to have UZR ratings at Fangraphs. From 2002 to 2007, Fangraphs reports Hillenbrand's UZR at third base at −21.4 in 3,839.2 innings, which works out to a z-score of −0.89. If we view UZR as the "ideal," it looks like DRA and DRS might have gotten this one right.

Two players in the table won Gold Gloves at third base, Ken Reitz and Jim Davenport, who won one apiece. As with second basemen, pW-L records seem to think more highly of the defense of the Gold Glove winners than either DRA or DRS. Actually, pW-L records think more highly of the defense of all four Gold Glove winners in the above table, although Joe Torre (C) and Pete Rose (OF) won their combined three Gold Gloves (1 by Torre, 2 by Rose) at positions other than third base.

Finally, Toby Harrah was among the top 150 players in innings played at two positions over the time period analyzed here. In addition to his 9,210.1 innings at third base, Harrah also played 6,690.1 innings at shortstop earlier in his career. As a shortstop, Harrah earned z-scores of 0.25 for DRA (vs. −2.07 at 3B), −0.76 at DRS (vs. −1.12 at 3B), and 0.16 in NFW (vs. −0.08 at 3B). The pW-L (NFW) numbers certainly seem to be the most consistent across the two positions.

Shortstop

The next table summarizes differences in z-scores for DRA, DRS, and NFW for the top 150 shortstops in innings played from 1953 through 2009.

	DRA v. DRS	DRA v. NFW	DRS v. NFW
Avg. (abs) Difference	0.59	0.59	0.47
Difference > 1	32	21	14

There are a total of 6 players for whom the difference in z-scores is greater than one (in absolute value) for both DRA vs. NFW and DRS vs. NFW. These players are shown in the next table.

Fielding Z-Score

	Innings	DRA (Humphreys)	DRS (Smith)	NFW (Thress)
Bud Harrelson	11,509.2	0.52	0.56	1.59
Ivan DeJesus	10,808.2	−0.39	−0.33	−1.49
Johnny Logan	10,571.2	1.04	1.02	−0.07
Tony Kubek	7,566.1	1.36	1.65	0.05
Pee Wee Reese	5,191.1	−0.54	0.80	2.27
Mario Guerrero	4,599.0	−0.87	−0.90	−2.65

The only Gold Glove winner in the above table was Bud Harrelson, who won one (in 1971).

Left Field

The next table summarizes differences in z-scores for DRA, DRS, and NFW for the top 150 left fielders in innings played from 1953 through 2009.

	DRA v. DRS	DRA v. NFW	DRS v. NFW
Avg. (abs) Difference	0.59	0.71	0.57
Difference > 1	31	43	27

There are a total of fifteen players for whom the difference in z-scores is greater than one (in absolute value) for both DRA vs. NFW and DRS vs. NFW. These players are shown in the next table.

Fielding Z-Score

	Innings	DRA (Humphreys)	DRS (Smith)	NFW (Thress)
Joe Rudi	9,691.2	−0.11	1.01	2.07
Kevin McReynolds	8,537.0	−0.51	−0.14	0.98
Cleon Jones	6,469.1	1.03	0.36	−0.80
Rondell White	6,066.0	0.72	0.68	−0.59
Ted Williams	5,858.0	−1.16	−1.10	−2.22
Pete Rose	5,841.0	1.39	1.74	0.07
Wes Covington	5,690.2	−2.30	−2.27	−1.26
Dave Collins	5,586.0	0.93	0.74	−0.78
Don Baylor	5,189.0	−0.38	−1.36	−2.66
Gene Richards	5,056.0	0.49	0.66	−0.61
John Lowenstein	4,503.0	−0.47	−0.78	−1.89
Tony Phillips	4,274.1	1.08	1.10	−0.26
Warren Cromartie	4,227.1	2.57	2.18	1.14
Jeff Burroughs	3,522.1	−1.42	−1.45	−2.62
Steve Braun	3,495.1	−0.77	0.11	1.44

Decomposition of Fielding Value

Most fielding measures focus primarily on what is almost certainly the most significant aspect of fielding: how well a fielder turns balls in play into outs. It is my understanding that this is the primary focus of both DRA and DRS. Both DRA and DRS do, however, attempt to incorporate infielders' ability to turn double plays and outfielders' ability to throw out runners and/or prevent baserunner advancement.

pW-L records assign fielding won-lost records within five components, which were discussed in detail in Chapter 4. Component 5 measures whether balls in play become hits or outs and is, therefore, perhaps most directly comparable to other fielding systems. Component 6 measures whether hits become singles, doubles, or triples. To the best of my knowledge, no other fielding system attempts to measure anything comparable to this. Component 7 measures whether ground balls are converted into double plays in double play situations (runner on first, less than two outs). I believe that both Humphreys (DRA) and Smith (DRS) make some attempt to incorporate similar information within their systems. Component 8 measures whether fielders are able to put baserunners out on the bases. Component 9 measures the extent to which baserunners are able to advance more or less than average on a particular play. Many fielding systems (including both DRA and DRS, I believe) make at least some effort to incorporate these latter two factors for outfielders. My system goes a step farther, however, and calculates Component 8 and 9 pW-L records for infielders as well.

Some of the differences, then, between how pW-L records view some players' fielding vis-à-vis DRA and DRS (and other systems) is that pW-L records are incorporating additional aspects of these players' fielding skills.

Of the fifteen players on the above list, only one—Pete Rose—would appear on a comparable list comparing net Component 5 fielding wins to DRA (excluding Arm ratings) and DRS, although he would be joined by one other player, Johnny Damon.

Right Field

The next table summarizes differences in z-scores for DRA, DRS, and NFW for the top 150 right fielders in innings played from 1953 through 2009.

	DRA v. DRS	DRA v. NFW	DRS v. NFW
Avg. (abs) Difference	0.52	0.68	0.54
Difference > 1	19	38	20

There are a total of fourteen players for whom the difference in z-scores is greater than one (in absolute value) for both DRA vs. NFW and DRS vs. NFW. These players are shown in the next table.

		Fielding Z-Score		
	Innings	DRA (Humphreys)	DRS (Smith)	NFW (Thress)
Tony Oliva	9,949.2	1.03	1.02	2.04
Dante Bichette	7,263.2	0.58	−0.46	−1.49
Bobby Murcer	7,105.2	−1.45	−1.54	0.02
Ellis Valentine	6,453.0	−0.32	1.18	2.67
Alex Rios	6,005.1	0.97	0.06	2.13
Michael Tucker	5,512.2	0.31	0.09	−1.32
Mike Marshall	5,412.2	−1.85	−1.06	0.00
Jim King	5,343.2	0.99	0.19	−0.82
Ron Fairly	5,094.1	−0.68	−0.46	0.57
Jim Rivera	4,240.1	−0.32	0.16	1.21
Jose Cruz, Sr.	4,075.2	1.01	0.74	−0.61
Jim Lemon	3,928.2	−1.15	−1.37	−2.71
Bobby Darwin	3,525.2	−1.40	−0.96	0.12
Larry Parrish	3,462.0	−3.00	−2.09	−0.28

Two players in the above table have played recently enough to have UZR calculated for them. Through 2009, Alex Rios had a calculated UZR value of 54.3 runs, which works out to a z-score of 1.42. Michael Tucker had a UZR value of −7.6 over his final 2,164.1 innings in RF, which produces a z-score of −0.55. Both of those ratings nicely split the difference between DRA and NFW.

Three players in the above table won a Gold Glove (exactly one apiece): Tony Oliva, Bobby Murcer (who played CF that season), and Ellis Valentine. All three players are better in pW-L records than in either DRA or DRS.

Bobby Murcer was among the top 150 players in innings played at two positions over the time period analyzed here, right field and center field. In 6,727.1 innings as a centerfielder, Murcer had z-scores of −1.14 in DRA (vs. −1.45 in RF), −0.76 in DRS (vs. −1.54 in RF), and −0.01 in NFW (vs. 0.02 in RF). pW-L records think more highly of Murcer's defense at both positions, although both DRA and DRS think that, contrary to what one would expect, Murcer was worse defensively in right field than in center field.

One other player in the above table was among the top 150 players in innings played at two positions, Larry Parrish, who played 8,768.2 innings at third base in addition to his 3,462 innings in right field. DRA, DRS, and NFW are in remarkable agreement about Larry Parrish's fielding at third base, with z-scores of –0.73, –0.77, and –0.79, respectively. That said, I don't know that one can draw too many conclusions about a player's likely fielding prowess in right field based on how well he played third base.

CENTER FIELD

The next table summarizes differences in z-scores for DRA, DRS, and NFW for the top 150 centerfielders in innings played from 1953 through 2009.

	DRA v. DRS	DRA v. NFW	DRS v. NFW
Avg. (abs) Difference	0.55	0.79	0.66
Difference > 1	18	50	30

There are a total of 21 players for whom the difference in z-scores is greater than one (in absolute value) for both DRA vs. NFW and DRS vs. NFW. This is the most players for any of the six positions compared here. These players are shown in the next table.

Fielding Z-Score

	Innings	DRA (Humphreys)	DRS (Smith)	NFW (Thress)
Willie Mays	22,927.2	1.12	1.45	0.05
Amos Otis	15,714.2	–0.95	–0.41	2.09
Garry Maddox	13,736.0	1.29	1.35	–0.54
Chet Lemon	12,425.1	1.38	1.46	–0.07
Richie Ashburn	11,011.1	1.36	0.67	–1.11
Willie Wilson	10,721.0	0.72	0.51	–0.54
Juan Pierre	10,176.1	–0.65	–0.50	–1.95
Jim Landis	9,310.1	1.37	0.85	–0.23
Del Unser	9,061.1	0.95	0.46	–0.66
Bill Tuttle	8,717.2	–0.83	–0.24	0.87
Al Oliver	7,246.1	–0.59	–0.73	–1.76
Matty Alou	7,123.1	–0.59	–1.30	0.52
Juan Beniquez	5,974.2	0.31	0.48	–1.18
John Shelby	5,823.0	–0.18	0.00	1.08
Vic Davalillo	5,797.1	1.04	0.69	2.34
Brian Hunter	5,548.0	0.85	0.68	2.43
Adolfo Phillips	4,613.1	1.18	0.57	–0.59
Don Demeter	4,355.0	–0.83	–0.22	0.91
Gary Geiger	4,324.2	–0.29	0.13	1.74
Ken Henderson	4,220.1	–0.71	0.09	–2.47
Jay Johnstone	3,961.1	0.07	0.81	–1.15

As with UZR, the numbers for centerfielders are the most idiosyncratic numbers for pW-L records. They are also harder to defend than most other positions.

I discussed the first name on the list earlier in this chapter. Let me discuss briefly, then, the next two names on the list: Amos Otis and Garry Maddox.

Amos Otis

I rate Amos Otis quite a bit more highly than either Humphreys or Smith. pW-L records view Amos Otis as an elite defensive center fielder, while Humphreys' and Smith's systems consider Amos Otis to have been a below-average defensive centerfielder over the course of his career.

Humphreys quotes Bill James calling Otis "a 'magnificent' fielding center fielder," and he did win 3 Gold Gloves in his career (in 1971, 1973, and 1974). But everybody can surely think of at least one fielder who won a Gold Glove award or two that he didn't deserve.

I think that one reason why my system loves Amos Otis's defense so much has to do with his home ballpark in Kansas City. The next table shows team ballpark factors for the Kansas City Royals in the 1970s (the seasons when Amos Otis was their everyday centerfielder). Numbers here are expressed in relation to the batting team with 100 being average, so, for example, a Doubles factor of 102 would mean that doubles are 2% more common in Royals games than in the AL in general (because of the ballparks, not the players). Ballpark factors are discussed in more detail in Chapter 10.

Season	Runs	Doubles	Triples	Home Runs
1970	98.6	102.1	104.4	93.6
1971	100.0	104.9	106.1	93.8
1972	99.7	98.4	103.6	92.8
1973	101.3	105.6	103.7	99.9
1974	101.0	106.2	106.7	96.2
1975	100.7	105.4	105.7	95.9
1976	98.7	103.4	99.0	97.4
1977	101.7	106.2	106.8	93.8
1978	101.5	105.4	107.4	95.4
1979	101.5	103.3	107.0	100.7

The numbers bounce around a bit from year to year but, in general, Kansas City's ballpark boosted run-scoring a little bit by boosting doubles and triples while suppressing home runs. The result is a higher-than-average number of balls in play in Kansas City with a higher-than-average number of these balls falling in for hits in general, and for extra-base hits in particular.

Because hits-in-play were more plentiful in Kansas City, the value of outs on balls-in-play there was greater than average. By measuring value using ballpark-specific win probabilities, my pW-L records (fielding, batting, baserunning, and pitching) implicitly adjust for ballpark context. So, my pW-L records like Amos Otis's defense better because he played in a ballpark where outfield hits were more common, making it a more difficult ballpark to play centerfield.

I think that this is a real advantage of my fielding (and batting, baserunning, and pitching) won-lost records.

Garry Maddox

One of the more troubling results I encountered when I was first evaluating my pW-L records was the fielding record of Garry Maddox. Garry Maddox won 8 consecutive Gold Gloves from 1975 through 1982 and was considered the gold standard of centerfield defense.

My pW-L records, on the other hand, show Garry Maddox to have been an average defensive centerfielder over the course of his career.

Now, as anyone familiar with Gold Gloves knows, they are not necessarily the best measure of fielding prowess—far from it in many cases. And similarly, one of the lessons of modern fielding metrics is that looks can frequently be deceiving when it comes to judging major-league fielding ability.

But DRA and DRS both agree with the consensus of the time: Garry Maddox was a great centerfielder. He led his league in DRS among centerfielders 4 times (1976, 1978–80) and finished second 3 other times (1975, 1977, and 1981). For his career, his z-score in DRA is 1.29 and for DRS it's 1.35. But for fielding pW-L records, his net fielding wins earn a z-score of –0.54.

This concerned me: it seemed like an obvious mistake on the part of my pW-L records. But then I read Michael Humphreys' entry on Garry Maddox in his book:

> [Maddox] was at best an average fielder when he came up with the Giants. Traded to the Phillies, he played next to possibly the worst outfielder of all time: Greg "The Bull" Luzinski. On almost all teams, the centerfielder takes all chances in the outfield that he can, including soft flies that could be handled in the gaps by the corner outfielders. But with The Bull, Maddox may have taken what would normally be fly ball chances of the left fielder. Maddux had only one good season when he wasn't playing next to Luzinski, the strike-shortened 1981 [*Wizardry*, p. 302].

The next table shows how Garry Maddox's career record looks in the "Range" component of DRA, DRS, and pW-L records (Component 5), all measured in z-scores. The seasons where Maddox was not teamed with Luzinski are bolded.

Fielding Z-Score

Season (Team)	Innings	DRA (Humphreys)	DRS (Smith)	NFW (Thress)
1972	810.1	–1.199	–0.467	0.027
1973	1,236	–1.146	0.766	–0.287
1974	1,124.1	0.337	0.000	–0.289
1975 (SFN)	122.2	0.671	4.630	1.094
1975 (PHI)	840.1	4.037	2.028	0.908
1976	1,240	2.537	2.901	–0.091
1977	1,204.2	2.748	1.729	–0.240
1978	1,324.1	2.462	2.287	–0.999
1979	1,194.1	2.923	2.853	0.109
1980	1,246.2	1.599	1.519	–0.399
1981	750	2.657	1.514	1.182
1982	903	–0.255	0.000	1.153
1983	736.1	0.403	–0.514	–1.225
1984	496.2	1.293	0.762	0.590
1985	492.1	–0.268	–0.385	–0.417
1986	14	–17.65	–27.04	–14.80
Total (w/ Luzinski)	7,050.1	2.637	2.229	–0.189
Total (w/o Luzinski)	**6,685.2**	**0.059**	**0.255**	**0.057**

My Component 5 numbers for Maddox are much more stable with and without Greg Luzinski as a teammate than either DRA or DRS. This stability of Maddox's Component 5 numbers suggests to me that my system does well in dealing with "ball hogs." Maddox is not being over-valued in my system, as compared to DRA and DRS, because he caught an inordinate number of fly balls to left-center field.

My numbers are more stable than DRA and DRS, but does that mean that my numbers are correct?

Let me pick out one season. I don't claim this season is representative, it's just the first one that I looked at. According to pW-L records, the 1979 Phillies accumulated a total of approximately 0.7 net fielding wins overall and the Phillies outfield accumulated approximately –0.8 net fielding wins. This ranked them 7th in the National League that year in net fielding wins. According to Baseball-Reference.com, on the other hand, the Phillies led the National League in Defensive Runs Saved with +54, with their starting outfield scoring a combined +24 (+26 by Maddox, +18 by Bake McBride, and –20 by Luzinski).

At the team level, we should be able to get a strong sense of how good a team's defense is by looking at the team's Defensive Efficiency Rating (DER, the percentage of balls-in-play turned into outs) (especially with regard to Component 5). According to Baseball-Reference, the Phillies ranked 6th in the NL in DER in 1979 at 0.703 vs. a league-wide value of 0.700. Those numbers are right in line with my assessment of the Phillies' team fielding—very slightly better than average. On the other hand, it seems somewhat unlikely to me that the best defensive team in the National League—as suggested by DRS—would be merely average at converting balls in play into outs.

Component 6

The above analysis, while entirely true, is, perhaps, somewhat misleading. The analysis above focused only on what I call Component 5—the ability to convert balls in play into outs. Another component of my fielding is Component 6—whether hits-in-play end up as singles, doubles, or triples. The next table shows Garry Maddox's Component 6 fielding record (as a CF only) divided into three segments: as a San Francisco Giant (at ages 22–25), as a teammate of Greg Luzinski (at ages 25–30), and as a Philadelphia Phillie without Luzinski as a teammate (at ages 31–36). The data here are all context-neutral and teammate-adjusted (although "teammate-adjusted" in my system means controlling for the team's pitchers, not for the other outfielders).

	eWins	eLosses	eWin Pct	Net eWins
San Francisco Giants	1.6	1.4	0.532	0.2
Philadelphia Phillies (w/ Luzinski)	3.5	4.9	0.414	–1.4
Philadelphia Phillies (w/o Luzinski)	1.9	2.3	0.460	–0.3

While Maddox's Component 5 records are very stable with and without Luzinski, the same does not seem to be the case with respect to Component 6–the extent to which hits on balls in play become doubles or triples. Although, while Maddox was better in Component 6 fielding without Luzinski as a teammate, this was mostly because he was good at preventing extra-base hits as a very young man playing with the San Francisco Giants. Even after Luzinski left the Phillies, Maddox remained below average in Component 6 fielding (outside of the 1982 season).

Hits Allowed by the 1979 Philadelphia Phillies

Returning to the 1979 Phillies, the Phillies led the National League in 1979 in both doubles (274, 2nd place was the Pirates with 260) and triples (59, next highest was the Cubs with 55) allowed. In contrast, the Phillies were one of only two National League teams in 1979 to allow fewer than 1,000 singles (987; the Houston Astros led the NL with 963 singles allowed).

If Garry Maddox was routinely running down doubles and triples that were Luzinski's fault, I may be under-rating Maddox and over-rating Luzinski. To try to assess this and dig a bit deeper into the Component 6 results, I took a closer look at all of the triples allowed in the National League in 1979. Leaguewide, I am able to identify a specific outfielder as the first fielder to handle 473 of the 518 triples hit in the National League in 1979 (91.3%). Of those triples for whom I can identify a specific outfielder, they broke down LF-CF-RF as follows 19.5%–33.2%–47.4%. This is what I would expect. Triples are most common to right field because the rightfielder has a longer throw to third base. The deepest part of most ballparks is center field, leading to the reasonably high number of triples to center. But triples to left field are relatively rare (92 of 473 identified triples in the 1979 NL) because the throw from left field to third base is relatively short.

I am able to identify a specific outfielder as the first fielder to handle 58 of the 59 triples allowed by the 1979 Phillies. The percentage breakdown by field, from LF to RF, was 15.5%–46.6%–37.9%. In other words, the vast majority of the "extra" triples allowed by the 1979 Phillies were hit to center field—or, more accurately, were eventually fielded by Garry Maddox (although 2 of the 27 triples hit to CF against the Phillies in 1979 were hit while Greg Gross was playing CF).

But were all of those triples Garry Maddox's "fault"?

One possible problem that my system might be having with the Luzinski/Maddox outfields could be if Maddox ended up tracking down a fair number of hits that were Luzinski's fault. Under my system, one key (perhaps "the key") defining characteristic of balls-in-play is the first fielder to touch the ball. Specifically, certain assumptions about the probability that a play could have been turned into an out and by whom are calculated based on who the first fielder was to touch the ball. So, for example, if a triple is fielded by the center fielder, the system assigns more "blame" for that triple to the center fielder than to the adjoining fielders.

Location data for balls in play in 1979 are extremely sparse. Of the 518 triples hit in the National League in 1979, 14 of them (2.7%) were identified as having been hit to left-center field and 22 (4.2%) were identified as having been hit to right-center field. For the Phillies, only 1 of the 59 triples they allowed was identified as having been hit to left-center field (1.7%) with 4 identified as having been hit to right-center field (6.8%). The evidence does not support the theory that Maddox is being charged with a lot of triples that should have been played by Luzinski, but, really, the data are simply too sparse to tell us anything.

Another possibility could be that Maddox had to shade more heavily to left field to cover for Luzinski (his right fielder most of this time was Bake McBride, who was a very good defensive outfielder—he even played over 3,000 innings in centerfield in his career), which helped convert some fly balls to outs but which resulted in more extra base hits on some balls that could, perhaps, have been cut off (or even caught) by somebody playing a more conventional centerfield. In other words, Maddox's Component 6 numbers may be "legitimate" in the sense that he did allow more extra-base hits than a conventional centerfielder but this may have still been because of Luzinski's presence.

While the data here suggest there may be some issues in who pW-L records "blames" for the extra-base hits allowed by the Phillies of this era, it is important to keep in mind that Component 5 is by far the more important factor than Component 6.

While I find the results here very interesting, I am somewhat reluctant to claim that I have established definitively that Garry Maddox was wildly overrated as a defensive centerfielder. But he might have been.

Conclusions

Overall, I am quite pleased with the results here. The overall correlation, across all six positions (900 players) investigated here, between Humphreys' DRA and my Fielding won-lost records—expressed in terms of z-scores—was 0.627 with disagreements of 1 or more in 206 cases (22.9%). The correlation between Smith's DRS and Fielding won-lost records was 0.772 with disagreements of 1 or more in 123 cases (13.7%). For a little context, the correlation between DRA and DRS was 0.742 and the two systems disagreed by more than 1 z-score in 148 cases (16.4%).

As discussed above, my results disagree with DRA and DRS more often for outfielders than for infielders. Even here, however, my overall correlations with DRA and DRS are 0.660 and 0.759, respectively. Moreover, as I discuss above, much of the lower correlation in this case is because I incorporate outfielders' (and infielders') individual ability to prevent extra-base hits. In this case, therefore, I believe this modestly lower correlation is an indication of the extent to which I am doing a somewhat better job of fully measuring the overall fielding value of these players.

8. Baseball Player Won-Lost Records vs. WAR

Having explained how pW-L records are calculated and what they show us, this chapter shows why Baseball pW-L records are the best measure of player value available—in essence, why Baseball pW-L records are the ultimate baseball statistic. This is done by comparing my results to what is currently the most popular all-inclusive baseball statistic: Wins above Replacement (WAR), as measured by Baseball-Reference.com and Fangraphs.com.

As I have explained in detail, I calculate Player wins and losses two ways. I begin by calculating pWins, which are tied directly to team wins, by construction. Having constructed these, I then also construct eWins, which are neutralized for context. Statistics derived from eWins—such as eWins over Positional Average (eWOPA) and eWins over Replacement Level (eWORL)—are conceptually comparable to other sabermetric "uber-statistics," including the various constructions of WAR (Wins above Replacement).

The relationship between team wins and pWins is perfect:

[Actual Wins minus Actual Losses] equals [pWins minus pLosses]

for any given team by construction. As such, there's not much "analysis" to be done there. But what about context-neutral wins (eWins)?

The object of analysis throughout most of this chapter will be net wins—Wins minus Losses—and/or wins above average (WOPA, in my vernacular; WAA, in the vernacular of WAR). I focus on wins relative to average for three reasons.

- First, wins above or below average are a real thing that can be empirically measured, whereas replacement level is more of a theoretical concept (although, once replacement level is set—at, say, .294 as is the case for Baseball-Reference and Fangraphs—it essentially becomes as empirically valid a measuring stick as .500).
- Second, for both pW-L records as well as for WAR, values are built up initially relative to average; comparisons to replacement level simply derive from a final step that shifts the comparison point from .500 to something else.
- Third, net wins, WOPA, and WAA are all centered on zero by construction. This simplifies the mathematics of the statistical analyses that I undertake here by eliminating the need for constant terms in any of my equations.

pW-L Records: eWins versus Team Wins

Having laid that out, we begin, then, with a basic equation that looks at the relationship between net team wins (actual team wins minus actual team losses) and net eWins (total eWins for the players on a team minus total eLosses for the players on a team):

$$\text{Net Team Wins} = a^*(\text{Net eWins})$$

This equation was fit using Ordinary Least Squares (OLS) with the following results.

Seasons	a	Standard Error	R^2
2003–2015	2.294	0.054	0.821

I chose the time period investigated here, 2003–2015, because Retrosheet data are generally consistent since that time at identifying the hit type (e.g., ground ball, fly ball, line drive) for all balls in play. I also investigated some longer time periods to see how consistent the results were over the longer time period. Generally speaking, the results presented here were fairly stable across earlier seasons as well.

The estimated coefficient, a, has a value of approximately two. This is, perhaps, twice what one might expect—that the coefficient in the above equation should be approximately equal to one. I discussed this relationship somewhat in earlier chapters, where I noted that the difference in player winning percentage between the winning and losing team within a game tends to be fairly narrow. Specifically the pWin winning percentage of players on a winning team will be .667 by construction (2 pWins vs. 1 pLoss). But the eWin winning percentage of players on a winning team has tended to be closer to .576 (1.9 wins vs. 1.4 losses per game before normalization). In other words, 0.076 net eWins (0.576–0.500) translate into 0.167 net pWins (0.667–0.500), a ratio of about 2.2, which is very similar to the number in the above table.

The standard error of the coefficient, a, measures the uncertainty of the coefficient estimate. Given certain assumptions, we would expect the true coefficient to fall within one standard error of the point estimate approximately two-thirds of the time and we would expect the true coefficient to fall within two standard errors of the point estimate approximately 95% of the time.

The value, R^2 measures the percentage of total variation in the *dependent* variable (net team wins) that is explained by the equation—i.e., that is explained by the *explanatory* variable(s) in the equation—net eWins, in this case. Overall, somewhat more than 80% of the variation in team wins can be explained by differences in eWins. The remaining differences can presumably be attributed to differences in the context in which player performance took place.

Teammate Interaction

For several components of pW-L records, responsibility is shared between players—either between batters and baserunners or between pitchers and fielders. The values of eWins are calculated controlling for the ability of one's teammates. For shared components, however, the team-level winning percentage is affected not only by the context-neutral winning percentages for the two sets of players sharing the components (e.g., pitchers and fielders), but also by the interaction of these two variables. This latter term is referred to by me as a "Teammate Adjustment." If both pitchers and fielders on a team are above average at something, the team, as a whole, will be better than either its pitchers or its fielders.

To account for this interaction, then, the next equation which I investigated added teammate adjustments to the previous equation as follows.

$$\text{Net Team Wins} = a_0 * (\text{Net eWins}) + a_1 * (\text{Teammate Adj.})$$

This equation was fit using OLS with the following results.

Seasons	a_0	Std Error	a_1	Std Error	R^2
2003–2015	2.239	0.054	3.899	0.854	0.830

The coefficient on Teammate Adjustments is approximately twice as large as the coefficient on net eWins. This is because of a difference in the nature of the two variables. Net eWins are equal to wins minus losses. So, for a record of, say, 90–72, net wins would be +18. Teammate adjustments are reported relative to .500, where 90 wins (out of 162) is only 9 games over .500 (81 out of 162 games). If the coefficient on Teammate Adjustments was constrained to be exactly equal to twice the coefficient on net eWins in the equation above, the coefficient on net eWins would be 2.227 (standard error of 0.051) and the R^2 of the equation would be 0.830.

Impact of Batting v. Baserunning v. Pitching v. Fielding on Team Wins

Having set up a basic equation to relate eWins to team wins, this equation can be extended to evaluate whether the four basic factors are weighted appropriately within pW-L records. That is, the basic equation laid out above:

$$\text{Net Team Wins} = a_0 * (\text{Net eWins}) + a_1 * (\text{Teammate Adj.})$$

can be replaced with the following equation:

$$\text{Net Team Wins} = a_b * (\text{Net Batting eWins}) + a_r * (\text{Net Baserunning eWins}) + a_p * (\text{Net Pitching eWins}) + a_f * (\text{Net Fielding eWins}) + a_1 * (\text{Teammate Adj.})$$

One might think, then, that if batting, baserunning, pitching, and fielding are weighted correctly, then the coefficients on these factors (a_b, a_r, a_p, and a_f) should be equal to each other (and should all be equal to the coefficient on net eWins from the earlier equation(s), a_0).

I re-arranged some terms in the basic equation outlined above to make the interpretation and analysis of the results somewhat more intuitive. Specifically, I fit the following equation (using OLS):

$$\text{Net Wins} = a_0 * [(\text{Net Batting eWins}) + (1 + a_{r0}) * (\text{Net Baserunning eWins}) + (1 + a_{f0}) * (\text{Net Fielding eWins}) + a_2 * (\text{Teammate Adj.})] + a_0 * (1 + a_{p0}) * (\text{Net Pitching eWins})$$

This equation is mathematically identical to the previous equation, but some terms have been re-arranged and coefficients have been re-presented to facilitate analysis.

- In this equation, a_0 is the same as in the equation relating net team wins to net eWins and we would expect this coefficient to be similar in magnitude across both equations.
- The coefficient on teammate adjustments in the earlier equation, a_1, is equal to $a_0 * a_2$ in this equation. As explained earlier, the coefficient here, a_2, has an expected value of two.

- The coefficients, a_{ro} and a_{fo}, measure the difference in the weight on these two factors (a_r and a_f) relative to the weight on the factor, batting (a_b). The expected coefficients on a_{ro} and a_{fo} are both zero.
- I have separated pitching from the other three factors for reasons that will become more obvious later in this chapter.

The final results of this equation are presented in the next table.

	2003–2015	
	Coefficient	Std Error
a_0	2.059	0.078
a_2	1.881	0.546
a_{ro}	−0.278	0.272
a_{fo}	0.042	0.164
a_{po}	0.216	0.063
R^2	0.838	

A few comments.

1. The general coefficient, a_0, is similar to earlier estimates, around 2.0.
2. Batting, baserunning, and fielding seem to generally be weighted correctly. The one possible exception is baserunning, with the coefficient on a_{ro} being about one standard error below zero (which implies that baserunning is, perhaps, somewhat over-weighted in pW-L records), although a difference of one standard error is generally not viewed as statistically significant.
3. The coefficient on teammate adjustments, a_2, is not significantly different from two.
4. Including the four factors separately improved the R^2 value of the equation somewhat, from 83.0% to 83.8%.
5. The coefficient on pitching, a_{po}, is significantly (3.5 standard errors) greater than zero. Over the most recent sample period, the coefficient on pitching here, 0.22, suggests that pitching is under-weighted in pW-L records by approximately 22%.

Obviously, comment 5) warrants some further discussion and analysis.

One of the key findings of my work is that player wins are not additive. In fact, they are something closer to multiplicative. This is mostly because of the result noted above that the players on a winning baseball team have an average context-neutral (eWin) winning percentage of .576, which translates into a pWin winning percentage of .667. As mentioned above, this is the reason why a_0 has a value of two in the equations presented so far. This multiplicative effect affects the expected impact of players who are somewhat above (or below) average. The impact of a player being slightly above average will translate into a greater impact on team wins. This effect is not taken account of in the net factor wins analyzed above. And it is this effect that explains the significant positive coefficient on a_{po}.

The multiplicative effect of player performance on team wins is incorporated into my calculation of eWins through an expected team win adjustment. This increases the expected player winning percentage based on the expected impact of the player's performance on the team's winning percentage. Expected team win adjustments are stronger for pitchers than for non-pitchers, because pitchers concentrate their performance into fewer games, so that the per-game impact of pitchers tends to be greater than the per-game impact of individual non-pitchers. The calculation of expected team win adjustments was discussed in more detail in Chapter 2.

From 2003 to 2015, pitching (including pitcher fielding) accounted for 33.2% of unadjusted player decisions. But pitchers accounted for 43.7% of pWins over replacement level (excluding pitcher offense). In other words, the impact of pitchers on team wins is 31.6% greater than the impact implied by simple, unadjusted pitching decisions (43.7% / 33.2%–1). Hence, the expected coefficient on a_{p0} is not zero, but is, instead, 0.316, which is not significantly different from the value of a_{p0} shown above.

In other words, my analysis here strongly suggests (to me) that the relative value of batting, baserunning, fielding, and pitching implied by pW-L records accurately reflect the relative value of these four factors on actual team wins.

Summary of Results

To summarize, then, I fit the following equation to relate actual team wins to (context-neutral, teammate-adjusted) eWins:

$$\text{Net Wins} = a_0 * [(\text{Net Batting eWins}) + (1 + a_{r0}) * (\text{Net Baserunning eWins}) + (1 + a_{f0}) * (\text{Net Fielding eWins}) + a_2 * (\text{Teammate Adj.})] + a_0 * (1 + a_{p0}) * (\text{Net Pitching eWins})$$

The next table repeats the results above for my final equation and contrasts the estimated coefficients with the expected coefficients, as they were derived above (except for a_0, for which the "expected" value is really an empirical question—i.e., the "right" coefficient is whatever comes out of the equation). That is, the second equation takes everything except a_0 as given and only estimates a coefficient for a_0.

	Statistical Estimates	*Expected Values*
a_0	2.059	1.963
(Std. Error)	0.078	0.044
a_2	1.882	2.000
(Std. Error)	0.546	–
a_{r0}	–0.278	0.000
(Std. Error)	0.272	–
a_{f0}	0.042	0.000
(Std. Error)	0.164	–
a_{p0}	0.216	0.316
(Std. Error)	0.063	–
R^2	0.838	0.837

None of the results in the first column are significantly different from the expected results in the right-hand column.

Taking all of this a step further, then, team wins over .500 can be related to eWins over positional average by the following equation:

$$\text{Team Wins over .500} = a_0 * (\text{eWOPA} + (\text{Teammate Adjustments}))$$

If eWOPA (and, by extension, eWORL) is calculated correctly, we would expect the coefficient in this equation, a_0, to match the coefficient of the same name in the previous equation, and we would expect the R^2 here to match the R^2 from that equation as well. The results are as follows.

Seasons	a_0	*Std Error*	R^2
2003–2015	1.837	0.045	0.814

The value of a_0 perhaps changed a bit more than expected and the value of R^2 is a bit lower, but, overall, the results are reasonably similar.

Wins Above Replacement (WAR) vs. Actual Team Wins

Having looked at how the factors underlying pW-L records—batting, baserunning, pitching, and fielding—related to team wins and whether, based on this analysis, these factors were correctly weighted in the calculation of pW-L records—specifically, wins over positional average (eWOPA, pWOPA) and replacement level (eWORL, pWORL), I will perform similar analysis for WAR (Wins above Replacement) as calculated and presented by Baseball-Reference (bWAR) as well as by Fangraphs (fWAR).

For both bWAR and fWAR, the basic calculation framework is the same. For non-pitchers (as well for the offensive contributions of pitchers), a player's contributions are expressed in terms of runs above average (runs below average being expressed as negative numbers) for the three non-pitching factors: batting, baserunning, and fielding. A fourth factor is then added into the mix, a positional adjustment, also expressed in runs above average (RAA). The positional adjustments are positive for "defense-first" positions (C, SS, 2B) and negative for "offense-first" positions (1B, LF, RF) (CF and 3B tend to have positional adjustments near zero). These four factors are added up to produce an aggregate RAA for the player. A final value, called Rrep by Baseball-Reference, based on playing time, is added to convert from runs above average (RAA) to runs above replacement level (RAR). RAA and RAR are then converted from runs to wins, based on the run-scoring environment in which the player played. In theory, one could apply the run-to-win converter to the individual components to create, in effect, separate values of WAA for batting, baserunning, and fielding (WAA_b, WAA_r, WAA_f).

Pitcher WAR is somewhat more complicated but is similar in concept: a pitcher's runs allowed are compared against average and converted into wins above average (WAA_p) and replacement (WAR_p). Baseball-Reference begins with RA9–runs allowed per nine innings—and adjusts for the team's fielding RAA; Fangraphs uses FIP—expected runs allowed per nine innings, based on strikeouts, walks, and home runs allowed. Both Baseball-Reference and Fangraphs adjust relief pitcher WAR to account for leverage. Baseball-Reference also calculates a unique run-to-win converter for each pitcher to reflect the impact of the pitcher on the run-scoring environment (I am not entirely sure what Fangraphs does in this regard).

Team WAR (or WAA) is then simply equal to the sum of the WAR (WAA) of the individual players on the team. In theory, I would expect the positional adjustments to balance out—every team has exactly one of every position in every inning of every game—so that, at the team level, I would expect a team's total WAA to equal the sum of WAA_b, WAA_r, WAA_f, and WAA_p.

To test, then, whether batting, baserunning, fielding, and pitching are weighted appropriately within WAR, I fit the following equation:

$$\text{Team Wins over .500} = a_b * WAA_b + a_r * WAA_r + a_f * WAA_f + a_p * WAA_p$$

For analysis purposes, I re-arranged the terms in the above equation, as I did in my analysis of pW-L records earlier in this article.

$$\text{Team Wins over .500} = (1 + a_0)*[WAA_b + (1 + a_{r0})*WAA_r + (1 + a_{f0})*WAA_f]$$
$$+ (1 + a_0)*(1 + a_{p0})*WAA_p$$

The next two sections present and discuss my results for both bWAR and fWAR.

Baseball-Reference: bWAR

Baseball-Reference has two pages on its website for every season which summarize position player and pitcher WAR for every team within the season.

For position players, Baseball-Reference provides data on Rbat (RAA for batting), Rbaser, Rdp (runs above average for batters at avoiding grounding into double plays—for this analysis, I combined Rdp and Rbat), Rfield, and Rpos (positional adjustments), along with total RAA (the sum of all of the aforementioned columns) and WAA, Rrep (replacement runs), RAR (RAA + Rrep), and WAR.

As I said above, in theory, I would have expected Rpos to be approximately zero at the team level. In fact, however, for the 2015 season, total Rpos across all 30 teams summed to +742 runs (+25 runs per team on average). Offsetting this, the combined total for Rbat was −700 runs. This is typical of the seasons which I examined (back to 1969). I am reasonably certain that the reason for this is that the average number of runs against which Rbat is measured excludes pitcher batting. But the sum of Rbat (and Rpos) for teams includes pitcher batting. For the 2015 NL, total Rpos was +847 vs. Rbat of −630; for the AL, total Rpos was −105 vs. Rbat of −70.

My intended analysis required that total WAA be limited to batting, baserunning, pitching and fielding, and that total WAA be equal to zero at the seasonal level, by construction. To do this, I distributed Rpos to Rbat such that the sum of Rbat across the league was exactly equal to zero—i.e., in 2015, since Rbat summed to −700, I adjusted that number up by +700; I did so proportional to the +742 Rpos—i.e., I added 94.3% (700/742) of Rpos to Rbat for every team. For Rrun, Rdp, and Rfield, I adjusted the numbers proportionally across all teams such that the sum for the season was equal to zero—e.g., in 2015, Rfield totaled +37; I therefore subtracted 1.2 runs (37/30) from each team's Rfield value; in 2015, Rrun and Rdp both summed to zero across the league, so that no adjustments were necessary to these numbers.

On Baseball-Reference's pitcher WAR page, they provided data for WAA, WAAadj, and WAR. The last of these was, of course, total pitcher WAR. The first two of these summed to zero at the league level in every season. I, therefore, set pitcher WAA equal to the sum of WAA and WAAadj. Based on Baseball-Reference's explanation of its WAR for pitchers, WAAadj is an adjustment made to account for reliever leverage. As I understand it, then, at the league/team level, WAAadj ends up essentially being rounding error to re-center WAA to zero.

Having set all of that up, I fit the above equation using Baseball-Reference data from 2003 to 2015. The equation being solved is repeated here for reference.

$$\text{Team Wins over .500} = (1 + a_0)*[WAA_b + (1 + a_{r0})*WAA_r + (1 + a_{f0})*WAA_f]$$
$$+ (1 + a_0)*(1 + a_{p0})*WAA_p$$

The results in the first column of the table were estimated using OLS. The results in the last column are what we would expect if the four factors—batting, baserunning, fielding, and pitching—were appropriately weighted in the calculation of bWAR.

	2003–2015	
	Statistical Estimates	Expected Values
a_0	0.080	0
(Std. Error)	0.043	–
a_{r0}	0.085	0
(Std. Error)	0.328	–
a_{f0}	–0.118	0
(Std. Error)	0.074	–
a_{p0}	0.013	0
(Std. Error)	0.035	–
R^2	0.817	0.815

None of the coefficients are significantly different from their expected value (zero) at a 95% significance level. The value for a_0 is nearly so, however (p=.064, meaning a_0 differs from zero at about a 93.6% significance level (1–p)). The value for a_{f0} (p=.114) is also at least suggestive if, perhaps not quite "significant."

A positive value of a_0 suggests that the impact of position player WAA (i.e., batting, baserunning, and fielding) on team WAA is greater than one-to-one. In this case, a coefficient of 0.080 suggests that team wins over .500 are, on average, 8% greater than implied by team-level position-player WAA. So, for example a team with players with a combined (position-player) WAA of +12 (and 0 pitching WAA) would be expected to finish 13 games over .500. This is the difference between a 93- and 94-win team in a 162-game schedule.

This is consistent with my discovery that player value is somewhat multiplicative at the team level—"players who are a little bit better than average will translate into a team that is a lot better than average." This is recognized in my work through the introduction of teammate adjustments and expected team win adjustments. There are, however, no such adjustments in the case of bWAR (or fWAR).

A negative value of a_{f0} suggests that the impact of player fielding on team wins is less than the impact of batting or baserunning. In this case, a coefficient of –0.118 suggests that fielding WAA are, on average, 12% less valuable than batting or baserunning WAA in translating into team wins.

> The top fielding team in MLB in 2015, according to Baseball-Reference, was the Arizona Diamondbacks at +68 Rfield. I translated that into a WAA_f of 6.5. Reducing that by the 12% implied by the estimated value of a_f would lower that to approximately 5.7 WAA–a reduction of just under one team win (0.8). Overall, Baseball-Reference calculated a total of 6.2 WAA for the 2015 D-Backs. Reducing that by 0.8 would lower it to 5.4 WAA. The 2015 D-Backs actually finished 79-83, 2 wins below .500.
>
> The worst fielding team in MLB in 2015, according to Baseball-Reference, was the Seattle Mariners at –68 Rfield. I translated that into a WAA_f of –6.7. Reducing that by the 12% implied by the estimated value of a_f would lower that (in absolute value) to –5.9–a reduction of 0.8 wins. Overall, Baseball-Reference calculated a total of –7.7 WAA for the 2015 Mariners. Adjusting that by 0.8 would raise it to –6.9 WAA. The 2015 Mariners actually finished 76-86, 5 wins below .500.

Correlation Between Pitching and Fielding

Baseball-Reference's treatment of pitching vis-à-vis fielding makes it difficult to evaluate the accuracy of bWAR as compared to fWAR or eWOPA. This is not a criticism of Baseball-Reference's treatment of pitching and fielding, merely a statement of fact. From the perspective of a team, Baseball-Reference begins with actual runs allowed, calculates an independent estimate of fielding runs above or below average, and attributes the difference between the two (i.e., total runs allowed minus (net) runs allowed by the team's fielders) to the team's pitchers. Baseball-Reference does not calculate WAR directly at the team level–WAR is constructed at the player level—and there are differences in the conversion from runs to wins for position players (where I understand the adjustment to be constant, or at least nearly-constant, across all players within a league) and pitchers (where the adjustment is calculated uniquely for each pitcher to reflect the impact of the pitcher on his own run-scoring environment). Because of these differences, it is not literally true that fielding WAA and pitching WAA can be traded off exactly one-for-one. But, it is the case, that, essentially, team-level pitching WAA and team-level fielding WAA will very nearly add up to a team-level defensive WAA based on actual runs allowed at the team level.

In other words, any errors in Baseball-Reference's calculation of fielding WAA will produce nearly-exactly offsetting errors in Baseball-Reference's calculation of pitching WAA—and vice versa. The mathematical term for this issue is Multicollinearity and this issue may affect the interpretation of the results in the above table (especially a_{fo} and a_{po}). Specifically (from the Wikipedia article on Multicollinearity), "One of the features of multicollinearity is that the standard errors of the affected coefficients tend to be large. In that case, the test of the hypothesis that the coefficient is equal to zero may lead to a failure to reject a false null hypothesis of no effect of the explanator, a type II error." In layman's terms, the standard errors associated with a_{fo} and a_{po} are artificially large, because of the way in which Baseball-Reference calculates bWAR.

Because of the way in which Baseball-Reference calculates fielding and pitching WAA, total WAA (or WAR), as calculated with Baseball-Reference will have virtually no "errors" on the defensive side, relative to actual runs allowed. Actual runs allowed may not track perfectly with team wins because of differences in timing (e.g., "clutch performance," "pitching to the score"), but these differences should generally be beyond the scope of fWAA and eWOPA, as well (but not pWins and pWOPA, which explicitly measure such factors, of course). This should make bWAR a more accurate measure of actual team performance than either eWOPA or fWAR, neither of which tie their defensive measures directly to actual runs allowed at the team level.

This makes it very difficult to evaluate Baseball-Reference's treatment of fielding and pitching at the player level by looking at the team-level accuracy of bWAR (or bWAA). Difficult, but not entirely impossible.

One thing worth looking at is the team-level correlation between pitching (WAA) and fielding (WAA). If there were systematic errors in Baseball-Reference's calculation of fielding WAA, this would lead to perfectly offsetting errors in Baseball-Reference's pitching WAA, which would lead to these two measures being negatively correlated. Hence, a negative correlation between fielding WAA and pitching WAA, at the team level, could be indicative of problems in the split between fielding and pitching.

pW-L records also calculate fielding and pitching measures controlling for each other. As with Baseball-Reference, a negative correlation between these two measures could indicate problems with this split.

One challenge, however, in evaluating correlations between pitching and fielding is to figure out what correlation we should expect. At one level, we might expect a correlation of zero: pitching and fielding are performed by entirely different players (outside of pitcher fielding, but (a) pitchers tend to have relatively few fielding opportunities compared to other positions, and (b) pitcher fielding is necessarily subsumed within "pitching" by Baseball-Reference, because of its decision to tie to actual runs allowed). On the other hand, good teams tend to be good at everything and bad teams—especially very bad teams—tend to be bad at everything. So, it might be reasonable to expect pitching and fielding to be positively correlated at the team level.

Fortunately for our analysis, one of the three systems being analyzed here–Fangraphs—estimates pitching and fielding independently, based on entirely independent statistics. Specifically, pitchers are evaluated based entirely on strikeouts, walks, and home runs (via FIP), while fielders are evaluated based entirely on balls in play (via UZR). The correlation between pitching WAA and fielding WAA, as measured by Fangraphs, should reflect the "true" correlation between these factors at the team level.

The next table calculates the correlation between pitching and fielding WAA for the three systems from 1969 through 2015.

Fangraphs	*Baseball-Ref*	*Player W-L*
6.67%	–13.07%	11.05%

As measured by Fangraphs, the correlation between pitching and fielding is fairly small, but is slightly (and somewhat significantly) positive—as one might expect for the reasons suggested above. As measured by Baseball-Reference, however, the correlation between pitching and fielding is negative—not greatly, but significantly, so. This suggests to me that Baseball-Reference may be systematically mis-allocating credit for runs allowed between pitchers and fielders.

And what of pW-L records? The correlation between fielding and pitching as measured by pW-L records is 11.05%. This is somewhat higher than the correlation identified by Fangraphs, which would seem to suggest that I am not mis-allocating credit for runs allowed between pitchers and fielders.

bWAR vs. Actual Wins Above Replacement

Both Baseball-Reference and Fangraphs use a replacement level of .294. As a final analysis, I compared bWAR to team WAR, where the latter was set equal to actual team wins minus the number of wins a .294 team would have won over that team's total games (47.6 per 162). For this experiment, I fit the following equation:

$$\text{Team Wins over .294} = a_0 + (1 + a_{pos})*WAR_{pos} + (1 + a_p)*WAR_p$$

As with the previous table, the results in the first column of the table were estimated using OLS. The results in the last column are what would be expected.

	2003–2015	
	Statistical Estimates	*Expected Values*
a_0	2.152	0
(Std. Error)	0.847	–
a_{pos}	–0.092	0
(Std. Error)	0.033	–
a_p	–0.039	0
(Std. Error)	0.036	–
R^2	0.798	0.793

The coefficients, a_0 and a_{pos} are both significant at a 95% confidence level (in fact, both are significant at more than a 98% confidence level).

The value of a_0, 2.15, indicates that a team that amassed an actual .294 winning percentage would be expected to earn 2 WAR rather than the 0 WAR implied by a replacement level of .294.

> The only sub-replacement team over the time period analyzed here was the 2003 Detroit Tigers, who went 43–119 for a .265 winning percentage, which works out to –4.3 wins over .294. Baseball-Reference shows them with +4.3 WAR.
>
> The next two worst teams over this time period were the 2004 Arizona Diamondbacks and the 2013 Houston Astros, who both finished 51–111 (.315), 3.4 wins over .294. According to Baseball-Reference, the players on the 2004 Diamondbacks accumulated 5.7 WAR and the players on the 2013 Astros had 8.4 WAR.

The value of a_{pos}, –0.092, indicates that position-player WAR translate into about 9% fewer team WAR—i.e., 11 position-player WAR translate into only 10 team WAR. This is broadly consistent with the earlier result suggesting that fielding WAA may be overstated by 12% or so.

The value of R^2 indicates that just under 80% of the variance in team wins (over .294) can be explained by player WAR as presented at Baseball-Reference.com.

Fangraphs: fWAR

Fangraphs has two pages on its website for every season which summarize position player and pitcher WAR for every team within the season.

For position players, Fangraphs provides data on Batting, Baserunning, and Fielding, as well as Positional values, expressed as runs above average. Fangraphs also has a column titled "League" which appears to reflect differences between the two leagues in a particular season (e.g., in 2015, AL teams are credited with approximately 22 league runs; NL teams are credited with approximately 11 league runs). Finally, Fangraphs has a column "Replacement," which converts the previous columns (including League) from runs above average (RAA) to runs above replacement (RAR). Fangraphs then shows RAR (which is the sum of the preceding aforementioned columns) and WAR.

For a season as a whole, the sum of Fangraphs' values for Batting, Baserunning, Fielding, Positional, and League add up to zero (or something exceptionally close to zero, most likely due to minor rounding issues). As was the case with Baseball-Reference, however, total Batting runs above average tend to be negative while Positional and League adjustments tend to be positive, on average, across all teams. To create WAA measures for Batting, Baserunning, and Fielding, all of which were centered at zero, therefore, I distributed Positional and League adjustments by team across Batting, Baserunning, and Fielding, such that the total number of Batting, Baserunning, and Fielding Runs (relative to average) were all exactly equal to zero for every season. I then converted these runs above average (RAA) measures into wins above average (WAA) measures using the ratio of WAR to RAR reported by Fangraphs.

Fangraphs' pitcher WAR pages provide team values for RA9-WAR (WAR based on actual runs allowed) and WAR (their preferred measure, based on FIP—i.e., based only on strikeouts, walks, and home runs allowed). Fangraphs does not provide any measures of either runs or wins relative to average (RAA or WAA). I converted Fangraphs' WAR estimates (using WAR, not RA9-WAR) to WAA by simply subtracting the same number of WAR from each team such that the sum equaled zero. So, for example, in 2015, total pitcher WAR, as reported by Fangraphs was 429.8. Dividing 429.8 by the 30 MLB teams, the "replacement" portion of WAR worked out to 14.3 "wins" per team. Subtracting each team's WAR by 14.3 produced a set of WAA measures which summed to zero across the 30 major league teams in 2015.

Having set all of that up, I fit the same equation as used earlier for eWins and bWAR, using Fangraphs data from 2003 to 2015. The equation being solved is repeated here for reference.

$$\text{Team Wins over .500} = (1 + a_0)*[WAA_b + (1 + a_{r0})*WAA_r + (1 + a_{f0})*WAA_f] + (1 + a_0)*(1 + a_{p0})*WAA_p$$

The results in the first column of the table were estimated using OLS. The results in the last column are what we would expect if the four factors—batting, baserunning, fielding, and pitching—were appropriately weighted in the calculation of fWAR.

	2003-2015	
	Statistical Estimates	*Expected Values*
a_0	−0.043	0
(Std. Error)	0.043	−
a_{r0}	−0.122	0
(Std. Error)	0.263	−
a_{f0}	−0.200	0
(Std. Error)	0.085	−
a_{p0}	0.190	0
(Std. Error)	0.051	−
R^2	0.802	0.790

The coefficients on fielding, a_{f0}, and pitching, a_{p0}, are both significantly different from their expected value (zero) at more than a 95% significance level.

A negative value of a_{f0} suggests that the impact of player fielding on team wins is less than the impact of batting or baserunning. In this case, a coefficient of −0.200 suggests that fielding WAA are, on average, 20% less valuable than batting or baserunning WAA in translating into team wins.

The top fielding team in MLB in 2003, according to Fangraphs, was the Seattle Mariners at +78.1 Fielding Runs (above average). I translated that into a WAA_f of 7.7. Reducing that by the 20% implied by the estimated value of a_{f0} would lower that to approximately 6.1 WAA—a reduction of 1.6 wins. Overall, Fangraphs calculated a total of 47.2 WAR for the 2003 Mariners. Reducing that by 1.6 would lower it to 45.6 WAR. The 2003 Mariners actually finished 93–69, which is 45.4 wins above the .294 replacement level used by Fangraphs (and Baseball-Reference).

The worst fielding team in MLB in 2003, according to Fangraphs, was the Toronto Blue Jays at −73.5 Fielding Runs. I translated that into a WAA_f of −7.2. Reducing that by the 20% implied by the estimated value of a_{f0} would lower that (in absolute value) to −5.8, a reduction of 1.4 wins. Overall, Fangraphs calculated a total of 33.6 WAR for the 2003 Blue Jays. Increasing that by 1.4 would raise it to 35.0 WAR. The 2003 Blue Jays actually finished 86–76, 38.4 wins above the .294 replacement level used by Fangraphs.

A positive value of a_{p0} suggests that the impact of pitching WAR on team wins is greater than the impact of position-player WAR on team wins. In this case, a coefficient of 0.190 suggests that pitching WAA are, on average, 19% more valuable than position-player WAA in translating into team wins.

The top pitching team in MLB in 2003, according to Fangraphs, was the New York Yankees with 28.6 WAR. I translated that into a WAA_p of 14.3. Increasing that by the 19% implied by the estimated value of a_{p0} would raise that to approximately 17.0 WAA and 31.3 WAR. Overall, Fangraphs calculated a total of 55.1 WAR for the 2003 Yankees. Increasing that by the additional 2.7 pitcher WAR derived above would raise it to 57.8 WAR. The 2003 Yankees actually finished 101–61, which is 53.6 wins above the .294 replacement level used by Fangraphs.

The worst pitching team in MLB in 2003, according to Fangraphs, was the Detroit Tigers with 2.9 WAR. I translated that into a WAA_p of –11.4. Increasing that (in absolute value) by the 19% implied by the estimated value of a_{p0} would raise that (in absolute value) to –13.6 WAA and 0.7 WAR. Overall, Fangraphs calculated a total of 1.7 WAR for the 2003 Tigers. Decreasing that by the additional negative pitcher WAA derived above (2.2) would lower it to –0.5 WAR. The 2003 Tigers actually finished 43–119, which is 4.6 wins below the .294 replacement level used by Fangraphs (i.e., an actual WAR of –4.6).

fWAR vs. Actual Wins Above Replacement

Both Baseball-Reference and Fangraphs use a replacement level of .294. As a final analysis, I compared fWAR to team WAR, where the latter was set equal to actual team wins minus the number of wins a .294 team would have won over that team's total games (47.6 per 162). For this experiment, I fit the following equation:

$$\text{Team Wins over } .294 = a_0 + (1 + a_{pos})*WAR_{pos} + (1 + a_p)*WAR_p$$

As with the previous table, the results in the first column of the table were estimated using OLS. The results in the last column are what would be expected.

	2003–2015	
	Statistical Estimates	Expected Values
a_0	–0.605	0
(Std. Error)	0.906	–
a_{pos}	–0.116	0
(Std. Error)	0.035	–
a_p	0.199	0
(Std. Error)	0.052	–
R^2	0.799	0.788

The coefficients, a_{pos} and a_p are both significant at a 99% confidence level.

The value of a_{pos}, –0.116, indicates that position-player WAR translate into about 12% fewer team WAR—i.e., 9 position-player WAR translate into only 8 team WAR. This is broadly consistent with the earlier result suggesting that fielding WAA is overstated by 20%. The value of a_p in this equation, 0.199, is virtually identical to the value of a_{p0} in the previous equation. Both coefficients suggest that pitcher WAR translates into 20% more team WAR—i.e., 5 pitcher WAR translate into 6 team WAR.

The value of R^2 indicates that just under 80% of the variance in team wins (over .294) can be explained by player WAR as presented at Fangraphs.com.

Measuring the Accuracy of bWAA, fWAA, and eWOPA

At the team level, one would expect bWAA, fWAA, and eWOPA to correlate at least reasonably strongly with actual team wins over .500. The correlation will not be perfect (as it is for pWOPA and pWORL, by construction), of course. On offense, none of bWAA, fWAA, nor eWOPA tie to actual runs scored. And even if they did, differences in the distribution of runs scored lead to a less-than perfect correlation between runs scored (and runs allowed) and team wins. On the other hand, there is no particular reason to expect any of bWAA, fWAA, or eWOPA to do a notably better job of incorporating these differences, since none of the three are designed to capture such differences.

There are, however, some expected differences across the three systems.

- As noted above, bWAA for pitching and fielding are constructed to tie to actual runs allowed at the team level, by construction. This might lead one to expect bWAA to correlate somewhat more strongly to actual team wins than either fWAA or eWOPA.
- Both bWAA and fWAA for relief pitchers incorporate the leverage in which relief pitchers pitched. To the extent that better relief pitchers pitch in more important situations, this should lead to a better correlation with team wins for bWAA and fWAA than for eWOPA, which does not adjust for pitcher leverage.
- While eWOPA are calculated based on context-neutral win probabilities, there are some plays—stolen bases, bunts, and intentional walks—which I do not neutralize for context. To the extent that these plays are incorporated within eWOPA based on their actual context, this may lead eWOPA to correlate somewhat better with actual wins than bWAA or fWAA.

But, overall, the best way to evaluate how accurate bWAA, fWAA, and eWOPA are, relative to one another, is to evaluate how close they come to actual wins over .500 at the team level.

The first table below repeats results presented earlier in this article that relate actual team wins to my eWOPA (eWins over positional average) and to WAR (Wins above Replacement), as calculated by Baseball-Reference (bWAR) and Fangraphs (fWAR). I evaluated WAR rather than WAA because the WAA values investigated here were at least partially constructed by me, as explained earlier in the chapter, and I did not want to seem to be influencing the results in any way.

For eWOPA, I fit the following equation:

$$\text{Team Wins over } .500 = a_0 * (\text{eWOPA} + (\text{Teammate Adj.}))$$

For bWAR and fWAR, I fit the following equation:

$$\text{Team Wins over } .294 = c + (1 + a_{pos}) * \text{WAR}_{pos} + (1 + a_p) * \text{WAR}_p$$

The equations were all fit over team data from 2003 through 2015.

	eWOPA	bWAR	fWAR
a_0	1.837	–	–
(Std. Error)	0.045	–	–
c	–	2.152	−0.605
(Std. Error)	–	0.847	0.906
a_{pos}	–	−0.092	−0.116
(Std. Error)	–	0.033	0.035
a_p	–	−0.039	0.199
(Std. Error)	–	0.036	0.052
R^2	0.814	0.798	0.799

In comparing the results, I would point out that the equation for eWOPA presumes that the various factors are weighted optimally (as, indeed, I showed that they are earlier in this chapter). For bWAR and fWAR, however, the equations correct for any mis-weighting between position players and pitchers. As such, to the extent the results here may be biased toward one or the other, they would be biased toward the WARs.

In spite of this possible bias, the highest R^2 (which measures the percentage of variance in actual team wins explained by the various equations) is for eWOPA.

There are several alternate ways to measure how "close" these measures come to actual team wins beyond the above table. The next table presents two such measures over two alternate time periods.

	bWAA	fWAA	Raw	eWOPA incl. Teammate Adj.
1969–2015	89.7%	88.4%	90.5%	91.0%
2003–2015	89.3%	88.8%	90.2%	90.8%
1969–2015	4.931	5.213	4.793	4.684
2003–2015	5.066	5.118	4.847	4.732

The first two rows present the simple correlation between team wins over .500 and the measures being evaluated here (bWAA, fWAA, eWOPA). Correlation is a measure that ranges from –1 to 1. Numbers greater than zero indicate that teams with higher values of bWAA (for example) tend to also have more actual wins over .500 (and vice versa). A correlation of 1 (or 100%) would mean that actual wins and the measure of interest move perfectly in synch, so that, for example, 5% more bWAA would translate into exactly 5% more wins over .500.

Statisticians often refer to correlation by the letter, r. The relationship between the "r" here and the R^2 in several of my earlier tables is not coincidental. In fact, for a univariate equation (i.e., y is a simple function of one variable, x), R^2 is the square of the correlation coefficient, r. Not surprisingly, then, the correlation results here tell the same basic story as the R^2 results told earlier: the relationships between team wins over .500 and bWAA, fWAA, and eWOPA are fairly similar, with eWOPA correlating somewhat better than bWAA and fWAA.

The last two rows calculate standard errors for bWAA, fWAA, and eWOPA. These are calculated as follows. For every team-season, the difference between team wins over .500 and the number of wins over .500 predicted by the relevant measure is calculated. For bWAA and fWAA, the "number of wins over .500 predicted" is simply equal to bWAA and fWAA, respectively. As discussed earlier, the relationship between net eWins and net team wins (and, by extension, between eWOPA and team wins over .500) is not one-to-one, but is closer to two to one. Hence, for this set of calculations, "the number of wins over .500 predicted by" eWOPA is equal to 2 times eWOPA. There is no strict mathematical reason why the number of wins over .500 predicted by eWOPA should be exactly equal to two times eWOPA. In fact, the correct relationship between team wins over .500 and eWOPA is an empirical question. To the extent, then, that this exact relationship may not be exactly two to one, the standard error associated with eWOPA calculated here will overstate the true error in the accuracy of eWOPA as a predictor of team wins.

These differences are squared and then summed. Squaring the errors has two effects. First, a square of any number is positive, so squaring the numbers has the effect of valuing 2 the same as –2, so that positive and negative errors do not simply cancel out. Second, squaring these numbers (as opposed to simply taking the absolute value) weights larger errors more strongly than smaller errors. For example, squaring errors of 1 and 4 would produce a sum of squared errors of 17 ($1^2 + 4^2$) while squaring errors of 2 and 3 (which have the same simple sum, 5) would produce a sum of squared errors of only 13 ($2^2 + 3^2$): being off by 4 half of the time is worse than always being off by 2 or 3. The sum of squared errors is then divided by the total number of observations (1,288 team-seasons from 1969 to 2015) and the square root is taken. The results, then, are, essentially, average absolute errors (weighted against large errors)—so lower numbers are better.

The conclusion from the standard errors is basically the same as the conclusion from the correlations: eWOPA is best. Over the most recent time period (2003–2015), the standard error associated with eWOPA (including teammate adjustments) is approximately 7% better than bWAA and 8% better than fWAA.

Comparing bWAA and fWAA, the results seem to clearly favor Baseball-Reference. This is as I would have expected, given that defensive bWAA are constructed based on actual runs scored. Given that, the fact that eWOPA is even more accurate than bWAA strikes me as truly impressive.

Comparison of Factors: Batting, Baserunning, Fielding, Pitching

Earlier in this chapter, I spent a great deal of time looking at the individual factors of player value—Batting, Baserunning, Fielding, and Pitching—and assessing whether these factors were properly weighted within eWOPA, bWAA, and fWAA. Those results are repeated below.

To review, I fit the following equation for eWins, bWAA, and fWAA by factor.

$$\text{Team Wins over }.500 = a_0 * [WAA_b + (1 + a_{r0}) * WAA_r + (1 + a_{f0}) * WAA_f + a_2 * (\text{Teammate Adj.})] + a_0 * (1 + a_{p0}) * WAA_p$$

The table below presents statistical results (estimated using OLS) as well as expected coefficients. All three equations were estimated over data from 2003 to 2015.

	pW-L Records		Wins Above Replacement (WAR)		
	Statistical Estimates	Expected Values	Baseball-Ref	Fangraphs	Expected Values
a_0	2.059	1.963	1.080	0.957	1.000
(Std. Error)	0.078	0.044	0.043	0.043	–
a_2	1.882	2.000	–	–	–
(Std. Error)	0.546	–	–	–	–
a_{r0}	–0.278	0.000	0.085	–0.122	0.000
(Std. Error)	0.272	–	0.328	0.263	–
a_{f0}	0.042	0.000	–0.118	–0.200	0.000
(Std. Error)	0.256	–	0.074	0.085	–
a_{p0}	0.216	0.316	–0.062	0.243	0.000
(Std. Error)	0.063	–	0.050	0.086	–
R^2	0.838	0.837	0.817	0.802	0.793 / 0.788

To review some key points from my earlier analysis. First, with respect to pW-L records:

- None of the coefficients in the equation for pW-L records are significantly different from their expected values.
- The impact of pitching on pW-L records is stronger (by 20–30 percent) than expected based on raw pW-L records. But this is accounted for in player eWins through adjustments for expected context and "team win adjustment."
- The relationship between net eWins and net Team wins is approximately 2-to-1.
- The relationship between eWins and team wins is strengthened by taking explicit account of teammate adjustments, to reflect the interactive relationship between pitchers and fielders (and, to a lesser extent, between batters and baserunners).

- Overall, approximately **84%** of the variance in team wins is captured within eWins.

As for the two WAR measures:

- Fielding is significantly over-weighted and pitching is significantly under-weighted within Fangraphs' fWAR framework.
- Because of the structure of its calculations—which tie to actual runs allowed at the team level—it is difficult to evaluate the appropriateness of Baseball-Reference's weighting of fielding and pitching. The evidence that exists, however, suggests that fielding is over-weighted by Baseball-Reference.
- Despite certain factors that should give the two WAR measures certain structural advantages vis-à-vis context-neutral eWins—relief pitcher leverage, Baseball-Reference's use of actual runs allowed—both WAR measures explain less of the actual variance in team wins than eWins, even when optimizing the weighting of batting, baserunning, pitching, and fielding.
- As presented by Baseball-Reference and Fangraphs, **less than 80%** of the variance in team wins is captured within either bWAR or fWAR.

Why Are pW-L Records Superior?

The math is very compelling. pW-L records are a better measure of actual team value—and, hence, by extension, are a better measure of player value—than WAR. Of course, I'm not the most objective observer here, but hopefully I have made a sufficiently compelling case that you agree with me.

Moving beyond the math, why are pW-L records superior to WAR?

The answer, I believe, is because I start from actual wins. I actually begin by calculating pWins, which tie to team wins by construction. I then pull out the context from pWins to create eWins. But starting from actual wins ensures that eWins still tie directly to team wins because eWins are still derived from actual team wins—albeit indirectly.

For example, starting from actual wins, I discovered that home runs are more valuable, relative to other hits, than conventional sabermetric wisdom believed. I first presented this result in Chapter 5 and discuss it further later in this chapter, where I compare the values of individual players as measured by pW-L records to values as measured by Baseball-Reference's WAR.

Starting from actual wins, my other big discovery is that the translation from player value to team value is not linear, but is, instead, largely multiplicative. Being a little bit better than average will translate into a lot of wins. By starting from actual team wins, I was able to incorporate this finding even into my context-neutral wins through what I call an **expected team win adjustment**. This recognizes that a player who is somewhat above (or below) average will have a non-linear, multiplicative, impact on his team's wins above (or below) average.

The extent to which this is true will depend on how concentrated a player's performance is within his team's games. Because pitchers concentrate their performance more heavily than position players, this leads to pitchers having stronger expected (and actual) team win adjustments. This leads me to (correctly) weight pitcher performance more heavily than may be suggested by a simple linear analysis.

Probably the most significant difference between my eWOPA and eWORL measures versus bWAR and fWAR is in the impact of fielding on team wins. As I showed and discussed above, both WAR measures overstate the impact of fielding on team wins, by perhaps as much as 25%. In contrast, the evidence strongly suggests that my weighting of fielding is entirely appropriate. As with batting and pitching, I believe that I have gotten this weighting right because I determined the appropriate split between pitching and fielding through an objective analysis that began from a framework tied to actual team wins.

Ultimately, if you want to understand what leads to wins in major league baseball, you have to look at actual wins in major league baseball. pW-L records begin by looking at actual team wins, unlike WAR, which begins by looking at theoretical run values. And that is why pW-L records produce the best estimate of player value, either in or out of context.

Player-Level Comparisons of WAR vs. pW-L Records

Having taken a systematic comparison of pW-L records to WAR at the team level, the remainder of this chapter extends this analysis to the level of detail at which pW-L records and WAR are actually calculated: the individual player.

Using Baseball-Reference's Play Index tool, I calculated career WAR values for players amassed over the seasons from 1949 through 2013. The range of seasons used here was chosen because it happened to be all of the seasons for which I had complete play-by-play data with which to calculate pW-L records at the time I originally performed this analysis several years ago.

Putting pW-L Records on the Same Scale as bWAR

The first thing to do in order to make a comparison with Baseball-Reference's WAR (bWAR) is to figure out what specifically to compare to bWAR.

I calculate two sets of pW-L records: pWins and eWins. The former of these, pWins, are context-dependent, and are constructed such that the sum of pWins by all players on a team are exactly equal to the number of games played by a team plus the number of team wins, by construction. The latter, eWins, on the other hand, are calculated adjusting for context, assuming a player played on an average team with average teammates. The contextual factors relating pWins and eWins were described in detail in Chapter 2.

Baseball-Reference's bWAR measure is generally calculated independent of context (with one exception, which is discussed below). Therefore, it is more comparable to eWins than to pWins. Because of this, my comparison statistic is constructed based on eWins.

In order to facilitate these player comparisons, I think it is probably helpful to be able to place pW-L records on the same scale as bWAR.

I calculate a measure of Wins over Replacement Level (WORL) based on both pWins and eWins: pWORL and eWORL, respectively. One might, therefore, think that a logical comparison would be to compare bWAR to eWORL. In fact, however, bWAR and eWORL are on somewhat different scales.

As discussed earlier in this chapter, eWins over positional average (eWOPA) do not relate to team wins over .500 on a one-to-one basis (as bWAA and fWAA do), but on something closer to a two-to-one basis, i.e.,

$$(\text{Wins over .500}) \sim \text{bWAA} \sim 2*\text{eWOPA}$$

But the difference between WAA (Wins above Average) and WAR (Wins above Replacement) and the difference between WOPA (Wins over Positional Average) and WORL (Wins over Replacement Level) are on the same scale, i.e.,

$$(\text{bWAR}-\text{bWAA}) \sim (\text{eWORL}-\text{eWOPA})$$

Hence, one can calculate the PWin or eWin-based equivalent of WAR by adding WOPA plus WORL.

Except for one detail: bWAR is calculated setting team replacement level at .294 (approximately 48–114 over a 162-game season). In contrast, my player-level replacement level is approximately 0.455. As I explained in Chapter 3, a player-level replacement level of 0.455 works out to a team-level replacement level of 0.366. Converting eWORL from a team-level replacement level of 0.366 to .294 (to match bWAR and fWAR) can be done as follows.

If player replacement level works out to 0.455 and wins over positional average (WOPA) work out to 0.500 (on average), then we can make two general statements:

(1) WORL−WOPA = 0.045*(Player Decisions)
(2) Wins−WORL = 0.455*(Player Decisions)

Given 2 pWins and 1 pLoss for every team win (and the reverse for every team loss), a team-level replacement level of .294 would work out a player replacement level of .431. To set player-level replacement level at .431, one would want to subtract 0.024*(Player Decisions) from WORL, or, from (2) above: (0.024/0.455)*(Wins−WORL), i.e.

$$\text{Wins over } 0.431 = \text{WORL} + 0.053*(\text{Wins}-\text{WORL}) = 0.053*\text{Wins} + 0.947*\text{WORL}$$

Combining the earlier result, then, that WAR ~ WOPA + WORL, we can get the pW-L version of WAR–eWAR–by fitting the following formula:

$$\text{eWAR} = 0.053*\text{eWins} + \text{eWOPA} + 0.947*\text{eWORL}$$

The player comparisons below compare eWAR, calculated as above, to bWAR. Just to clarify: I am not suggesting that eWAR is a better measure than either eWOPA or eWORL; it just makes for a more informative comparison to put eWins on the same scale as bWAR and it is easier for me to do this by constructing eWAR rather than trying to construct the bWAR equivalent of eWOPA or eWORL.

The top 10 players in bWAR are compared to the top 10 in this adjusted version of pW-L records (which I will call eWAR for the remainder of this chapter) over the time period from 1949 to 2013 in the table below.

	eWAR			bWAR	
1	Barry Bonds	166.0	1	Barry Bonds	162.4
2	Roger Clemens	136.4	2	Willie Mays	156.2
3	Hank Aaron	135.7	3	Hank Aaron	142.6
4	Willie Mays	134.4	4	Roger Clemens	139.4
5	Greg Maddux	133.3	5	Alex Rodriguez	116.0
6	Mickey Mantle	123.9	6	Rickey Henderson	110.8
7	Joe Morgan	123.6	7	Tom Seaver	110.5

		eWAR			*bWAR*
8	Alex Rodriguez	122.4	8	Mickey Mantle	109.7
9	Mike Schmidt	108.4	9	Frank Robinson	107.2
10	Frank Robinson	108.0	10	Greg Maddux	106.9

Eight players are in the top 10 in both eWAR and bWAR over the time period being considered here. The two players in the top 10 in bWAR but not eWAR are Rickey Henderson and Tom Seaver, who ranked 11th and 15th in eWAR over this time period, respectively. The two players in the top 10 in eWAR but not bWAR are Mike Schmidt and Joe Morgan, who ranked 11th and 13th in bWAR over this time period, respectively.

At a sufficiently high level, eWAR and bWAR are very similar; one might even say that they're more similar than different.

bWAR versus eWAR

To allow for a more detailed analysis, I compiled lists of the top 1,000 players by eWAR and bWAR from 1949 to 2013. Actually, rounding both eWAR and bWAR to one decimal place, there were 1,003 players who earned at least 17.4 bWAR and 1,004 players who earned at least 17.2 eWAR. I won't bore you by actually listing all of these players, but will simply summarize the results. Overall, 863 players made the list for both eWAR and bWAR over this time period. A total of 141 players made the list for eWAR but not bWAR, and another 140 players made the list for bWAR, but not eWAR.

For each of the 1,144 players who made one or both of these two lists, I calculated the positions they played. I weighted the positions by the share of Player wins earned at the position. The next table breaks down the mix of positions played by the players who made the cut in eWAR and the players who made the cut in bWAR, and calculates the differences.

Position Distribution, All Players

Position	*eWAR*	*bWAR*	*Difference*
SP	33.2%	31.5%	1.7%
RP	3.4%	6.6%	−3.2%
C	4.7%	5.4%	−0.7%
1B	7.9%	7.7%	0.2%
2B	7.2%	6.3%	0.9%
3B	7.8%	7.8%	0.0%
SS	7.4%	7.1%	0.3%
LF	9.1%	8.6%	0.5%
CF	7.8%	8.7%	−0.9%
RF	9.0%	8.1%	0.9%
DH	2.5%	2.2%	0.3%

Position Distribution, Players in Only One List

Position	*eWAR*	*bWAR*	*Difference*
SP	37.6%	25.9%	11.7%
RP	4.2%	27.7%	−23.5%
C	4.2%	9.7%	5.4%
1B	5.8%	4.3%	1.5%
2B	11.5%	4.8%	6.7%
3B	5.4%	5.2%	0.2%
SS	7.3%	5.2%	2.1%
LF	7.5%	4.0%	3.5%

Position	eWAR	bWAR	Difference
CF	3.8%	9.6%	–5.8%
RF	9.5%	3.2%	6.3%
DH	3.1%	0.4%	2.7%

Pitchers

By far the largest difference between the two lists is in their treatment of relief pitchers. Relief pitching accounts for 27.7% of the player wins earned by players who made the cut in bWAR but not in eWAR, but only 4.2% of the player wins for the reverse group. The primary reason for this is a difference in the treatment of context in calculating eWins vis-à-vis bWAR. In general, bWAR is a context-neutral measure. This is why the measure of pW-L records to which I am comparing it here is based on eWins, which are also context-neutral. There is one exception, however: bWAR takes into account leverage in valuing relief pitchers. That is, bWAR gives closers (and other relief pitchers) credit for pitching in higher-context situations.

Relief Pitchers

JOHN HILLER

The player rated highest in bWAR who failed to make the cut in eWAR was John Hiller, who was the relief ace for the Detroit Tigers in the mid–1970s. Hiller recovered from three heart attacks in a single day in early 1971 at the age of 27 to put together an impressive four-year run from 1973 to 1976 that is a fascinating throwback to the old "fireman" model of relief pitching. In 1973, Hiller pitched 65 games, all in relief, of which he finished 60 of them, pitching 125.1 innings (nearly two innings per appearance). He earned a traditional won-lost record of 10–5 and a then-record 38 saves while posting a 1.44 ERA. The next year, he pitched 59 games, all in relief, finishing 52 of them, pitching 150 innings with a 2.64 ERA. His save total fell dramatically, to 13, but he posted a traditional won-lost record of 17–14, all in relief. His workload declined fairly dramatically in 1975, to only 70.2 innings pitched, but not from a change in the Tigers' treatment of him, but because he suffered a season-ending pulled muscle on July 25th. He returned healthy in 1976 and pitched 112.1 innings in relief, with a traditional record of 11–8, 13 saves, and an ERA of 2.57. He also made one start that year (on October 1st): a complete-game, 4-hit shutout

Baseball-Reference credits John Hiller with 31.2 bWAR for his career, which ranks him tied (with Ted Kluszewski and Bill Russell) for 422nd over the time period analyzed here (1949–2013). In contrast, his eWAR total of 10.4 ranks a much more pedestrian 1,550th in eWAR over the same time period.

I do, however, also calculate pW-L records with context taken into account via pWins and pLosses. Incorporating actual context into John Hiller's record increases his player decisions by 29%. That alone would boost Hiller's eWAR from 10.4 to 13.3, although this would still leave Hiller almost 4 eWORL below the level needed to make the top 1,000 cut.

In addition to simply multiplying a player's context-neutral record by a context multiplier, pWins also adjust for the timing of a player's performance. In his career, John Hiller performed better in higher-context situations than in lower-context situations. Calculating a variation of eWAR based on John Hiller's career pWins, pWOPA, and pWORL produces a pWAR value of 20.7, which is still somewhat less than Baseball-Reference's 31.2 bWAR.

While I calculate the average context in which John Hiller performed in his career at 1.29, Baseball-Reference adjusts Hiller's record based on an average leverage of 1.91.

The context in which Hiller performed is overstated by Baseball-Reference for two reasons. First, leverage is comparable only to inter-game context. As I explained in Chapter 2, inter-game context measures the importance of a situation relative to other situations within the same game. But I also account for intra-game context, which adjusts the number of player decisions to be constant across games. As I discussed in Chapter 2, inter-game and intra-game context are negatively correlated as high-leverage situations lead to more player decisions within games with a large number of high-leverage situations than in games with relatively few high-leverage situations. As a result of this, intra-game context will tend to be lower in games with a large number of high-leverage situations. As a rough approximation, inter-game context (leverage) tends to over-state total context by about 50%. In fact, Baseball-Reference cuts leverage in half before applying it to its calculation of bWAR. Because of this, Baseball-Reference's treatment of leverage actually ends up very similar to my calculation of context.

There is an additional issue, however, that is more specific to John Hiller. Baseball-Reference calculates leverage based on the leverage when a relief pitcher first enters a game and then applies that leverage to the pitcher's entire appearance. Based on this, Baseball-Reference estimates the average leverage for John Hiller's career at 1.91—i.e., they increase Hiller's value by half of 91%, i.e., by about 46%.

pW-L records implicitly calculate a unique context for each batter faced by John Hiller in his career. In his prime, John Hiller was typically brought into the game by the Tigers at a key moment—generally in a close game, often with runners on base. But, in general, once Hiller entered a game, he stayed until the finish. In his four-season peak (1973–76), Hiller finished 192 of his 215 relief appearances (89.3%), which frequently meant pitching two or more innings (he averaged just over 2 innings per appearance across these four seasons). But once the high-pressure situation in which Hiller entered the game was past (either because Hiller got out of the inning or, on rare occasions, because Hiller allowed inherited runners to score), the leverage for the rest of Hiller's appearance was generally considerably lower than when he entered the game.

Fangraphs reports leverage calculated four ways: gmLI is defined as "Average Leverage Index when entering the game"; exLI is defined as "Average Leverage Index when exiting the game"; inLI is defined as "Average Leverage Index at the start of the inning"; and, pLI is defined as "Average Leverage Index." The measure of leverage that corresponds to pW-L records is pLI, which is also what Fangraphs uses to calculate its fWAR.

Fangraphs only presents leverage data since 1974, so it is missing the first 8 seasons of John Hiller's career, including the first year of his four-year prime. Even with that missing data, however, Fangraphs basically agrees with Baseball-Reference regarding what Fangraphs calls Hiller's gmLI, 1.98. But Fangraphs estimates Hiller's pLI at only 1.69. Adjusting that 1.69 down to incorporate intra-game context (and to recognize that Hiller's average context was somewhat lower earlier in his career) would produce a figure fairly close to my estimate for Hiller's overall context of 1.29.

Fangraphs calculates its version of WAR two ways: based on actual runs allowed and based on FIP (Fielding Independent Pitching, i.e., expected runs allowed based on Hiller's strikeouts, walks, and home runs allowed). Fangraphs calculates Hiller's fWAR based on actual runs allowed (RA9-WAR) at 26.2. Fangraphs calculates Hiller's fWAR based on FIP (WAR) at 14.9. As I said above, calculating a WAR-equivalent based on pWins, pWOPA, and pWORL—i.e., incorporating context—John Hiller had a pWAR of 20.7, almost exactly between Fangraphs's two estimates, which makes perfect sense to me: walks, strikeouts, and home runs allowed are the most important factors affecting pitching, but pitchers do have some impact on the other aspects of run prevention.

Dick Hall

Although relief pitchers are much more frequent in the bWAR top 1,000 (1,003, to be precise) than in the eWAR top 1,000 (1,004), there is actually one player for whom over half of his player wins were earned as a relief pitcher who makes the eWAR cut, but not the bWAR cut, Dick Hall.

Dick Hall actually made the major leagues as an outfielder with the Pittsburgh Pirates in the 1950s. In his third season, 1954, he appeared in 112 games with 351 plate appearances as the Pirates' fourth outfielder. Hall batted only .239/.304/.310 that season, and he was destined to play only 4 more games in the outfield in the rest of his major-league career. Instead, in 1955, Hall appeared in 15 games as a pitcher, including 13 starts, earning a traditional won-lost record of 6–6 and a 3.91 ERA in 94.1 innings. Hall spent the next few years swinging between the bullpen and the starting rotation. His top games started came with the 1960 Kansas City Athletics, for whom Hall started 28 games in 29 games pitched. He moved to the Baltimore Orioles the next year, and after starting 13 of 29 games in his first season in Baltimore, he settled into a career mostly as a relief pitcher.

For his career, Hall pitched in 495 games, 422 of them in relief, with 93 traditional pitcher wins, 71 saves, and a 3.32 ERA in 1,259.2 innings pitched.

Putting everything together, including his ill-fated career as an outfielder, I calculate that Dick Hall earned 17.9 eWAR. Baseball-Reference, in contrast, credits Hall with only 16.4 bWAR. This is not a big difference, of course, but the cut-offs for the top 1,000 lists were 17.2 eWAR, which Hall just passed, and 17.4 bWAR, which Hall just misses. As with Hiller, the difference here is one of context. If I calculate a WAR-equivalent based on Hall's pWins, pWOPA, and pWORL, I get a pWAR for Hall of 15.6. So, Baseball-Reference neatly splits the difference between Hall's eWAR and pWAR.

Starting Pitchers

While relief pitchers are more heavily represented in the bWAR top 1,000, starting pitchers are more heavily represented in the eWAR top 1,000.

The reason for this is also because of the treatment of context in the two measures. Technically, eWins are not calculated using no context. Rather, they are calculated incorporating expected context. For non-pitchers, expected context has a very minor effect. For pitchers, however, expected context actually serves to increase the context for starting pitchers and decrease the context for relief pitchers. This higher expected context for starting pitchers serves to increase the level of eWins for starting pitchers.

For example, Ed Figueroa just sneaks onto the bottom of the top 1,000 in eWAR with 17.4, while just missing the top 1,000 in bWAR with 16.0. What pushes him into the top 1,000 is that his starting pitching gave him an expected context of 1.06 which boosted his value by 6%. Removing that expected context would push Figueroa's eWAR down to 16.4, just out of the top 1,000 and quite close to his bWAR. Fully incorporating the actual context in which Ed Figueroa performed in his career, a pWin-based version of WAR would give Figueroa 17.4 pWAR, exactly equal to his 17.4 eWAR.

Position Players

Outside of pitchers, the differences in the position distribution of the two lists are fairly minimal.

Catchers are the least-represented fielding position in both lists. This is because catchers tend to play fewer games than players at other positions, both within single seasons and also over their careers. It is also because the parts of catcher fielding which are measured by both pW-L records and WAR measures—stolen bases, passed balls, and fielding on balls in play—are fairly minor. The reason why somewhat fewer catchers show up in my list than in the bWAR list is probably because I divide credit for stolen base attempts and wild pitches and passed balls between pitchers and catchers, whereas I believe catchers' fielding ratings in bWAR give 100% of the credit for these things to catchers.

The other big difference among infielders is second basemen. The shares of second basemen, third basemen, and shortstops in the eWAR list—7.2%, 7.8%, 7.4%—seem like a more even distribution than in the bWAR list, where second basemen seem to me to be under-represented at 6.3% versus 7.8% for third basemen and 7.1% for shortstops. On the other hand, the split of outfielders seems more even in the bWAR list—8.6%, 8.7%, 8.1%—than in the eWAR list—9.1%, 7.8%, 9.0%.

Player-Specific Differences in Valuation

While there are some differences in the positional mix of the top 1,000 players in bWAR vis-à-vis eWAR, the overwhelming majority of players on only one of the two lists are there simply because of differences in how these players' performances were evaluated by bWAR versus pW-L records.

For example, 7.8% of player wins were earned at third base by the players on both lists. But there are 8 players who made the cut in bWAR but not eWAR who played a majority of their career at third base (Ken Oberkfell has the most bWAR of the 8 at 22.3 versus 15.7 eWAR). And there are a different 7 third basemen who made the cut in eWAR but not bWAR (headed by Larry Parrish, 24.3 eWAR vs. 15.5 bWAR).

The rest of this chapter looks at two player comparisons. The first comparison is of the highest-ranked non-pitcher in bWAR outside the top 1,000 in eWAR versus the highest-ranked player in eWAR outside the top 1,000 in bWAR. The second comparison compares two shortstops, one in the top 1,000 in bWAR but not eWAR and one in the top 1,000 in eWAR but not bWAR.

Adam Dunn vs. Lance Johnson

Adam Dunn

The highest-rated player as measured by eWAR who is not among the top 1,000 players in bWAR is OF/1B/DH Adam Dunn. Dunn's 45.4 eWAR ranks 245th over the time period evaluated here while his bWAR total of 16.7 falls just short of the top 1,000 (17.2 was needed to make the top 1,000).

The decomposition of Adam Dunn's values as measured by Baseball-Reference and pW-L records are compared in the next table.

	Batting	Net Wins Baserunning	Fielding
Baseball-Reference	19.3	-1.5	-15.4
pW-L Records	33.0	-1.6	-5.2

pW-L records like two aspects of Adam Dunn's game more than bWAR: batting and fielding.

For batting, the issue is how Adam Dunn generated most of his batting value: home runs. One of the results that I discovered, in looking at the net win values of various offensive events is that home runs are more valuable than run-based systems, such as linear weights, rate them. This is because, in addition to the average number of runs generated by a particular event, the value of a win is also affected by the certainty of those runs scoring and home runs, of course, are guaranteed to produce runs.

As for fielding, the difference here is one of scale. I agree with Baseball-Reference that Adam Dunn was well below average as a fielder. In fact, he rates among the 20 worst fielders for whom I have calculated pW-L records, as measured by net wins, at both first base and left field. But defensive pW-L records are shared between pitchers and fielders, even on balls in play. The result is that my fielding records tend to be less extreme than those that underlie bWAR (and fWAR).

Put it together and I think that Adam Dunn was much more valuable in his career than Baseball-Reference rates him. But, one could argue, that's just one man's opinion. Is there an objective way to evaluate who is right in this case?

Earlier in this chapter, I showed why my weighting of fielding is superior to the weighting underlying bWAR (and fWAR). One of the key tools of this evaluation which I introduced there was to evaluate how closely bWAA, fWAA, and eWOPA tied to actual team wins over .500 at a team level by looking at standard errors associated with each of these measures. Weighting the teams on which Adam Dunn played in his career by the number of games he played for them, the standard error for bWAA (Baseball-Reference's measure of Wins above Average) was 6.52 wins. For eWOPA (including teammate adjustments), the standard error for Adam Dunn's teams was 5.30 wins. In other words, on average, pW-L records tended to be about 1.2 wins (almost 20%) closer to actual team wins than Baseball-Reference for Adam Dunn's teams through his career.

Lance Johnson

The highest-rated position player as measured by bWAR who did not make the cut in eWAR is former major-league centerfielder Lance "One Dog" Johnson. Johnson's 30.1 bWAR ranks 438th over the time period evaluated here while his eWAR total of 14.5 falls short of the top 1,000.

The decomposition of Lance Johnson's values as measured by Baseball-Reference and pW-L records are compared in the next table.

	Batting	*Net Wins* *Baserunning*	*Fielding*
Baseball-Reference	−2.1	3.3	7.7
pW-L Records	−11.4	3.9	2.7

The Lance Johnson story is basically the Adam Dunn story in reverse. Baseball-Reference thinks much more highly of Lance Johnson's offense and fielding.

As with Dunn, the defensive issue is one of valuation not evaluation. Baseball-Reference rates Johnson among the top 5 centerfielders in his league five times in his career. pW-L records rate him that high four times. From 1990 to 1997, the seasons in which Johnson played 100 or more games, he ranks second in net fielding wins in center field behind only Kenny Lofton.

For his career, Lance Johnson batted .291/.334/.386. According to Baseball-Reference, that was good for an OPS+ of 95—which is consistent with their bWAR breakdown. Johnson's offensive game revolved around balls in play. His career highs in the "three true outcomes" were 58 strikeouts, 42 walks, and 10 home runs. He had some non-home-run pop, however, leading his league in triples 5 times.

Johnson's best offensive season was 1996, his first (and only full) season with the New York Mets. That season, Johnson led his league in hits for the second straight season, with 227, his only season of more than 200 hits. He led his league in triples for the fifth time, with a career-high 21. In addition, he had career highs in runs scored (117), doubles (31), RBI (69), stolen bases (50), batting average (.333), on-base percentage (.362), and slugging percentage (.479). Baseball-Reference credits Lance Johnson's offense that season (including double-play avoidance) as being worth 2.3 wins above average. Coupled with his usual excellent baserunning and defense, Baseball-Reference credits Lance Johnson with 7.2 WAR in 1996, the ninth-highest total in the National League that season.

In contrast, pW-L records give Lance Johnson a (context-neutral, teammate-adjusted) batting won-lost record of 13.8–12.8 in 1996, only 1.0 net batting wins, and an overall eWAR value of only 4.2.

According to an article at Beyond the Box Score (http://www.beyondtheboxscore.com/2011/1/4/1912914/custom-woba-and-linear-weights-through-2010-baseball-databank-data), the relative linear weights for singles, doubles, triples, and home runs (denominated in runs) in 1996 were the following.

Singles	*Doubles*	*Triples*	*Home Runs*
0.484	0.783	1.056	1.398

These numbers suggest that one home run is equal in value to 1.8 doubles or 1.3 triples.

Using these numbers, then, Lance Johnson's 166 singles, 31 doubles, 21 triples, and 9 home runs in 1996 were equivalent in value to 99.7 home runs.

In contrast, these are the net win values for singles, doubles, triples, and home runs for the 1996 National League.

Singles	*Doubles*	*Triples*	*Home Runs*
0.035	0.058	0.075	0.136

These numbers suggest that one home run was equal in value to 2.4 doubles or 1.8 triples.

Using these numbers, then, Lance Johnson's league-leading 227 hits were equivalent in value to 77.1 home runs. In other words, pW-L records value Lance Johnson's hits as 23% less valuable than suggested by linear weights.

That explains why bWAR and eWAR are different. But which is correct? As with Adam Dunn, I looked at the teams for which Lance Johnson played in his career. The average standard error for bWAA (weighted by the games played by Johnson) was 6.14 wins per season. Using eWOPA (plus teammate adjustments) produces a standard error of 4.55 wins per season.

REY SANCHEZ VS. JOSE OFFERMAN

As I said above, the vast majority of the differences in the bWAR top 1,000 and eWAR top 1,000 are not differences based on position, but differences in the valuation of players. The Johnson and Dunn examples highlight some of these differences. My final example is perhaps the clearest example of this difference because it is a direct comparison of two players at the same position.

Rey Sanchez was a brilliant defensive shortstop who lasted 15 seasons in the major leagues with over 5,000 career plate appearances despite a career batting line of .272/.308/.334. Sanchez played through the heart of the "sillyball" era of the late 1990's and early 2000's, so that translated into an OPS+ of 69. In an era where seemingly every middle infielder in baseball could hit 15–20 home runs per season, Sanchez hit 15 in his career. But, despite (surprisingly to me) never winning a Gold Glove, Sanchez's defense was brilliant enough that he appeared in 95 or more games in eleven consecutive seasons from 1993 through 2003.

Jose Offerman was an exact contemporary of Sanchez. Offerman played 29 games in 1990, but otherwise his career perfectly overlapped with Sanchez's (Offerman missed the 2003 season, so that he and Sanchez ended up playing an identical 15 seasons). Like Sanchez, Offerman arrived in the major leagues as a shortstop. Unlike Sanchez, Offerman was ***not*** a "brilliant defensive shortstop" and Offerman ended up playing his last game at shortstop at age 27 in 1996. But Offerman's bat was solid enough—career batting line of .273/.360/.373 (OPS+ of 94)—that teams were willing to move Offerman to second base and, eventually, first base, to keep him in the lineup. Offerman even played 100 games as a designated hitter.

Rey Sanchez, brilliant defensive middle infielder (in addition to shortstop, he also played 480 games at second base and was brilliant defensively there as well) played in 1,490 games in his career and amassed 5,246 plate appearances. According to his Baseball-Reference page, Sanchez won no major awards (including, as I said, no Gold Gloves), made no All-Star teams, and earned $13.5 million in his major-league career.

Jose Offerman, defensively-challenged middle infielder, played in 1,651 games in his career and had 6,582 plate appearances. According to his Baseball-Reference page, Offerman made two All-Star teams (in 1995 and 1999) and earned $32.7 million in his major-league career.

The next table compares the careers of Rey Sanchez and Jose Offerman, as measured by Baseball-Reference's bWAR calculation and pW-L records.

	Batting	Net Wins *Baserunning*	*Fielding*	*WAR*
Rey Sanchez				
Baseball-Reference	–17.8	1.3	13.5	**20.5**

	Batting	Net Wins Baserunning	Fielding	WAR
pW-L Records	−22.0	−0.5	6.2	10.0
Difference	4.2	1.8	7.3	10.5
Jose Offerman				
Baseball-Reference	−0.5	0.0	−6.3	17.0
pW-L Records	−5.7	−1.5	−2.8	18.0
Difference	5.3	1.5	−3.4	−1.0

pW-L records value both Sanchez's and Offerman's offense less than Baseball Reference. This is for the same reasons as were outlined earlier in this article with respect to Adam Dunn and Lance Johnson–Sanchez and Offerman were largely singles hitters who hit a combined 72 career home runs.

But the difference in offensive value between the two players is basically the same, measured either by Baseball Reference or by pW-L records.

The big difference, then, between Sanchez's and Offerman's career values in bWAR vis-à-vis eWAR is because of the difference in the valuation of their fielding. But it is important to understand that the difference here is one of **valuation** not **evaluation**. pW-L records rate Rey Sanchez as one of the top 15 defensive shortstops and Jose Offerman as one of the 20 worst defensive shortstops for whom I have calculated pW-L records. Neither played enough second base to rank that highly at that position, but their relative defensive performances as second basemen were comparable to their relative performances as shortstops.

The difference in the fielding value shown here between Sanchez and Offerman, then, is not because of a difference in the evaluation of their specific fielding performance, but is due to a difference in the overall value which Baseball Reference and I place on fielding. As I explained earlier when discussing Dunn, the relative value of fielding vis-à-vis batting, baserunning, and pitching in pW-L records was not assigned by me, but was, instead, an output of my work. The relative value of offense to pitching to fielding (roughly 3 to 2 to 1) which I end up with are the relative values which the data tell us.

So which is the correct weighting of fielding? Obviously, I think that my numbers are correct.

As with Dunn and Johnson, I looked at the teams for which Offerman and Sanchez played (including the 2002 Boston Red Sox for whom they both played) and calculated how closely Baseball-Reference and pW-L records came to their actual records. The standard error for bWAA for Offerman and Sanchez's teams were 5.48 and 5.56, respectively. For eWOPA (including teammate adjustments), the standard errors for their teams were 5.15 and 4.71, respectively.

Let me also throw out one other piece of information. There are clear and obvious issues with relating player compensation to player value, most directly because of the timing of player compensation based on major league baseball's arbitration and free-agent systems. And it has certainly been the case historically that many front offices have made serious mistakes with regard to player evaluation and player compensation. But overall, for his career, Baseball Reference estimates that Rey Sanchez earned $0.7 million per bWAR while Jose Offerman earned $1.9 million per bWAR. In contrast, I estimate that Rey Sanchez was paid $1.3 million per eWAR versus $1.8 million per eWAR for Jose Offerman. And, in case you were curious, the numbers for Adam Dunn (through 2013) were $5.9 million per bWAR vs. $2.2 million per eWAR.

The relative valuation of batting, baserunning, pitching, and fielding as determined by pW-L records are generally consistent with the relative valuation of batting, baserunning, pitching, and fielding as paid for by major league front offices. In my opinion, it is clearly the case that Major-League front offices can, and frequently do, overpay for specific players based on specific misevaluations of player value (e.g., Adam Dunn and the Chicago White Sox), but I find it far less likely that major league baseball, as a group, would consistently misevaluate the relative importance of specific components of the game across all major-league players as Baseball-Reference's fielding numbers (and most other sabermetric fielding measures) implicitly claim.

I take a more systematic look at how player salaries compare to pW-L records next.

Salary vs. pWORL: Measuring Player Value

In my day job, I am an economist. In economics, the definition of "value" is very straightforward. The "value" of a good or service is whatever somebody is willing to pay for it. Applying this to baseball players, the economic "value" of baseball players can be measured by what baseball owners are willing to pay them.

There are a number of reasons why this may not be a particularly useful "value" measure of major league baseball players.

- Players' salaries are set in advance based on expected, not actual, performance.
- The economic value of player performance may not be constant across all teams and all situations. For example, a team's 85th win, which could significantly improve the team's playoff prospects could be more valuable than a win that improves a team from 61–101 to 62–100. As Branch Rickey reportedly said about Ralph Kiner and the 1953 Pittsburgh Pirates, "We finished last with you, we can finish last without you."
- Finally, and perhaps most importantly, the labor market for major league baseball players is not an entirely free market. Players are restricted to their original team—and American players are assigned to their original team via a draft—until they have accumulated six years of major-league experience, so that "what baseball owners are willing to pay" players may be considerably more than what baseball owners actually do pay players.

Because of this, it is probably not a good idea to attempt to estimate either the value of an individual player based on that player's salary or even, necessarily, to attempt to draw conclusions about the marginal dollar value of a win from overall player salaries.

What may be reasonable, however, is to use relative salaries as a basis for measuring the relative value placed on different aspects of baseball player value by major-league general managers.

Sean Lahman produces an annual database of baseball statistics which he makes available on the Internet. The last version of the database which I downloaded included data on player salaries for many (probably most) players from 1985 to 2014. I have added these salaries to my database. The next table compares the distribution of player value and player salary by the four basic factors for which player value is accumulated: batting, baserunning, pitching, and fielding. Player salaries are distributed across the four factors in proportion to their relative proportion of that player's value.

The table has four columns. The first two represent the distribution of pW-L records.

The first column is calculated based simply on the sum of pWins and pLosses. The second column is based on pWins over replacement level (pWORL). The numbers here only include players for whom I have salary data.

The last two columns then are calculated based on two measures of salary. The first is simply total salary. The second is salary above the minimum (which was $500,000 in 2014). My thinking is that this would correspond to wins over replacement level: replacement-level players are not technically "freely available," they're available for the major-league minimum.

| | *Player Decisions* | | *Salary* | |
Factor	Total	over Repl	Total	over Min
Batting	46.9%	40.7%	42.0%	42.6%
Baserunning	4.2%	3.6%	3.4%	3.4%
Pitching	30.9%	41.2%	40.1%	39.5%
Fielding	18.0%	14.5%	14.5%	14.5%

I think that the relevant comparison is between the second (pWORL) and fourth (Salary above Minimum) columns. Overall, the share of salary paid seems fairly close to the share of value for all four factors, although batting appears to be somewhat over-valued and pitching somewhat under-valued, in terms of salaries.

As I mentioned earlier, major league baseball players' salaries are limited in their earliest seasons, and players are not eligible for free agency—and, hence, a fully free labor market—until they have played six full major-league seasons. To account for this, the next table only includes players whose major-league debut was at least 7 years before the season in question (my thinking is that most players don't play a full season in their first year, so most players will have appeared in parts of seven seasons before qualifying for free agency).

| | *Player Decisions* | | *Salary* | |
Factor	Total	over Repl	Total	over Min
Batting	49.9%	43.7%	43.7%	43.8%
Baserunning	4.2%	3.7%	3.4%	3.4%
Pitching	28.4%	38.1%	38.4%	38.2%
Fielding	17.5%	14.4%	14.5%	14.5%

Focusing only on veteran players here, the salary mix between batting, baserunning, pitching, and fielding (over the minimum) is nearly perfect as compared to the mix of value as measured by pW-L records (over replacement level). As an economist, I could not ask for a better endorsement of pW-L records than that table.

9. Win Probabilities

The basic concept that underlies my construction of pW-L records is the concept of Win Probability, which, as far as I know, was first developed by Eldon and Harlan Mills in 1969 and published in their book, *Player Win Averages*. The concept has been developed further by many people over the years. Notable proponents of Win Probability Advancement concepts in recent years include Tom Tango, Dave Studenmund at the Hardball Times, Keith Woolner at Baseball Prospectus (*Baseball Prospectus 2005*), and many others (e.g., Fangraphs, Baseball Prospectus). This list is not close to being exhaustive.

The basic concept underlying win probability systems is elegantly simple. At any point in time, the situation in a baseball game can be uniquely described by considering the inning, the number and location of any baserunners, the number of outs, and the difference in score between the two teams. Given these four things, one can calculate a probability of each team winning the game. Hence, at the start of a batter's plate appearance, one can calculate the probability of the batting team winning the game. After the completion of the batter's plate appearance, one can once again calculate the probability of the batting team winning the game. The difference between these two probabilities, typically called the Win Probability Advancement or something similar, is the value added by the offensive team during that particular plate appearance (where such value could, of course, be negative).

If we assume that the two teams are evenly matched, then the initial probability of winning is 50% for each team. At the end of the game, the probability of one team winning will be 100%, while the probability of the other team winning will be 0%. The sum of the Win Probability Advancements for a particular team will add up to exactly 50% for a winning team (100% minus 50%) and exactly –50% for a losing team (0% minus 50%). Hence, Win Probability Advancement is a perfect accounting structure for allocating credit for team wins and losses to individual players.

This basic concept is used here to develop pW-L records for individual players based upon their contributions during major league baseball games. The technical calculation of Win Probabilities is described in this Chapter.

Understanding Win Probabilities

Win Probabilities are a very popular analytical tool. They are also an important component in my construction of pW-L records. It is important, however, to understand that win probabilities have two very distinct purposes, which require different assumptions.

First, win probabilities can be used to assess specific in-game strategies. What is the cost/benefit of intentionally walking Mike Trout? When does it make sense to attempt to steal home in the bottom of the ninth inning of a tie game? To properly answer these questions, one needs to evaluate the actual win probabilities that exist, given the actual players involved. In other words, the question of whether to walk Trout depends not simply on the location of the baserunners, the number of outs, the score, and the inning, it also depends on who the on-deck hitter is, who the pitcher is, who's available in the bullpen, maybe even how the wind is blowing. Here, the specifics of who is involved are crucial to making a proper evaluation.

Alternatively, however, win probabilities can be used as a tool to help one evaluate the value of individual players. This is what I am doing here, creating a value-based system using win probabilities. In order to evaluate the value of individual players, however, I need to begin by assuming that everybody is average. That is, the probability of winning when batting with runners on 1st and 2nd, one out, in a tie game in the last of the ninth has to be the same for everybody. If I calculate a unique probability for every player based on what his actual performance was, then I'll just find that everybody is a 0.500 player—everybody is exactly as valuable as an average player, if the average player is him. The key here is to assume that everybody is average—for the league as a whole. A player's value, measured in this way, doesn't depend, therefore, on the quality of the on-deck hitter, or the speed of the baserunners, or even on the quality of the pitcher. One could, and perhaps should, attempt to adjust for such things—that is, a 0.500 hitter who faced above-average pitching is better than a 0.500 hitter who faced below-average pitching. I have made some attempts to make some adjustments of this nature, although other such adjustments are beyond the scope of my research thus far.

In fact, however, I believe that this initial round of research that I have done here is a necessary first step before one could begin to accurately make such adjustments.

Looking at win probabilities in these two ways can lead to different results. For example, there may be a situation (say, runner on first, nobody out) where a successful sacrifice bunt reduces win probability for an average hitter (i.e., the expected win probability is lower with a runner on second and one out than with a runner on first and nobody out). In that same situation, however, a successful bunt may well increase the expected win probability for some hitters (e.g., a bad-hitting but good-bunting pitcher with a tendency to ground into double plays, with an excellent lead-off hitter coming up next). In such a case, a value-based system such as I have devised here will assign a negative value (i.e., player losses) to the latter hitter for sacrificing, even though, given who he is, a bunt may have been the right strategic decision. While this may seem wrong, in fact, it is perfectly reasonable. The only reason why the bunt was the right decision for that hitter was because he was a below-average hitter. This should be reflected in the value of that player. His ability to bunt will be credited to him, insofar as the losses charged for the sacrifice bunt will be less than the expected losses that would have been charged had he not bunted, but still, from the team's overall perspective, the bunt was not a positive event—it cost the team an out. The team suffered because this was a below-average hitter, and this is properly reflected in the value assigned to this player.

By the same token, however, one should be cautious about using average win probabilities to assess the value of specific events. For example, it is often noted that there are very few situations where Win Probabilities say that the correct average event is to sacrifice bunt. This is true. Of course, this is why sacrifice bunts are never attempted in most situations and are only rarely used in most other situations. To use average win probabilities to assess whether a particular strategy was a good idea or not misses, in my opinion, the point. Strategies are chosen for specific plays, based on the specific players involved.

For example, in my research, I have found that, on average, in most seasons (but not for the last several seasons), stolen base attempts are slight net negative events—total player wins from successful stolen bases are slightly less than total player losses from being caught stealing and picked off. Does this mean that teams and/or players' specific decisions to attempt to steal bases were bad, on average, or, at the extreme, that players should just never bother attempting a stolen base? Not necessarily. You would have to look at the specific players involved—the pitcher, the on-deck hitter, and the day-specific game conditions—to be able to say whether or not a specific stolen base attempt was a good or a bad play. Ditto for intentional walks, sacrifice bunt attempts, and any other strategic decisions employed by teams.

Calculating Win Probabilities

The basic concept of win probability posits that the situation in a baseball game can be uniquely described by considering the inning, the number and location of any baserunners, the number of outs, and the difference in score between the two teams. Given these four things, one can calculate a probability of each team winning the game.

The most obvious way to calculate win probabilities would be based purely on empirical observations, i.e., to determine the probability of a team winning when they lead by 4 runs with runners on 2nd and 3rd base with two outs in the top of the 8th inning, one could simply look at every time that a team has had runners on 2nd and 3rd base with two outs and a four-run lead in the top of the eighth inning and calculate what percentage of those teams ended up winning those games.

This approach has several problems. Because of the relative infrequency of many events, such a technique will lead to idiosyncratic results, whereby positive events may inadvertently decrease win probabilities or negative events may inadvertently increase win probabilities.

Compounding this problem, the true probability of winning in any given situation depends on the run-scoring environment in which the game is taking place. A 2-run lead was much easier to overcome in Coors Field in the late 1990s than it would have been in Dodger Stadium in the mid–1960s. Because of this, an ideal system would use a unique win probability matrix for each ballpark for each season to reflect differences in run-scoring environment. This is all but impossible using direct empirical observation, however, because of severe data limitations.

Finally, a system that makes empirical calculations based on the score-differential and the inning cannot begin with an assumption that the initial probability of winning is 50% for each team. This is because home teams actually win about 54% of major-league baseball games. Hence, teams that bat with nobody on and nobody out in a tie game in the top of the first inning do not win 50% of the time; they only win about 46% of the time.

This is a problem, however, if one's goal is to accurately and completely account for all of a team's wins and allocate them to the players on the team. In effect, the team's home ballpark will get some credit for home wins (and take some of the blame for road losses). But, the reason that more teams win at home is because players tend to play better at home: hitters tend to hit better at home and pitchers tend to pitch better at home, regardless of where home is. But, it seems clear to me that the players should get credit for this.

Hence, empirical calculations based on historical results using score-differential and inning are not, in my opinion, a proper starting point for calculating the win probabilities necessary to construct pW-L records.

In fact, however, the only empirical observations one needs to calculate a complete set of win probabilities are what I call a Base-Out Transition Matrix: the position of the baserunners and the number of outs before and after an event (typically a plate appearance). Given a Base-Out Transition Matrix, one can impute a full Win-Probability matrix in four "easy" steps.

1. Given a Base-Out Transition Matrix, one can compute a Base-Out Probability Matrix.
2. Given a Base-Out Probability Matrix, one can compute a Run Probability Matrix.
3. Given a Run Probability Matrix, one can compute an Inning Probability Matrix.
4. Given a Run Probability Matrix and an Inning Probability Matrix, one can compute a Win Probability Matrix.

Base-Out Probability Matrix

The basic base-out transition matrix is 24 rows by 28 columns (24 × 28). The 24 rows identify the number of outs (0, 1, or 2) and the position of the baserunners (8 possibilities, identified here as 0, 1, 2, 3, 1–2, 1–3, 2–3, and 1–2–3) at the beginning of the event. The 28 columns identify the number of outs and the position of the baserunners at the end of the event. The four additional columns represent the additional possibility that this event results in the third out of the inning. The third out gets four columns to also reflect the number of runs which score on the play (0, 1, 2, or 3—a team cannot score more than 3 runs while also making the third out). This breakdown of third-out plays is important in the next step, converting the base-out transition matrix to a run-probability matrix.

Throughout my work, I refer to base-out states in the following format (o,b/r), where o is the number of outs, and b/r is either the position of the baserunners, or the number of runs scored on the play if o is equal to 3. For example (0,0) indicates no outs and the bases empty (1,2) indicates one out and a runner on second base (2,2–3) indicates two outs and runners on second and third base, and (3,1) indicates three outs with one run scoring on the play on which the third out was recorded.

The initial base-out transition matrix simply includes the number of occurrences of a particular event in each cell. That is, the value in row (0,0), column (0,0) is equal to the number of times a plate appearance began with nobody on and nobody out and ended with nobody on and nobody out (i.e., in this particular example, this is the number of times a batter hit a home run leading off an inning).

The first step in converting the base-out transition matrix into a win-probability matrix is to convert the base-out transition matrix into a base-out probability matrix.

The base-out probability matrix is also 24 rows by 28 columns. Here, the value of each cell (r,c) is equal to the probability that a play will end in base-out state c, given that it started in base-out state r. The base-out transition matrix is converted into a base-out probability matrix by simply dividing the value in each cell of the base-out transition matrix by the sum of the values for that row of the base-out transition matrix. Hence, each row of the base-out probability matrix will sum to 100% by construction.

Individual base-out transition matrices are actually constructed for each individual ballpark for each individual season for which pW-L records are calculated as described in Chapter 10.

Run Probability Matrix

The second step in converting a base-out transition matrix into a win-probability matrix is to convert the base-out probability matrix into a run-probability matrix. That is, given the initial base-out state, what is the probability of scoring exactly zero runs over the remainder of the inning, what is the probability of scoring exactly one run, what is the probability of scoring exactly two runs, etc.?

If all of the events within the base-out probability matrix are plate appearances (i.e., stolen bases, wild pitches, et al. are not considered separate events), then each cell of the base-out probability matrix will generate a specific number of runs scored. The number of runs scored within a particular cell is equal to one (which represents the batter) plus the number of initial baserunners plus the number of initial outs minus the number of baserunners at the end of the play minus the number of outs at the end of the play (if less than three). In words, if the batter and baserunners can't be accounted for as either additional outs or baserunners after the play, then they must have scored. For example, if a play begins with one out and runners on first and second (1,1–2) and ends with two outs and a runner on third (2,3), then the number of runs scored is equal to one (1+2+1−1−2).

Knowing how many runs are scored from a specific event, then, one can calculate the probability of scoring any given number of runs given any initial base-out state. This is done recursively as follows.

We Begin with the Initial State, Two Outs and the Bases Loaded (2,1–2–3)

The probability of scoring exactly zero runs is equal to the probability of transitioning from (2,1–2–3) to (3,0) (i.e., 3 outs, zero runs scored), because any other transition will necessarily involve at least one run scoring.

As an example, on average, between 2000 and 2006, the probability of this happening was 66.81%.

Next, consider the initial state (2,2–3)

The probability of scoring exactly zero runs is equal to the probability of transitioning from (2,2–3) to (3,0) PLUS the probability of transitioning from (2,2–3) to (2,1–2–3) (which produces no runs scored) times the probability of scoring zero runs from

(2,1–2–3) (which was solved for above). Again, any other final base-out state except for these two will have involved at least one run scoring.

Between 2000 and 2006, the major-league-wide probability of transitioning from (2,2–3) to (3,0) was 58.63%, the probability of transitioning from (2,2–3) to (2,1–2–3) was 20.51%, and the probability of scoring zero runs from (2,1–2–3) was 66.81% (as stated earlier). Hence, the probability of scoring zero runs from an initial base-out state of (2,2–3) is equal to 58.63% plus (20.51% times 66.81%) for a total probability of 72.33%.

Continuing Onward, We Can Work Up to the Initial State (2,1)—Two Out and a Runner on First

The probability of scoring exactly zero runs is equal to the probability of transitioning from (2,1) to (3,0) plus the probability of transitioning from (2,1) to (2,1–2) times the probability of scoring zero runs from (2,1–2) plus the probability of transitioning from (2,1) to (2,1–3) times the probability of scoring zero runs from (2,1–3), ….

Eventually, one works back recursively to the initial state (0,0)—nobody on and nobody out. The probability of scoring zero runs is equal to the sum of the product of the probabilities of transitioning to each base-out state for which no runs score (i.e., any base-out state except for (0,0), which would produce one run) times the probability of scoring exactly zero runs from that base-out state. This works, without creating any kind of circular logic because, for every base-out transition state, if the initial and final base-out transition states are the same, then a run must score.

Having done this for zero runs scored, one can then do the same thing for one run scored. For any given base-out state, the probability of scoring exactly one run is equal to the sum of the product of the probabilities of transitioning to a state that generates exactly one run times the probability of scoring exactly zero runs from that state plus the sum of the product of the probabilities of transitioning to a state that generates exactly zero runs times the probability of scoring exactly one run from that state.

Generalizing further, the probability of scoring exactly X runs (for X greater than or equal to four) is equal to the sum of the product of the probabilities of transitioning to a state that generates exactly four runs times the probability of scoring exactly X–4 runs from that state, plus the sum of the product of the probabilities of transitioning to a state that generates exactly three runs times the probability of scoring exactly X–3 runs from that state, plus the sum of the product of the probabilities of transitioning to a state that generates exactly two runs times the probability of scoring exactly X–2 runs from that state, plus the sum of the product of the probabilities of transitioning to a state that generates exactly one run times the probability of scoring exactly X–1 runs from that state, plus the sum of the product of the probabilities of transitioning to a state that generates no runs times the probability of scoring exactly X runs from that state.

It is theoretically possible to score any number of runs in a single inning, even an infinite number of runs. As a practical consideration, however, in my work, I calculate exact probabilities, as outlined above, for scoring anywhere from 0 to 14 runs. I then estimate the probability of scoring exactly 15 runs as simply being equal to 1 minus the sum of all of the other probabilities. The choice of 15 runs was chosen arbitrarily as being sufficiently large that the probability of scoring 15 runs, calculated in this way, was always calculated to be less than the probability of scoring 14 runs, calculated correctly.

Once the run-probability matrix is constructed, an inning-probability matrix is constructed showing the probability of a team winning given the score differential at the start of an inning.

Inning Probability Matrix

Once the run-probability matrix is constructed, what I call an inning-probability matrix can be constructed, based upon the run-probabilities for the base-out state (0,0) — nobody on and nobody out. As with the run-probability matrix, the inning-probability matrix is constructed recursively.

The probability of a team winning that is trailing by X runs leading off the bottom of the ninth inning (or later) is equal to the probability of scoring X+1 or more runs given a base-out state of (0,0) plus 50% times the probability of scoring exactly X runs given a base-out state of (0,0).

So, for example, the probability of a team winning that is trailing by one run leading off the bottom of the ninth inning is equal to the probability of scoring 2 or more runs given a base-out state of (0,0) — 13.69% on average from 2000 to 2006 — plus 50% times the probability of scoring exactly 1 run (15.58%), for an overall probability of 21.48%. The probability of a team winning that is trailing by two runs leading off the bottom of the ninth inning was equal to 10.00% over this same time period.

Working backwards, the probability of a team winning if they lead by, say, one run leading off the top of the ninth is equal to the probability of scoring exactly zero runs times (one minus the probability of the batting team winning if they trail by one run entering the last of the ninth), plus the probability of scoring exactly one run times (one minus the probability of the batting team winning if they trail by two runs entering the last of the ninth), plus the probability of scoring exactly two runs times (one minus the probability of a team winning if they trail by three runs entering the last of the ninth), ..., plus the probability of scoring fifteen runs times (one minus the probability of a team winning if they trail by sixteen runs entering the last of the ninth).

For major league baseball from 2000 to 2006, this becomes 70.73% times (1–21.48%) plus 15.58% times (1–10.00%) plus 7.36% times (1–4.58%) plus 3.49% times (1–2.03%) plus 1.61% times (1–0.87%) plus ... 0.00% times (1–0). If one works through the arithmetic, then, the probability of a team winning when leading by one run leading off the top of the ninth inning was equal to 82.82% on average over this time period.

In actuality, teams won 84.74% of the time when leading by exactly one run leading off the top of the ninth inning between 2000 and 2006. I suspect that this difference is because teams are more likely to use their closer to pitch the bottom of the ninth inning in such a situation and the average major-league closer is an above-average pitcher. It seems to me to be entirely appropriate to credit this above-average win probability to the above-average pitchers who are responsible for it.

Given the probabilities for the top of the ninth, one can calculate probabilities for the bottom of the eighth using the same logic as the preceding paragraph. Repeating this, one can ultimately work all the way back to the probability of winning leading off the top of the first inning (50%, by construction, as is the probability of winning leading off the top of any inning when the score is tied).

A complete win-probability matrix can then be constructed from an inning-probability matrix and a run-probability matrix.

Win Probability Matrix

Given an inning-probability matrix, giving the probability of winning given the score differential at the start of any inning, and a run-probability matrix, which gives the probability of scoring any number of runs through the end of the given inning given the current base-out state, one can build a complete win-probability matrix.

Given a run differential of r, an initial base-out state b, and half-inning j, the probability of the batting team winning is equal to the probability of scoring exactly zero runs times the probability of the half-inning j batting team winning given a run differential of r leading off half-inning j+1 (i.e., one minus the probability of the team batting in half-inning j+1 winning given a run differential of –r), plus the probability of scoring one run times the probability of the half-inning j batting team winning given a run differential of r+1 leading off half-inning j+1, plus the probability of scoring exactly two runs times the probability of the half-inning j batting team winning given a run differential of r+2 leading off half-inning j+1, plus the probability of scoring exactly three runs times the probability of the half-inning j batting team winning given a run differential of r+3 leading off half-inning j+1, plus the probability of scoring exactly four runs times the probability of the half-inning j batting team winning given a run differential of r+4 leading off half-inning j+1, ..., plus the probability of scoring exactly fifteen runs times the probability of the half-inning j batting team winning given a run differential of r+15 leading off half-inning j+1.

The final win-probability matrices used here are 432 rows (24 initial base-out states times 18 half-innings) by 31 columns (run differential of –15 to +15, including zero). The win-probabilities for extra innings are identical to those for the ninth inning—both top and bottom.

Individual win-probability matrices are actually constructed for each individual ballpark for each individual season for which pW-L records are calculated. The construction of ballpark-specific win-probability matrices are described in Chapter 10.

Pennants Won

The job of a major league baseball player is to help his team win games, for the ultimate purpose of making the playoffs and winning the World Series. That is the first sentence of this book. And it's true. So, logically, if the goal of a team is to make the playoffs and win the World Series, shouldn't we be measuring how a player contributes to that goal, not simply the goal of winning individual games?

The concept of Win Probability that underlies my work here begins with the assumption that not all runs are created equal. A run in the ninth inning of a tie game is more valuable than a run in the ninth inning of a blowout. But, by the same token, not all wins are created equal. A win over your closest division rival when you are tied for the division lead with two games left in the season is obviously worth a lot more than a win over a 100-loss team in the middle of July. Given this, wouldn't it make sense to move from Win Probabilities to Pennant Probabilities, judging players based on how they increase their team's odds of winning the pennant?

There is certainly some merit to this argument. At a basic level, it is certainly logically compelling. I have chosen to not evaluate Pennant Probabilities here, however. My reason for this decision is a fundamental difference between Win Probabilities and Pennant Probabilities. This difference is best illustrated by an example.

From 1949 to 1958, the New York Yankees won 9 pennants. In those 9 pennant-winning seasons, they won between 92 and 99 games every year. The only season over that time period when the Yankees won over 100 games was in 1954, when the Yankees won 103 games. The 1954 Yankees, however, despite winning more games than any Yankee team between 1942 and 1961, was the only Yankees team between 1949 and 1958 to not win the pennant. Why? Because they had the misfortune to play in the same league as a Cleveland Indians team that won a then–American League record 111 games that year.

The 1953 New York Yankees split their season series with the Cleveland Indians, 11-11, but went 88-41 against the rest of the league, while the Indians went 81-51 against the same teams and finished 8½ games behind the Yankees. The 1954 Yankees again split their season series with the Cleveland Indians, 11-11, and improved their record against the rest of the American League to 92-40. But the 1954 Indians went an astounding 100-32 against the rest of the American League and beat the Yankees by 8 games.

The 1954 Yankees did more to ensure themselves a pennant than the 1953 Yankees did. They played equally well against their chief rival and played better against the rest of the American League.

With Win Probabilities, the sum of the contributions of the players on a team will always add up to 50% when a team wins a game and to –50% when a team loses. Win Probabilities are a perfect accounting structure for team wins and losses.

Pennant Probabilities are not and cannot be a perfect accounting structure for team pennants. The 1954 Yankees did more to contribute to a pennant than the 1953 Yankees. The reason that the 1954 Yankees did not win a pennant had nothing to do with the 1954 New York Yankees and everything to do with the 1954 Cleveland Indians. The 1954 New York Yankees lost the pennant because the Cleveland Indians improved from 9-13 against the Boston Red Sox in 1953 to 20-2 against the Red Sox in 1954.

So who gets the Pennant Losses for the 1954 Yankees? The Red Sox? The 1954 Yankees won more games against the Red Sox (13) than had the 1953 pennant winners (11). The Indians? Certainly, the Indians deserve credit for doing what they needed to do to win the pennant in 1954. But the Yankees did more in 1954 than they had the year before, too. From 1947 to 1967, the only American League team other than the Yankees to win more than 103 games was the 1954 Cleveland Indians. If the 1954 and 1959 Yankees teams (the latter of which went 79-75 and finished in 3rd place) traded places, the Yankees would have won one more pennant in the 1950s (the pennant-winning 1959 Chicago White Sox had the same record in both 1954 and 1959: 94-60).

If we think about the 1953 Yankees and the 1954 Yankees as both starting the season with a 12.5% (1 in 8) chance of winning the pennant, there's simply going to be no way to fairly allocate +87.5% Pennants Added to the 1953 Yankees and –12.5% Pennants Added to the 1954 Yankees, when the 1954 Yankees out-performed the 1953 Yankees in every meaningful way in which they controlled their own fate. Teams that split with their closest rival and play 0.669 baseball for the season will win the pennant far more often than they will lose it.

From 1900 to 1968 (when winning a pennant involved simply having the best regular season record), only 27 teams had better winning percentages than the 1954 Yankees. And of those 27 teams, only 2—the 1909 Chicago Cubs and 1942 Brooklyn Dodgers—failed to win a pennant. In fact, after the Yankees you have to go down to the 45th best winning percentage during these years—the 1915 Detroit Tigers—to find the next best non-pennant winner. Moreover, in all three of these cases, the Cubs, Dodgers, and Tigers all lost the season series to the team that won the pennant (the Pirates, Cardinals, and Red Sox, respectively). The odds of the 1954 Yankees winning the pennant was certainly greater than 90% and given that they split with the Indians (and won the season series from everybody else) was probably greater than 95%.

But what good is a Pennants Added system that gives the 1954 Yankees the +80% or so Pennants Added that they likely deserve, when, after all, they didn't actually win the pennant? Not much, and that's why I don't use one.

Am I saying that players do not deserve extra credit for performing better against their team's top rivals? Not at all. I am simply saying that I do not believe there is a simple objective means of evaluating how much credit that should be worth. Should players get bonus points for making the playoffs? All other things being equal, sure. Within a season, I can see valuing a playoff-making performance over a non-playoff performance.

But the 1980 Baltimore Orioles won 100 games while the 1987 Minnesota Twins won 85 games. Even though the Twins won a World Series, I find it hard to blame the Orioles for having the misfortune of being in the same division in the same year as a New York Yankees team that won 103 games (especially since the Orioles actually won their season series from the Yankees 7–6). I suppose you can blame the Orioles for not going 9–4 against the Yankees (which would have given them the division title with 102 wins to 101 for the Yankees) but ultimately the requirements for making the playoffs change every year and, more importantly, are not known until the season is over.

And, how fair is a system that punishes the Orioles for only going 7–6 against their closest rival, while rewarding the Twins for going 5–8 against their closest rival (the Kansas City Royals, who would have beaten the Twins if they could have only gone 10–3 against them that year)?

As the season is unfolding, all a player can do is work toward winning the game at hand, taking the season day by day and game by game. And ultimately, that is what is reflected in the pW-L records that I have developed here.

10. Ballpark Adjustments to Player Won-Lost Records

In this chapter, I discuss how I control for differences across ballparks and how pW-L records can help to identify and are influenced by ballpark effects.

Controlling for Ballpark Effects: Constructing Ballpark-Specific Base-Out Transition Matrices

The core of my pW-L records is the concept of win probability. The probability of winning, given a base-out-score-inning state, is very much dependent on time and place. Individual positive offensive events are less valuable in higher-offense environments than in lower-offense environments. Hence, the win probability matrix to be used within a particular baseball game should be specific to the specific league (by which I intend to differentiate between, for example, the 2004 American League and the 2004 National League as well as the 2003 American League and the 2004 American League), and the specific ballpark in which the game takes place. For example, as estimated by me, a team had a 30% chance of winning a game in which they trailed by one run entering the bottom of the ninth inning if the game was played in Coors Field in 2000, whereas a team had only an 14.5% chance of winning the same game if it were played in Dodger Stadium in 1968. (These percentages are for an average team in the 2000 National League and 1968 National League, respectively, not specifically for the 2000 Rockies and 1968 Dodgers.)

I construct a unique base-out transition matrix—from which I construct a unique win-probability matrix—for each ballpark, for each year, for each league that I consider.

Why 1 Year?

The use of one-year ballpark factors is fairly widely disdained in sabermetric circles as being generally inappropriate because of the large degree of noise which is inherent in a single year's worth of data. If one's primary purpose is prospective, then I think that this is probably true. Even if one's primary purpose is explanatory, if one is only considering a single-value run factor along the lines of "Ballpark A increases runs scored by 5%," then the noise inherent in a single season of data might well be sufficiently large that one would be better off using a multi-year park factor.

In fact, however, I am doing neither of these things. My purpose is explanatory—I am measuring the value of what actually happened—but I am looking at a much finer level of detail of data than simply looking at runs scored. As such, my "sample size" for a particular ballpark is not the 800–900 runs that were scored at that ballpark that year, but instead is the 6,000–7,000 plate appearances that took place at that ballpark that year.

The purpose of pW-L records is to measure the actual value of individual baseball players. That actual value, however, depends on what a ballpark actually did, not what it averaged. Technically, day-specific base-out transition matrices would be appropriate if possible, but, alas, they are not. There are many reasons why the run-scoring environment of a ballpark may change from year to year including,

1. the league's run-scoring environment may change,
2. the efficiency of run-scoring may change (i.e., the expected runs (XR, RC, whatever) may not change, but the actual runs do, perhaps because teams hit better or worse than expected with runners in scoring position, for example),
3. the conditions of the ballpark may change (wind, temperature, change in field dimensions), or
4. hitters (or pitchers) may simply perform somewhat differently from one year to another.

For many purposes, it may be desirable to try to remove some of these reasons, particularly numbers 2 and 4. For my purposes, however, *all* of these reasons are valid reasons and will legitimately affect the win probabilities.

Having said that, it is still extremely important to attempt to control for anomalous results as much as possible in constructing ballpark-specific base-out transition matrices, and it is important to utilize as much data as possible. The technique I use to construct ballpark-specific base-out transition matrices is outlined next.

Constructing a Ballpark-Specific Base-Out Transition Matrix

STEP 1

The first step in constructing a ballpark-specific base-out transition matrix is to construct a league-wide base-out transition matrix. Call this BO_L.

For a particular ballpark, call it ballpark p, find all team combos that met in this ballpark as well as in at least one other ballpark. Teams that only played each other in one ballpark are not used in this calculation. In addition, inter-league games are not used here, since games played at American League ballparks use the designated hitter rule while games played at National League ballparks do not, which affects the relative run-scoring environments of the two leagues. To be precise, I consider all games played in American League ballparks to be "American League" games and all games played in National League ballparks to be "National League" games. Hence, inter-league games played between two teams at an American League ballpark are not considered to be in the same "league" as games played between the same two teams at a National League ballpark.

STEP 2

For each team combination within the same league which met in ballpark p and at least one other ballpark, calculate a base-out transition matrix for all of their games against each other in ballpark p. For teams j and k, call this BO^p_{jk}. Construct a second base-out transition matrix, then, for all games between teams j and k that did not take place in ballpark p. Call this matrix $(BO')^p_{jk}$.

STEP 3

Re-size each of these base-out transition matrices so that all of the BO^p_{jk} and $(BO')^p_{jk}$, for all teams j and k, are the same size (by "size" I mean they should include the same number of events—i.e., plate appearances). That is, multiply each element of BO^p_{jk} by the ratio of the desired number of elements (call it E) to the raw number of elements in BO^p_{jk}. For example, suppose that BO^p_{jk} was a 3-by-3 matrix as shown below (in reality, BO^p_{jk} will be a 24-by-28 matrix):

$$\begin{matrix} 13 & 5 & 10 \\ 8 & 2 & 2 \\ 11 & 6 & 3 \end{matrix}$$

The size of BO^p_{jk} in this example is 60 (13+5+10+8+2+2+11+6+3). If the value of E to which one wanted to re-size this matrix was 12, then each element of this matrix would be multiplied by (12/60) = 0.2. Hence, the re-sized matrix would be the following:

$$\begin{matrix} 2.6 & 1.0 & 2.0 \\ 1.6 & 0.4 & 0.4 \\ 2.2 & 1.2 & 0.6 \end{matrix}$$

STEP 4

Sum all BO^p_{jk} for ballpark p (the ballpark of interest here). Call this BO_p. This is, in effect, a home-game transition matrix for ballpark p.

Re-size this sum, BO_p, to be the same size as each of the $(BO')^p_{jk}$. Sum all of the $(BO')^p_{jk}$ and the re-sized BO_p, and call this $(BO')_p$. The home-game transition matrix, BO_p, is included here with the same weight as other ballparks. This creates, in effect, a league-wide transition matrix for the teams that played in ballpark p $(BO')_p$.

STEP 5

Now, re-size BO_p and $(BO')_p$ so that they are both the same size as BO_L. The initial estimate of the base-out transition matrix for ballpark p is then equal to the following:

$$BO_p = BO_L + (BO_p - (BO')_p)$$

In some cases, the difference $(BO_p - (BO')_p)$ may be very large relative to BO_L for some cells. At the extreme, in fact, it is theoretically possible that $(BO_p - (BO')_p)$ may be a negative number which is greater in absolute value than BO_L. Hence, it is theoretically possible for some cells of BO_p to become negative given this formula. This problem is avoided by restricting the maximum size of the $(BO_p - (BO')_p)$ term. The restriction is that the term $(BO_p - (BO')_p)$ cannot exceed T% of the corresponding cell of BO_L, where T is equal to 1.96 times the (weighted) standard deviation of the percentage difference between $(BO_p - (BO')_p)$ and BO_L for all cells across all of the ballparks of interest (the 1.96 figure was chosen because 95% of all data points will be within 1.96 standard deviations of the mean (zero in this case) for a data series which is normally distributed).

A unique value is calculated for T for every league. For the 2004 National League, for example, T had a value of 78%, so that no element of any ballpark-specific base-out transition matrix could be more than 78% greater or less than 78% less than the league-wide base-out transition matrix. This restriction was binding in about 20% of all cells for the 2004 National League. By construction, these 20% of cells account for approximately 5% of the total events within the league.

Step 6

Finally, after calculating values for BO_p for every ballpark, all of the BO_p matrices are summed, and re-sized, such that the size of the sum of the BO_p matrices is equal to the size of BO_L.

Let n equal the number of ballparks and let BO_{ALL} be the sum of the BO_p. The final base-out transition matrix for ballpark p is then equal to the following:

$$BO_p = BO_p + (BO_L - BO_{ALL}) / n$$

The final term $(BO_L - BO_{ALL}) / n$, is again restricted to be no greater (in absolute value) than the T figure constructed above.

Summary

In words, what I do here is to construct a normalized base-out transition matrix for a ballpark and a normalized base-out transition matrix for all games played by the same teams at all of the ballparks at which they played (in effect, a ballpark-specific league-transition matrix). I then adjust the league base-out transition matrix by the difference between the ballpark-specific transition matrix and this latter transition matrix (i.e., the ballpark-specific league-transition matrix).

This basically becomes my ballpark-specific base-out transition matrix, subject to two general restrictions: (1) that the ballpark-specific matrix can't be too different from the league-wide base-out transition matrix, and (2) that the sum of the ballpark-specific base-out transition matrices should be approximately equal to the league-wide base-out transition matrix.

Ballpark factors based on base-out transition matrices are explored in the remainder of this chapter. First, ballpark run factors are explored. Event-specific component park factors are then explored, as well as road park factors for teams which play unbalanced schedules.

Finally, three additional analyses are undertaken. First, the stability of my ballpark factors across seasons is explored. Next, I look at how the same ballpark played in different leagues. Finally, I look at some park factors for ballparks which only hosted a handful of games.

Ballpark Run Factors

pW-L records are normalized by ballpark. This is done by calculating ballpark-specific win probability matrices, as described above. Ballpark-specific base-out transition matrices are much richer than more traditional ballpark factors, which are typically expressed as a single number representative of the aggregate effect of a ballpark on runs scored, or even than component ballpark factors, which measure the impact of a ballpark on specific events, such as home runs.

Ballpark-specific base-out transition matrices can be converted directly into traditional ballpark factors, however. Each ballpark-specific base-out transition matrix generates a unique expected number of runs scored per inning. The process for converting a base-out transition matrix to a run-probability matrix was described in Chapter 9. These run figures can be compared across ballparks in the same way as traditional ballpark factors. Ballpark-specific base-out transition matrices can also be converted into event-specific component park factors, which are discussed later in this chapter.

Ballpark Run Factors

Calculating run factors for ballparks is incredibly straightforward. Based on the ballpark-specific run probability matrix, one can calculate an expected number of runs scored per half-inning at the particular ballpark. Dividing this number by the average number of runs scored per half-inning for the league as a whole and multiplying by 100 will produce a ballpark-specific run factor.

A set of such numbers for the 2009 National League is shown in the table below. Expected runs below are per team per 9 innings.

Ballpark	*Expected Runs*	*Ballpark Run Factor*
Atlanta: Turner Field	4.27	93.7
Chicago: Wrigley Field	4.89	107.2
Cincinnati: Great American Ballpark	4.53	99.4
Denver: Coors Field	5.39	118.3
Houston: Minute Maid Park	4.25	93.3
Los Angeles: Dodger Stadium	4.18	91.7
Miami: Pro Player Stadium	5.02	110.1
Milwaukee: Miller Field	4.49	98.6
New York: Citi Field	4.14	90.8
Philadelphia: Citizens Bank Ballpark	4.77	104.7
Phoenix: Bank One Ballpark	5.20	114.0
Pittsburgh: PNC Park	4.52	99.2
San Diego: Petco Park	3.53	77.4
San Francisco: Pac Bell Park	4.98	109.2
St. Louis: Busch Stadium II	4.46	97.8
Washington: Nationals Park	4.32	94.8

Team Run Factors

Traditionally, park factors are expressed with respect to teams rather than ballparks (despite their name). That is, the "Park Factor" shown for, say, the 2009 Colorado Rockies at Baseball-Reference.com of 112 measures the average run-scoring context in which the Rockies played, i.e., it is an average of the impact of Coors Field for 81 games and 81 games at other ballparks. Because such a figure is tied to a team rather than a ballpark, I think it is more accurate to describe this as a Team Run Factor.

While I believe Team Run Factors have been calculated by several different people using somewhat different formulae, the general construction is fairly universal. A good description of their version of this process can be found at Baseball-Reference.com. Of note, park run factors are typically converted into team run factors by assuming that a team played all of its road games in an average ballpark (excluding the team's home park). In recent years, however, major league baseball teams tend to play unbalanced schedules, with significantly more games played against inter-division rivals than against teams in other divisions. In such cases, the assumption that a team's road games were played in "average" ballparks may be invalid.

For example, looking at the table above, 3 of the 5 teams in the 2009 NL West played in hitters' parks, including the two most extreme hitters' parks in the 2009 National League: Colorado (118.3) and Arizona (114.0). The NL West is also home to the ballpark with the lowest Ballpark Run Factor, Petco Park in San Diego, with a Ballpark Run Factor of (77.4).

A traditional park factor, which assumed average road parks, would produce a Team Run Factor for the San Diego Padres of about 89 (this compares, for example, to Baseball-Referece.com's Run Factor for the Padres of 90). In fact, however, because of the unbalanced schedule and the preponderance of hitters' parks in its division, I find that the Padres' average road game was played in a park with a Park Run Factor of 103.7. This makes their overall Team Run Factor only 90.6, somewhat closer to neutral (albeit not by all that much).

Nevertheless, while the differences are likely to be small in almost all cases, one can calculate Team Run factors more accurately by taking a weighted average of the Ballpark Run Factors for the ballparks in which teams actually played, where the weights used would be games played. A few cases where Road Run Factors make a difference in assessing player value are discussed later in this chapter.

Team Run Factors, as well as average home and road Ballpark Factors, are shown for 2009 for all 30 major-league teams below. The table also lists the Team Run Factors calculated by Baseball-Reference.com.

Team	Team Run Factor			Baseball-Reference.com Park Factor
	Overall	Home	Road	
American League				
Anaheim	101.1	101.4	100.9	98.5
Baltimore	100.7	101.5	99.9	101.5
Boston	102.0	104.3	99.6	105.5
Chicago	99.2	98.3	100.1	105
Cleveland	95.8	90.6	101.0	95
Detroit	100.3	101.5	99.2	101.5
Kansas City	102.1	105.4	98.7	98
Minnesota	101.0	102.1	99.9	98.5
New York	99.7	100.0	99.4	104
Oakland	97.3	94.4	100.3	99
Seattle	98.8	97.7	100.0	95
Tampa Bay	99.8	98.8	100.9	97.5
Texas	105.4	111.3	99.4	104
Toronto	96.8	92.8	100.8	99.5
National League				
Arizona	106.6	114.0	99.1	105.5
Atlanta	97.2	93.7	100.8	98.5
Chicago	102.7	107.2	98.3	106.5
Cincinnati	99.5	99.4	99.7	100
Colorado	108.3	118.3	98.3	112
Florida	104.3	110.1	98.5	102
Houston	97.4	93.3	101.4	98

| | Team Run Factor | | | Baseball-Reference.com |
Team	Overall	Home	Road	Park Factor
Los Angeles	96.9	91.7	102.2	95.5
Milwaukee	99.1	98.6	99.6	98
New York	95.7	90.8	100.6	97
Philadelphia	101.7	104.7	98.7	100.5
Pittsburgh	99.8	99.2	100.5	98.5
San Diego	90.6	77.4	103.7	90
San Francisco	104.2	109.2	99.2	102
St. Louis	98.5	97.8	99.1	97.5
Washington	97.4	94.8	100.1	100

Baseball-Reference.com park factors are simple averages of batting park factor (BPF) and pitching park factor (PPF).

The Base-Out Team Run Factors (i.e., my team run factors) are generally similar to Baseball-Reference.com's Run Factors. Overall, the simple correlation between Base-Out Team Run Factors and Baseball-Reference.com's Park Factors (which are 3-year park factors) is 0.807. My Home Ballpark Factors correlate slightly better with Baseball-Reference.com's numbers (0.815). The difference between these two correlations is because of my use of team-specific Road Run Factors. The stability of ballpark run factors is addressed later in this chapter.

Event-Specific Park Factors

Beyond simply modeling expected runs scored, ballpark-specific base-out transition matrices enable one to assess more subtle differences between ballparks.

For some events, it is possible to deduce ballpark factors from these base-out transition matrices. For example, in general, a plate appearance which ends with the bases empty and the same number of outs as when the plate appearance started will have been a home run. Hence, one can estimate the relative home run frequencies across ballparks implied by the base-out transition matrices here.

Other less-obvious ballpark effects can also be induced. For example, based on a base-out transition matrix, one could impute park factors associated with on-base percentage (that is, plays that do not result in an out), doubles, triples, and even double plays (although double-play park factors calculated in this way tend to be highly erratic and exhibit only limited year-to-year correlation by ballpark). One could then combine some of these factors (OBP, Doubles, Triples, Home Runs) to make a factor that roughly corresponds to slugging percentage (SLG) (note: this will not be exactly the same as SLG since the OBP factor here doesn't distinguish between singles, walks, and ROE [reached on errors]).

Park factors for all of these things, as well as runs, are presented below for all ballparks for 2009.

Component Park Factors Imputed from Base-Out Transition Matrices: 2009
American League

City	Ballpark	Runs	OBP	SLG
Anaheim	Angel Stadium	101.4	100.5	101.5
Arlington	Rangers Ballpark	111.3	106.6	108.3

City	Ballpark	Runs	OBP	SLG
Baltimore	Oriole Park at Camden Yards	101.5	99.7	101.5
Boston	Fenway Park	104.3	97.3	101.1
Chicago	U.S. Cellular Field	98.3	99.6	99.9
Cleveland	Jacobs Field	90.6	97.9	95.1
Detroit	Comerica Park	101.5	101.2	98.2
Kansas City	Kauffman Stadium	105.4	106.8	103.7
Minneapolis	Metrodome	102.1	99.3	98.8
New York	New Yankee Stadium	100.0	101.8	101.8
Oakland	Oakland Coliseum	94.4	96.1	94.7
Seattle	Safeco Field	97.7	99.8	99.0
St. Petersburg	Tropicana Dome	98.8	98.7	99.4
Toronto	Skydome	92.8	94.7	97.0

City	Ballpark	Doubles	Triples	Home Runs	Double Plays
Anaheim	Angel Stadium	96.2	86.0	110.5	103.9
Arlington	Rangers Ballpark	107.6	112.3	114.8	106.3
Baltimore	Oriole Park	99.7	100.9	109.9	90.7
Boston	Fenway Park	119.9	102.6	104.8	99.0
Chicago	U.S. Cellular Field	99.5	97.7	101.4	82.6
Cleveland	Jacobs Field	93.7	89.8	85.9	90.4
Detroit	Comerica Park	95.4	94.4	88.4	97.2
Kansas City	Kauffman Stadium	113.4	106.6	85.2	112.8
Minneapolis	Metrodome	96.7	108.8	97.3	93.1
New York	New Yankee	90.1	100.2	108.7	103.9
Oakland	Oakland Coliseum	93.3	94.9	90.2	103.6
Seattle	Safeco Field	94.8	95.6	98.9	105.9
St. Pete	Tropicana Dome	101.0	107.4	100.2	92.4
Toronto	Skydome	98.8	102.7	103.9	118.2

National League

City	Ballpark	Runs	OBP	SLG
Atlanta	Turner Field	93.7	98.1	96.0
Chicago	Wrigley Field	107.2	101.9	101.1
Cincinnati	Great American Ballpark	99.4	100.1	102.8
Denver	Coors Field	118.3	106.6	107.7
Houston	Minute Maid Park	93.3	100.9	101.0
Los Angeles	Dodger Stadium	91.7	95.2	94.6
Miami	Pro Player Stadium	110.1	105.6	103.2
Milwaukee	Miller Field	98.6	97.7	103.1
New York	Citi Field	90.8	95.7	97.4
Philadelphia	Citizens Bank Ballpark	104.7	101.0	101.2
Phoenix	Bank One Ballpark	114.0	104.8	105.2
Pittsburgh	PNC Park	99.2	100.7	101.5
San Diego	Petco Park	77.4	92.9	89.0
San Francisco	Pac Bell Park	109.2	103.7	102.9
St. Louis	Busch Stadium II	97.8	99.9	97.0
Washington	Nationals Park	94.8	95.2	96.2

City	Ballpark	Doubles	Triples	Home Runs	Double Plays
Atlanta	Turner Field	86.6	89.0	94.2	94.7
Chicago	Wrigley Field	104.4	96.0	96.6	114.5
Cincinnati	Great American	105.8	101.6	113.2	81.5
Denver	Coors Field	114.9	136.5	102.4	101.1
Houston	Minute Maid Park	83.3	97.2	113.6	130.7
Los Angeles	Dodger Stadium	101.1	86.7	89.1	106.9
Miami	Pro Player Stadium	99.0	65.7	102.4	74.6
Milwaukee	Miller Field	107.7	118.2	120.8	97.0

City	Ballpark	Doubles	Triples	Home Runs	Double Plays
New York	Citi Field	92.0	95.1	109.0	86.9
Philadelphia	Citizens Bank	103.7	113.4	98.4	117.8
Phoenix	Bank One Ballpark	121.9	121.5	93.0	103.6
Pittsburgh	PNC Park	99.1	87.2	109.0	100.8
San Diego	Petco Park	78.3	94.8	77.8	116.2
San Fran	Pac Bell Park	109.5	106.4	94.5	94.9
St. Louis	Busch Stadium II	96.3	66.4	90.2	101.2
Washington	Nationals Park	96.4	124.4	95.6	77.9

The next set of numbers are average component park factors since 2000 for those ballparks which have been primary home parks for at least six seasons over this time period.

Component Park Factors Imputed from Base-Out Transition Matrices: 2000–2015

City	Ballpark		Runs	OBP	SLG
Anaheim	Angel Stadium				
		Mean Values	97.8	99.3	98.6
		Std. Deviation	4.2	2.3	2.5
Arlington	Rangers Ballpark				
		Mean Values	104.8	102.1	103.0
		Std. Deviation	5.1	2.4	2.7
Baltimore	Oriole Park at Camden Yards				
		Mean Values	101.7	100.4	100.7
		Std. Deviation	4.4	2.3	2.6
Boston	Fenway Park				
		Mean Values	103.2	101.4	101.8
		Std. Deviation	3.6	2.1	1.8
Chicago	U.S. Cellular Field				
		Mean Values	102.6	100.8	101.8
		Std. Deviation	4.7	2.5	2.8
Cleveland	Jacobs Field				
		Mean Values	97.7	99.7	99.1
		Std. Deviation	4.2	2.7	2.5
Detroit	Comerica Park				
		Mean Values	100.2	100.8	99.4
		Std. Deviation	5.7	2.6	2.8
Kansas City	Kauffman Stadium				
		Mean Values	103.1	101.8	101.4
		Std. Deviation	5.1	2.3	2.7
Minneapolis	Metrodome				
		Mean Values	100.2	99.0	99.3
		Std. Deviation	4.9	2.1	1.7
New York	Yankee Stadium				
		Mean Values	100.9	99.8	100.7
		Std. Deviation	1.8	0.9	0.8
Oakland	Oakland Coliseum				
		Mean Values	95.5	97.7	97.1
		Std. Deviation	4.9	2.3	2.7
Seattle	Safeco Field				
		Mean Values	93.9	97.5	96.4
		Std. Deviation	4.6	2.6	2.5
St. Petersburg	Tropicana Dome				
		Mean Values	97.2	99.1	98.8
		Std. Deviation	4.0	2.0	2.0
Toronto	Skydome				
		Mean Values	100.3	99.2	100.8
		Std. Deviation	3.8	2.6	2.1

City	Ballpark	Doubles	Triples	Home Runs	Double Plays
Anaheim	AngValuesel Stadium				
	Mean Values	96.5	96.2	97.3	99.8
	Std. Deviation	5.1	6.8	7.5	6.6
Arlington	Rangers Ballpark				
	Mean	102.2	108.7	106.1	101.4
	Std. Deviation	6.1	7.1	7.8	7.1
Baltimore	Oriole Park at Camden Yards				
	Mean Values	95.1	95.2	105.7	98.9
	Std. Deviation	6.1	6.4	6.5	6.6
Boston	Fenway Park				
	Mean Values	113.1	98.4	96.8	99.3
	Std. Deviation	4.0	7.2	6.5	6.6
Chicago	U.S. Cellular Field				
	Mean Values	97.3	95.4	109.3	98.0
	Std. Deviation	5.2	7.1	6.0	8.4
Cleveland	Jacobs Field				
	Mean Values	100.2	94.5	96.4	103.3
	Std. Deviation	6.8	7.8	7.2	8.3
Detroit	Comerica Park				
	Mean Values	94.9	107.5	95.9	100.4
	Std. Deviation	5.5	6.9	9.2	7.4
Kansas City	Kauffman Stadium				
	Mean Values	106.8	104.1	96.3	104.8
	Std. Deviation	4.3	8.1	7.6	8.0
Minneapolis	Metrodome				
	Mean Values	100.9	106.0	98.7	99.7
	Std. Deviation	3.3	8.0	3.0	5.1
New York	Yankee Stadium				
	Mean Values	96.4	95.1	107.8	94.4
	Std. Deviation	3.6	6.2	3.8	6.1
Oakland	Oakland Coliseum				
	Mean Values	99.7	100.2	92.5	103.8
	Std. Deviation	6.2	6.8	8.1	6.0
Seattle	Safeco Field				
	Mean Values	94.2	94.4	93.6	100.7
	Std. Deviation	5.2	6.8	7.0	7.1
St. Petersburg	Tropicana Dome				
	Mean Values	97.5	101.9	97.5	95.6
	Std. Deviation	4.6	6.2	6.2	6.8
Toronto	Skydome				
	Mean Values	104.9	101.8	105.0	100.9
	Std. Deviation	6.1	8.6	6.9	9.0

City	Ballpark	Runs	OBP	SLG
Atlanta	Turner Field			
	Mean Values	98.0	100.1	99.4
	Std. Deviation	7.3	2.7	3.2
Chicago	Wrigley Field			
	Mean Values	102.6	100.8	101.5
	Std. Deviation	7.7	2.7	3.6
Cincinnati	Great American Ballpark			
	Mean Values	102.5	99.8	102.5
	Std. Deviation	6.2	2.6	3.1
Denver	Coors Field			
	Mean Values	123.4	108.3	110.8
	Std. Deviation	9.4	3.6	3.7
Houston	Minute Maid Park			
	Mean Values	102.6	100.4	102.1
	Std. Deviation	6.0	2.1	2.8

10. Ballpark Adjustments to Player Won-Lost Records

City	Ballpark	Runs	OBP	SLG
Los Angeles	Dodger Stadium			
	Mean Values	94.7	97.3	97.3
	Std. Deviation	6.2	3.9	3.5
Miami	Pro Player Stadium			
	Mean Values	94.6	99.2	97.1
	Std. Deviation	6.5	2.4	2.7
Milwaukee	Miller Field			
	Mean Values	101.4	99.4	101.6
	Std. Deviation	4.3	2.9	3.0
New York	Shea Stadium			
	Mean Values	95.3	97.8	96.5
	Std. Deviation	4.0	2.7	1.9
New York	Citi Field			
	Mean Values	92.3	96.7	96.7
	Std. Deviation	4.1	2.4	1.8
Philadelphia	Citizens Bank Ballpark			
	Mean Values	102.6	100.5	101.6
	Std. Deviation	4.8	1.8	2.9
Phoenix	Bank One Ballpark			
	Mean Values	107.8	102.4	103.8
	Std. Deviation	7.3	2.8	3.4
Pittsburgh	PNC Park			
	Mean Values	98.9	100.3	99.1
	Std. Deviation	6.2	2.4	3.3
San Diego	Petco Park			
	Mean Values	85.8	95.5	93.3
	Std. Deviation	5.4	2.6	3.9
San Francisco	Pac Bell Park			
	Mean Values	96.2	99.7	97.4
	Std. Deviation	8.6	3.0	4.5
St. Louis	Busch Stadium II			
	Mean Values	95.8	99.4	97.1
	Std. Deviation	2.5	1.4	2.1
Washington	Nationals Park			
	Mean Values	100.5	100.7	100.5
	Std. Deviation	2.9	3.1	2.3

City	Ballpark	Doubles	Triples	Home Runs	Double Plays
Atlanta	Turner Field				
	Mean Values	99.0	96.2	97.1	99.3
	Std. Deviation	10.3	14.0	8.6	9.7
Chicago	Wrigley Field				
	Mean Values	99.4	98.8	106.3	105.6
	Std. Deviation	8.0	15.5	11.9	9.5
Cincinnati	Great American Ballpark				
	Mean Values	97.4	88.2	119.6	100.2
	Std. Deviation	7.1	16.2	9.9	11.1
Denver	Coors Field				
	Mean Values	110.4	130.3	118.5	105.8
	Std. Deviation	6.4	14.2	13.7	10.4
Houston	Minute Maid Park				
	Mean Values	99.2	101.2	111.5	100.7
	Std. Deviation	8.0	13.9	6.1	16.1
Los Angeles	Dodger Stadium				
	Mean Values	93.9	75.4	103.1	97.3
	Std. Deviation	7.4	14.8	9.3	9.5
Miami	Pro Player Stadium				
	Mean Values	94.1	112.2	88.0	89.2
	Std. Deviation	8.5	20.0	8.3	10.8
Milwaukee	Miller Field				

City	Ballpark	Doubles	Triples	Home Runs	Double Plays
	Mean Values	98.9	94.7	113.9	94.4
	Std. Deviation	7.8	17.0	10.9	17.1
New York	Shea Stadium				
	Mean Values	97.5	83.7	93.0	94.7
	Std. Deviation	6.0	18.1	9.7	9.6
New York	Citi Field				
	Mean Values	93.2	92.3	99.3	94.5
	Std. Deviation	4.1	17.0	13.7	10.5
Philadelphia	Citizens Bank Ballpark				
	Mean Values	100.4	92.7	108.6	102.0
	Std. Deviation	6.1	12.5	13.4	10.8
Phoenix	Bank One Ballpark				
	Mean Values	107.1	124.6	104.2	101.1
	Std. Deviation	8.3	16.3	14.1	9.6
Pittsburgh	PNC Park				
	Mean Values	106.1	87.3	91.1	103.8
	Std. Deviation	9.2	13.5	11.4	8.5
San Diego	Petco Park				
	Mean Values	89.4	107.7	84.4	100.8
	Std. Deviation	7.0	12.7	13.3	11.7
San Francisco	Pac Bell Park				
	Mean Values	104.4	113.0	81.0	102.6
	Std. Deviation	8.5	18.2	15.0	7.7
St. Louis	Busch Stadium II				
	Mean Values	97.0	91.0	88.2	100.2
	Std. Deviation	7.8	14.2	7.1	8.3
Washington	Nationals Park				
	Mean Values	104.8	90.4	98.2	107.4
	Std. Deviation	7.6	27.2	12.9	13.5

One thing worth pointing out is that these are aggregate value factors. If, for example, a ballpark generates 10% more home runs than average to left field but 10% fewer home runs than average to right field, this park would show up as having a Home Run Factor here of exactly 100 (assuming the same number of balls hit to left and right field). This is consistent with all of my work here, which attempts to measure pure value, not "true talent." In other words, these numbers do not say that any player who played in a ballpark with a Doubles Factor of 95 (e.g., Florida) and moved to a ballpark with a Doubles Factor of 110 (e.g., Colorado) would be expected to hit 16% more doubles (110 ÷ 95−1). These numbers say that a player who hit 30 doubles in Florida is as valuable (all other things being equal) as a player who hit 35 doubles in Colorado.

One more note here: the numbers here are ballpark factors. That is, the numbers shown above for Colorado refer entirely to games played in Coors Field, not (as park factors are often reported) to all games played by the Colorado Rockies.

The next table shows two ways by which one can measure how stable these sorts of ballpark factors are from year to year.

The first of these is the standard deviation of these ballpark factors across all ballpark-seasons. This is calculated as follows: for every ballpark, average ballpark factors are calculated over the entire life of the ballpark. These are then used as the means in calculating the variance of these factors for each ballpark. That is, if the average home run factor in Anaheim Stadium was 100 over its 40+ year history (and it was), then for each of those 40+ seasons, the value 100 was used as the mean at Anaheim for calculating variance. The average home run factor in Wrigley Field, on the other hand, was 109, so that is used as the mean for calculating variance for seasons at Wrigley.

The second row shows year-to-year correlations for ballpark factors for ballparks that were in existence in consecutive years (e.g., Memorial Stadium in Baltimore in 1979 and 1980, Memorial Stadium in 1980 and 1981, etc.).

Year-to-Year Consistency of Event Ballpark Factors

	Runs	OBP	SLG	D	T	HR	DP
Std Deviation	17.9	16.9	17.0	18.4	20.4	21.2	18.6
Yr-to-Yr Correlation	51.6%	42.0%	56.5%	48.0%	46.8%	59.5%	9.5%

Keep in mind that all of these ballpark factors are expressed relative to all other ballparks. If other ballparks change, we shouldn't expect the ballpark factors of the remaining ballparks to stay unchanged, however. For example, in 1993, the run factors for the 12 National League parks that had been used in 1992 went down by an average of 3.1 with 7 of the 12 parks having lower run factors. The reason for this, of course, was because the National League expanded in 1993, adding a team in Colorado, which played its home games in Mile High Stadium which had a ballpark run factor in 1993 of 133.5. Other, less extreme, changes in ballparks have occurred in the past as well (the opening of Dodger Stadium, the Mariners moving from the Kingdome to Safeco Field, the Braves moving from Milwaukee to Atlanta, etc.).

In addition, I have not gone to the trouble of figuring out when ballparks may have been modified, which could lead to an expected change in ballpark factors. For example, the fences at Hiram Bithorn Stadium were moved out 30 feet between the 2003 and 2004 seasons. This had the perfectly predictable effect of decreasing the home run factor for Hiram Bithorn Stadium from 133 to 86. I'm sure there are other examples of ballparks that were changed in ways that led to predictable and understandable changes in some of these factors.

In other words, there's no reason why we would expect these standard deviations to actually be zero or year-to-year correlations to be 100%. Given this fact, I am quite satisfied with the consistency of most of these results, with the possible exception of double plays.

Road Park Factors

Traditionally, park factors are expressed with respect to teams rather than ballparks (despite their name). That is, the "Park Factor" shown for, say, the 2009 Colorado Rockies at Baseball-Reference.com measures the average run-scoring context in which the Rockies played, i.e., it is an average of the impact of Coors Field for 81 games and 81 games at other ballparks. More specifically, it is calculated assuming 81 games played at Coors Field and 81 games played at an average (non–Coors) ballpark.

Because pW-L records are calculated on a game-by-game basis using ballpark-specific win probability matrices, pW-L records go well beyond this, however, and adjust each individual player's record based on the specific mix of ballparks in which that particular player played. In some cases, this can have a significant impact on a player's apparent performance. Two such cases are discussed next: Roger Clemens in 2004 and Ryan Howard in 2006.

Roger Clemens, 2004

In the 2003–04 offseason, the Houston Astros talked Roger Clemens out of retirement by offering him special considerations to play for the Astros. These considerations included a promise that they would attempt to play him in Houston as much as possible and that he would not have to travel with the Astros on road trips in which he was not scheduled to pitch.

Because of this accommodation, Roger Clemens ended up starting 20 games in Minute Maid Park in 2004 in which he pitched 133 innings, while starting only 13 road games (81⅓ innings pitched).

Roger Clemens posted a traditional won-lost record of 18–4 in 2004, with a 2.98 ERA and won the National League Cy Young Award. His 2.98 ERA was fifth in the National League that year. Adjusting for Houston's team run factor (101 according to Baseball-Reference.com), Clemens's adjusted-ERA+ was calculated to be 145, which was also good for fifth in the National League.

Minute Maid Park in Houston was a strong hitters' park in the four seasons it was open before 2004 with an average ballpark run factor of 107.9 for those four seasons. Over its entire history, Minute Maid Park has an average ballpark run factor of 102.9.

Because Clemens made 61% of his starts and pitched 62% of his innings at Minute Maid Park in 2004, he pitched in a stronger hitters' environment, on average, than he would have had he pitched only half of his games at Minute Maid Park.

Roger Clemens v. Carlos Zambrano

As noted above, Roger Clemens ranked fifth in the National League in both earned run average (ERA) as well as park-adjusted ERA+. One pitcher who ranked ahead of him in both of these, with an ERA+ of 160 was Carlos Zambrano of the Chicago Cubs. A 15-point edge in ERA+ is pretty significant. In addition, Zambrano led Clemens in Baseball-Reference.com WAR, 6.7–5.5. Lee Sinins' Sabermetric Encyclopedia credits Zambrano with 42 Runs Saved above Average (RSAA) versus 32 RSAA for Clemens.

Based on my research here, I disagree with those who ranked Zambrano as having had the better season (and I say this a little bit sadly, as I was a big fan of Carlos Zambrano at that time). I calculate Roger Clemens as having amassed a (context-neutral) won-lost record of 12.2–9.3 (0.567 winning percentage, 1.7 Wins over Positional Average) as a starting pitcher in 2004 (excluding batting and baserunning), compared to a record of 11.7–9.7 for Zambrano (0.546, 1.3 WOPA).

Roger Clemens' Impact on Minute Maid Park's Run Factor

Even having controlled for how often Roger Clemens started at home, the above record might well understate Roger Clemens's 2004 season value. From 2000 to 2006, excluding 2004, Minute Maid Park had ballpark run factors that ranged from a low of 102.9 to a high of 112.0.

In fact, however, the ballpark run factor for Minute Maid Park in 2004 was only 97.7. In 2003, Minute Maid Park had a ballpark run factor of 103.7; in 2005 (when Clemens made a more normal 17 of 32 starts at home), Minute Maid Park's run factor was 102.9. The extent to which Minute Maid Park was a hitters' park in 2004 is understated here in part because the Astros' best pitcher, Roger Clemens, pitched 63.5% more innings in Minute Maid Park than he did elsewhere.

In 2004, the Houston Astros scored 405 runs and allowed 347 runs in Minute Maid Park versus 398 runs scored and 351 runs allowed on the road. Simply dividing the former two by the latter two produces a basic run park factor for Minute Maid Park of 100.4. The runs allowed by Astros pitchers in 2004 can be split as follows:

	Home		Road	
	IP	RA	IP	RA
Clemens	133	44	81.1	32
Others	604	303	624.2	319

If we substitute the average of the other Astros pitchers into Clemens' innings, it would look as follows instead:

	Home		Road	
	IP	RA	IP	RA
(Clemens)	133	*67*	81.1	*42*
Others	604	303	624.2	319

This would have led the Astros to have allowed 370 runs in Minute Maid Park versus 361 on the road for a basic run park factor for Minute Maid Park of 102.1 ([405+370] / [398+361]). Roger Clemens' own performance, which was achieved disproportionately at home, single-handedly serves to lower Minute Maid Parks' Run Factor by two percent!

Ryan Howard v. Albert Pujols, 2006

In 2006, the National League East consisted of four teams who played their home games in pitchers' parks: Atlanta (ballpark run factor of 87.6), Florida (93.5), New York (90.7), and Washington (91.9), and one team that played in a hitters' park: Philadelphia, with a ballpark run factor of 104.2. The result of this, coupled with the unbalanced schedule that had the Phillies playing inter-divisional opponents more often than intra-divisional opponents, was that the average ballpark run factor for Phillies' road games was 97.2.

A context-neutral measure which fails to recognize this may under-rate the offensive performance of Phillies hitters by penalizing them for their home ballpark without making an offsetting adjustment to reflect the fact that they played their road games in disproportionately difficult parks in which to hit.

In 2006, Ryan Howard was elected Most Valuable Player of the National League. The consensus by most sabermetric observers was that Albert Pujols had a better season than Ryan Howard.

Pujols had slightly better raw rate stats than Howard: .327/.429/.568 vs. .313/.425/.659, while Howard produced slightly better counting stats because he played 16 more games than Pujols and accumulated 70 more plate appearances. For example, Ryan Howard led the National League in Runs Created in 2006 with 169 versus 151 for Pujols.

Baseball-Reference.com considers Pujols' park factor to have been 99 versus 105 for Howard. This serves to make the difference in rate stats even greater between Pujols and Howard (e.g., Pujols leads Howard in OPS+ 178–167) and, as measured by most sabermetric measures, more than offsets Howard's 70 plate-appearance advantage, so that Pujols leads Howard in most offensive measures. For example, Baseball-Reference.com has Pujols leading Howard in Batting Runs 66–62.

Rather than assuming average road games, pW-L records are calculated given the actual ballparks in which players performed. Hence, pW-L records recognize that the Phillies played a disproportionately high number of road games in pitchers' parks. Knowing this, Ryan Howard's (context-neutral) batting won-lost record in 2006 is calculated as 17.1–10.3, or 3.4 wins over .500, versus Albert Pujols' record of 15.5–9.9, only 2.8 wins over .500. Howard's 70 additional plate appearances led to 2.0 more batting decisions for Howard as well, so this difference would increase slightly if the comparison were to a lower standard, such as replacement level.

Beyond simple batting, however, Pujols amassed better records as both a baserunner and fielder than Howard. Hence, even recognizing that Ryan Howard did not play in as strong a hitters' environment as one might think, Albert Pujols still led Ryan Howard in pWORL 5.5 to 3.7 and would still have been my choice for Most Valuable Player in the 2006 National League.

Stability of Ballpark Factors

As I have noted and I think is well understood by most people who are familiar with ballpark factors, one complication in assessing the stability of ballpark factors over time is that such factors would be expected to change over time due to changes in the ballparks to which a particular ballpark is being compared. For example, as I said earlier in the chapter, in 1993, the ballpark run factors for the 12 National League parks that had been used in 1992 went down by an average of 3.1 with 7 of the 12 parks having lower run factors. The reason for this, of course, was because the National League expanded in 1993, adding a team in Colorado, which played its home games in Mile High Stadium, which had a Ballpark Run Factor in 1993 over 130. A decline in the existing 12 parks of 3.1 each is exactly what you would expect if none of these other parks changed at all relative to each other.

In studying the stability of ballpark run factors it may, therefore, be helpful to focus on periods of time when the ballparks used in major league baseball remained relatively unchanged.

The most recent period of relative stability is probably the American League from 2000 (the year Comerica Park in Detroit opened) through 2008 (the last season for Yankee Stadium). Over these nine seasons, the primary ballparks for all 14 American League teams remained the same every year. Even over these seasons there were a few minor changes in the ballparks in which American League teams played: Boston and Oakland played two games in Tokyo in 2008, Tampa Bay played series in Lake Buena Vista, Florida in 2007 and 2008, and several National League teams changed ballparks (most notably the Montreal Expos / Washington Nationals which played in four home ballparks during this decade). Nevertheless, this is a stable enough and long enough time period that I think looking at the American League over these nine seasons will be helpful in judging just how stable my ballpark run factors are.

The tables below show ballpark run factors for the primary home ballparks of American League teams from 2000 to 2008. I also show the ballpark factors for these teams presented by Baseball-Reference.com, which calculates its park factors over 3-year time periods.

Ballpark Run Factors Based on Base-Out Transition Matrices, American League Home Ballparks, 2000–2008

Team	2000	2001	2002	2003	2004	2005	2006	2007	2008
ANA	100.3	105.9	97.9	93.7	99.6	99.7	97.3	105.3	96.2
					Mean	99.5		Std. Dev.	4.0
BAL	96.1	98.8	102.8	95.2	100.1	97.9	103.3	107.1	101.8
					Mean	100.3		Std. Dev.	3.8
BOS	99.1	103.7	96.5	107.6	101.9	98.6	98.7	106.5	105.2
					Mean	102.0		Std. Dev.	4.0
CHI	104.0	107.2	104.7	99.1	105.2	100.7	101.6	104.7	104.7
					Mean	103.5		Std. Dev.	2.5
CLE	101.9	101.3	97.7	96.1	94.1	95.2	101.0	98.1	101.9
					Mean	98.6		Std. Dev.	3.1
DET	94.3	96.8	90.5	96.9	96.6	95.7	100.4	103.0	108.4
					Mean	98.1		Std. Dev.	5.2
KC	106.2	110.1	110.4	107.1	97.1	98.2	107.6	97.8	91.7
					Mean	102.9		Std. Dev.	6.8
MIN	107.1	97.4	92.7	102.9	103.2	104.8	101.7	98.6	91.4
					Mean	100.0		Std. Dev.	5.4
NY	99.2	99.4	100.7	102.1	99.8	101.8	98.4	103.3	103.7
					Mean	100.9		Std. Dev.	1.9
OAK	95.9	99.6	103.3	93.4	98.6	100.6	94.3	86.9	96.8
					Mean	96.6		Std. Dev.	4.8
SEA	90.1	80.8	96.4	98.0	93.2	99.9	93.6	98.6	94.1
					Mean	93.9		Std. Dev.	5.8
TB	99.4	100.3	98.0	94.4	93.6	103.4	103.1	95.3	101.2
					Mean	98.7		Std. Dev.	3.6
TEX	106.5	96.0	107.7	108.9	109.0	103.7	101.4	98.6	105.0
					Mean	104.1		Std. Dev.	4.6
TOR	100.1	102.9	100.5	104.7	107.8	99.8	97.5	95.7	97.9
					Mean	100.8		Std. Dev.	3.8
Avg.					Mean	100.0		Std. Dev.	4.2

Team Run Factors Based on Base-Out Transition Matrices, American League, 2000–2008

Team	2000	2001	2002	2003	2004	2005	2006	2007	2008
ANA	99.9	101.6	99.2	96.4	99.9	100.3	98.8	102.7	98.1
					Mean	99.7		Std. Dev.	1.9
BAL	98.2	99.3	101.1	97.8	100.5	99.7	100.9	103.0	101.1
					Mean	100.2		Std. Dev.	1.6
BOS	99.2	102.1	97.9	103.6	101.4	99.5	99.0	102.7	102.6
					Mean	100.9		Std. Dev.	2.0
CHI	102.0	103.7	101.8	99.9	102.3	100.1	101.2	102.2	102.0
					Mean	101.7		Std. Dev.	1.2
CLE	101.0	101.2	99.0	99.2	96.8	97.5	100.8	99.3	101.0
					Mean	99.5		Std. Dev.	1.6
DET	97.0	99.3	95.8	98.9	98.7	98.1	100.5	101.1	103.4
					Mean	99.2		Std. Dev.	2.3
KC	103.1	105.2	104.2	103.2	98.0	99.2	103.9	98.9	96.5
					Mean	101.4		Std. Dev.	3.2
MIN	103.7	99.6	96.3	101.1	101.4	101.8	101.4	99.3	95.7

Team	2000	2001	2002	2003	2004	2005	2006	2007	2008
					Mean	100.0		Std. Dev.	2.6
NY	99.3	99.5	100.2	100.7	100.0	100.9	99.1	102.0	101.9
					Mean	100.4		Std. Dev.	1.1
OAK	98.6	98.9	101.9	96.7	99.6	100.3	97.1	93.6	98.7
					Mean	98.4		Std. Dev.	2.4
SEA	95.1	90.8	98.8	98.7	97.0	99.3	96.9	98.8	96.7
					Mean	96.9		Std. Dev.	2.7
TB	99.4	100.2	99.3	97.4	97.4	101.4	101.0	98.7	100.8
					Mean	99.5		Std. Dev.	1.5
TEX	103.7	97.1	103.7	103.7	103.5	101.8	100.6	99.1	102.0
					Mean	101.7		Std. Dev.	2.4
TOR	99.6	101.1	100.4	102.1	103.3	99.9	98.7	98.5	99.4
					Mean	100.3		Std. Dev.	1.6
Avg.					Mean	100.0		Std. Dev.	2.0

Team Run Factors from Baseball-Reference.com, American League, 2000–2008

Team	2000	2001	2002	2003	2004	2005	2006	2007	2008
ANA	102.5	101.0	99.5	97.5	97.0	97.5	100.0	100.5	102.5
					Mean	99.8		Std. Dev.	2.1
BAL	95.5	95.5	95.5	99.0	98.5	99.0	99.5	101.5	101.5
					Mean	98.4		Std. Dev.	2.4
BOS	103.5	101.5	102.5	104.0	105.5	104.0	104.5	105.5	107.0
					Mean	104.2		Std. Dev.	1.7
CHI	102.0	103.5	101.5	102.0	102.0	103.0	104.0	104.0	105.0
					Mean	103.0		Std. Dev.	1.2
CLE	100.5	100.0	97.5	96.5	94.0	96.0	98.5	100.5	98.0
					Mean	97.9		Std. Dev.	2.2
DET	95.0	94.0	93.5	94.0	95.5	98.0	100.0	101.5	103.0
					Mean	97.2		Std. Dev.	3.6
KC	103.0	107.5	110.5	107.5	102.5	100.0	102.0	100.5	99.0
					Mean	103.6		Std. Dev.	4.0
MIN	104.5	102.0	100.0	100.5	102.5	102.0	98.0	95.0	96.0
					Mean	100.1		Std. Dev.	3.2
NY	98.5	101.0	99.5	97.5	97.5	97.5	100.0	100.5	102.5
					Mean	99.4		Std. Dev.	1.8
OAK	95.5	98.0	97.5	98.5	98.5	100.5	97.0	94.0	95.0
					Mean	97.2		Std. Dev.	2.0
SEA	94.0	93.5	96.0	95.0	97.5	95.5	97.0	96.5	97.0
					Mean	95.8		Std. Dev.	1.4
TB	99.5	99.0	98.0	96.0	97.0	99.5	100.0	99.0	101.0
					Mean	98.8		Std. Dev.	1.5
TEX	102.0	104.5	106.5	111.0	108.5	106.0	101.0	101.0	102.0
					Mean	104.7		Std. Dev.	3.6
TOR	103.0	102.5	104.0	104.0	104.0	102.0	100.0	99.5	97.5
					Mean	101.8		Std. Dev.	2.3
Avg.					Mean	100.0		Std. Dev.	2.4

*Park Factors shown here are the average of Batting Park Factors (BPF) and Pitching Park Factors (PPF). Factors shown here are 3-year averages as used by Baseball-Reference.com.

The average standard deviation for Baseball-Reference.com's park factors for American League teams from 2000 through 2008 was 2.4. The average standard deviation for my team run factors for the same teams over the same time periods is 2.0. If anything, I certainly would have expected Baseball-Reference.com's run factors to be more stable than mine, since Baseball-Reference.com calculates 3-year park factors. The fact that my team run factors are actually more stable than Baseball-Reference.com's team park factors over this time period is a very pleasant surprise.

One Complication: Kauffman Stadium, 2004

Even when a team keeps its home ballpark, it may change things about that park which may lead to changes in how the ballpark affects offensive levels. One example of this actually did occur in the American League over the nine-year period considered above. According to an article on MLB's website relating the history of Kansas City's ballpark, prior to the 2004 season, "the outfield fences in the gaps and in straight-away center field were moved back 10 feet to their original dimensions of 387 and 410, respectively, making Kauffman Stadium [in Kansas City] one of the most spacious parks in major league baseball." The impact of this change is readily apparent in the above tables, where my ballpark run factor for Kauffman Stadium shifts from 108.5 from 2000 through 2003 to 98.5 from 2004 through 2008. In fact, the change in these park factors is what prompted me to check to see if anything changed about Kauffman Stadium that season.

Removing Kansas City from the calculations, the average standard deviation of my team run factors falls to 1.9 while the average standard deviation for Baseball-Reference.com's team park factors falls to 2.2.

Overall, I am quite satisfied with the ballpark adjustments that underlie by pW-L calculations.

Same Ballpark, Different League

Throughout this chapter, I have discussed ballpark factors based on the ballpark-specific win probability matrices that I use in my work. The ballpark factors are relative to other ballparks in the same league, for the same season. Because of this, strictly speaking, one cannot compare these factors across leagues and draw conclusions about whether, say, Wrigley Field (average Ballpark Run Factor = 105.7 over all seasons for which I have calculated pW-L records) or Fenway Park (average Ballpark Run Factor = 104.9) is a better hitting environment (of course, one probably shouldn't draw any conclusions given how similar those two numbers are anyway).

The only way in which one could make comparisons across leagues would be if a ballpark happened to host games in both leagues within a particular season. Fortunately, this has happened on several occasions during the seasons over which I have calculated pW-L records. Unfortunately, the number of such instances is relatively small. So, great caution should, of course, be taken in trying to draw meaningful conclusions. Nevertheless, I thought it might be instructive (or at least fun) to look at the few cases where a ballpark hosted both American League and National League games, just to see what they suggest.

1940s and 1950s

In the middle of the twentieth century, American and National League teams shared a ballpark in two cities: Philadelphia, where the A's and Phillies both played in Shibe Park (aka Connie Mack Stadium) from 1938 through 1954 (after which the A's moved to Kansas City), and St. Louis, where the Cardinals and Browns both played in Sportsman's Park from 1920 through 1953 (after which the Browns moved to Baltimore). I have calculated pW-L records for every game as far back as 1945. This yields nine years of shared games in St. Louis (1945–1953) and ten years of shared games in Philadelphia (1945–1954). A comparison of various Ballpark Factors for these stadiums for American League versus National League games are shown in the table below.

	Runs	OBP	SLG	HR
Shibe Park (PHI), 1945–1954				
American League (A's)	101.5	101.0	101.2	100.0
National League (Phillies)	95.0	98.2	98.2	90.7
AL / NL–1	6.9%	2.8%	3.1%	10.2%
Sportsman's Park (STL), 1945–1953				
American League (Browns)	105.0	102.1	102.5	104.0
National League (Cardinals)	101.1	102.0	100.7	88.2
AL / NL–1	3.9%	0.1%	1.8%	17.9%

All things considered, the results for Shibe and Sportsman's Parks tell a reasonably similar story: in general, National League parks were somewhat better run-scoring parks and much better home run parks than American League parks in the late 1940s and early 1950s.

1960s

The next time that AL and NL teams shared a ballpark was for four years in the early 1960s, 1962–1965, when the Angels and Dodgers shared Dodger Stadium.

American League vs. National League, Based on Common Ballparks				
	Runs	OBP	SLG	HR
Dodger Stadium (LA), 1962–1965				
American League (Angels)	95.7	99.6	97.3	87.7
National League (Dodgers)	85.9	97.1	92.4	67.9
AL / NL–1	11.5%	2.6%	5.3%	29.1%

The results for Dodger Stadium in the early 1960s are broadly similar to the results for Shibe Park and Sportsman's Park a decade earlier. American League versus National League Park Factors over these time periods are summarized in the table below.

Averages, AL/NL–1				
	Runs	OBP	SLG	HR
Shibe Park (PHI), 1945–1954	6.9%	2.8%	3.1%	10.2%
Sportsman's Park (STL), 1945–1953	3.9%	0.1%	1.8%	17.9%
Dodger Stadium (LA), 1962–1965	11.5%	2.6%	5.3%	29.1%
Average, 1945–1965	7.2%	1.8%	3.3%	18.2%

Common ballparks produced Ballpark Run Factors about 7% higher in the American League than in the National League, with OBP Factors 2% higher, SLG Factors 3% higher, and Home Run Factors 18% higher in the American League.

Honestly, the consistency of these results is quite surprising to me, considering that major league baseball expanded into seven new cities over the time period being looked at here: Baltimore, Houston, Kansas City, Milwaukee, Minnesota, Los Angeles, and San Francisco.

What Does This Imply About the Average American League Ballpark Versus the Average National League Ballpark Over This Time Period?

If a ballpark has a higher ballpark run factor in the American League than in the National League, this means that the other ballparks in the National League must have higher ballpark run factors. Backing into what the implied league-wide ballpark run factors would be for the AL versus the NL over these time periods is a little bit convoluted. Let me try to walk through it.

From 1962 to 1965, there were 10 teams in each of the American and National Leagues. The average ballpark run factor for a league will always be exactly equal to 100 by definition. If the ballpark run factor for Dodger Stadium is 95.7 (as it was in the AL), then the average ballpark run factor for the other 9 AL ballparks must be 100.5 (since (9*100.5 + 95.7)/10 = 100). Doing the same thing for the NL, the average ballpark run factor for the other 9 NL ballparks over these same four seasons must be 101.6 (since (9*101.6 + 85.9)/10 = 100). Now, assume that Dodger Stadium really played the same in both the AL and NL in absolute terms (which may or may not be true for a variety of reasons), then we can re-calculate an average ballpark run factor for the American League, substituting, say, 100 for Dodger Stadium's 95.7; this produces an "absolute" ballpark run factor for the American League of 100.4 ((9*100.5 + 100)/10). Doing the same for the National League gives us 101.4 ((9*101.6 + 100)/10). So, on average, the average National League ballpark produced about 1.0% more runs than the average American League ballpark over these four seasons (101.4 ÷ 100.4 – 1).

Doing this for all of the seasons considered here (remembering that there were 8 teams in the AL and NL from 1946 to 1954, and two shared ballparks from 1946 to 1953) and then averaging across the seasons, I estimate that National League ballparks produced about 1% more runs than American League ballparks over this time period on average.

Estimated Impact of Ballparks on Offensive Events, 1945–1965
Additional Events in National League Ballparks (on average)

Runs	OBP	SLG	HR
1.1%	0.3%	0.5%	2.5%

So, in the 1950s and 1960s, it appears that scoring was approximately 1% higher in the National League than in the American League, due primarily to home runs being 2.5% more common, because of differences in the ballparks (and cities) in which the two leagues played. While an interesting result, it is important to note that this difference has absolutely no impact on the relative values of hitters or pitchers, in either the American or National League, over this time period.

Shared Ballparks Since 1965

Since the Angels moved to Anaheim and became the California Angels for the 1966 season, there have only been two seasons in which two teams shared a home ballpark, 1974 and 1975. For those two seasons, the Yankees shared Shea Stadium with the Mets while Yankee Stadium was being renovated. Average ballpark factors for Shea Stadium for the American and National Leagues for the 1974 and 1975 seasons are shown next.

American League vs. National League,
Based on Common Ballparks, Shea Stadium (NY), 1974–75

	Runs	*OBP*	*SLG*	*HR*
American League	98.7	99.4	100.3	103.8
National League	95.6	97.8	97.6	99.9
AL / NL–1	3.3%	1.6%	2.8%	3.9%

Shea Stadium looks to have uniformly higher AL park factors, by about 3%, suggesting that the average NL ballpark other than Shea generated somewhat greater offense than the average non–Shea AL ballpark in these two seasons.

There have been two other ballparks to host American League and National League games in the same season (excluding interleague games): U.S. Cellular Field in Chicago in 2004, which, in addition to being the home ballpark of the Chicago White Sox of the American League also hosted two games between the Montreal Expos and Florida Marlins of the National League (the Marlins were technically the "home" team for these two games) which were moved due to a hurricane; and Miller Park in Milwaukee in 2007, which, in addition to being the home ballpark of the Milwaukee Brewers of the National League also hosted three games between the Cleveland Indians and Anaheim Angels of the American League (the Indians were the "home" team), which were moved because of a snowstorm.

In both of these cases, we are talking about extremely small sample periods for the non-host league. So, we should be even more careful than usual about drawing any kinds of conclusions here. Nevertheless, here are relative Ballpark Run Factors in the two leagues for U.S. Cellular Field in 2004 and for Miller Park in 2007.

American League vs. National League,
Based on Common Ballparks, Since 1975

	Runs	*OBP*	*SLG*	*HR*
U.S. Cellular Field (CHI), 2004				
American League	105.2	101.3	102.8	110.9
National League	105.8	102.6	101.2	106.5
AL / NL–1	–0.6%	–1.3%	1.5%	4.1%
Miller Park (MIL), 2007				
American League	103.4	104.0	102.2	106.0
National League	96.8	98.9	99.9	105.8
AL / NL–1	6.7%	5.1%	2.3%	0.2%

Obviously, one has to be extremely cautious at drawing too many conclusions from such small sample sizes. With that caveat, it appears based on these results that the average ballpark in the American League and National League are probably similar in recent years.

Milwaukee County Stadium

Three other ballparks have served as the home ballpark for both an American League team and a National League team at some point during the seasons for which I have calculated pW-L records. The first of these is RFK Stadium in Washington, D.C., which served as the home ballpark of the Washington Senators of the American League from 1962 through 1971 (average ballpark run factor of 99) and as the home ballpark of the

Washington Nationals of the National League from 2005 through 2007 (average ballpark run factor of 91). Given the 34-year gap between the time that RFK Stadium was an AL park and when it was an NL park, I am doubtful as to how informative such a comparison is.

The second ballpark which has hosted both AL and NL teams is more interesting: County Stadium in Milwaukee. From 1953 through 1965, County Stadium was the home stadium of the Milwaukee Braves. In 1966, the Braves moved to Atlanta. Two years later, however, County Stadium re-emerged as an American League ballpark, hosting 20 Chicago White Sox games in 1968 and 1969 combined. Then, in 1970, County Stadium became the home stadium of the newly relocated Milwaukee Brewers.

Ballpark Factors for County Stadium for 1965 (its final season as an NL park) and 1968, 1969, and 1970 (its first season as a full-time home ballpark for an AL team) are shown in the next table.

Ballpark Factors, Milwaukee County Stadium

	Runs	OBP	SLG	HR
1965 (NL, 81 games)	105.8	102.2	103.4	112.2
1968 (AL, 9 games)	98.1	101.0	101.6	100.9
1969 (AL, 11 games)	98.9	98.6	97.7	93.9
1970 (AL, 81 games)	96.6	97.0	98.2	98.8
AL Average, 1968–1970 (101 games)	**97.0**	**97.5**	**98.4**	**98.4**

More recently, County Stadium moved from the home ballpark of an American League team to the home ballpark of a National League team when the Brewers moved from the AL to the NL between the 1997 and 1998 seasons. Ballpark Factors for those two seasons are shown next.

Ballpark Factors, Milwaukee County Stadium

	Runs	OBP	SLG	HR
1997 (AL)	105.5	103.3	102.4	98.0
1998 (NL)	109.6	104.0	102.5	97.8

Finally, Houston's Minute Maid Park moved from the home ballpark of a National League team to the home ballpark of an American League team when the Astros moved from the NL to the AL between the 2012 and 2013 seasons. Ballpark Factors for those two seasons are shown next.

Ballpark Factors, Minute Maid Park, Houston

	Runs	OBP	SLG	HR
2012 (NL)	97.9	98.9	99.2	104.3
2013 (AL)	103.8	101.0	101.3	109.8

In both of the above cases, the ballpark run factor increased by 4–6 percent after the teams switched leagues. Note, however, that the two league shifts were in opposite directions, so the implications regarding AL vs. NL parks in these two cases essentially cancel out.

Overall, the results in the last two tables both strike me as reasonably stable. Compared to year-over-year changes in ballpark factors for ballparks that stayed within the same league, the changes in Milwaukee's and Houston's ballpark factors here would probably not strike anybody as being at all remarkable. Coupled with the 2004 and 2007 results shown earlier, it appears that the average ballpark in the two leagues is probably fairly similar in recent years.

Small-Sample Park Factors

Player wins and losses are based, in part, on win probabilities with unique win probabilities being calculated by ballpark for each league and season. For most ballparks, these calculations are based on a ballpark having served as a team's home ballpark for a full season: i.e., they are based on approximately 81 games per season. There are, however, a few cases where a ballpark is only used for a very limited number of games in a particular season. I think that sometimes it can be interesting to look at these smaller, less reliable sets of data to see what, if anything, they might tell us about the system as a whole.

Between 2000 and 2010, there were three ballparks that did not serve as a principal home ballpark for any team but which nevertheless hosted major league baseball games in that league. I thought it might be interesting to look at these ballparks and see what, if anything, the data tell us.

Tokyo Dome

The Tokyo Dome hosted two games between the Chicago Cubs and New York Mets to start the 2000 season, two games between the Tampa Bay Devil Rays and the New York Yankees to open the 2004 season, and two games between the Oakland A's and the Boston Red Sox to open the 2008 season. Park factors for Tokyo for these three seasons are shown below.

Component Park Factors Imputed from Base-Out Transition Matrices: Tokyo Dome

	Runs	OBP	SLG	D	T	HR	DP
2000 NL	99.8	100.0	100.1	100.1	100.4	100.3	100.0
2004 AL	98.9	99.5	99.5	105.5	99.4	95.9	102.0
2008 AL	94.1	98.5	98.0	97.2	91.2	97.6	103.9

For the 2000 National League, the Tokyo Dome basically shows up as an average ballpark. I think this is due, in large part, to the restrictions which I impose to prevent extreme deviations from league-wide transition matrices. The story is similar for the 2004 American League, although the Tokyo Dome shows up here as something of a slight pitchers park, especially with respect to home runs.

Technically, these two park factors are not really comparable as none of the comparison ballparks are the same. In contrast, the 2008 American League shared 15 ballparks with the 2004 American League, including the Tokyo Dome. The results in the 2008 American League are the most extreme of the three seasons, with the Tokyo Dome having a ballpark run factor of 94. Most of the ballpark event factors are fairly similar in 2004 and 2008: OBP (99.5 v. 98.5), Home Runs (95.9 v. 97.6), DPs (102.0, 103.9). Still, there are some differences, most notably the ballpark doubles factor which fell from 105.5 in 2004 to 97.2 in 2008. While it's easy to point to a change from 105 to 97 and chalk it all up to small sample size, it may be worth noting that this was not the biggest change in ballpark doubles factor between these two years. The doubles factor for Comerica Park in Detroit, for example, changed from 86 to 97 between these same two seasons.

Hiram Bithorn Stadium

The first major-league game played at Hiram Bithorn Stadium in San Juan, Puerto Rico, was between the Toronto Blue Jays and the Texas Rangers in 2001. In 2003 and

2004, Hiram Bithorn Stadium served as a second home for the Montreal Expos, who played a total of 43 home games there over those two seasons. More recently, the Florida Marlins hosted the New York Mets in a 3-game series at Hiram Bithorn Stadium in June 2010. Park factors for these four seasons are shown below.

Component Park Factors Imputed from Base-Out Transition Matrices: Hiram Bithorn Stadium, San Juan, Puerto Rico

	Runs	*OBP*	*SLG*	*D*	*T*	*HR*	*DP*
2001 AL	91.5	98.2	96.5	95.4	90.0	91.3	82.1
2003 NL	104.9	102.6	107.3	103.2	79.3	133.5	82.3
2004 NL	81.2	94.4	91.2	80.8	87.4	85.7	113.5
2010 NL	93.5	95.4	95.2	96.8	59.9	98.9	103.3

In 2003, Hiram Bithorn Stadium was the fourth best hitters' park in the National League behind Denver, Phoenix, and Montreal. The Expos and their opponents combined to score 10.86 runs per game in Puerto Rico versus 8.49 runs per game in Expos games played elsewhere. San Juan was the easiest ballpark in the National League in which to hit home runs (Coors Field had a home run factor of 130) with 75 home runs being hit in 22 games that year.

In 2004, Hiram Bithorn Stadium was the best pitchers' park in the National League. The Expos and their opponents combined to score only 6.38 runs per game in Puerto Rico, while combining to hit only 24 home runs in the 21 games played there.

My first thought, seeing these differences, was that they must have moved the outfield fences after the 2003 season, perhaps in response to the large number of home runs in 2003. Sure enough, a little Googling uncovered a USA Today article from February 25, 2004, which states, "Improvements have been made for the 2004 season: A new artificial turf is being laid, and fences that are 30 feet farther from home plate should help keep the home runs from flying out at breakneck speed."

Given that information, the numbers suddenly seem to make some sense. Deeper fences mean a lot fewer home runs and a few fewer doubles (what had been fly balls off the wall now become fly outs), both of which serve to reduce both OBP and SLG. A better turf could also explain the dramatic increase in double plays, although shifts in double play factors are not unusual (albeit not usually nearly that big). Put it all together, and you get a great hitters' park turning into a great pitchers' park. The results for 2010 are similar to 2004, but show more of a good, not necessarily great, pitchers' park.

THE BALLPARK AT DISNEY'S WIDE WORLD OF SPORTS IN LAKE BUENA VISTA, FLORIDA

The Tampa Bay Rays played an early-season 3-game series at Disney's Wide World of Sports Complex in the 2007 and 2008 seasons (against Texas and Toronto, respectively).

Ballpark factors for these two seasons are shown below.

Component Park Factors Imputed from Base-Out Transition Matrices: The Ballpark, Lake Buena Vista, Florida

	Runs	*OBP*	*SLG*	*D*	*T*	*HR*	*DP*
2007 AL	107.2	104.9	104.8	105.0	95.3	105.7	104.1
2008 AL	104.7	101.7	101.3	94.1	112.3	102.5	112.2

In my opinion, the results here are quite consistent considering we're talking about 3 games played here in each of these two seasons. Just to emphasize how small these sample sizes are: in 2007, two triples were hit in three games in Lake Buena Vista's ballpark; in 2008, there were three triples hit. That's it. And even with that, the run factor changed by only 2 points—from 107 to 105.

Overall, while the results for these four ballparks do show some changes over time, I'm actually quite reassured by these results given the extremely small sample sizes that we are looking at here.

I hope you enjoyed reading about Baseball pW-L records as much as I enjoyed writing about them. You can look up pW-L records for players, teams, and leagues, look at leaderboards, and compare players at my website at http://baseball.tomthress.com. I hope you'll come to visit!

Glossary

BABIP Batting Average (BA) on Balls in Play (BIP).

Background Losses Sum of context-dependent player losses (pLosses) for a team minus team losses; equal to one loss per team game played.

Background Wins Sum of context-dependent player wins (pWins) for a team minus team wins; equal to one win per team game played.

Ballpark Factors Factors which measure the relative likelihood and/or value of certain events, including run-scoring, across different ballparks within the same league and season. Ballpark factors are typically expressed as indices, relative to 100, reflecting differences in average runs scored in the ballpark relative to league average.

Base-Out Probability Matrix Matrix showing the probability of transitioning from a particular starting base-out state to a particular ending base-out state.

Base-Out State Number and location of baserunners and the number of outs at the start of a particular plate appearance. There are 24 possible initial base-out states; 28 possible ending states (the ending state may include 3 outs; the 4 ending base-out states associated with 3 outs vary based on the number of runs that scored on the inning-ending play, 0–3).

Baserunning Losses Losses accumulated by a player as a baserunner.

Baserunning Wins Wins accumulated by a player as a baserunner.

Batting Losses Losses accumulated by a player as a batter.

Batting Wins Wins accumulated by a player as a batter.

BIP Balls in Play. This refers to batted balls which are handled by a fielder (i.e., it excludes home runs).

bWAR Wins above Replacement (WAR) as calculated by and presented at Baseball-Reference.com.

Component Each of the nine steps in the process of calculating pW-L records.

Component 1 Base stealing (stolen bases, caught stealing, pickoffs, balks). Component 1 decisions are allocated to baserunners, pitchers, and catchers.

Component 2 Wild pitches and passed balls. Component 2 decisions are allocated to baserunners, pitchers, and catchers.

Component 3 Balls not in play: strikeouts, walks, hit-batsmen. Component 3 decisions are allocated to batters and pitchers.

Component 4 Batted balls, including home runs. Component 4 decisions are allocated to batters and pitchers.

Component 5 Hits vs. Outs on balls in play. Component 5 decisions are allocated to batters, pitchers, and fielders.

Component 6 Singles vs. Doubles vs. Triples on hits in play. Component 6 decisions are allocated to batters, pitchers, and fielders.

Component 7 Double Plays. Component 7 decisions are allocated to batters, baserunners, pitchers, and fielders.

Component 8 Baserunner Outs. Component 8 decisions are allocated to batters, baserunners, and fielders.

Component 9 Baserunner Advancement. Component 9 decisions are allocated to batters, baserunners, and fielders.

Context Importance of a specific play in terms of determining team victories relative to a play of average importance.

Context-Dependent Player decisions calculated such that player wins and losses are tied to team wins and losses. Context-dependent player wins and losses are referred to as pWins and pLosses in my work.

Context-Neutral Player's expected record if his performance had happened in a typical context with average teammates. Context-neutral player wins and losses are referred to as eWins and eLosses in my work.

Correlation Relationship between two series, expressed as a number between –1 and +1. A correlation of 1 means that two series move perfectly together. Literally, if two series have a correlation of 1 it means that one of them can be expressed as a linear function of the other. A correlation of 0 means that there is no relationship between the two series. A correlation of –1 means that two series move in exactly opposite directions.

DIPS Defense-Independent Pitching Statistic. DIPS measures expected Earned Run Average as a function of only those events which are not affected by defense: strikeouts, walks, hit batsmen, and home runs. DIPS was developed by Voros McCracken based on a theory that major-league pitchers have very little, if any, control over balls in play.

DRA Defensive Regression Analysis and/or Defensive Run Analysis. Measure of player fielding, denominated in runs, developed and explained by Michael Humphreys in his book, *Wizardry: Baseball's All-Time Greatest Fielders Revealed*.

DRS Defensive Runs Saved. Measure of player fielding, denominated in runs, developed by Sean Smith, originally presented at hardballtimes.com. DRS values for players are now available online at Baseball-Reference.com

e Prefix meaning "expected." Statistics with an "e" prefix have been adjusted to reflect expected performance in a typical context with average teammates.

eLosses Player's expected losses if his performance had happened in a typical context with average teammates.

Event Probability Probability of a particular event occurring. For example, the probability of a particular ball in play being a triple, given the hit type (ground ball, fly ball, line drive) and location of the hit.

eWins Player's expected wins if his performance had happened in a typical context with average teammates.

eWOPA Wins over Positional Average (WOPA) calculated using eWins and eLosses.

eWORL Wins over Replacement Level (WORL) calculated using eWins and eLosses.

Expected Context Expected context. Expected product of inter-game and intra-game context based on the position(s) played by a player.

Expected Win Adjustment Expected intra-game win adjustment based on player's individual performance, assuming that the rest of his team consisted of average major-league players.

Fielding Losses Losses accumulated by a player as a fielder.

Fielding Wins Wins accumulated by a player as a fielder.

FIP Fielding-Independent Pitching. A statistic based solely on the factors which are affected only by the pitcher—strikeouts, walks, hit-by-pitches, and home runs—scaled to mirror ERA (earned run average). The formula for FIP is the following:

$$FIP = c + (13 \cdot HR + 3 \cdot (BB + HBP) - 2 \cdot K) / IP$$

where c is set to a unique value for each season-league, such that league-wide FIP is equal to league-wide ERA.

fWAR Wins above Replacement (WAR) as calculated by and presented at Fangraphs.com.

fWORL Fielding Wins over Replacement Level.

Harmonic Mean The Harmonic mean of A and B is equal to $2 \cdot (A \cdot B) / (A + B)$. Frequently, in my work, the 2 in the above formula would end up dropping out, so I simply use $(A \cdot B) / (A + B)$.

Hit Type Type of batted ball for a ball in play: bunt, ground ball, fly ball, or line drive.

Inning Probability Matrix A matrix indicating the probability of a team winning a game given the specific difference in score at the start of a particular inning.

Inter-Game Within a single game. Relative importance of situations within the same game on that game's final outcome.

Inter-Game Context Inter-game context measures the average importance of the situations in which the player participated within the context of the game.

Inter-Game Win Adjustment Adjustment to player's winning percentage based on the timing of his performance within games.

Intra-Game Across games. Relative importance of situations within one game as compared to the importance of comparable situations across all games.

Intra-Game Context Intra-game context normalizes player decisions so that total player decisions are equal across all games.

Intra-Game Win Adjustment Adjustment to player's winning percentage based on the timing of his performance relative to his team's performance.

Leverage Relative importance of a situation. Conceptually, leverage is the same as inter-game context, as I use the term. Leverage was developed by Tom Tango.

Linear Weights Run-scoring estimator which is constructed by estimating the number of runs generated by each possible offensive event (single, double, triple, home run, etc.). Summing up this value for each event generated by a player or team then represents an estimate of the total number of runs generated by that particular player/team. Linear Weights were first developed by Pete Palmer for his series of Total Baseball books.

Losses Player decisions which contribute toward the player's team's probability of losing.

Multicollinearity The case where two or more explanatory variables in an equation are highly correlated with one another. The presence of multicollinearity can affect the interpretation of certain statistical properties from linear regression methods such as Ordinary Least Squares (OLS) and Weighted Least Squares (WLS).

Net Wins Total player wins minus total player losses associated with a particular play or plays.

Opportunity Cost Economic concept designed to measure the cost of forgoing alternative uses of one's resources. The opportunity cost of a choice is the value of the best alternative forgone, where a choice needs to be made between several mutually exclusive alternatives given limited resources. Assuming the best choice is made, opportunity cost is the cost incurred by not enjoying the benefit that could have been had by taking the second best choice available.

Ordinary Least Squares (OLS) A technique for estimating unknown parameters in a linear equation of the form, $y = \beta X + \varepsilon$, where X may be a single explanatory variable or a matrix of variables. In the latter case, β will be a vector of coefficients associated with the elements of X. OLS solves for the value(s) of an estimate of β, b, which will minimize the sum of the squared residuals ($e = y - bX$) of the equation. The basic OLS equation solves for b using the following formula:

$$b = (X'X)^{-1}X'y$$

p Prefix standing for "Player." Statistics with a "p" prefix are adjusted such that player wins and losses tie to team wins and losses.

Pennant Probability Probability of a team winning the pennant, given their current record, the current records of their opponents, and the number of games remaining in the season.

Persistence Equation Equation measuring the extent to which a statistic (typically, a Player's won-lost winning percentage in my work) persists over time. The persistence of a statistic can be viewed as the extent to which something represents a real skill as opposed to being the result of simple random chance.

Pitcher Losses The traditional baseball statistic assigned to a single pitcher on the losing team in a game.

Pitcher Wins The traditional baseball statistic assigned to a single pitcher on the winning team in a game.

Pitching Losses Losses accumulated by a player as a pitcher. This is not to be confused with the traditional baseball statistic, Pitcher Losses.

Pitching Wins Wins accumulated by a player as a pitcher. This is not to be confused with the traditional baseball statistic, Pitcher Wins.

Player Win Average Player valuation method developed by Eldon and Harlan Mills in their book of the same name, which first introduced the concept of Win Probability.

Playoff Probability Probability of a team making the playoffs, given their current record, the current records of their opponents, and the number of games remaining in the season.

pLosses Player losses calculated such that player losses are tied to team losses. For a team, the sum of player losses will be equal to team losses (plus 0.5 pLosses per tie game) plus team games played.

Positional Average Average winning percentage expected for a player who played the same position(s) as a particular player.

Positional Replacement Level Replacement Level performance of freely available players who could have been found to play the same position(s) as this player. Set equal to one standard deviation below Positional Average.

pWins Player wins calculated such that player wins are tied to team wins. For a team, the sum of player wins will be equal to team wins (plus 0.5 pWins per tie game) plus team games played.

pWOPA Wins over Positional Average (WOPA) calculated using pWins and pLosses.

pWORL Wins over Replacement Level (WORL) calculated using pWins and pLosses.

Pythagorean Winning Percentage Estimated team winning percentage based on a team's runs scored and runs allowed. Bill James first observed that a team's winning percentage could be estimated by the formula, $RS^2 / (RS^2 + RA^2)$, where RS is runs scored and RA is runs allowed. The formula was named because of its similarity to the Pythagorean Theorem in geometry that relates the length of the sides of a right triangle. More recent refinements have suggested that the optimal exponent is closer to 1.83 than to 2 and that the ideal exponent varies in relation to the average runs scored per game.

Replacement Level Level of play which could be achieved by a player who is freely available to any major-league team. The term, which was first coined by Bill James, comes from the concept that a player who plays at replacement level or below, can be easily replaced by a cheap minor-leaguer or journeyman major-leaguer.

Run Probability Matrix A matrix indicating the probability of scoring X runs within an inning given the current base-out state.

Run-Scoring Environment Average runs scored per game for a particular set of games. Run-scoring environments can vary by ballpark (Coors v. Petco), because of differences in rules (DH v. pitchers hitting), or because of differences across seasons (1968 v. 2000). The run-scoring environment can also be affected by the level of play (little league v. major-league, etc.), although this latter factor is irrelevant to the work presented here, which deals exclusively with major league baseball.

Standard Deviation Statistical measure of the spread of a range or distribution. Standard deviation is equal to the square root of the variance. In a normal distribution, approximately 65% of all values will fall within one standard deviation of the mean, 95% of all values will fall within two standard deviations, and 99% of all values will fall within three standard deviations of the mean.

Statistical Significance Term used by statisticians to indicate a result which is strong enough to prompt one to reject one's null hypothesis. The term is perhaps most commonly used to indicate the extent to which an estimated coefficient is different from some value (commonly, zero). Statistical significance can be used in either of two ways. One can make a general claim of statistical significance relative to a set likelihood (frequently 95%) or one can use it in reference to a specific percentage, to assess the likelihood of a particular result not happening by chance.

T-Statistic The ratio of a coefficient estimate and its standard error. Under certain statistical assumptions, a t-statistic will follow a t-distribution, which is very similar to a normal distribution. As a general statistical rule of thumb, a t-statistic greater than two (in absolute value) is frequently used to establish the statistical significance of a result.

Teammate Adjustments Effect of a player's teammates on his won-lost record based on shared responsibilities for certain plays between batters and baserunners and/or between pitchers and fielders.

Three True Outcomes Strikeouts, walks (or hit-by-pitch), and home runs. These are the only outcomes of a plate appearance that involve only the pitcher and the batter.

UZR Ultimate Zone Rating. A measure of fielding, denominated in runs. UZR was developed by Mitchel Lichtman. It rates fielders by evaluating plays based on the location and other factors associated with balls in play and comparing players' success in converting balls-in-play to outs relative to league-wide averages, given the same location and other characteristics of the play.

Variance Statistical measure of the spread of a range or distribution. Variance measures the average squared difference of a set of numbers from their mean.

WAR Wins above Replacement. Measure of total player value developed by Sean Smith, available at Baseball Reference. An alternate measure, also called WAR, is calculated by Fangraphs.

WARP Wins above Replacement Player. Measure of total player value developed by Baseball Prospectus.

Weighted Correlation Measure of correlation, weighted by the relative size of the individual observations of the sample being measured.

Weighted Least Squares A variant of Ordinary Least Squares (OLS), where individual observations may be given different weights and the coefficient(s), b, are solved minimizing the weighted sum of squared residuals.

Weighted Standard Deviation Measure of standard deviation, weighted by the relative size of the individual observations of the sample being measured.

Weighted Variance Measure of variance, weighted by the relative size of the individual observations of the sample being measured.

Win Adjustment Difference between a player's context-dependent and context-neutral winning percentage based on the timing of his performance.

Win Probability Matrix A matrix indicating the probability of a team winning a game given the current base-out state, the current score differential, and the current inning.

Win Probability A concept whereby the probability of a team winning a baseball game is estimated based on the current inning, baserunners, outs, and score differential.

Win Shares Estimated wins contributed by a player. The players on a team receive 3 Win Shares per team win and 0 Win Shares per team loss. Win Shares were developed by Bill James and described in his 2002 book of the same name.

Wins Player decisions which contribute toward a player's team's probability of winning.

WOPA Wins over Positional Average.

WOPA_b Batting wins relative to expected batting wins accumulated by non-pitchers.

WOPA_p Pitching wins relative to expected average pitching wins.

WOPA_r Baserunning wins relative to expected baserunning wins accumulated by non-pitchers.

WORL Wins over Replacement Level.

WPA Win Probability Advancements. A statistic which allocates net changes in win probability to individual players, typically batters and pitchers.

Z-Score A transformation of a variable to allow one to compare two or more variables on a similar scale. The formula for a z-score is $(x - m) / s$, where m is the mean of the statistic and s is the standard deviation. Z-scores will be distributed around zero, by construction. If the variable is normally distributed, one would expect approximately two-thirds of all z-scores to be between -1 and $+1$ and 95% of all z-scores between -2 and $+2$.

Bibliography

Albert, Jim. "Comments on 'Underestimating the Fog.'" *By the Numbers: The Newsletter of the SABR Statistical Analysis Committee* 15, no. 1 (February, 2005).

Allen, Erik, Arvin Hsu, and Tom M. Tango. "Solving Dips." Tangotiger.net (website). http://www.tangotiger.net/solvingdips.pdf.

"The Baseball Gauge." Seamheads.com. http://www.seamheads.com/baseballgauge/index.php.

"Baseball-Reference.com WAR Explained." Baseball-Reference.com. http://www.baseball-reference.com/about/war_explained.shtml.

Birnbaum, Phil. "Clutch Hitting and the Cramer Test." *By the Numbers: The Newsletter of the SABR Statistical Analysis Committee* 15, no. 1 (February, 2005).

Dewan, John, and Ben Jedlovec. *The Fielding Bible*, Vol. III. Chicago: ACTA, 2012.

_____. *The Fielding Bible*, Vol. IV. Chicago: ACTA, 2015.

"The Fangraphs UZR Primer." Fangraphs (website). http://www.fangraphs.com/blogs/index.php/the-fangraphs-uzr-primer/.

Fast, Mike. "Confessions of a DIPS Apostate." Hardballtimes.com, March 4, 2009. http://www.hardballtimes.com/main/article/confessions-of-a-dips-apostate/.

"fWAR and rWAR." Fangraphs (website). http://www.fangraphs.com/library/war/differences-fwar-rwar/.

Gassko, David. "Evaluating the Evaluators." Hardballtimes.com, February 3, 2006. http://www.hardballtimes.com/main/article/evaluating-the-evaluators/.

_____. "A Treatise on True Talent," Hardballtimes.com. July 30, 2009, http://www.hardballtimes.com/main/article/a-treatise-on-true-talent/.

Green, Christopher D. "Jim Rice, the Hall of Fame, and the Numbers," Baseballanalysts.com. http://baseballanalysts.com/archives/2008/12/jim_rice_the_ha.php.

Greene, William H. *Econometric Analysis*, Fifth Edition. Upper Saddle River, NJ: Prentice-Hall, 2003.

Hilliard, Larry, and Hilliard, Rob. "John Hiller." SABR Baseball Biography Project. http://sabr.org/bioproj/person/bf95ab65.

"The History of Kaufmann Stadium." Official Site of Major League Baseball. http://mlb.mlb.com/kc/ballpark/history.jsp.

"Hit a Home Run—In the Caribbean." *USA Today*. February 25, 2004.

Humphreys, Michael. "Ghosts in the Outfield." Hardballtimes.com, August 24, 2007. http://www.hardballtimes.com/main/ghosts-in-the-outfield/.

_____. *Wizardry: Baseball's All-Time Greatest Fielders Revealed*. New York: Oxford University Press, 2011.

James, Bill. *The New Bill James Historical Baseball Abstract*. Free Press, 2001.

_____. "Underestimating the Fog." *Baseball Research Journal*. Volume 33 (2004): 29–33.

James, Bill, and Jim Henzler. *Win Shares*. Morton Grove, IL: Stats Publishing, 2002.

Keri, Jonah, ed. *Baseball Between the Numbers: Why Everything You Know About the Game Is Wrong*. New York: Basic Books, 2006.

Klaassen, Matt. "Custom Woba and Linear Weights Through 2010: Baseball Databank Data Dump 2.1." Beyondtheboxscore.com. http://www.beyondtheboxscore.com/2011/1/4/1912914/custom-woba-and-linear-weights-through-2010-baseball-databank-data.

Lichtman, Mitchel G. "How Important Is Bayes in Advanced Defensive Metrics?" MGL on Baseball (website). http://mglbaseball.com/2016/03/04/how-important-is-bayes-in-advanced-defensive-metrics/.

McCracken, Voros. "Pitching and Defense: How Much Control Do Hurlers Have?" Baseball Prospectus.com, January 23, 2001. http://www.baseballprospectus.com/article.php?articleid=878.

Mills, Eldon G., and Harlan D. Mills. *Player Win Averages: A Complete Guide to Winning Baseball Players*. New York: A.S. Barnes, 1970. Available for download from the Harlan D. Mills Collection, University of Tennessee, Knoxville. http://trace.tennessee.edu/utk_harlan/6.

Morong, Cyril. "Clutch Hitting Links." CyrilMorong.com. http://cyrilmorong.com/Clutch Links2.htm.

"Park Adjustments." Baseball-Reference.com. http://www.baseball-reference.com/about/parkadjust.shtml.

Pinto, David. "Probabilistic Model of Range Explanation." Baseballmusings.com, November 19, 2006. http://www.baseballmusings.com/archives/018496.php.

"Pitcher WAR Calculations and Details." Baseball-Reference.com. http://www.baseball-reference.com/about/war_explained_pitch.shtml.

Ruane, Tom. "The Value Added Approach to Evaluating Performance." Retrosheet.Org. http://www.retrosheet.org/Research/RuaneT/valueadd_art.htm.

Schwarz, Alan. *The Numbers Game: Baseball's Lifelong Fascination with Statistics*. New York: Thomas Dunne Books, 2004.

Silver, Nate. "Is David Ortiz Really Mr. Clutch?" ESPN.com. http://sports.espn.go.com/espn/page2/story?page=betweenthenumbers/ortiz/060405.

Smith, Sean. "Measuring Defense for Players Back to 1956," Hardballtimes.com, January 10, 2008. http://www.hardballtimes.com/main/article/measuring-defense-for-players-back-to-1956/.

Studeman, Dave. "But I Regress..." Hardballtimes.com, January 4, 2007. http://www.hardballtimes.com/main/article/but-i-regress/.

———. "The One About Win Probability." Hardballtimes.com, December 27, 2004. http://www.hardballtimes.com/main/article/the-one-about-win-probability/.

———. "What's a Batted Ball Worth?" *2006 Hardball Times Baseball Annual*.

Tango, Tom M. "Crucial Situations." Hardballtimes.com, May 1–June 29, 2006. http://www.hardballtimes.com/main/article/crucial-situations/.

———. "How Much Is Each Pitcher's BABIP Affected by His Fielders That Day?" Insidethebook.com, August 31, 2012. http://www.insidethebook.com/ee/index.php/site/comments/how_much_is_each_pitchers_babip_affected_by_his_fielders_that_day/.

———. "Suzr V Buzr." Insidethebook.com, December 12, 2008. http://www.insidethebook.com/ee/index.php/site/comments/suzr_v_buzr/.

———. "Tango on Baseball," http://www.tangotiger.net.

Tango, Tom M., Mitchel G. Lichtman, and Andrew E. Dolphin. *The Book: Playing the Percentages in Baseball*. N.p: TMA Press, 2006.

Thorn, John, and Pete Palmer. *The Hidden Game of Baseball*. New York: Doubleday, 1985.

Tippett, Tom. "Can Pitchers Prevent Hits on Balls in Play?" Diamond-Mind.Com, July 21, 2003. http://diamond-mind.com/blogs/baseball-articles/tagged/baseball-research.

Walsh, John. "Best Outfield Arms of 2007." Hardballtimes.com, January 7, 2008. http://www.hardballtimes.com/main/article/best-outfield-arms-of-2007/.

Wyers, Colin. "How to Measure a Player's Value (Part 1)." Hardballtimes.com, January 22, 2009. http://www.hardballtimes.com/main/article/how-to-measure-a-players-value-part-i/.

Index

Aaron, Hank 13, 16–17, 27–28, 102–103, 126, 137, 139, 144, 146, 148, 150, 188–189, 233
Abbott, Jim 118
Abreu, Bobby 14, 131, 137, 144
Adair, Jerry 141
Adams, Bobby 135
Adams, Sparky 128, 141
Adcock, Joe 126, 128
Affeldt, Jeremy 5, 8
Aguirre, Hank 180
Aikens, Willie 128
Ainge, Danny 135, 142
Alfonzo, Edgardo 129
Alicea, Luis 124
Allen, Dick 117, 123, 147, 150
Allen, Ethan 110, 119, 137
Alomar, Roberto 14, 148, 183
Alomar, Sandy, Jr. 97
Alomar, Sandy, Sr. 135, 141
Alou, Felipe 96, 137
Alou, Matty 106, 137, 143, 209
Alou, Moises 198–199, 202
Amoros, Sandy 110
Anderson, Brian 123
Anderson, Garret 118, 126
Andrus, Elvis 125
Ankiel, Rick 200
Aparicio, Luis 14, 88, 92, 96, 109, 129, 133, 136, 142, 148, 185, 190–191
Appier, Kevin 163
Appleton, Pete 127
Appling, Luke 14, 100, 121, 132
Armas, Tony 111, 120
Arroyo, Bronson 107
Ashburn, Richie 100, 106, 122, 139, 186, 209
Ashby, Alan 181
Astroth, Joe 134
Atkins, Garrett 4, 6, 8–9
Auker, Elden 127
Ausmus, Brad 97, 107, 127, 189
Averill, Earl 186
Azcue, Joe 127, 140

Baerga, Carlos 123, 128, 141
Bagwell, Jeff 104, 128, 141, 146, 150
Bailey, Bill 127
Baines, Harold 132, 139

Baker, Dusty 118
Baker, Jeff 8
Baldelli, Rocco 200
The Ballpark at Disney's Wide World of Sports 279–280
Banks, Ernie 15, 110, 128
Barber, Steve 180
Bard, Josh 8
Barfield, Jesse 40, 111, 131, 137, 144, 188, 189
Barmes, Clint 198
Barr, Jim 97
Barrett, Michael 6, 8
Bartell, Dick 136, 142
Battey, Earl 93
Bauer, Hank 119
Bautista, Jose 137, 144, 199–200
Bay, Jason 185
Baylor, Don 41, 185, 207
Belanger, Mark 40–42, 109, 136, 142, 184, 190, 191
Bell, Buddy 109, 184, 190
Bell, David 197
Bell, George 136, 143
Bell, Gus 41, 186
Bell, Heath 6, 8
Belliard, Ron 128
Beltran, Carlos 15, 110, 119, 130, 148, 191, 201–202
Beltre, Adrian 14, 109, 184, 190
Bench, Johnny 16, 28, 93, 107, 180–182
Benedict, Bruce 97
Beniquez, Juan 209
Berkman, Lance 147, 150
Berra, Yogi 16, 18, 96–97, 127, 134, 140
Berroa, Angel 198
Berry, Ken 119
Bichette, Dante 41, 188, 208
Bigbee, Carson 130
Biggio, Craig 14, 96, 106, 121, 183
Billingham, Jack 133, 140
Bishop, Max 109
Blair, Paul 119, 130, 137, 143, 186–187, 191
Blanco, Henry 93
Blasingame, Don 122, 128, 135, 141
Blauser, Jeff 185

Blue, Vida 107
Blum, Geoff 6, 8, 198
Blyleven, Bert 18, 29, 101, 163
Boggs, Wade 101, 126, 129
Bonds, Barry 13, 16–17, 27–28, 40, 100, 102–103, 110, 118, 143, 146, 150, 185–186, 190–191, 233
Bonds, Bobby 96, 133, 148
Bonilla, Bobby 129
The Book: Playing the Percentages in Baseball 156–157
Boone, Bob 93, 180, 189
Bordick, Mike 124, 136, 142
Boswell, Ken 205
Bottomley, Jim 128
Boudreau, Lou 109, 129, 136, 142, 184, 190–191
Bourn, Michael 122, 200
Bowa, Larry 109, 190–191
Boyer, Clete 109, 124, 142
Boyer, Ken 124
Branca, Ralph 107
Brandt, Ed 180
Braun, Steve 136, 143, 207
Bream, Sid 108
Brett, George 14, 18, 29, 117, 132, 135, 139, 150
Bridges, Tommy 118
Brinkman, Ed 110, 129
Broaca, Johnny 123
Brocail, Doug 8
Brock, Greg 128, 134, 141
Brock, Lou 14, 40, 88, 92, 106, 117–118, 122, 133, 148
Brookens, Tom 206
Brosius, Scott 129
Brown, Kevin 16, 27, 29, 104, 118, 162
Brown, Ollie 131
Bruce, Jay 111
Bruton, Bill 119, 139
Bryant, Clay 127
Buchholz, Taylor 5, 8
Buehrle, Mark 92, 97
Buford, Don 96
Buhl, Bob 106
Buhner, Jay 188
Bumbry, Al 119
Bunning, Jim 97, 127, 163
Burdette, Lew 97
Burkett, John 97

289

Burks, Ellis 186
Burrell, Pat 130
Burris, Ray 133, 140
Burroughs, Jeff 41, 188, 207
Bush, Guy 107
Butler, Brett 106, 119, 121, 133, 139

Cabrera, Asdrubal 198
Cabrera, Miguel 103, 147, 150
Cairo, Miguel 124
Caldwell, Mike 123, 140
Callison, Johnny 111, 117, 131, 137, 144, 188–189
Cameron, Mike 8, 90, 93–94, 110, 119, 191, 201
Camilli, Dolph 117, 147
Caminiti, Ken 124
Campanella, Roy 108, 134, 140
Campaneris, Bert 92, 96, 133, 136, 139, 148, 191
Campbell, Bruce 119
Candelaria, John 97, 133, 140
Cano, Robinson 128, 141
Cardenal, Jose 126
Cardenas, Leo 129
Carew, Rod 106, 133, 139
Carey, Andy 124
Carleton, Tex 127
Carlton, Steve 14, 16–17, 28, 92, 101, 122, 158, 163
Carrasquel, Alex 133
Carroll, Clay 133, 140
Carroll, Jamey 6–9
Carter, Gary 93, 97, 180–181, 189
Carty, Rico 126, 139
Case, George 136–137, 143
Cash, Dave 135, 141
Cash, Norm 123, 147, 150
Castilla, Vinny 109, 129, 198
Castillo, Luis 122
Castillo, Welington 134, 140
Cavarretta, Phil 122
Cedeno, Cesar 92, 118–119, 137, 143, 148
Cespedes, Yoenis 130, 143
Cey, Ron 135, 142
Chambliss, Chris 134
Chandler, Spud 118
Chapman, Sam 130
Charles, Ed 129
Chavez, Endy 200
Chavez, Eric 109, 129, 197–198
Chiozza, Lou 128
Chipman, Bob 127
Christman, Mark 124
Church, Ryan 136, 143
Cirillo, Jeff 109, 124
Clark, Brady 5–6, 8
Clark, Jack 123, 131, 137, 144
Clark, Tony 91, 126
Clark, Will 108, 123, 134, 141, 182, 190

Clayton, Royce 136, 142
Clemens, Roger 14, 16–17, 27–28, 101, 104, 106, 158, 162, 167–175, 233, 268–269
Clemente, Roberto 14, 40, 106, 117, 119, 131, 137, 144, 186, 188–189
Clift, Harlond 135, 142
Cochrane, Mickey 107, 127, 134, 140
Colavito, Rocky 118
Colbert, Nate 128
Coleman, Jerry 128
Coleman, Vince 92, 143, 148
Collins, Dave 207
Colon, Bartolo 97
Concepcion, Dave 136, 142, 190–191
Cone, David 163
Cooper, Mort 127
Cooper, Scott 206
Cooper, Walker 126
Coors Field 4, 247, 255, 259, 262, 264–267, 279
Cora, Alex 124–125
Corpas, Manuel 6, 8
Coscarart, Pete 135
Cotto, Henry 136
Counsell, Craig 108
Covington, Wes 207
Cowens, Al 137, 144, 189, 204
Crandall, Del 93, 97
Crawford, Carl 92, 110, 117–118, 121, 136, 148, 191
Crisp, Coco 110–111
Critz, Hughie 108
Cromartie, Warren 130, 207
Crosetti, Frankie 122
Crowder, Alvin 122
Cruz, Jose, Sr. 106, 118, 208
Cruz, Julio 109
Cuccinello, Tony 128
Cuddyer, Mike 131, 199
Cullenbine, Roy 131, 144
Curtright, Guy 136
Cuyler, Kiki 111

Dahlgren, Babe 126
Dalrymple, Clay 140
Damon, Johnny 92, 110, 119, 121, 148, 200–201, 208
Danning, Harry 126
Dark, Alvin 125
Darwin, Bobby 208
Dauer, Rich 135
Davalillo, Vic 96, 119, 137, 143, 187, 209
Davenport, Jim 109, 206
Davis, Eric 92, 148
Davis, Jody 93
Davis, Rajai 148
Davis, Willie 14, 110, 119, 130, 133, 139, 148, 186, 191
Dawson, Andre 14, 137, 143

Dayley, Ken 180
DeCinces, Doug 124, 135, 142
DeJesus, Ivan 185, 206
Delgado, Carlos 156, 182
Demeter, Don 209
Dempsey, Rick 93, 107, 180, 189
Dent, Bucky 110
DeShields, Delino 128, 135, 141, 148
Dickey, Bill 93, 107, 180, 189
Dietz, Dick 181
DiMaggio, Dom 122, 130, 143–144, 187
DiMaggio, Joe 16–17, 28–29, 117, 119, 130, 137, 143–144, 147, 150, 186–187, 191
DiMaggio, Vince 111, 137, 143–144, 186–187
DIPS (Defense-Independent Pitching Statistic) 102, 159, 164–165, 195, 282
DiSarcina, Gary 129
Dobson, Joe 103
Doby, Larry 55, 119, 132, 139
Dodger Stadium 247, 255, 259, 262, 265, 267, 274–275
Dominguez, Matt 135, 142
Donaldson, John 129
DRA (Defensive Run Average) 113, 203–214, 282
Drew, J.D. 199
Driessen, Dan 134
DRS (Defensive Runs Saved) 113, 186, 203–214, 282
Drysdale, Don 118, 133, 140, 163
Ducey, Rob 137
Duncan, Dave 181
Dunn, Adam 102, 239, 242–243
Dykes, Jimmie 124
Dykstra, Lenny 110

Easley, Damion 124
Eckersley, Dennis 96, 101
Edmonds, Jim 111, 130, 143, 186, 191, 201
Edwards, Hank 137
Edwards, Johnny 108, 126
Elliott, Bob 124, 132, 139
Ellis, Mark 108, 182
Ellsbury, Jacoby 148, 200, 202
Encarnacion, Edwin 135, 142
Ennis, Del 130
Ensberg, Morgan 7–8
Erstad, Darin 110, 122, 126
Espinosa, Danny 124
Espinoza, Alvaro 125
Estalella, Bobby 127
Estes, Shawn 123
Ethier, Andre 120, 196
Evans, Darrell 15, 129
Evans, Dwight 14, 29, 118, 120, 137, 144, 147, 150, 188–189
Everett, Adam 110
Evers, Hoot 136, 143

Fain, Ferris 101, 128
Fairly, Ron 131, 134, 208
Falk, Bibb 110
Fast, Mike 164
Felder, Mike 118
Feliz, Pedro 109
Feller, Bob 16, 103–104, 163
Fermin, Felix 130
Fernandez, Sid 106
Fernandez, Tony 136, 142, 191
Ferrell, Rick 101, 107, 127, 140
Ferrell, Wes 103, 127
Fielder, Cecil 182
Fielder, Prince 182
Figgins, Chone 135
Figueroa, Ed 238
Fingers, Rollie 133
Finley, Chuck 122, 180
Finley, Steve 14, 121
FIP (Fielding Independent Pitching) 220, 224–225, 237, 282
Fisk, Carlton 97, 107, 127
Fitzsimmons, Freddie 107
Fletcher, Darrin 97
Fletcher, Scott 124–125
Flood, Curt 110, 119, 186, 191
Floyd, Cliff 198
Fogg, Josh 4–5, 8
Foiles, Hank 134
Foli, Tim 122, 124, 136, 142, 185
Fondy, Dee 123
Ford, Whitey 16, 18, 106, 122, 163
Foster, George 110
Fowler, Dexter 186
Fox, Nellie 101, 108, 182–183, 190–191
Fox, Pete 119, 137, 189
Foxx, Jimmie 16, 18, 28–29, 103, 126–127, 146, 150
Franco, John 133
Francoeur, Jeff 131, 137, 144
Francona, Tito 132, 139
Freehan, Bill 97, 107
Freisleben, Dave 140
French, Larry 133
Frey, Lonny 108, 122, 124, 183
Friend, Bob 96, 118, 163
Friend, Owen 124
Fryman, Travis 129
Fuentes, Brian 6, 8, 10
Fukudome, Kosuke 199
Furillo, Carl 40, 111, 188–189, 191

Gaetti, Gary 109, 124, 129, 190
Gagne, Greg 110
Galan, Augie 100, 122, 133
Galarraga, Andres 106, 128
Gant, Ron 110
Gantner, Jim 124
Garcia, Mike 103, 118
Garciaparra, Nomar 55

Gardenhire, Ron 129
Gardner, Brett 110
Garr, Ralph 119
Garrett, Wayne 135, 142
Garver, Ned 118
Garvey, Steve 108, 123, 128
Garza, Matt 180
Gehrig, Lou 16, 18, 27, 29, 100, 103, 132, 134, 141, 146, 150
Gehringer, Charlie 28–29, 100, 124, 126, 128, 190
Geiger, Gary 137, 143, 209
Geronimo, Cesar 130, 137, 143, 187
Giambi, Jason 147, 150, 182
Gibbs, Jake 97
Gibson, Bob 16, 18, 28–29, 104, 118, 163
Gilbert, Wally 142
Giles, Brian 5–10
Gilkey, Bernard 110, 118, 130, 143, 185
Gilliam, Jim 101, 109, 122
Giuliani, Tony 127, 140
Glanville, Doug 137
Glaus, Troy 142
Glavine, Tom 16, 18, 28, 42, 92, 96, 107, 118, 158, 163, 179
Gomez, Lefty 103
Gonzalez, Adrian 5–6, 8–11, 108, 123, 134, 141, 182, 190
Gonzalez, Luis 14, 110
Gonzalez, Tony 110
Gonzalez, Wiki 127
Gooch, Johnny 127, 134, 140
Gordon, Alex 110, 130, 136, 143, 185
Gordon, Joe 109, 124, 135, 141, 183
Gordon, Sid 119
Goslin, Goose 130, 136, 143
Grace, Earl 127
Grace, Joe 131
Grace, Mark 108, 134, 141, 181, 190
Green, Dick 135, 141
Green, Lenny 119
Green, Shawn 126, 188
Greenberg, Hank 118, 147, 150
Greene, Khalil 6, 8, 198
Greenwell, Mike 130
Greinke, Zack 101, 107
Grich, Bobby 28, 109, 128, 190
Grieve, Tom 136, 143
Griffey, Ken, Jr. 14, 28–29, 102, 130, 137, 143, 147, 150, 200–201
Griffey, Ken, Sr. 106, 188
Grissom, Marquis 92, 148, 201
Gross, Greg 131, 213
Grote, Jerry 107
Grove, Lefty 16, 18, 103–104, 163
Grubb, Johnny 136
Grudzielanek, Mark 124

Guerra, Mike 134
Guerrero, Mario 185, 206
Guerrero, Pedro 182
Guerrero, Vladimir 21, 67
Guidry, Ron 163
Guillen, Jose 131
Guillen, Ozzie 96, 109, 122, 192
Gumbert, Harry 107, 118
Gura, Larry 127
Gutierrez, Franklin 110, 200
Gutierrez, Ricky 40, 185
Guzman, Cristian 122
Gwynn, Tony 14, 106, 111, 119, 188–189

Hack, Stan 100, 122, 135, 142
Hadley, Bump 103
Haefner, Mickey 133, 140
Hairston, Scott 6–9, 11
Hall, Dick 97, 237
Halladay, Roy 20–21, 101, 104, 163
Haller, Tom 107
Hamels, Cole 101
Hamilton, Josh 200
Hamlin, Luke 180
Hamner, Granny 136, 142
Hampton, Mike 123
Hanna, Preston 41
Hansen, Ron 125, 129, 142
Harder, Mel 93, 103, 118, 163
Hardy, J.J. 110, 198
Haren, Danny 101
Hargrove, Mike 123
Harper, Tommy 92, 133, 139, 148
Harrah, Toby 129, 133, 135, 139, 142, 148, 206
Harrelson, Bud 109, 206–207
Harris, Dave 136
Hartnett, Gabby 93, 134
Hatteberg, Scott 197
Hawkins, LaTroy 6, 8
Hawpe, Brad 6–8, 188
Hayes, Frankie 127, 180
Headley, Chase 7–8, 129
Heath, Jeff 117
Hebner, Richie 96
Helton, Todd 4–5, 7–8, 104, 108, 123, 128, 146, 150
Hemsley, Rollie 134, 140
Henderson, Dave 111, 137, 143, 186
Henderson, Ken 209
Henderson, Rickey 14, 16–17, 28, 88, 92, 100, 110, 117–118, 133, 136, 139, 147–148, 150, 185, 190, 233–234
Henrich, Tommy 119, 144
Herges, Matt 6, 8–9
Herman, Babe 118
Herman, Billy 123, 133, 135, 139, 141
Hermida, Jeremy 120, 199
Hernandez, Felix 101, 163

Hernandez, Keith 108, 128, 134, 141, 182, 190
Hernandez, Livan 97, 107, 127, 133, 140, 180
Hernandez, Ramon 97
Herr, Tom 123, 135, 141, 205
Hershberger, Mike 131
Hershiser, Orel 163
Heving, Joe 180
Heyward, Jason 122, 199
Hidalgo, Richard 144
Higgins, Pinky 184
Higginson, Bobby 130, 143
Hill, Aaron 205
Hillenbrand, Shea 206
Hiller, John 235–237
Hiram Bithorn Stadium 267, 278–279
Hoag, Myril 131
Hobson, Butch 184
Hodges, Gil 108, 123, 128, 141, 182, 190
Hodgin, Ralph 122
Hoffman, Trevor 7–8, 10, 43
Hogan, Shanty 134, 140
Holliday, Matt 5, 7–9, 11
Hoover, Joe 129
Hornsby, Rogers 1, 126
Horton, Willie 118
Hostetler, Chuck 131
Hough, Charlie 106, 133
Howard, Elston 108, 134, 140
Howard, Frank 41, 103, 117, 139, 185
Howard, Ryan 132, 269–270
Howell, Roy 96
Hrbek, Kent 132, 139
Hubbard, Glenn 108, 124
Hubbell, Carl 163
Hudlin, Willis 103
Hudson, Johnny 128
Hudson, Orlando 108
Hudson, Tim 28, 104, 163
Hughson, Tex 127
Humphreys, Michael 186, 193, 201–214, 282
Humphries, Johnny 133, 140
Hundley, Randy 97, 140
Hundley, Todd 181
Hunt, Ron 135
Hunter, Brian 130, 143, 209
Hunter, Catfish 97, 106
Hunter, Torii 15

Inge, Brandon 109

Jackson, Danny 133, 140
Jackson, Darrin 111
Jackson, Reggie 14, 16, 18, 28, 40, 102, 132, 139, 146, 150
Jackson, Travis 129
Jacobs, Mike 197
James, Bill 21, 43, 53, 56, 58, 77, 84, 210

Javier, Julian 122, 128, 135, 141
Javier, Stan 92
Jeffcoat, Hal 119, 130, 143
Jenkins, Fergie 16, 18, 97, 101, 106, 163
Jenkins, Geoff 110, 119, 130, 185
Jensen, Jackie 119
Jeter, Derek 14, 16–17, 29, 41, 43, 55, 106, 126, 148, 185
John, Tommy 18, 29, 103–104, 118, 163
Johnson, Charles 93, 97
Johnson, Dan 123
Johnson, Deron 134, 141
Johnson, Indian Bob 130, 136, 143, 185, 191
Johnson, Kelly 124
Johnson, Lance 110, 148, 239–241
Johnson, Randy 15–17, 27–28, 101, 104, 158, 162
Johnson, Roy 131
Johnstone, Jay 209
Jolley, Smead 130
Jones, Adam 130, 137, 143, 187, 200
Jones, Andruw 42, 110, 112, 130, 137, 143, 186–187, 191, 200–202
Jones, Chipper 14, 16–17, 28–29, 124, 146, 150
Jones, Cleon 207
Jones, Randy 97, 107
Jordan, Brian 111, 120, 188–189
Joseph, Caleb 134
Joyner, Wally 123, 128, 134, 141
Julio, Jorge 7–9

Kaat, Jim 180
Kaline, Al 14, 16, 18, 28, 40, 96, 111, 119, 137, 144, 146, 150, 188–189
Karkovice, Ron 93
Kauffman Stadium 210, 262–264, 273
Kearns, Austin 111
Kell, George 109, 135, 142
Keller, Charlie 110
Kelly, George 123
Keltner, Ken 109, 129, 142
Kemp, Matt 200
Kennedy, Adam 108
Kennedy, Bob 144
Kennedy, Terry 97
Kennedy, Vern 93
Kershaw, Clayton 163
Kessinger, Don 136, 142, 192
Key, Jimmy 133
Kiermaier, Kevin 63
Killebrew, Harmon 15, 102–103, 146, 150
Kinder, Ellis 140
Kiner, Ralph 41, 147, 150, 185
King, Jeff 108, 129, 208
Kingman, Dave 103

Kinsler, Ian 108
Kirkland, Willie 137, 144
Klein, Chuck 119, 144
Kluszewski, Ted 139
Knepper, Bob 122
Knoop, Bobby 135, 141
Kolloway, Don 128
Koosman, Jerry 133, 140
Koshansky, Joe 8
Kotsay, Mark 130, 200–201
Kouzmanoff, Kevin 5–6, 8
Kranepool, Ed 134, 141
Kreevich, Mike 110
Kress, Red 129
Kreuter, Chad 134
Kubek, Tony 206
Kuhel, Joe 122, 126
Kurowski, Whitey 124

Laabs, Chet 118, 122
Landis, Jim 209
Landreaux, Ken 96
Lane, Jason 8
Langston, Mark 93
Lanier, Hal 129
Lanier, Max 92, 103
Lannan, John 123
Larkin, Barry 16, 92, 96, 126, 148
Lary, Lyn 136, 142
Lavagetto, Cookie 124
Lazzeri, Tony 135, 141
Lee, Big Bill 103, 118
Lee, Carlos 185, 198–199
Lee, Cliff 163
Lee, Derrek 108, 134, 141
Lee, Hal 136
Lee, Thornton 103
LeFlore, Ron 92, 119, 148
Leibrandt, Charlie 140
Leiter, Al 123
Lemke, Mark 109
Lemon, Bob 103
Lemon, Chet 209
Lemon, Jim 188, 208
Leonard, Dutch 103–104
Leonard, Jeffrey 119, 143
Leverage 31, 33, 43–44, 70, 220–221, 228, 231, 235–236, 283
Levey, Jim 136
Levy, Ed 130
Lewis, Buddy 131
Lezcano, Sixto 120
Lichtman, Mitchel G. 156, 192, 195, 201–202
Lind, Jose 135
Linear Weights 152–153, 239–241, 283
Livingston, Mickey 127, 140
Lockhart, Keith 141
Lockman, Whitey 141
Lofton, Kenny 92, 122, 130, 133, 139, 143, 148, 191

Index

Logan, Johnny 142, 206
Lolich, Mickey 63, 93
Lollar, Sherm 97
Lombardi, Ernie 128, 132, 139–140
Loney, James 123
Long, Dale 134, 141
Longoria, Evan 109, 124, 184
Lopes, Davey 92, 139, 148
Lopez, Al 93, 107, 180, 189
Lopez, Hector 206
Lowell, Mike 109, 135, 198
Lowenstein, John 207
Lugo, Julio 136, 142
Luque, Dolf 93
Luzinski, Greg 41, 185–186, 211–213
Lynn, Fred 132
Lyons, Ted 103, 106, 118, 163

Maddox, Elliott 131
Maddox, Garry 188, 209–214
Maddux, Greg 14, 16–17, 27–28, 42, 96, 101, 104, 107, 118, 158, 162, 167–175, 179–180, 233–234
Madlock, Bill 184
Mahler, Mickey 41
Malzone, Frank 184
Mantle, Mickey 14, 16–17, 27–28, 55, 102–103, 110, 126, 146, 148, 150, 233–234
Marichal, Juan 16, 18, 97, 101, 104, 118, 127, 163
Marion, Marty 110, 129
Maris, Roger 111, 120, 189
Marquis, Jason 123
Marshall, Mike 107, 208
Marshall, Willard 131
Martin, Al 185
Martin, Leonys 130
Martin, Pepper 122
Martinez, Dennis 107
Martinez, Edgar 147, 150
Martinez, Pedro 16, 18, 27, 29, 101, 104, 162
Martinez, Tino 108, 123, 182, 190
Masi, Phil 108
Masterson, Walt 123
Mathews, Eddie 14, 16–17, 27–28, 103, 126, 129, 146, 150
Matsui, Kazuo 5, 7–8
Matthews, Gary, Sr. 41, 185
Mattingly, Don 134, 141, 182
Maxwell, Charlie 110
Mayberry, John 123
Maye, Lee 96
Mayne, Brent 108
Mays, Willie 13, 16–17, 27–28, 55, 59, 96, 102–103, 106, 117, 119, 137, 143, 146, 148, 150, 186–188, 209, 233
Mazeroski, Bill 124, 183, 190

McAuliffe, Dick 133, 139
McBride, Bake 119, 212–213
McCann, Brian 107
McCormick, Frank 108, 128, 182
McCosky, Barney 122
McCovey, Willie 102–103, 132, 139, 146, 150, 182
McCracken, Voros 164–165
McCutchen, Andrew 119
McDowell, Roger 133, 140
McDowell, Sam 92, 180
McGee, Willie 106
McGehee, Casey 135, 142
McGraw, Tug 133, 140
McGriff, Fred 102, 128, 132, 139, 147, 150, 182
McGwire, Mark 102–103, 108, 146, 150
McKeel, Walt 63
McLemore, Mark 124
McMillan, Roy 109, 129, 192
McNertney, Jerry 108
McQuinn, George 108, 134, 141, 190
McRae, Hal 117
McReynolds, Kevin 207
McWilliams, Larry 127, 140
Medwick, Joe 106, 117, 132
Melillo, Ski 128, 135, 141
Melton, Cliff 118
Merced, Orlando 131
Merullo, Lennie 136, 142
Metkovich, Catfish 137
Miksis, Eddie 135
Millan, Felix 128, 135, 141, 205
Miller, Damian 134, 140
Miller, Eddie 109, 125, 185
Miller, Stu 107
Millette, Joe 129
Mills, Eldon G. 18, 245, 283
Mills, Harlan D. 18, 245, 283
Milner, John 126
Milwaukee County Stadium 276–277
Minoso, Minnie 40, 118, 130, 133
Minute Maid Park 259, 262, 264–265, 268–269, 277
Mirabelli, Doug 97–99
Mitchell, Dale 126
Mize, Johnny 128, 146, 150
Molina, Bengie 127
Molina, Yadier 93, 134, 180
Molitor, Paul 14, 92, 106, 122, 124, 126, 129, 139, 148
Monbouquette, Bill 97
Mondesi, Raul 119, 137, 144
Montanez, Willie 123
Monteagudo, Rene 180
Montero, Miguel 134
Moore, Charlie 108
Moore, Gene 111, 189
Moore, Jo-Jo 118, 130, 136, 143, 185, 191

Moore, Mike 93
Moore, Terry 130, 143
Mora, Andres 136, 143
Morgan, Joe 14, 16–17, 27–28, 92, 100, 126, 147–148, 150, 190, 233–234
Morgan, Mike 93
Morneau, Justin 108
Morris, Hal 123
Morris, Jack 107
Morrison, Jim 129
Morton, Bubba 136, 143
Moses, Wally 111, 189
Moyer, Jamie 96, 107, 127
Multicollinearity 223, 283
Munson, Thurman 93, 134, 140
Murcer, Bobby 208
Murphy, Dale 137
Murphy, Dwayne 137, 143
Murray, Eddie 14, 126, 128, 132, 139, 141
Musial, Stan 14, 16–17, 27–28, 100, 103, 106, 117, 146, 150
Mussina, Mike 16, 18, 27–28, 101, 104, 107, 162
Myer, Buddy 122
Myers, Greg 108, 134, 140
Myrow, Brian 8

Nady, Xavier 199
Neal, Charlie 205
Nettles, Graig 14, 129
Newcombe, Don 106
Newhouser, Hal 118, 123, 133, 140, 180
Newsom, Bobo 92, 123
Newsome, Skeeter 142
Nicholson, Bill 119, 126, 139
Niekro, Joe 127, 140
Niekro, Phil 14, 41, 93, 107, 118, 158, 180
Nixon, Otis 91–92, 148
Nixon, Trot 199
Nolan, Joe 134
North, Billy 111

Oberkfell, Ken 238
O'Brien, Charlie 97
O'Brien, Pete 108, 123
Offerman, Jose 241–243
Office, Rowland 119
Oglivie, Ben 118
Olerud, John 108, 126, 134, 141, 181, 189
Oliva, Tony 111, 137, 144, 188–189, 208
Oliver, Al 186, 209
OLS (Ordinary Least Squares) 216, 283
O'Neill, Paul 111, 189
Oquendo, Jose 109
Ordonez, Rey 125, 136, 142
Orsulak, Joe 119
Orta, Jorge 183

Ortiz, David 43, 48–49, 52, 67–74, 147, 150
Ortiz, Ramon 7–8
Osteen, Claude 92, 97, 118
Oswalt, Roy 163
Otis, Amos 92, 110, 148, 186, 191, 209–210
Ott, Mel 14, 16–17, 27–28, 100, 103, 111, 119, 126, 146, 150, 188–189, 191
Owen, Mickey 127, 140

Pagnozzi, Tom 93
Palmeiro, Rafael 14, 147, 150
Palmer, Dean 55, 184
Palmer, Jim 16, 18, 28, 42, 103–104, 107, 127, 163
Pappas, Milt 107
Parker, Dave 14, 96
Parker, Wes 108, 123
Parrish, Lance 93, 189
Parrish, Larry 208–209, 238
Partee, Roy 127
Pascual, Camilo 133, 140
Passeau, Claude 103, 118, 127
Patek, Freddie 136
Patterson, Corey 122
Paul, Josh 127
Payton, Jay 198
Peavy, Jake 4–6, 8, 163
Pedroia, Dustin 108, 182
Pena, Tony 93, 180, 189
Pendleton, Terry 109, 135, 184, 190
Pennington, Cliff 125, 198
Perez, Marty 141
Perez, Neifi 124
Perez, Tony 14
Perkins, Cy 127
Perry, Gaylord 14, 18, 28, 92, 101, 104, 158, 162
Perry, Jim 92
Pesky, Johnny 133, 139
Peters, Gary 127, 140
Petry, Dan 127
Pettis, Gary 110, 130
Pettitte, Andy 93, 123, 163, 175–177
Petty, Jesse 133
Phelps, Babe 181
Philley, Dave 131
Phillips, Adolfo 209
Phillips, Brandon 197, 202
Phillips, Bubba 124
Phillips, Tony 205, 207
Piazza, Mike 39–40, 83, 86, 97, 134, 180
Pierce, Billy 163
Pierre, Juan 91, 122, 148, 186, 200–201, 209
Piersall, Jim 110, 137
Pinson, Vada 14, 106, 117, 133, 137, 139, 143
pitchers: starting v. relief 26, 31–35, 59–61, 65–67, 159–162, 175–177, 235, 237–238; wins 1, 13, 158, 167, 237, 283
Pizarro, Juan 127
player win averages 18, 245
Podres, Johnny 107
Podsednik, Scott 200
Polanco, Placido 109
Potter, Nels 127
Powell, Boog 132, 139
Power, Vic 108, 128, 134, 141, 182, 190
Presley, Jim 184
Priddy, Jerry 135
Prothro, Doc 142
Puckett, Kirby 106, 130
Pujols, Albert 14, 16, 18, 28–29, 102–103, 108, 123, 134, 141, 146, 150, 181, 189, 269–270
Purkey, Bob 127
Pytlak, Frankie 134, 140

Quinones, Rey 125

Rader, Dave 128, 135, 142
Raines, Tim 14, 88, 92, 118, 126, 133, 139, 148
Ramirez, Aramis 63, 184
Ramirez, Hanley 185
Ramirez, Manny 14, 16, 18, 28–29, 40, 59, 72, 102–103, 117, 146, 150
Ramirez, Rafael 185
Randa, Joe 124
Randolph, Willie 100, 123, 126, 135, 141, 183, 190
Ransom, Cody 74
Reddick, Josh 111
Redus, Gary 148
Reese, Pee Wee 16, 18, 40, 109, 125, 133, 139, 184, 190–191, 206
Reese, Pokey 108
Reimer, Kevin 117
Reitz, Ken 135, 142, 206
Retrosheet 1, 79–80, 111–112, 144, 152–153, 183, 192–193, 201, 203, 216
Reuss, Jerry 118
Reyes, Jose 92, 122, 148, 185
Reynolds, Allie 103
Reynolds, Carl 111
Reynolds, Mark 184
Rice, Del 107
Rice, Jim 130
Rice, Sam 111, 122
Richards, Gene 130, 207
Richardson, Bobby 123, 135
Rigney, Bill 135, 142
Rios, Alexis 111, 144, 189, 208
Ripken, Billy 124
Ripken, Cal 14, 16, 18, 28, 109, 124, 129, 184–185, 190–191
Rivera, Jim 208
Rivera, Juan 136, 143

Rivera, Mariano 16, 104, 163, 175–177
Rivers, Mickey 106, 148
Rizzuto, Phil 122, 125
Roberts, Brian 197
Roberts, Robin 15, 18, 29, 97, 106, 158, 163
Robinson, Brooks 14, 40, 42, 109, 184, 190–191
Robinson, Eddie 128
Robinson, Frank 14, 16–17, 27–28, 102–103, 126, 133, 139, 146, 150, 234
Robinson, Jackie 16, 109, 128, 141
Robles, Oscar 8
Rocco, Mickey 134, 141
Rodgers, Buck 93
Rodriguez, Alex 14, 16–17, 27–28, 55, 67–74, 102, 104, 146, 148, 150, 233–234
Rodriguez, Aurelio 109, 124, 129, 135, 142, 184, 190
Rodriguez, Francisco 31, 33, 35–36
Rodriguez, Ivan 93, 134, 140, 180, 189
Rogell, Billy 126
Rogers, Kenny 92, 107, 122
Rogers, Steve 163
Rojas, Cookie 135, 141
Rolen, Scott 109, 184, 190
Rolfe, Red 109
Rollins, Jimmy 92, 125, 148
Rosar, Buddy 93, 97, 127
Rose, Pete 13, 100, 128, 135–136, 141, 143, 206–208
Ruane, Tom 152, 154
Rudi, Joe 110, 118, 136, 143, 185, 191, 207
Rueter, Kirk 107, 133, 140
Ruffing, Red 28, 103, 163
Ruiz, Carlos 97
Rush, Bob 103
Russell, Bill 109, 191
Russell, Jack 133, 140
Russell, Rip 129
Ruth, Babe 16, 21, 28, 104, 132, 139, 146, 150
Ryan, Brendan 125
Ryan, Mike 127, 140
Ryan, Nolan 14, 18, 28, 101, 104, 158, 162, 180

Sabathia, C.C. 20–21, 101, 163
Saberhagen, Bret 93, 104, 107, 163, 180
Salmon, Tim 137, 144, 189
Samuel, Juan 117, 183
Sanchez, Freddy 197
Sanchez, Rey 109, 241–243
Sandberg, Ryne 108, 133, 139, 148, 183, 190
Sanders, Reggie 111, 119, 131, 189

Sanguillen, Manny 96–97
Santana, Johan 101, 163
Santo, Ron 129
Sauer, Hank 130
Saunders, Joe 21
Sax, Steve 183
Schalk, Ray 107
Schatzeder, Dan 123
Schilling, Chuck 205
Schilling, Curt 28, 101, 104, 162, 164–165
Schmidt, Mike 14, 16–17, 27–28, 102–103, 109, 129, 146, 150, 184, 190, 234
Schneider, Brian 83–84, 93
Schoendienst, Red 123, 126, 139, 190
Schofield, Dick, Jr. 136
Schumacher, Hal 107, 118
Schumaker, Skip 197
Scott, George 108, 134
Scutaro, Marco 198
Seaver, Tom 14, 16–17, 27–28, 101, 104, 106–107, 158, 162, 233–234
Seitzer, Kevin 124, 135, 142
Shantz, Bobby 107
Shawkey, Bob 140
Shea Stadium 265–266, 275–276
Sheffield, Gary 14, 41, 103, 126, 146, 150, 199
Shelby, John 119, 209
Shibe Park 273–274
Siebern, Norm 132, 139
Siebert, Dick 128
Simmons, Al 110, 126, 139
Simmons, Andrelton 124
Simmons, Curt 97
Simmons, Ted 107
Singleton, Ken 188
Sisti, Sibby 124
Sizemore, Grady 119
Sizemore, Ted 124, 135, 141
Skowron, Bill 123
Slaught, Don 97, 140
Slaughter, Enos 15, 106, 117
Sledge, Terrmel 8
Smith, Al 133
Smith, Lonnie 130, 133, 148
Smith, Ozzie 14, 40, 59, 92, 109, 125, 129, 136, 142, 148, 184, 190–191
Smith, Reggie 119
Smith, Sean 203–214, 282, 285
Smith, Seth 5, 8
Smith, Zane 123
Smoltz, John 16, 18, 28–29, 42, 101, 104, 163
Snider, Duke 16, 28–29, 55, 102, 110, 139, 146, 150, 186
Snyder, Chris 134
Snyder, Cory 131
Solomon, Eddie 41

Soriano, Alfonso 130, 183, 198
Sosa, Sammy 14, 102, 111, 189
Spahn, Warren 14, 16–17, 27–28, 93, 103–104, 106, 118, 122, 158, 162
Span, Denard 200, 202
Speier, Chris 192
Speier, Ryan 5, 8
Spiezio, Scott 135, 142
Spilborghs, Ryan 5–6, 8
Splittorff, Paul 107
Sportsman's Park 273–274
Stanhouse, Don 133, 140
Stanky, Eddie 100
Stanley, Mickey 119, 137
Stanton, Giancarlo 111
Stargell, Willie 102, 130, 132, 143, 146, 150
Staub, Rusty 14–15, 18, 131–132, 137, 139, 144
Stennett, Rennie 108
Stephens, Gene 119
Stieb, Dave 106–107
Stillwell, Kurt 185
Stobbs, Chuck 127
Stringer, Lou 135, 141
Stripp, Joe 122
Stuart, Dick 182
Stubbs, Drew 200
Studenmund, Dave 152–153, 245
Suder, Pete 128
Suhr, Gus 118, 123, 134, 141
Sullivan, Cory 8
Sullivan, John Paul 129
Sundberg, Jim 93, 127, 140, 180, 189
Surhoff, B.J. 110, 118, 130, 136, 143, 185, 191
Sutton, Don 14, 18, 28–29, 101, 104, 106, 158, 162
Suzuki, Ichiro 20, 40–41, 90, 93–94, 106, 111, 121, 126, 137, 148, 188–189, 191
Suzuki, Kurt 97
Swindell, Greg 97

Tabor, Jim 124, 129
Tango, Tom M. 31, 156, 202, 245, 283
Tartabull, Danny 188
Tatis, Fernando 124, 129
Taveras, Frank 129, 136, 142
Taylor, Tony 183
Teixeira, Mark 108
Tejada, Miguel 96, 185
Temple, Johnny 183
Templeton, Garry 109, 191
Terry, Bill 108
Terry, Ralph 106
Thatcher, Joe 7–8
Thomas, Frank 28–29, 59, 103, 146, 150, 182
Thomas, Gorman 119

Thome, Jim 28–29, 102–103, 146, 150
Thompson, Jason 134, 141
Thompson, Robby 123
Tiant, Luis 96, 107
Tillman, Bob 181
Todd, Al 127, 134, 140
Tokyo Dome 278
Torgeson, Earl 134
Torre, Joe 127, 129, 142, 206
Torrealba, Yorvit 5–6, 8
Trammell, Alan 96, 109, 124, 127, 185, 190–191
Travis, Cecil 126
Traynor, Pie 124
Tresh, Mike 93, 108, 122
Trosky, Hal 123
Trout, Dizzy 103, 127
Trucks, Virgil 133
Tucker, Michael 208
Tucker, Thurman 122
Tudor, John 93
Tulowitzki, Troy 5, 7–8, 124, 198
Tuttle, Bill 130, 143, 209

Uggla, Dan 183
Unser, Del 130, 209
Upton, B.J. 111, 200
Urbanski, Billy 136, 142
Uribe, Jose 125, 136, 142
Uribe, Juan 109, 129
Utley, Chase 108, 122, 128, 183, 205
UZR (Ultimate Zone Rating) 104, 112–113, 116, 178, 192–203, 205–206, 208–209, 224, 285

Valentin, Jose 96, 124, 136
Valentine, Ellis 119, 131, 137, 144, 188–189, 208
Valenzuela, Fernando 93
Valo, Elmer 100
Vander Meer, Johnny 180
Van Slyke, Andy 130, 137, 143, 187
Varitek, Jason 97
Vaughan, Arky 28, 100, 117, 122, 126
Vazquez, Javier 101, 107
Venable, Will 137
Ventura, Robin 109, 124, 135, 142, 184, 190
Verban, Emil 128
Vernon, Mickey 117, 182
Versalles, Zoilo 130, 136, 142
Victorino, Shane 137, 143
Vina, Fernando 123
Viola, Frank 92
Virgil, Ozzie 181
Vizquel, Omar 14–15, 109, 185, 190–191

Wagner, Hal 181
Wagner, Leon 185

Wakefield, Tim 98
Walker, Bill 180
Walker, Dixie 126, 132
Walker, Gee 186
Walker, Larry 106, 118, 131, 137, 144, 146, 150, 188
Walker, Todd 183
Wallach, Tim 109, 135, 142, 184, 190
Walters, Bucky 103
Waner, Lloyd 110, 126
Waner, Paul 101, 111, 126, 189
Wang, Chien-Ming 164–165
WAR (wins above replacement) 18, 43, 67, 215, 220–221; from Baseball-Reference (bWAR) 167, 195, 221–225, 228–242, 268; from Fangraphs (fWAR) 195, 224–232
Ward, Gary 110
Warneke, Lon 106–107
Warstler, Rabbit 129
Wasdell, Jimmy 128
Washington, Claudell 119, 188
Weaver, Monte 123
Webb, Brandon 164–165
Webb, Earl 120
Weeks, Rickie 183, 197
Weiland, Bob 122
Wells, David 101
Wells, Vernon 201
Werber, Billy 129
Wert, Don 109, 206
Werth, Jayson 20–21
Wertz, Vic 126
Westbrook, Jake 123

Whitaker, Lou 16, 18, 96, 108, 128, 148, 182, 190–191
White, Bill 182
White, Devon 111, 119, 122, 148
White, Frank 108, 183, 190
White, Rondell 207
White, Roy 110, 119, 191
Wietelmann, Whitey 128
Wieters, Matt 97
Wigginton, Ty 184
Wilhelm, Hoyt 104
Williams, Bernie 126, 186
Williams, Billy 14, 96, 130, 132, 139, 147, 150
Williams, Matt 109
Williams, Ted 14, 16–17, 27–28, 96, 100, 102–103, 106, 126, 132, 139, 146, 150, 185, 207
Willis, Dontrelle 37–38
Wills, Maury 88, 110, 139, 148
Wilson, Dan 97
Wilson, Glenn 131, 144
Wilson, Jack 110, 122, 129, 142
Wilson, Jimmie 107
Wilson, Mookie 148
Wilson, Preston 186
Wilson, Willie 88, 92, 106, 110, 122, 133, 139, 148, 185, 191, 209
win shares 21, 43, 58, 77, 285
Wine, Bobby 125
Winfield, Dave 14, 120, 139, 188–189
Winford, Jim 180
Winn, Randy 121, 198–199
Witt, Bobby 123

Wizardry: Baseball's All-Time Greatest Fielders Revealed 186, 193, 201, 203, 211
WLS (weighted least squares) 50, 83, 285
Wolf, Randy 97
Womack, Tony 148
Woods, Al 136, 143
WPA (win probability advancements) 4, 7–10, 19, 72, 245, 285
Wright, Glenn 129
Wright, Taffy 122
Wynn, Early 15, 103, 158

Yastrzemski, Carl 14, 18, 28, 96, 100, 103, 130, 132, 136, 139, 143, 146, 150, 156, 191
Yeager, Steve 93
York, Rudy 128, 141
Yost, Eddie 100, 122, 184
Youkilis, Kevin 108
Young, Babe 123, 128
Young, Del 135
Young, Eric 128
Young, Kevin 108, 134, 141
Young, Michael 198
Yount, Robin 14, 29, 126, 133, 139, 148

Zahn, Geoff 93
Zambrano, Carlos 268
Zeile, Todd 184
Zimmerman, Ryan 129
Zito, Barry 164–165

www.ingramcontent.com/pod-product-compliance
Lightning Source LLC
Chambersburg PA
CBHW081541300426
44116CB00015B/2716